D1504376

FREE MEN *and* DREAMERS

VOLUME FOUR

OH, SAY CAN YOU SEE?

FREE MEN *and* DREAMERS

VOLUME FOUR

OH, SAY CAN YOU SEE?

L.C. LEWIS

WALNUT SPRINGS PRESS

Walnut Springs Press, LLC
110 South 800 West
Brigham City, Utah 84302
http://walnutspringspress.blogspot.com

ISBN:978-1-935217-82-4

To Tom,
Tommy, Amanda, Adam, and Josh,
for helping me believe.

ACKNOWLEDGEMENTS

Creating a work of historical fiction is like building a house. History sets the foundation, while the stories of the people are the materials from which historians reframe the past. It is upon these scholars' research that the novelist primarily relies as he or she designs a story. The necessary tools are gleaned from supportive colleagues and editors, and then one's friends and family provide the inspiration that adds life and tenderness to the project. So it has been in the production of this series.

Great thanks goes to these National Park Service employees who generously shared their own brilliant research or who guided me to splendid resources: author/historian Scott Sheads of Fort McHenry, Eric Vobril of Baltimore's Flag House Museum, and the docents at the Frederick County Historical Society and the Taney House. Once again, my appreciation is boundless for the exhaustive research of historian Anthony Pitch, author of *The Burning of Washington*, and for the work of George J. Svejda, Ph.D., whose fascinating *History of the Star Spangled Banner from 1814 to the Present* provided many of the historical details for this work.

I am grateful for the generosity of James Gillispie of the Sheridan Libraries of Johns Hopkins University, for chasing down R. E. Lee Russell's original map of the Battle of Baltimore and for allowing me to include it in this volume. I also extend my gratitude to Rachel Frederick of the Manuscript Division at the Library of Congress, and to Jennifer King at the George Washington University Library for chasing down much needed information.

Oh, Say Can You See? proved to be the most daunting of the volumes in the series because it is the keystone upon which all the other volumes rest. As I dedicated all my energies to this project, my sweet, supportive husband, Tom, generously endured a greatly altered routine at home. Thanks for smiling through the chaos, Honey. We're almost finished!

As always, I'm grateful to my children—Tom and Krista, Amanda and Nick, Adam and Brittany, and Josh—for their love and support. Like my husband, my daughter Amanda endures my daily angst. Her insight and suggestions inspired major changes to the series. Thanks, Mandy! And to my sweet grandchildren—Tommy, Keira, Christian, Brady, and Avery—I hope Grandma's book will inspire you to face the world with hope and courage.

An author never knows how her work will be received until someone else's eyes are on the project. So many friends helped improve this volume by proofing it before it went to the editors. Incredible thanks go to my volunteer beta readers: Stephanie Mortenson, Judi Stull, Ernest Runge, Lynette Johnson, Melinda Grenier, Jamie Wing, Heather Halliday, Kay Edwards, Dr. and Mrs. Wayne Allgaier, and super-proofer Michelle Mebius. I'm also very grateful to my talented colleagues, Braden Bell and Liz Adair, who took time from their own projects to read the manuscript and provide endorsements.

Thanks to all my LDStorymakers and ANWA colleagues for sharing their professional wisdom and providing moral support. Continued thanks go to Angela Eschler, who fanned my sometimes-waning enthusiasm to keep the series alive over the long haul. I'm so grateful to Garry Mitchell for adopting this project, and to the superwomen of the Walnut Springs team—Linda Mulleneaux for a beautiful, insightful edit that added greatly to this book; and Amy Orton for the spectacular cover, layout, and marketing plan. Thanks also to Matt Heinemeyer for maintaining my website.

Special thank you's to all the readers who have continued on the *FREE MEN and DREAMERS* journey with me, and whose beautiful, encouraging letters have provided a much-needed lift when the work became tedious. And to any and all new readers—welcome to the family! I hope you enjoy this glimpse of history.

On a personal note, my gratitude is without measure for the courageous men and women who lived through these events, and whose lives are reflected in this work. Their continued belief in America, even when hope seemed thin, preserved the republic. The similarities between the issues of our day and theirs stagger me. We are already repeating many of the mistakes of our past, and if we do not quickly learn from them, I fear we may well find ourselves defending our soil once more.

FICTIONAL CHARACTERS

THE AMERICANS

Residing at the Willows Plantation along the Patuxent River in Maryland

JED PEARSON: the twenty-four-year-old owner of the plantation; a lieutenant in the Maryland Militia

HANNAH STANSBURY PEARSON: Jed's twenty-year-old wife; rejected by her parents for marrying Jed

FRANNIE PEARSON: Jed's twenty-three-year-old sister; a former musical entertainer

MARKUS O'MALLEY: the twenty-seven-year-old Irish foreman of the Willows; a flotillaman

BITTY: the thirty-seven-year-old former slave who raised Jed and Frannie

JACK: a forty-one-year-old former slave; Bitty's brother and Jed's best friend

ABEL: a former slave set free by Jed; Bitty's husband; in his late thirties

JEROME (DECEASED) AND SARAH: Abel's aged parents

CALEB, ELI, GRANDY, AND HELEN: Abel's children and Bitty's stepchildren

BABY PRISCILLA: Abel and Bitty's infant daughter

ROYAL AND MERCY: a married slave couple

SOOKIE: a male slave in his early thirties

Residing at White Oak Plantation, the neighboring farm

STEWART STRINGHAM (DECEASED): original owner of White Oak; father of Frederick

FREDERICK STRINGHAM: current owner of White Oak; Stewart's recently crippled son; former beau of Frannie

PENELOPE STRINGHAM: Frederick's wife

Residing at Coolfont Farm, southeast of Baltimore

BERNARD STANSBURY: owner of Coolfont Farm; downtrodden husband of Susannah Stansbury; father of Beatrice, Myrna, and Hannah

SUSANNAH STANSBURY: crazed wife of Bernard; Hannah's mother; abused Hannah as a child

Others

MYRNA STANSBURY BAUMGARDNER: narcissistic sister of Hannah and Beatrice; separated from her husband, Harvey Baumgardner; resides at Harvey's country estate north of Baltimore

HARVEY BAUMGARDNER: Myrna's estranged husband; legal counsel to the mayor of Baltimore

DR. SAMUEL RENFRO: friend of Jed, Hannah, and Timothy; a surgeon

CAPTAIN ANDREW ROBERTSON: a bright, twenty-six-year-old career army officer from New York; formerly engaged to Hannah Stansbury

TIMOTHY SHEPARD: twenty-five-year-old college chum of Jed Pearson; former beau of Frannie; currently serving in Senator Gregg's office and as an aide to Dolley Madison, the First Lady

BEATRICE STANSBURY SNOWDEN: sister of Hannah; married to Major Dudley Snowden; currently resides in Tunbridge, Vermont

MAJOR DUDLEY SNOWDEN: husband of Beatrice Stansbury Snowden; American military officer captured at the surrender of Ft. Detroit; currently imprisoned in Melville Island Prison in Halifax, Nova Scotia

TITUS: an escaped slave; member of the Pennsylvania Militia

JENNY TYLER: the twenty-two-year-old friend of Frannie's who also sang at Le Jardin de Chanteuses

MR. WEST: the resident of Upper Marlborough who carried the news of Dr. Beanes's capture to Francis Scott Key

THE BRITISH

The household of the Earl of Whittington

LORD WHITTINGTON (EVERETT SPENCER): the Earl of Whittington; member of the House of Lords; British noble; widower

DANIEL SPENCER: the Viscount of Whittington; twelve-year-old son of Lord Whittington

The Ramseys of London, England

STEPHEN RAMSEY: a wealthy entrepreneur now in his fifties

ARTHUR RAMSEY: Stephen's son; a former divinity student who enlisted in the British Army

Others

SEBASTIAN DUPREE: Creole freedman; former pawn of a British entrepreneur; attempted to murder the Pearsons and take control of the Willows

JERVIS: a British sailor who joined Dupree's band; now an enemy of Arthur Ramsey

MRS. MCGOWAN: the young widow of a murderer; engaged to Stephen Ramsey

LORD NORTHRUP: member of the House of Lords; cousin to Lord Whittington

HISTORICAL FIGURES

THE AMERICANS

JOHN QUINCY ADAMS: eldest son of President John Adams and his wife, Abigail; served as the chair of the American delegation during peace negotiations with Great Britain

MAJOR GEORGE ARMISTEAD: commander of Fort McHenry in Baltimore

SECRETARY JOHN ARMSTRONG: U.S. secretary of war under President Madison

COMMODORE JOSHUA BARNEY: captain of the American vessel *Rossie;* later served as the commander of the Chesapeake Bay Flotilla

DR. WILLIAM BEANES: Scottish-born physician; leader of Upper Marlborough, Maryland; taken prisoner by the British on their retreat from Washington; friend of Francis Scott Key

CHARLES AND FERDINAND DURANG: brothers attributed with the first musical performance of "The Star-Spangled Banner"

CAPTAIN JOHN FERGUSON: captain of the *President*, the vessel Francis Scott Key and John Skinner were aboard as they watched the bombardment of Fort McHenry

LIEUTENANT JAMES GRAMMATT: first mate on board the *President* during the bombardment of Fort McHenry

THOMAS JEFFERSON: third president of the United States; dear friend of the Madisons

EDWARD JOHNSON: mayor of Baltimore in 1814

FRANCIS SCOTT KEY: an American lawyer; the district attorney for the District of Columbia; writer who is best known for his poem "In Defence of Fort McHenry" (put to music as "The Star-Spangled Banner"), written during his shipboard detention during the attack on Baltimore

POLLY KEY: wife of Francis Scott Key

LIGHT HORSE HARRY LEE: father of Robert E. Lee; a Revolutionary War hero and friend of George Washington; tortured in the Baltimore riot of 1812

CAPTAIN STEPHEN MACK: brother of Lucy Mack Smith and founder of Pontiac, Michigan; served in Fort Detroit during Hull's surrender in 1812

JAMES MADISON: fourth president of the United States

DOLLEY MADISON: First Lady and wife of James Madison

HENRY MCCOMAS: young Baltimore sharpshooter who, along with Daniel Wells, is attributed with killing British Major General Robert Ross

CAPTAIN (JUDGE) JOSEPH HOPPER NICHOLSON: brother-in-law of Francis Scott Key; captain over the Baltimore Fencibles and second-in-command at Fort McHenry

STEPHEN PLEASANTON: clerk and aide to Secretary of State Monroe; saved the original Declaration of Independence

RED JACKET: chief of the Seneca Indians; persuaded his people to change their loyalties from the British to the Americans

COLONEL JOHN SKINNER: U.S. prisoner exchange agent who accompanied Francis Scott Key to negotiate for the release of Dr. William Beanes

JOSEPH SMITH JR.: Prophet and founder of The Church of Jesus Christ of Latter-day Saints

DR. NATHAN SMITH: surgeon; dean of Dartmouth Medical School; credited with performing the surgery that saved Joseph Smith Jr.'s leg

CAPTAIN JOHN RODGERS: commander of Baltimore's Batteries; planned the blockade of the Patapsco River

MAJOR GENERAL SAMUEL SMITH: commander of the Baltimore defenses

GENERAL JOHN STRICKER: commander of the Third Brigade of the Third Division, Maryland Militia

DR. WILLIAM THORNTON: designed the U.S. Capitol Building; saved U.S. Patent Office during the attack on Washington

GEORGE WASHINGTON: first president of the United States

DANIEL WELLS: young Baltimore sharpshooter who, along with Henry McComas, is attributed with killing British Major General Robert Ross

GENERAL WILLIAM WINDER: commander of U.S. forces at Bladensburg; led troops to Baltimore to battle the British

THE BRITISH

ADMIRAL SIR ALEXANDER COCHRANE: succeeded Admiral Warren as British commander in chief of the North American Station; commanded the British forces during the final stages of the Chesapeake campaign, including the Burning of Washington and the Battle of Baltimore

ADMIRAL GEORGE COCKBURN: British second-in-command during the Chesapeake campaigns of the War of 1812; served under Admiral John Borlase Warren and then under Cochrane; driving force behind the Burning of Washington

ADMIRAL EDWARD CODRINGTON: captain of the British fleet during the operations against Washington, Baltimore, and New Orleans during the War of 1812

LIEUTENANT GEORGE GLEIG: scholar, author, and British patriot; trained as a clergyman

PRINCE REGENT (LATER KING GEORGE IV): ruled Great Britain when his father, King George III's, health rendered him unable to fulfill his duties as monarch

MAJOR GENERAL ROBERT ROSS: highest-ranking British leader once the British forces came ashore: known as a gallant and generous man; beloved by his men; Irish born

CHAPTER 1

Thursday, August 25, 1814, 11:00 PM
One day after the Burning of Washington

Dear God, please, don't let it be true. It was the silent prayer of Judge Joseph Hopper Nicholson as he hurried home to Baltimore, the smoke growing thicker with each passing mile. His horse was restless over the scent, straining at the bit and wanting to turn off the road. As debilitated as he felt, Hopper feared to give the animal his head and allow him to lead as he normally would.

Several times, Nicholson nearly slipped from his mount. Fatigue and the heat only added to his previous distress, brought on by a feverish malady during his stay in New York, when the fearsome news arrived of the British landing near Washington. Concerns for his wife and family, and for his volunteer artillerists, the Baltimore Fencibles—who would surely have rushed to the defense of Fort McHenry—drew the forty-four-year-old militia commander from his sickbed to begin an anxious return home to Baltimore.

As he headed south, increasingly grim details of the invasion assaulted him at each stop along the way—the American army had fled at Bladensburg, the president and his cabinet had been evacuated, and the city of Washington had been captured and set ablaze. Baltimore was eerily quiet when Nicholson entered. Slowing his horse to a trot, he followed Belle Air Avenue southwest, gazing down the side streets to assess the city's mood. A smoky haze hung in the air as he urged his mount up onto Hampstead Hill, the highest rise near the city. A cry caught in the back of Nicholson's throat as he gasped at the scene. Far off to the southwest, in the direction of Washington, seethed the source of the smoldering air.

"It's true . . ." he groaned as he absorbed the cruel reality of it all.

He had been warned. As much as he had tried to discount the wild tales, how could he have doubted their general veracity after so many similar reports? A few facts had differed—British troop figures, how quickly they defeated the Americans at Bladensburg, the number and names of the magnificent Washington buildings torched, the amount of time required to mindlessly destroy a republic's capital. In the deepest corner of Nicholson's heart, he had hoped it had been a grotesque exaggeration. But it wasn't. Glowing surreally, like a distant campfire emitting a forty-mile-long trail of soot and ash, the capital city still burned.

He leaned forward on his horse and scanned the harbor area to be sure Baltimore was still sovereign and safe, but it too was eerily illuminated, and his stomach tightened. He studied the light until he could identify the reason for the unnerving glow—dozens of small campfires. But whose? Peering more intently, Nicholson studied the star-shaped Fort McHenry, scanning the outline for the flag pole and then . . .

A loud release of breath escaped him as he saw the defiant outline of the American flag, fluttering boldly above the fort. He eyed it thankfully for several long seconds. Never before had he become emotional at seeing the red, white, and blue banner that designated American territory, but today his gratitude was full. His head instinctively turned toward the Pickersgill home, number 60 Albemarle Street, on the corner of East Pratt. He wondered if the widowed Mrs. Pickersgill and the other women of the family, whose hands had created the glorious ensign, had determined to remain in the city at such a perilous time as this.

Despite the presence of the American flag, Nicholson couldn't shake his worry over the state of Baltimore. Delaying the arrival to his home, he set off straight to Fort McHenry. Innumerable militia soldiers were bivouacked around the fort's five-sided perimeter. A private saluted him at the sally port as he hurried through, past his own quarters in the junior officers' barracks to the dimly lit barracks where Major Armistead and his family lived.

He rapped on the door and the major answered quickly. "You look dreadful, Joseph."

"A touch of the grip, but you look none better, Major. I hurried home as soon as I heard."

The grim-faced officer opened the door wide, encouraging Judge Nicholson to enter. "Washington is a devastating loss. We're bracing for the worst here, but we've made our preparations. Still, I've moved Louisa to Gettysburg to keep her and the baby out of harm's way. Did I tell you I dreamed the child she carries is a son? I pray I get to meet him."

"Of course you will, George. What is the mood in the city? All seems calm."

"Panic, initially, particularly as news of Alexandria's plan to capitulate reached here. Some of the citizens are fleeing, and some are calling for us to surrender as well. I'd like to shoot such cowards, but sadly, they still retain the privilege to exercise their freedom to speak, even if it is in a manner that would deprive them of that very right!"

"Not a single sentry met me on my ride in, as if there has been a deliberate plan to surrender Baltimore without a struggle."

Armistead sighed in exasperation. "It did appear that way a few days ago, but things are improving somewhat. We've over a thousand militia camped around our perimeter, and Major General Smith is amassing new volunteers every day to defend the city against an attack by land. He strengthened the militia and Fort McHenry prior to my arrival, and he continues to work for the defense of this city. We owe him such gratitude for all this! There are also citizens' groups springing up amongst those determined to remain and defend Baltimore."

"What do your instincts tell you, Major? Do you think those volunteers will hold their lines, or will this be a repeat of Bladensburg and Washington?"

The major's hand reached up and pressed against his tense mouth. Tiny shakes of his head gave the reply he dared not utter. Then he looked Nicholson in the eye. "I don't know, Joseph. Only time will tell. Only time will tell."

CHAPTER 2

Monday, August 29, 1814, 4:00 PM
Base of the Chesapeake Bay, near Virginia

His resources were minimal, but they would have to do. He'd had an epiphany of sorts. As ludicrous as the event might seem to some, it had been real enough to him, offering him a sliver of something—hope, comfort, or maybe even enlightenment. And so he made a modest plan that he knew he must begin this day.

The cuff was smooth except for the iron lock's bulge and the weld where the link attached. He placed the weld in the needed position, pressed it to the wood, and began to scrape. Fourteen passes produced an obvious gash in the wood, perceptible to the touch but invisible to the eye in the dimming light that shone only through the knotholes in the decking above.

One mark . . . day one.

He heard voices above him, the voices of sailors adjusting lines and hoisting the white, billowing sails determined to carry him away from everyone he loved. One British voice caught his attention—the voice of his new oppressor. The prisoner struggled to repress the anger still smoldering in him from their earlier encounter as he recalled the abuse he had suffered.

"What'll ya give me for this prize? Two bits? Four bits? I'm told he's considered a handsome cuss." The middle-aged ensign jerked on the rope wrapped around the man's burned neck, eliciting a pained yelp as the captive obeyed the demand to step up and join his tormenter on a crate, placed on full display before the blue-and-white-uniformed sailors swarming the British *Iphigenia*'s deck.

Ten minutes earlier, the American's greatest fear had been that he would die an ignominious death in the filth of Britain's notorious Dartmoor Prison. It wasn't dying that frightened him. He had faced death before, when pride and honor mattered more to him than life. But he was married now, a man whose twenty-fourth birthday had passed with the news that a child was on the way, and for those reasons he vowed to bear whatever cost was required to survive Dartmoor Prison. But that had been ten minutes earlier.

His burned, muscular frame towered over his captor, who enjoyed taunting the shackled and bound man. The American pushed his fury and pride down deep. No sense in mourning justice denied. He had survived the explosion of the bridge, and he meant to survive whatever else came.

The ensign grabbed a hank of the American's dark, tangled hair and pulled his face close, raining rancid spittle on the captive's cheeks. "Who are you?"

"Jed Pearson," came the controlled reply.

"No. Who are you really?"

This was before Jed's epiphany, and his anger momentarily got the best of him. Chuckling sarcastically at the old ensign he said, "Forgive me for forgetting that truth means nothing here."

The ensign was taken aback for a few moments, then broke loose with a heinous laugh. "I'll tell you who you are." He jerked on the rope again, turned to his naval audience, and crowed, "I'll tell everyone who you really are! What we've got 'ere, men, is one authentic American, upstart of an aristocrat! A slave owner getting a taste of what it feels like to stand on the block. 'E's a little charred." He slapped the younger man on his burned back, offering a feigned apology when the prisoner crumpled in agony.

After dragging Jed back to his feet, the ensign continued, "But 'e's not without 'is talents. 'E's a farmer, might even've worked a mite alongside 'is poor slaves on 'is grand plantation. And we know 'e's a crack shot. Pity 'e got 'isself blowed up in the process, but it were a great deal better than 'e gave to our men!" The auctioneer removed his cap, placing it reverently over his heart. "God rest their souls."

Angry jeers and spittle were hurled at Jed, but he stood defiantly, making no attempt to deflect the assault. He steeled himself against the promises of death and torture that filled the air, knowing Dartmoor was no longer his foremost concern. The question now was whether he'd leave the American coast alive. He saw the malice in the ensign's sunburned face, and then, as the noise began to quickly dim to silence, the sailor's face paled. The cause was instantly clear as an impeccably clad British officer moved through the ranks to where the ensign stood. Before a word escaped the officer, the ensign stepped down and snapped to attention, his demeanor shifting from fear to humiliation.

"What goes on here?" the British captain snarled.

The ensign's eyes diverted to avoid his superior's gaze. "We're just . . . 'avin' us a li'le fun, Cap'n. No 'arm done. Adm'ral Cockburn never minded the crew 'avin' a bit o' fun with the pris'ners. He always felt it made for good morale amongst the ranks."

The captain's eyes narrowed, indicating that this was, perhaps, the most profoundly wrong reply that could have been uttered. In a voice resembling a growl, the captain said, "This is not one of Admiral Cockburn's plunder-and-burn missions, Ensign Stonesifer. We sail under Major General Ross's diplomatic orders to convey the official report of the Washington campaign to London. Am I making my point quite clear?"

Three seconds of apparent rebellion delayed the reply that came out forced and obstinate. "Aye, Cap'n Smith. Yer point is indeed quite clear, sir."

"Very good." Captain Smith raised his glance to the prisoner. "Who is this man?"

Stonesifer clamped his hand over Jed's manacled arm and jerked him forward. With hands and feet tethered and little slack between, Jed was unable to break his fall. His head snapped hard to the deck, leaving him lying in an awkward sprawl. "This 'ere is Lieutenant Pearson, the assassin what killed members of our peace delegation as they entered Washington."

Moments of silence passed. "Get him up," Smith said.

Two sailors dragged Jed to a tottering stand and held him in place until the captain waved them and the ensign away. The American and the British officer sized one another up, and Jed saw something in the captain's eyes that made him dare to appeal to this man. "I'm not the man who fired on that delegation," Jed said softly.

With only a slight raise of an eyebrow, the officer responded in a voice intended only for their ears. "I'm Captain Smith, Mr. Pearson, Major General Ross's attaché. Listen carefully. This crew is already in a lather because their plans to attack Baltimore have been denied. They're filled with fire and looking for fight. I advise you not to give them further cause to notice you."

One phrase from Captain Smith's warning caused Jed's heart to pound with hope. "Are you saying the planned assault on Baltimore is cancelled altogether?"

"Calm yourself, soldier," Captain Smith whispered sharply. "Just mind what I've said."

"I will . . . I will, sir. Just . . . please, please tell me about Baltimore."

"Do not press me, Lieutenant."

"Please, sir. I'll cause you no further concern. Please, what of Baltimore?"

The captain chose his words carefully. "Your Baltimore is safe, but I've said all I'll say on the matter!"

Jed's body sagged with relief as a smile broke free.

"Wipe that grin off your face, Pearson. You pose a great liability to me if you do not heed my warning. I'm ordered to deliver you to Dartmoor Prison, which I intend to do, but these are Cockburn's men. They feel no loyalty to me. Rile them, and I will be unable to assure your safety."

Moments later, Jed was shoved down the ladder into the *Iphigenia*'s dank hold, where his legs were shackled and chained to iron rings fastened to the ship, with just enough slack to stand and reach the waste bucket that sat in the middle of the floor. British soldiers took every opportunity to jeer at him, spit on him, and worse. They had judged and sentenced him, calling him a murderer and a coward, debasing him in dreadful, diverse ways. He felt like less than a man, less than a dog. He remembered stories of surviving such a horror. Who told them? What was he? He hadn't been a soldier. He had been a . . . *He had been a slave!*

The shame and horror of this revolting understanding stung him as fiercely as his fear. In his mind's eye Jed saw Jerome, the aged Negro man. Jed was not the one who had bushwhacked the young seminary student on a beach in Barbados, beating him unconscious and then tossing his previously free body into the hold of a ship. Most importantly, Jed was not the one who had deprived Jerome the expression of his brilliant, educated mind, stilling a tongue that knew five languages and the complete works of Shakespeare. Other men had done that. But Jed *was* the last man to own Jerome, and the admission rocked Jed's sensibilities.

It helped little that he had come to love Jerome as a father, or that he had set all his slaves free. Aside from Jed's wife Hannah, his sister Frannie, and his Irish friend and farm manager, Markus O'Malley, he loved none better. But still, he had owned *people.* And though he was not the coward who had fired on the British negotiation delegation, everything else the sailor had said was true. Jed was a wealthy, young American landowner, and he had once been the master of slaves—the owner of human beings. It wasn't illegal, but it was immoral. Jerome's eyes had made that clear.

"You must hate me," Jed had confessed on the night he first heard the sad tale of the brilliant scholar's seizure, ashamed that he could have ever thought to own another man.

"No. Hate is the very worst, master. It imprisons the heart and mind as well as the body."

The voice seemed so clear that Jed's eyes darted around, almost expecting to see the man.

"'Who knoweth whether thou art come to the kingdom for such a time as this,'" the biblical scholar had whispered reverently. "Perhaps God is leading you . . ."

"Leading me?" The memory had chilled Jed. As he pondered it he had heard the scraping of the rising anchor as it was drawn from the deep. Voices called out orders to unfurl the sail, and then he had felt the lurch and pitch of the vessel. They began sailing away from the shore—away from home—and the slosh of the bay against the hull deepened his despair. He had tried to recall the sweet smells of his farm, the Willows, to drive the stink of his oppression away, but only Jerome's face could be summoned. Closing his eyes, Jed had whispered, "Is He leading me now, Jerome?"

In his mind's eye, Jed had seen the beloved brown face from whose wrinkled lips came the comforting words, the wellspring of his epiphany. But the words were not from a previous memory. They were coming to him as he prayed; he was certain of that.

Place your trust in the Lord, Jed. Let him show you what He can make of you.

One tear had welled in Jed's eye. "I hear you, Jerome. Oh, please forgive me, old friend. I pray that you and God will forgive me. I will trust in Him. I will see what God will make of me."

In that moment Jed had vowed to endure, to survive, to trust in the Lord.

The other American prisoners had been sent to the British prison on Melville Island in Nova Scotia, where Jed's brother-in-law, Dudley Snowden, was being held. But due to the crimes of which Jed was accused, he was being sent to England, to a place even more dreaded.

He pushed the thought away and rubbed his fingers over the first hash mark in the ship's hull—his record of this journey. Yes, day one was nearly past. The gentleness of the waves assured him they were still in Chesapeake Bay, perhaps nearer to Hampton. He thought about tomorrow but he dared not think beyond. How would he fill the morbid hours? With his dream.

Since his epiphany, the dream had come over and over throughout the day. There were slight alterations on occasion— the color of his wife Hannah's dress; the size of her increasing belly that brought the most tender smiles to her beautiful, young face; the styling of his sister Frannie's auburn hair; the sight of Markus and Jack waving muskets or rods, calling Jed to join them on a hunt or a fishing trip. Sometimes Jed saw Bitty's gentle scowl after she caught him pinching the end off a loaf of her freshly baked bread, or poking a finger into a pie. He saw the brown faces of the children, who tugged at his shirttail, cajoling him into a game of Blind Man's Bluff. He held fast to the dream wherein Jerome came to him and wiped away his tears.

Jed continued to feel his old friend near, entreating him to surrender his heart to God. Jerome was the only person in Jed's circle truly capable of understanding his current pain. Except for Hannah. She too knew much about suffering, and for her he vowed to keep fighting to live another day.

CHAPTER 3

Monday, August 29, 1814, 4:00 PM
Baltimore, Maryland

Markus O'Malley drove his wagon away from Benedict, Maryland, the weight of his completed assignment still wearing heavily on his broad twenty-six-year-old shoulders. The grey haze loomed ahead of him, testifying that the nightmarish attack on America's capital had indeed occurred. Markus needed no proof. The images of the blazing Capitol Building, the torched President's House, the Arsenal at Greenleaf's Point, the rope works, and the Washington Naval Yard were forever etched in his mind. He had been there, and his scarred body attested to the sorry tale.

The fires and their smoke had driven the animals away from their swampy habitats around Foggy Bottom and Washington's tidal basin, scattering many of them east toward the Patuxent River. A pair of quivering calico kittens cried from just inside the cover of a downed log. From their size, Markus figured them to be about ten weeks old. Seeing no mother, he assumed the family had somehow become separated. He pulled back on the reins and stopped the wagon to investigate, but as he leapt to the ground the kittens disappeared into the hollow log. When he stuck his hand in to scoop them out, he quickly pulled back a bloodied finger.

Markus chuckled at his foolishness, enjoying the normalcy of this moment after so many abnormal months. He barely regarded the wound. After all, in the last two weeks alone he had been marched nigh to death, gun shot, rocket burned, and bayoneted at Bladensburg. Even worse were the pains that sorrowed his heart, but he pushed those thoughts away.

Markus ran a hand through his loosely tied red hair and came up with an idea. He pulled a piece of dried beef from his shirt pocket and went fishing for kittens. Barely half a minute passed before he felt the determined tugs and heard the brave hissing of the babies. In a few minutes the pair were tucked happily into his shirt. He felt awash in warmth, not just from their furry little bodies but from the feeling of being so close to life after spending so many days surrounded by death and the dying. A lump formed in his throat. Cradling the mewing bundle close to his muscled chest, he climbed into the wagon box and slapped the reins to urge the team on.

"One of you'll be for Hannah," he whispered to the kittens in his soft Irish brogue, "and one of you'll be for Frannie. Now mind yourselves and be kind ta them. The poor dears will be needin' a bit o' comfort." He wiped a tear away. "But don't we all."

The anchors in Markus's life were disappearing. He wouldn't have believed it was possible to hurt more deeply than he had after British pirates murdered his father. But six years later the enemy killed his sweet bride, leaving him utterly alone without root or branch. It was Jed Pearson who had given him the will to carry on—to see a brother and a family where only friends once stood. Markus pushed his anger down deep, using it to motivate him to fight, to prevent his fate from befalling anyone else.

No matter how deeply he had hurt, no matter what he had lost, there was always the order and promise of America. Two years ago he would have wagered all he had that America would prevail in this war. But now? He just wasn't sure anymore. He longed to grab Jed and take a stand together at Baltimore as they had at Bladensburg, only he dreamed that this time the battle line would hold. This time they wouldn't be betrayed by their own. Markus felt sick again at the thought.

The knot in his stomach grew bigger with each dreary mile he placed between himself and the British fleet. Twice he pulled the rig off the road, ready to return to Benedict, where the British fleet was still docked, but he knew it would do him no good. While the bulk of the fleet rested and restocked to deliver the final death blow to America's eastern coast, the anchors were being raised on the Britain-bound *Iphigenia,* the ship that held Jed Pearson. And the only thing Markus could do to help free the friend he loved as a brother would involve breaking the very promise he had made to him. It was a dilemma that made Markus thirst for a drink.

Shame was riding him hard this day—shame for his part in Jed Pearson's imprisonment, shame for being so wrong about Arthur Ramsey, shame for his cowardice in facing Hannah and Frannie to explain their men's fates, and most of all, shame for seeking solace in a drink—a remedy those two brave women would never pursue.

Markus gave that some thought and chuckled sadly. *Well, Hannah never would, but Frannie?* If he knew one thing about Jed's sister it was that the headstrong young filly was likely to do just about anything.

Markus drove the team south along the sweltering western shore of the Patuxent, headed for the ferry that ran across the river to Sandy Point. From there it would only be a short ride to the Willows, where he would have to face the women. He constantly scanned ahead for signs of British defectors. The roads were filled with people wasting no time in preemptively running from the next expected target on the British campaign—Baltimore.

But there were also signs of hope, as some sooty survivors of the failed Washington campaign mingled with others heading northeast to make a stand at Fort McHenry. Markus scowled at those with clean faces and clothes. Some had just arrived from Virginia and parts west, but some, he knew, were the very cowards who had run at the first suggestion of retreat at Bladensburg, leaving only a few hundred of Commodore Barney's flotillamen and Captain Miller's marines to stand between the British hordes and the nation's capital. They had all fought valiantly but it hadn't been enough, and in the end, they too had finally been ordered to retreat.

Markus thought again about that drink. Nearly every inn and shop along the shore was closed and dark, except for a shabby old place with a crooked sign that read Moorehouse's Inn. Twenty or more rigs surrounded the place, but Markus spied an empty spot on the rear side of the building, situated his rig, and hoisted his short, broad body into the back of the wagon. He nested the kittens into the makeshift bed that still bore the imprint of a man's body. He paused upon seeing the bloodstained blankets.

With a shiver, he jumped down and fetched some hay and water for his team. "Poor ol' dears," he crooned to the mares in his Irish lilt as he ran a loving hand along their haunches. "You did fine today. We leastwise gave Arthur a fighting chance, didn't we? Now you just rest up a mite."

He entered the dark and smoky inn. When his eyes adjusted and he was finally able to read the drink prices scrawled on the board behind the rudimentary bar, Markus nearly cussed. "Is this some kinda joke, man? Why don't ya at least use a gun and be honest about yer intentions?"

The proprietor didn't flinch as he pointed to a shot glass. "That's good as gold right there. Who knows when the next ship carrying good British ale will sail in here?"

"Thanks to Jimmy Madison!" snarled a customer as he threw back the last swallow in his glass. Several of his compatriots growled approvingly before downing their own ales.

"Lovely clientele you've got here," Markus said.

"The mayor of Alexandria surrendered to the British this morning. Turned everything over to the scoundrels—ships, warehouse stores, munitions, and money. They promised not to burn the city or molest the residents. The city's women are serving the enemy refreshments!"

"What? Are they raising no defense at all?"

"Hold on . . ." The proprietor reached below the bar and retrieved a rumpled piece of paper. "The Common Council of Alexandria released a statement . . . yes, yes, here's how the mayor and his fancy advisors explained it. They say they acted 'from the impulse of irresistible necessity and solely from a regard to the welfare of the town.'"

Markus's gaze fell blankly to the floor. "They chose to save a few buildings rather than defend their liberty?"

"And spare the women and children!" cried a man in the back.

Markus turned in his seat and eyed all the men in the room, wondering where they were standing five days ago when the last American line broke on the bloody fields at Bladensburg. "The women and children? Is that whose necks they were tryin' to save? Or was it their own?" He turned back around, fished a coin from his pocket, and tossed it on the bar. "Gimme a beer."

The proprietor filled a mug and handed it over.

A white-haired man made his way through the crowd, which parted as he pressed forward. He took the seat next to Markus and struck up a conversation. "President Madison and his cabinet are back in Washington City. He replaced that buzzard, Secretary of War Armstrong, with Secretary James Monroe, and he's reassembling the army now. I heared tell that the president ordered the big cannons at Greenleaf Point to be placed so's they'll blast them British devils out of the water if they try to make a second run on the city."

A man in a ruffled-sleeved shirt snorted in response to the report. "It's tragic comedy at its finest—Jimmy Madison placing the cannons *after* the city is burned!"

Several men in the crowd began to snicker until Markus turned and shot them a glaring rebuke. "Who's the fool spoutin' off over there?" he asked the establishment's owner.

"That fine gentleman would be one of our illustrious senators—from New Hampshire."

Markus's aged neighbor sidled over to challenge the New Hampshire delegate. "I ain't particularly pleased with President Madison or his cabinet right now, but shame on the rest of you for making light of what's befallen us. I was with General Washington at Valley Forge during that awful winter of 1777. It was the most awful, and the proudest chapter in my life. We suffered terrible to give you the freedom you got to jest and criticize, but why would you want to? Sure as I can tell, Mr. Madison is still the president of these United States. We've got to make some defense if we're goin' ta save the republic."

The senator huffed in derision, pounding his ruffled fist on his table. "The British didn't come here to conquer us, you fool!"

"How can ya say that? They've burned our capital to the ground?"

"All they wanted was to expand their trade rights and prevent us from aiding France. Madison and his party rushed into this war unnecessarily. We brought this debacle on ourselves."

It was the man's great misfortune that the first person to reach him was a fiercely angered Markus O'Malley, who in one sweeping motion grabbed the man by the lapels of his tailored coat, spun him around, and hoisted him onto the bar, placing his face mere inches from his.

"Take your hands off me!" the man yelled. "I'm a United States senator!"

"Then act like one! Today, I watched my best friend be dragged on board a British prison ship to pay for a crime he didn't commit. There was no trial. They didn't care that he was too injured to have committed the crime. He got their justice, not ours! He's a farmer, a good man with a child on the way. All he wanted was to love his wife and see his child be born. So don't plead the British case to me!"

The aged patriot shook a crooked finger at the New Hampshire senator. "I hoped we'd never have to go to war again, but I lost my youngest boy four days ago at Bladensburg. I'd like to think his dyin' counted for something, but it will just have been a waste— all of it, the Revolution, too—if the only spit men like you have is aimed at your own government!"

Several silent seconds passed and then the crowd began to disperse. The senator squirmed on the bar top, still under the scrutiny of the old man.

"I think you owe this man an apology for belittlin' the sacrifice of 'is son," Markus said to the senator.

Head bent low, his eyes shifting from the floor to the old man, the senator slid down and stood before him. "Please forgive me, sir," he began sheepishly, "for allowing a bottle of spirits to loosen my tongue so. And forgive my shortsightedness on many matters which you have most rightly clarified for me. I pledge to do better in honoring the post I hold."

He turned to Markus and sized him up, making Markus acutely aware of his own shabby appearance, from his loosely bound mane of wild red hair that flowed over his blue neckerchief, to his torn, round-necked shirt that was so covered with dirt and soot and blood that one could scarcely see the stripes. Markus saw sympathy cross the senator's face as his eyes fell to Markus's knee britches, which were equally filthy and ragged after months shipboard and two harrowing weeks spent shifting into a soldier's life.

"You're a flotillaman, aren't you, Captain?" the senator asked, obviously recognizing the remnants of Markus's uniform. "One of Commodore Barney's brave men?"

"Aye," Markus answered cautiously. "I served with the commodore."

The senator nodded to the old soldier. "Then we have two heroes before us. Innkeeper, neither of these men's money is any good here today. I'll pay for whatever they desire—food, drink" —he shot Markus a gentle wink— "or a bed and bath." He pulled out a ten-dollar note and laid it on the counter. And then with a tip of his hat, he exited the inn.

The stiff attitude of the owner melted into solicitous kindness as he pushed Markus's previously offered coins back to him. "So you're a flotillaman, are you?"

"Aye, I'm a flotillaman, but I'm no hero."

The innkeeper's eyes rested on the crimson stain on Markus's sleeve. "Pshaw!" He called out across the room. "Gents? We've got us here a flotillaman. One of Barney's brave few!" A soft buzz filled the room and the owner's voice softened with admiration. "I suppose you're on your way to Baltimore. A man can't fight on an empty stomach. What'll you have, Captain?"

The reminder that the surviving flotillamen were heading east to defend Baltimore opened a new emptiness in Markus's gut. At the thought of Hannah and Frannie, and of his promise to Jed, Markus pressed the ache down once again. Some of the emptiness was pure hunger. He had been too numb to recognize it before, but the moment of civility had eased the knot in his stomach enough to allow his hunger to rise. "What've ya got on the spit?"

The proprietor beamed. "A venison roast. And the wife's got a kettle of chicken stew, the best this side of the Patuxent. And how about some hot rolls and honey butter, Captain? Or would you prefer some apple butter?" He was scurrying about, displaying each selection.

Markus smacked his lips. "I believe I'll take a mite of each, if you please."

"Of course! Of course! And how about a bath?"

The mere idea of a hot bath was delicious to Markus, but a bath meant home to him, and home was the Willows, where his onerous errand lay. His smile faded and his voice fell even again. "I've no time for a bath, sir. Just the vittles, if you please."

"And another pint of our best stout?"

The beer no longer appealed to him. "Just tea, please. And a pitcher of cold water."

Markus wound his way past the curious onlookers to a secluded table in the rear of the room. In short order his food arrived, and he tore into it with relish. The crowd shifted as men left and others arrived. Markus paid little attention to anything except his meal, the first real food he'd eaten in four days and the finest he'd eaten in weeks.

There was a loud bang as a man in a fine suit burst through the door, struggling to carry a limp woman clothed in a blue satin gown. "A cup of water please! This woman has collapsed!"

A portly young man rose from a table, offering his assistance. "I'm a physician, sir." To a pair of customers he said, "You two, help me move these tables together so he can lay her down."

The two men dragged tables side by side and the man laid the pale wisp of a woman down. The scene raised Markus's curiosity, but having troubles enough of his own and seeing that the woman was being attended to, he continued to eat his supper, eyeing things from afar.

Markus heard the surgeon's hackles rise and watched as he barked to the owner, "Bring me a pitcher of water and some broth!" Then the physician unloosed his anger on the man who had brought the woman in. "What are you to this woman?"

"I'm . . . I'm . . . her guide."

"Her what?" With one mighty fist the physician grabbed the man by his fancy lapels and jerked his face near. "How long has she been in your care? She's nearly starved to death!"

"It's not my fault! I just recently met her. She came to me in this condition and hired me to help her find the Willows Plantation."

The very mention of the Willows sent a chill down Markus's spine. "The Willows?" he repeated as he barreled over men to see the woman. *Frannie? Hannah?* The pale, sunken face was unknown to him and he gasped in relief.

"Markus?" said the doctor, whose face now reflected hope.

Looking up, Markus gazed into the familiar eyes of Jed's good friend, Samuel Renfro. "Dr. Renfro?" He took hold of the doctor's free hand. "It's wonderful to see you!"

Samuel Renfro released the guide and caught Markus up in an emotional embrace. "Markus! What a blessing to find a friend! I've just come from Washington. There's nothing but pain and loss wherever one looks. Just look at this pitiful woman. Do you know her? This man claims she's trying to get to the Willows."

Markus studied her face more thoughtfully. Her hair was the color of summer wheat against her sickly, wan face. He shook his head. "I've never seen her before, but I'll help ya get 'er to the Willows. It'd do Hannah and Frannie a world o' good to see ya."

"Hold on!" interrupted the black-suited man as he pushed in between Markus and Samuel. "I brought this woman in here to revive her before continuing on. I've no intention of abandoning her to you."

The proprietor delivered the water and broth to Samuel, who handed it over to the man. "Then be sure you do not move her until she's taken every drop, do you understand?"

The man smiled at Samuel and asked, "How far is it to the Willows? Five miles? Ten? I've heard it's owned by a very wealthy man. Surely she would fare better there than here in a saloon." The man set the broth aside. "Sadly, I have other commitments that also require my immediate attention. Perhaps we can come to some agreement to benefit my client."

Markus's skin prickled and his fists curled in response. Samuel glanced his way, then asked the guide, "Really? Such as?"

The man's eyes widened, darting to the woman's hand. "She promised me that ruby ring as payment for safely delivering her to her destination. Allow me my fee, and you can carry her on yourselves. Her host will reward you handsomely when you reach the Willows."

Markus's eyes narrowed into slits. "I have an arrangement for you. Leave this place now, or I'll—"

"Do not interfere, Mr.—"

Markus bullied up, dwarfing the reedy man. "The name's O'Malley. Markus O'Malley."

"Be careful who you make your enemy, Mr. O'Malley."

"I hope I never live ta see the day I fear a spineless coward who preys on women."

The man curled his lips. "Very well, Mr. O'Malley, have your way today, but one way or another, I will have my fee. These are lawless times. One stray ball is all it would require. With all the chaos in these parts, who'd even notice?" He snickered as he sidestepped toward the door. Feigning the firing of a pistol, he whispered, "Bang!" as he slipped outside.

The knot returned to Markus's gut, and a quick glance at Samuel informed him that the good doctor had experienced a similar eerie feeling. "What d'ya make of that?"

Samuel was already drizzling broth into the woman's mouth. "I've got worries enough right here. See if you can bring her around. Dip that cloth in the water and press it to her brow."

Markus reached for the cloth, then stalled, studying the rough, sorry state of his hands.

"She can't see them. They'll do just fine," Samuel reassured him.

With one strong hand Markus dipped the cloth and squeezed it out. With the other he tentatively, gingerly brushed the blond wisps away from the woman's pale brow. When he applied the cool cloth, her eyes fluttered as she uttered a barely audible sigh.

"Now that's better." Samuel set the bowl aside. "The poor thing can't be but twenty-two. So pretty, but she's known some hard times."

"Is she sick or just hungry?"

"Look at her skin, particularly her hands—all tanned and dry. Despite her satin dress, she's no pampered lady. It just doesn't add up. And how did she end up with a beast like him?"

Markus's brow furrowed with a new worry. "We don't know anythin' about her. Maybe she's no better than 'im. We could just be bringin' more trouble to the Willows."

"We can't just leave her here alone, can we?"

"I'm not sayin' that. But Hannah and Frannie have to be my first concern."

"Agreed. Drive slowly while I sit in the back to tend to her. We can probably leave soon."

Markus was slow to agree to the arrangement. "All right, but I have a bad feelin' about this. You handle the doctorin'. I'll handle the powder and balls."

CHAPTER 4

Monday, August 29, 1814, late afternoon
The Willows Plantation along Maryland's Patuxent River

"Sweltering" was the only word that justly described the oppressive mugginess plaguing the region. Hannah Stansbury Pearson hung a cool cloth around her neck and eased her rounded frame into a porch chair. As her expanded belly shifted, she smiled, not even noticing how her hand instinctively moved there to caress the growing babe within. She felt a momentary longing for her childhood country home on the eastern fringe of Baltimore. The large house, shaded by enormous trees, also had a large, deep icehouse that provided enough ice for cool drinks and chilled soaks in the porcelain tub. Hannah's eyes closed. The only person who'd ever benefited from those cool soaks was her crazed, malevolent mother, and no comfort the ice brought was worth the browbeating her father took until it was supplied, or the labor demanded of the overworked, mistreated slaves who cut and dragged the blocks.

Hannah stood, stretched, and shuffled on. She'd just tolerate the heat the same as everyone else.

Leaning against the porch post, Hannah closed her eyes as a river breeze combed through her long, dark hair. The gentle wind calmed her. She needed that right now, especially since the courier had delivered her sister Myrna's letters. Perhaps that's why her parents and home were on Hannah's mind this day. Myrna's letters were the only contact Hannah had with her parents anymore.

Interestingly, she felt closer to her eldest sister, Beatrice, who lived far away in Tunbridge, Vermont, where she moved after Dudley's imprisonment following the fall of Fort Detroit. Beatrice was nearly as severed from her parents as Hannah now, but this painful bond of being the wives of Americans held captive by the British had made the two as close as sisters could become.

On the other hand, Myrna busybodied herself so completely that nothing seemed able to touch her. Rumors held that her husband, Harvey Baumgardner, had packed up—lock, stock, and barrel—and moved back into the town home he had occupied before marrying Myrna. *Poor Harvey.* Myrna had turned herself inside out to win him, and the consequent wealth and freedom becoming Mrs. Baumgardner would bring, but as soon as the vows were said she dropped the ruse, and Harvey Baumgardner was trapped like a Christmas pig.

Hannah debated opening Myrna's latest dismal installation in the wretched series of weekly communications Hannah sarcastically referred to as *Myrna's Tales of Woe.* But with all that had recently happened in Washington, Myrna would actually have cause for her fretting and worry. Taking a deep breath, Hannah pulled the letter from her pocket and began to read.

Friday, August 26, 1814

Dearest Sister,

> *I am besieged by the utmost terror. I can see smoke rising in the direction of Washington City from the porch of my husband's country home. What are we to do? The capital is lost! The government is dissolved! And I am here alone because my dear husband, Mr. Baumgardner, moved off our farm and*

into our town home to be more readily available to General Smith and the militia. It has been a terrible sacrifice for us to be apart this way, but I suppose it is no more than dear Dolley Madison has borne. I rode to the city to ask Mr. Baumgardner what he thinks of my assessment of our nation's current situation. He utterly denies that the government has crumbled, but I believe he shares his more optimistic view only to spare my delicate feelings from the horror of the truth. Or he is dreadfully naive, and I informed him of as much.

Did you hear rumors about slave uprisings? I sent Mr. Barclay, the overseer, out to shackle all our Negroes up. And you there, milling about with them as if they were your friends! I fear you will be murdered in your sleep, and I will be forced to drive there in my state of mourning, to offer you a proper funeral.

Mother and Father are in a complete dither. Though my dear husband is in harm's way, preparing to meet the enemy at any hour, I took no thought for my own troubles and instead visited our dear parents. And what did I find? Mother was standing in the lawn wearing only her chemise and a pair of riding boots! She was carrying Father's rifle, fully intending to murder the British if they approached. I dare say she very nearly shot and killed the groomsman and the butler because they were wearing red!

I was, at first, appalled, and then I began to chuckle, until I saw Father's worried face. He

44

had been searching for her for some time, worried she'd do herself harm. Fortunately for us, no one from polite society visits Coolfont Farm or our parents anymore, and therefore no one who could ridicule the Stansbury name saw her. We were blessed.

I am not one to complain, mind you, but I do so wish you hadn't gotten yourself ostracized by our parents. With Beatrice in Vermont awaiting Dudley's return from that British prison, and you essentially cut off, the burden of our parents' happiness and the management of their large staff falls solely to me. And with the fall of Washington, and Mr. Baumgardner's entrance into the militia, I do not know how I will manage.

I know you are far nearer the capital than I, and therefore in somewhat more danger, but you are also privy to so much more news. I envy you that. Please do share. Did your husband survive the assault?

I wish you well.

Your loving sister,
Myrna

Hannah shook her head in awe that a single person could be so narcissistic. But that was Myrna—a paragraph about her worries over the Stansburys' brush with exile from polite society over their crazed mother's antics, but no mention of Hannah's coming baby, and only a gossipy interest in whether Jed was even alive after Washington. Hannah considered balling the page up and tossing it into the yard for the goats to chew, but she loved her goats too much.

The thought made her chuckle, and that caused the baby to kick again. Her humor restored, she thought once more on names for the expected little one. Hannah had no sure name if the baby was a girl, but if it was a boy, he would be named for his father. But she wouldn't call him "Jed," the affectionate nickname of her husband, Jonathan Edward Pearson III. Her first son would be the fourth to bear that name, but she would see that he was simply called Johnny. She knew Jed wouldn't mind. She had talked it over with him that very morning, and a smile had broken across his lips, signaling his approval.

She wondered if anyone thought she was as mad as her mother. She knew Bitty, Jack, and Sarah accepted her gift—the ability to *feel* things and *know* things. It went beyond mere intuition, though it wasn't a constant knowledge, except during these last few days since Jed had been taken away. At first the images were terrible, drawing Hannah's spirit down and making it hard for her to keep her promise to be brave and carry on. But today was different. Today, though the images were still dark and heavy, she felt hope break through, and as she lay in bed she spoke to Jed as if he were there beside her, and she knew her words carried to him somehow.

A flood of relief washed over her, and she thanked God heartily for her renewed hope, asking for forgiveness for her constant struggle with doubt and weakness. She knew she should be beyond those feelings by now, as she had been blessed with the gift since childhood. This sensitivity had provided her with a connection to Jed even then, during her oppressed, abused childhood. She had always loved him, for as long as she was capable of feeling love. It took years before Jed confessed he had always felt the same, and despite every imaginable obstacle, they were finally married.

A parade of little, dark, singing children followed Reverend Charles Myers from the river to the chapel site. His blond hair and fair skin distinguished him less from his predominantly Negro congregation than did his classical vibrato, which contrasted sharply with the slurred, Southern styling characteristic of the dark-skinned Willows residents' voices. The reverend had only arrived the day before, but it was clear the children already loved him.

"It's hard without our menfolk isn't it?" Bitty asked as she tucked her tiny frame against Hannah's tall, lean body.

"So who is seeing things now?" Hannah teased as she ruffled the tuft of cottony black hair peeking out beneath Bitty's bandana. She noticed gray in Bitty's hair, the first to appear in Bitty's thirty-seven years. Hannah wondered if all the Willows women wouldn't be gray before long.

"It doesn't take any special gift to see when a woman is missing her man."

"I suppose not," Hannah replied, giving Bitty a little squeeze. "You had less warning about losing Abel and Caleb than I had about losing Jed."

"I saw it comin', I just didn't want to admit it. My freedom papers made me feel free, but it wasn't that way with Abel. I knew he wouldn't rest until he had the respect of others. Joining the real army was his way of getting that for hisself, for Caleb, and for our family."

"You could go along to Fort McHenry with them. You're so skilled with healing herbs."

Bitty appeared to ponder the notion. "I can't leave the other children to chase after a hard-headed man and a son who longs to be just like him." She sniffed and ran a handkerchief under her nose. "No. Abel's a smart man." She ducked her head and chuckled. "He's probably smarter than most of those white commanders who'll be orderin' him about."

Hannah enjoyed her first hearty laugh in weeks. "You're right! Jerome taught him very well. I wonder if he'll tell them he can read and write—in several languages?"

Bitty's eyes widened and she sobered quickly. "Whites don't take kindly to free Negroes. I expect they'll be even less inclined to appreciate a free Negro who's learned."

"Don't worry, Bitty. Sergeant McCoy was pleased to have Abel and Caleb in his company, and Abel is as wise as he is smart. He'll handle himself well."

"I suppose." Bitty smiled as both women watched the merry dance Reverend Myers was leading. "It looks like the reverend's fittin' in well."

"Yes, but he's no Jerome," Hannah said.

"There'll never be another man like Jerome, but havin' a reverend to keep the children's learnin' goin' has been a real comfort to Sarah. She thinks his arrival is a gift from God."

Hannah didn't dispute Sarah's interpretation of the event. A company of Pennsylvania militia had arrived in Washington too late to spare the nation's fallen capital from its scorched fate, so they, and a young clergyman serving them, turned around and headed for Baltimore, bivouacking at the Willows for a night. Their group enchanted Bitty's husband, Abel, and their oldest son, Caleb, who joined their ranks. Abel's mother, Sarah, did some enchanting of her own. After she told Reverend Myers about Jerome's dream of providing a Christian foundation for the children, the reverend agreed to serve the Willows in her deceased husband's stead.

"Jack and the other men will have the old chapel site cleared tomorrow," Hannah explained. "They can start building the new one as soon as the house is repaired and the cabins are finished."

Hannah turned to survey the burned section of the house. The band of mercenaries who murdered Jerome also set the residents' cabins and the corner of the main house ablaze. Jed and the men had made structural repairs before he left to fight in Washington, but the roof leaked and painting would need to be done before the rainy season compromised the wood.

"The house is sound for now, but it is awfully crowded in there with all our women and children living under one roof. Perhaps the men should complete the chapel first. Some families could move in there until the cabins are rebuilt."

Bitty smiled. "With the baby comin', you're feelin' the need to get your nest in order."

Hannah's green eyes sparkled. "I think I conceived when Jed and I went to Washington in April, but my body was never normal again after I miscarried last winter."

"Well, I think we're gonna be greetin' this baby before the harvest is over." Hannah's eyes widened and Bitty rushed on. "You've been feelin' life for some time now."

A nervous thrill made Hannah shiver. "A new baby by Christmas."

"More likely a new baby in November."

Hannah leaned back against the post, her face glowing with contentment. "I can't wait to hold my baby in these empty arms, Bitty. Somehow I know I'll feel closer to Jed when I do."

"Every baby's a miracle, a gift of hope. We need a bit of that around here. Have you seen how my Priscilla's taken a shine to Frannie? The two of them have either been bangin' on the piano or playing with Frannie's old dolls since my baby woke up from her afternoon nap. I think it's been healin' for Frannie. That poor thing is sufferin' too."

"Where's Markus? I believe Jed is all right, but I want to hear that from Markus's lips. And Frannie won't let go of Lieutenant Ramsey unless she's certain he's passed away."

The women stood quietly for a time, breathing in the sounds of the children's singing, allowing the cool afternoon breeze to wick the sweat away from their brows.

Bitty sighed. "Sarah and Mercy are puttin' a cold supper together tonight. It should be ready shortly. Comin' in?"

"In a while," Hannah answered. "I just need a moment more."

With a nod of her head, Bitty disappeared around the corner and into the house. Hannah counted down the weeks between this day and mid-November on her fingers. "Perhaps as few as ten weeks and then our baby will be here. Do you hear that, Jed? You'll be arriving in England, or perhaps you'll already be in Dartmoor when our baby is born. Don't despair, Jed. Think of home and be brave, my darling. I need you to come home to me—to us."

CHAPTER 5

Monday, August 29, 1814, early evening
Near Calverton, Maryland, five miles north of the Willows

Samuel's horse was tied to the back of Markus's wagon, where a soft bed of fresh blankets was arranged for the woman, near the rescued kittens. Her eyes fluttered open again and Samuel attempted to explain their plans, but before he finished she had fallen back asleep.

Markus was not nearly as comfortable. Unable to shake the feeling they were being watched, he scoured the road for any sign of the woman's "guide," while keeping his musket at the ready. Once they had safely loaded onto the ferry, the two men relaxed and caught up on the news.

"What brought you this way, Dr. Renfro?"

"Please, Markus, we're better friends than that. Call me Samuel. A group of surgeons were sent to Bladensburg to check on the wounded. I made my way into the capital to visit the field hospitals, which was a dismal experience." He shuddered. "I did manage to see Timothy Shepard for a moment. He was sorely pressed for time—searching for a Mr. Francis Scott Key—to see to the release of a Dr. Beanes, who was taken prisoner by the British. Timothy was very worried about Frannie. He mentioned that she had fallen in love with a British lieutenant."

"Arthur Ramsey." Markus sighed. "'E was caught in a terrible blast at the Arsenal. Dr. Beanes is the American physician who cared for 'im when 'is own surgeons left 'im for dead."

"Such a tragedy. Poor Timothy has been pursuing Frannie since soon after he and Jed graduated from the university, and now she's grieving for a dead British officer."

"'E's still alive," Markus corrected, "leastwise 'e was the last I saw 'im."

"Timothy said you and Frannie raced away with Ramsey, seeking medical attention for the lieutenant. Frannie is blessed to have you, Markus. I wonder if she realizes what a difficult thing that had to have been for you, considering the hurt the British have caused you."

The observation, however delicately stated, sent a chill coursing through Markus. He stood and gazed out at the muddy water. "I've been blunt in my disgust regardin' her relationship with him. In the end, it was Arthur's goodness that changed my thinkin'. I hope the good Lord spares 'im. Despite the pain men in 'is uniform have wrought, the world needs more of 'is kind."

Silent moments hung in the air. Samuel leaned his head back against the rail and squinted at the bright sun. "Timothy told me Jed and Hannah are expecting their first child."

Markus studied Samuel's face, anxious to know if he had heard the rest of the tale. "Did Timothy also tell ya that Jed's a British prisoner and that I'm the one that got 'im captured?"

"He said only that you had been the bravest of patriots and a true friend to Jed."

Markus dropped back down onto the wagon bed. "It was still my fault."

"Timothy loves Jed as a brother too. He wouldn't spare the truth. He said Jed was caught in an explosion, and you were the first on the scene to tend to him—getting him back into the city and placing him in a home where he'd be able to rest safely away from the British."

"Aye." Markus chuckled sadly, and then his brogue became more accentuated by his sorrow. "Fine job I did pickin' 'im a safe house. I left 'im deaf and dazed in the very home that was harborin' the sharpshooter who fired upon the British peace delegation! Who knows what would have happened if that shot 'ad never been fired. Maybe the British would have taken tribute money for their prize and left the city intact. But once that murderous shot was fired, they were determined to burn down half the city, and they wanted their shooter at any cost. Well, they leveled the city, left the gems of America in smoke and flames, but instead of gettin' their shooter, they got themselves a scapegoat—hurt, confused Jed, who I placed in harm's way."

"But you couldn't have known, Markus. Who could have foreseen the day's events?"

"It's little comfort to me whilst Jed's on a ship headed for prison."

Suddenly Samuel turned to Markus and brightened. "Timothy was seeking Mr. Key to secure the release of an American prisoner. He has considerable influence with Senator Gregg and the Madisons as well. Perhaps he can convince them to petition for Jed's release!"

Markus's eyes remained fixed on the wagon bed. "It's too late. The ship Jed was hauled aboard was pullin' up anchor for Dartmoor as I was escorted away."

"Dartmoor?" Samuel's face went slack at the revelation. "I didn't know."

Markus buried his head in his hand and Samuel laid a sympathetic hand on his shoulder. "Then we need a victory while peace is negotiated in Ghent, Markus. If the British go to Baltimore and we stop them at Fort McHenry, perhaps they'll be more inclined to sign the treaty."

"Fort McHenry is ready," Markus said. "The question is whether or not the ground troops will learn from Bladensburg and finally hold."

"If they don't—if Britain takes control of Baltimore—they'll be able to write anything they want into that treaty, and we'll be powerless to negotiate."

The woman in blue moaned softly, her voice rising in agitation as if she were experiencing a nightmare. Then she began thrashing about, her cries becoming more panicked. Samuel scooped her into his ample arms, helpless to comfort her. Looking to Markus, he reached out. "You'll have to take her. I need to pull a sedative powder from my bag."

The idea was onerous to Markus. He had buried his sorrows under the tedious demands of war, filling every moment, every energy, so there was little time for loneliness or remembering. He didn't want to recall the way a woman's soft, rounded body fit so naturally into the curve of his arms, or the way her hair tickled his neck and chin. He wanted to forget the way Lyra had made him feel simultaneously vulnerable and invincible. And most of all, he didn't want to long for the fire of a woman's touch.

"Please, Markus, for her sake."

Reluctantly, awkwardly, Markus opened his arms to receive the woman. Sorrow tinged his youthful, bearded face as he tentatively pressed her struggling body to his chest. The more she tensed the tighter he held her until the muscles rose on his arms and shoulders. He began humming the little Irish ditty his mother sang him to sleep with, "Shule Agra." In seconds the young woman quieted, the lines of her brow softening and the set of her mouth relaxing. He felt his eyes burn but he dare not stop the song even though the sound of it both pierced and warmed his heart. From the corner of his eye he saw Samuel glance at him with moist eyes.

"It was once our song—mine and Lyra's." The words came out choked and hoarse.

"You're doing fine there, Markus. Just fine. Look how safe and calm she feels."

Markus reached his arms out to return the patient to Samuel, who shook his head and whispered, "Let's not move her again just now. I'd prefer not to have to medicate her while she's in such a fragile state. We're halfway across the river. She'll be jostled badly enough when we reach the shore."

A few peaceful minutes passed. As Markus enjoyed the gentle lapping of the water, he worried over the unknown situation awaiting him at the Willows. Nudging Samuel's foot with his own, he asked, "Did Timothy know anythin' about our military's plans for Baltimore?"

Samuel appeared perplexed by the question. "He said the able-bodied flotillamen were heading there. I just assumed you'd be among them."

The comment caused Markus to tense. "I can't. I'm needed at the Willows. I promised Jed I'd watch over his family 'til he comes home."

Samuel pulled his pipe out of his mouth, then stuck it back in. "Oh, of course. I see."

"I promised 'im, Samuel! It's th' only thing left I can do for 'im."

Samuel pulled the pipe back out, waving it to emphasize his points. "Ending this war quickly will bring Jed home, Markus, and that will serve Hannah's and Frannie's interests best."

"One man's contribution matters little in battle, but it counts dearly on a farm."

"Some men matter more than others in critical circumstances. You are such a man, just like Jed is, but I won't argue the point. War and farming are your areas of expertise."

Markus allowed the conversation to lag. He didn't want to argue a point on which he was already conflicted. But he had made a promise to Jed, and he could not, *would not* let his friend down again. He was relieved when the ferryman called out a warning, followed by a firm bump as they docked on the east bank of the Patuxent, a few miles north of the Willows.

Markus gently eased the woman from his arms and onto the blanket laid out in the wagon bed. He paid the ferryman and took the lead horse's bridle, guiding her off the dock and into the grass. Just then, he heard the snort of another horse somewhere in the brush. He dismissed it, knowing the roads were filled with travelers, but when no wagon or rider broke through the tree line, Markus grabbed his musket and ventured into the brush, fully expecting to see the woman's "guide." Finding no demons or devils, Markus climbed into the driver's box and began the last five miles toward the Willows to keep his promise—the hardest thing he'd ever have to do in his life.

"I'm sorry if I upset you," Samuel said. "Were I in your shoes, I would be equally torn."

Markus didn't reply for a time, but the words settled his heart somewhat. "I wish you could stay on a while at the Willows. Hannah and I barely met a few days ago when she and Frannie came to Washington to try to save Jed. I know she loves you dearly, and with Jed gone and the baby due, all she has left is Frannie, Jack, Bitty, and the other freed slaves."

"So her family made good on their threat to disown her for marrying Jed?"

"She's an outcast ta her parents. She has two sisters. Beatrice moved ta Vermont, and then there's Myrna . . ." He heard Samuel groan. "I see you've met the woman."

"No, but her reputation for misery precedes her. So the Willows and its people are all Hannah has to comfort her now."

"Or to protect her. Jed was hard pressed to go to war himself after the mercenaries attacked the Willows. There's only freedmen on the farm now, and those freedom papers may have emancipated them legally, but we both know they won't change a thing in some men's eyes. They'll be powerless to protect the women if push comes to shove."

The wagon lumbered into the town of Calverton, where a ruckus of some sort was commencing on the steps of the mercantile. The local center of trade, Calverton, was a draw to all sorts of people with diverse and unyielding opinions—slavers and anti-slavery proponents as well as Federalists and their opposing Democratic-Republicans. Having experience with Calverton's fist-to-fist politics, and knowing the recent defeat at Washington had the citizenry lathered up, Markus knew a fight could be incited at any moment.

Samuel's concern echoed his own. "Look at that crowd! Let's drive straight through."

Markus urged the horses on until his attention was drawn to a fellow perched on the steps, angrily shaking a newspaper at the assembly and shouting above the cacophony of the crowd. Markus turned to Samuel, who had already come to the same conclusion. "That's Timothy!" they both exclaimed as Timothy seemed to also catch sight of them.

Markus urged the team to a secluded spot as Timothy began a new tirade. "I was there, friends! I watched helplessly as they fired their rockets into the windows of our Capitol, denying my petitions to spare it, and setting it ablaze. As if that weren't a sufficiently vulgar act, they entered and deliberately set fire after fire with the intentions of sparing nothing of our nation's beginnings! And then they marched to the president's own house, mocking not only the Madisons, but regarding our country's highest office as naught. And with the utmost pleasure, they piled the personal belongings of our president and his dear wife among the gifts foreign nations bequeathed to our own—the treasures of our republic—and set them ablaze for sport." Timothy's voice broke with emotion, then rose in fury.

"*The Boston Patriot* decries the burning of our Capitol as barbarism, calling it a wanton piece of destruction without parallel in modern war!" Timothy shook the paper and the crowd roared. "Consider that Bonaparte has been in possession of almost every capital in Europe, but he spared the ornamental edifices unrelated to war and warring. Did he burn libraries?"

"No!" the angry crowd shouted in reply.

"Did he wage war on science? On the arts? On civilization?" Timothy shouted louder.

"No!" the crowd roared back again.

"Did he burn the palaces of the emperor of Austria? Or the king of Prussia?"

Timothy joined the people's mighty shout of "No!" as he continued to whip them into a frenzy. Now he allowed the crowd to settle to a low rumble as he drove his concluding points straight into their sorrowing hearts.

"Even the Goths and vandals who sacked Rome left her ornamental buildings standing. But Britain refused to take her example from either the cruel or the civilized nations. Oh, no! By burning our beautiful, ornamental Capitol they have set an altogether new example of barbarism for themselves, one that cannot—must not—go unanswered. Baltimore, that beautiful port city on the Patapsco, will be the next city placed under siege. Can we allow her to fall? I say no, we cannot." In a booming voice, he shouted, "Will we allow her to fall?"

The crowd became a moving entity as it hoisted the man upon its shoulders while shouting, "No! No! No! No!" and firing muskets into the air. Timothy motioned to his friends with a wave of his arms.

After a careful check on the woman, Markus and Samuel jumped to the ground and stood near the wagon to await their friend. The rowdy minutes seemed endless, and Markus worried over their decision to stop. One by one, wagons filled and horses were mounted. Some of the angry men sped off to prepare to head to Baltimore, but most hurried away to safety.

Finally, Timothy broke away from his adoring followers and made his way toward Markus and Renfro, waving with boyish pleasure as he ran to them.

"Did you see that? Did you see how excited they were?" he asked breathlessly.

"Oh, you got them riled up," Samuel said. "You're a born politician."

Timothy was obviously wounded by the remark. "That wasn't politics, friends. That was righteous American indignation!" He looked south and gasped. "Most of them are still fleeing away! Why aren't they heading back to Baltimore to defend their city? I started reading this article from *The Boston Patriot,* and their sense of patriotism seemed to swell within them. Why didn't they allow that patriotic spirit to spur them back to Baltimore to fight?"

"You did your best. No sense in floggin' yourself over their cowardice," Markus said.

Timothy seemed dumbfounded. "I don't understand what's happening to our country."

Markus understood those feelings so completely.

"What are you doing here in the first place?" Samuel asked. "Did you find Mr. Key?"

"I did. He has an appointment to meet with President Madison and Colonel Skinner, our prisoner exchange agent, to draft the demand for Dr. Beanes's release. I actually came this way looking for you, Markus. The delegation will need a captain to sail them out to the flagship of the British fleet. We need someone courageous and trustworthy. I recommended you."

"Me? But I promised Jed—"

Timothy placed his hands on Markus's shoulders, his earnest eyes boring into his Irish friend's. "This is important, Markus. It's not just Dr. Beanes's life that's at stake here. These envoys will send a critical message to the British—that though our capital has been destroyed, our government and our Constitution have survived. They need a valiant captain, but they need a savvy guard as well. You see how few men I can trust right now. So promise me that you'll sail Mr. Key and his associate safely to the British fleet, and I'll help you keep your promise to Jed."

Markus couldn't deny that the offer intrigued him. He noticed that Timothy's eyes were drawn to the wagon.

"We've got a sick woman in the wagon. We're takin' her to the Willows."

Timothy's eye's narrowed. "I don't see a woman. I see a man—"

A terrified shriek erupted from the back of the wagon, spinning Markus and Samuel around. All three men prepared to leap into the wagon to attend to the woman when the "guide" rose on his knees, positioning Markus's musket upon his shoulder until it pointed at the Irishman's chest. In his other hand he displayed his trophy—the woman's ruby ring.

"I told you I'd have my fee, O'Malley. Now, hands up, gentlemen!" He purposely moved the ring to catch and reflect the sunlight. "Not as cocky as you were at the inn now, are you?"

Markus shook with fury. "If you harmed that woman, I'll . . ."

"You'll what?" the man shot back as he stood. "I believe I have the upper hand now."

"There's three of us. You'll get one at best, but you'll never get away from here alive."

The man slipped the ring into his pocket, withdrawing a small pistol. "Two rounds should handle two of you quite nicely. And I'll secure the third round from one of your dead friends. I'll need your guns, gentlemen." To Samuel and Timothy he ordered, "Open up your jackets, one at a time, the good doctor first and then the politician. Let's have a look at what's hiding under there. And you, Mr. O'Malley? So much as flinch and I'll be delighted to shoot you first."

Markus saw movement in the corner of the wagon as the woman huddled behind the man in the first show of lucidity Markus had witnessed in her.

The gunman, obviously thinking she posed no threat, remained focused on securing the men's pistols, hardly regarding her at all. But there was something in her eyes that told Markus she had more grit than any of them suspected. Their eyes met, and a small shift in her brow told him she had an idea. He subtly returned her signal, and a moment later he saw her black-booted foot swing into the back of the man's knee.

It was a weak kick, but enough to throw the gunman off balance. Markus sprang onto the wagon like a cat, plunging straight into the man's knees, both of them crashing to the floor in a tangled heap. He could hear the scrape of feet off to the side and knew Timothy and Samuel were coming to his aid. Before they arrived, Markus had easily subdued the man, pressing his back against the wagon bed before securing the gun. A shot rang out and the woman's scream was followed by a groan and the huff of a pained exhale.

Time seemed to stop as Markus registered the burn in his side and the warm trickle spreading beneath his shirt. He felt the breathless man groan beneath his weight as he flailed wildly, attempting to dislodge Markus. The woman was the first to arrive at Markus's side, followed by Timothy, who cried out for Samuel to hurry while he cocked and pressed his own pistol to the assailant's head, threatening to shoot him if he didn't lie still.

Samuel rolled Markus over and paled when he saw the location of the wound. Pointing to the gunman he shouted, "Take him to the sheriff while I tend to Markus." Without the exchange of a single word, the woman opened Samuel's bag and began laying out the correct supplies.

"Are you a nurse?" Samuel asked as he ripped Markus's shirt open. The woman shrugged and handed him a bottle of alcohol and a batch of cloth bandages. "Markus! Markus!" Samuel called out. Markus grimaced in reply. Samuel half laughed, half cried when he cleared the blood enough to check the wound. "Markus O'Malley, you're the luckiest cuss I've ever met. That's a one-in-a-million miracle right there—a ball fired point blank hit a side rib and went clean through. You'll hurt like the dickens, but nothing vital has been damaged."

Eyes closed, his face tight with pain, Markus offered a taut smile. "The luck of the Irish."

Samuel's relief was palpable. "I suppose. Let's hope all our luck is about to change."

The woman slid back into the wagon corner while Samuel worked to stop the bleeding. A second later she returned with her petticoat in her hands. "Will this do for a bandage?"

Samuel smiled appreciatively. "Good girl. That will do fine."

She began tearing the cloth into wide strips that she tied one to another. "I'm sorry about your friend. I never meant to cause anyone any trouble."

Looking at her squarely, Samuel said, "Ma'am, now is not the time, but we're soon going to need some answers from you." In response she retreated back into her corner of the wagon.

By the time Timothy returned with the sheriff, Markus was wrapped and ready to travel.

The sheriff offered his hand to Markus. "I'm sorry this happened. The whole region is riled up. After I question your assailant I'll head to the Willows to talk to you and the lady."

Samuel nudged Timothy. "Let's leave here before I end up with another patient. Tie your horse on the back and drive the wagon. I'll tend these two back here."

The last few miles took nearly two hours owing to the snail's pace Samuel insisted on. The woman sat mutely in the corner. When they passed the last bend before the Willow's property, Markus insisted on sitting up front with Timothy to survey the farm. All three men gawked, noting the devastating toll the past year had taken on the once-pristine plantation.

"The dock is gone. Jed told me they blew it up to prevent attacks from the river."

The scorched fields, the burned fences, the missing dock, the debris scattered along the shore from July's tornado—all of it testified to how badly Markus was needed here. As the wagon rounded the bend, the little company stopped. Afforded their first full view of the charred three-story mansion house, they surveyed the damage.

Built nearly fifty years earlier by Jed's grandfather, the first Pearson in America, the large, white frame home had been among the grandest in the region in its day. The right half still looked lovely. Its white paint, hand-carved cornices, and black shutters were only partially marred by soot and smoke, but sooty patterns around the windows indicated that most of the rooms on the left side had been affected. The trampled front lawn looked as if a thousand head of cattle had been pastured there, and the burned fields ran within a hundred feet of the three-story mansion house.

Samuel sucked in a loud rush of air that confirmed every one of Markus's thoughts. "Those filthy mercenaries really did try to kill them, even the women and children!"

"Jed could hardly speak about the slaughter Dupree attempted. Jack, Abel, and the other freedmen stood with 'im. So did Arthur Ramsey. Even Frederick Stringham fought by 'is side."

"Frederick Stringham showed some spine?" Timothy asked. "I thought the Stringhams were aiding the mercenaries."

"Jed and Hannah offered sanctuary to Frederick's wife, so Frederick chose ta take 'is stand here, against 'is father's wishes. In the end, the tornado turned the fire back ta White Oak Farm, killin' both of Frederick's parents. 'E owns what's left of the place, and from what Jed says, 'e is convinced half the county that 'e saved the Willows single-handed. And now you see why Jed needs me here. There's so much rebuildin' to do."

Four armed freedmen soon appeared on the porch, followed by three women—two white and one Negro. Timothy slapped the reins and urged the team onward. As one of the women flew down to greet the wagon, he handed the reins to Samuel and leapt to the ground to greet the auburn-haired girl who had stolen his heart years ago—Frannie Pearson.

She filled Timothy's outstretched arms, but her eyes searched only for Markus O'Malley, who offered her a slight nod and a knowing smile. The female passenger rose shyly to stand behind

Markus, and Frannie regarded her with curiosity. "Who's that poor thing, Timothy?"

"We hoped you'd know. She hasn't said much. She fell in with some charlatan who was exploiting her in return for delivering her here. The pair crossed paths with Samuel and Markus."

Frannie neared the wagon, studying the woman carefully. Suddenly recognition lit Frannie's face. "Jenny? Jenny Potter?"

"I'm sorry, Frannie. I—I had nowhere else to go."

"Don't apologize. It's wonderful to see you!"

Much to the chagrin of all the men, Frannie climbed into the wagon unassisted, catching Jenny up in a hug from which the weak girl recoiled. "You poor dear, you're skin and bones," Frannie said.

Jenny stumbled from fatigue and Markus rushed to steady her, groaning as he did so.

"Dear, Mr. O'Malley." Jenny gasped. "I've already caused you so much distress. I should never have come."

"There, now." Markus yielded her to Frannie. "She's not well. Be gentle with Miss—"

"It's actually *Mrs.*, Mr. O'Malley." Jenny cast her eyes downward. "Mrs. Jeremiah Tyler." She turned to Frannie and explained, "I was just married last year."

"Oh, I see. Well, congratulations." Frannie's eyes arched curiously as she surveyed her friend's pitiful appearance. "And where is Mr. Tyler?"

"He best have a good excuse for leavin' a young wife to her own defenses at such a time," Markus said sharply. "Get 'er set up in a room, Frannie girl. I think we all need a bit o' rest."

Frannie noted the fatigue in his voice. It was then that she saw the fresh blood on his shirt. "Oh, Markus! What's happened to you?"

"It's my fault," Jenny said as she shrank back.

"'Twas no such thing," Markus replied softly. "Tell them, Samuel."

"Right now, I need to get you two into the house where I can attend to you properly."

Frannie took the reins and drove the team up the lane, leaving Timothy running alongside. At the top stood Hannah, a study in peace, who contrasted sharply with her sister-in-law's gregarious nature. Her rounded torso threw her posture back, and her long dark hair hung in a thick braid, making her appear more like a little girl than a twenty-year-old mother-to-be. Behind her stood her dark-skinned protectors—Jack, Sookie, Jubal, and Royal—and the most fierce protector of them all, Bitty, the tiny freed woman who had raised Frannie and Jed.

The freedmen lowered their muskets while the three white men waited to see to whom Hannah's attentions would turn. She greeted each one, but it was her dear friend Samuel who won her gaze. He lumbered down from the wagon and caught her in his broad embrace. "How's my girl?"

"I'm so glad you're here," she answered as she held on tightly. Several moments passed before she pulled back. "We're so glad to see all of you!"

"Hannah, I'd like to meet my dear friend, Jenny Potter," Frannie said. "We sang together in Philadelphia, at Le Jardin de Chanteuses. She'll be our guest for a while. Isn't that lovely?"

Jenny immediately spoke up. "I—I—I didn't come to be your guest. I'll gladly be your servant. With a day's rest, I'll be fit to work, and I'll work hard for my keep. I promise!"

Frannie's face melted with mercy. "No one is a servant here, Jenny. We all work together. Isn't that right, Hannah?"

Jenny looked to Hannah for affirmation.

"There's always room for one more, Jenny. I'm not quite sure where we'll situate you right now. Since the fire destroyed all the residents' cabins we've moved everyone into the two houses." She looked at Markus, who smiled knowingly, understanding that his house was one of the two filled with displaced residents.

"Hannah, I need to get Markus inside," Samuel said. "He's been shot."

The news sent everyone scurrying to attend to the newcomers. Samuel supported Markus's left side and Frannie slid in under his right, taking advantage of the moment. With wide eyes steeled for the worst, she asked, "Did Arthur make it to the ship alive?"

"Aye, darlin'. He was alive when I left 'im, and my last words to' im were of you."

Tears sprang to Frannie's eyes at the news. "And Jed? Did you see him too?"

"Aye, but let's save that news for Hannah too, shall we? And by the way, lest I forget, I have a little something in the bed of the wagon for you and Hannah."

"Markus . . ."

"Now it isn't much, just a couple of calico kittens, but I thought you both could use a little somethin' sweet to hold right about now."

Frannie tightened her hold on his good arm. "You do know me well."

Bitty quickly added a few peach tarts to the cold menu while Samuel patched up Markus. Frannie attended to Jenny, coercing the debilitated woman into eating a bowl of soup and half a peach. Clearly exhausted, Jenny fell asleep between mouthfuls, so Frannie withdrew to allow her to rest.

After supper, every resident on the farm came to the front porch to enjoy the luxury of company and news from Washington. Hannah sat flanked by Samuel and Markus, who hovered over her. Bitty was anxious to hear about President and Mrs. Madison, and where they would be living since the President's House had been burned to its shell. Timothy was able to answer nearly every query. He rattled on about President Madison's call to convene the Congress to begin a full inquiry into the cause of the loss at Bladensburg and the fall of the city. But his greatest lamentation was over the loss of the great library housed in the Capitol Building.

"Over three thousand volumes gone," Timothy cried. "Some of the greatest works in the world, burned to ash. Barbarians! I don't know how we'll rebuild it. Who knows what more this war will cost us? The national budget can barely meet its pledges to the military, and then there's so much rebuilding to be done. I fear books will be far down on the list of national priorities."

"Perhaps individuals will make private donations from their libraries," Frannie said.

"But many of the lost books were rare volumes personally selected by President Jefferson. They'll be hard to replace. Our only hope is if he can reconstruct a partial list."

Hannah fussed nervously with her hands, drawing attention to herself. "I probably sound dreadfully cold, Timothy, but books are the last thing I want my government fretting over at such a time. When will we know if the British are attacking Baltimore? And how are the peace negotiations going in Ghent? The news takes so long to travel from there to here and back that we could have a treaty and not know it, and still be warring with Britain."

Timothy sobered immediately. "Forgive me, Hannah, for prattling on about my own pet interests. You're right. Rebuilding the library pales beside the points you've raised. I'll do my best to answer them. To begin with, our peace delegation is making good progress. John Quincy, the son of President Adams, leads our delegation, and he is far and away superior to any delegate Britain has sent. But therein lies the problem. John Quincy is ready and fully empowered to set the treaty, but Britain's delegates are of such minor status that they must run each jot and tittle by the powers in London, thus stalling the treaty, which we believe is exactly Britain's plan. Our only course is to exact a sufficient toll in men, gold, and public opinion to make it advantageous for them to hurry the negotiations along. We don't yet know how the barbarism in Washington will play in London, and strategists are divided about Britain's next move. Some think they will most certainly attack Baltimore. Others say they may not wish to risk their great victory at Washington by suffering a defeat there. We simply don't know."

"What is their ultimate aim?" Hannah asked. "They claimed Washington was in retaliation for our sacking of York. All right, we're tit for tat. What do they now want?"

"It's about trade rights now, and we think their aim is control of the Mississippi River. Battle lines remain active along the northern borders and the New England waters, but if a treaty isn't reached shortly, the battle will eventually shift to the south."

"And the longer it goes on, the more men will die and suffer in prisons. My sister Beatrice writes to me, sending snippets of her communications from Dudley, who has been held in Melville Island Prison for almost two years now. How much longer can a man remain in such conditions? How long can any man . . ."

Samuel placed a comforting hand over Hannah's, and everyone sat as silent seconds passed with no one knowing how to fill them.

Finally, Timothy broke the stillness. "Frannie, would you join me for a stroll?" He stood, extending his hand to her. Frannie glanced at Hannah and the women's sad eyes met before Frannie took Timothy's hand and rose. Both women knew the hour had come when more painful explanations would have to begin.

"You look so troubled," Samuel observed as Hannah's eyes followed Frannie and Timothy to the river. "With all you have to deal with, you still worry over everyone else."

"She's my sister now, in every important way."

"And she's in pain. I had lunch with Timothy in Washington at the home of a Stephen Pleasanton, Secretary Monroe's clerk at the State Department. He had a niece there, Lucinda Bainbridge.

Timothy had evidently already confided in her about Frannie's romantic entanglement with Lieutenant Ramsey. When we were alone, she told me Timothy loved Frannie in a way no other woman could ever fill. It makes the current situation all the more difficult."

Hannah raised an eyebrow.

"I saw that, little lady," Markus said, clearly pleased for an opportunity to lighten the conversation. "What's goin' on in that mind of yours?"

"What am I missing here?" Samuel asked.

Markus chuckled. "Hannah's too polite to say it, but I believe she's a tad curious about Miss Bainbridge's interest in the state of Timothy's heart."

"You got all that from a single look? Clearly, I do not understand women." Samuel sighed. "Speaking of women, I hope we haven't brought more trouble to your door by delivering that Mrs. Tyler here. Markus raised valid concerns, but I wouldn't listen."

"Don't fret, Samuel. We'll sort it all out."

"I have another matter to sort out with you, Hannah. It involves Markus and his prom—"

"Not tonight," Markus scolded.

"No," Hannah said. "I want to hear what Samuel has to say."

Samuel shrugged at Markus and carried on. "Markus promised Jed he'd stay close to the farm and watch over things, but Timothy needs him in Baltimore. Mr. Key is going to petition the British to release Dr. Beanes, and he needs a good captain to ferry him to the fleet."

"Then of course he must go. Perhaps he'll be able to free Jed as well!"

"I asked you not to do this, Samuel!" Markus said roughly. "You've given her false hope."

No reproof was needed as Samuel's face twisted with sorrow. "I'm sorry. Markus is right. Mr. Key can't help Jed because his ship already set sail. But assuring the British that our government is still operating and suing for its citizens' rights will also serve Jed's cause."

Hannah's face fell as the reality of the words sank in. "Of course it will. Markus should go."

Samuel squeezed her hand. "Timothy has agreed to stay on until Markus's return."

"He's likely a complete loss as a farmer," Markus said, "but he'll keep you ladies well entertained, and if trouble comes riding in, who better to talk the varmint to death?"

"Very true." Hannah laughed and squeezed Markus's shoulder. "We'll be fine until you return. When will you be leaving?"

"I'll let my side knit another day or so. Timothy says a courier will come bringing word of when I'm to meet Mr. Key in Baltimore."

"And you, Samuel? Can you stay on a while?"

"If the British make a run on Baltimore, I'll be needed there. Until then, there's nowhere else I'd rather be. Right now I recommend we all turn in. Both of you need to rest."

"Oh, off with ya, Samuel!" Markus interjected. "What do you think of that, Hannah? This mornin' he was my friend, this afternoon he became my physician. Is he now tryin' to be my mother?"

Samuel waved off the joke and headed for Markus's crowded cabin.

"I've been waitin' for the right moment to speak to you about Jed." Markus looked at Hannah carefully.

Hannah's eyes darted about for a moment, settling on her hands. "I have these feelings about him—that's he's all right—and I want to hold on to those, Markus. Maybe I need to believe that to carry on. I—I just don't want you to tell me anything that will take that away from me."

Markus took her hand. "I saw 'im, Hannah, right before 'e boarded. 'E asked me to pass 'is love on to ya. You and the wee bairn are on 'is mind every minute. You mark my words: those

British won't break the spirit of Jonathan Edward Pearson III. 'E'll come home to ya."

Timothy noted how Frannie maintained a steady distance from him as they walked. He kept his hands clasped behind him, resisting his desire to take her hand.

"Was Mrs. Tyler somewhat improved when you last checked on her?" Frannie asked.

"We hardly spoke before she collapsed asleep."

"Odd that you didn't recognize her when you first saw her."

Frannie looked pensive. "She's so different now, so thin and sad. She was once the happiest person you'd ever wish to meet, full of plans and dreams."

"It would seem much has happened to her in the years since you parted."

"She speaks only of our Le Jardin days, and I haven't felt inclined to press the point."

"She appears to have been on her own or at least in poor company for some while now," Timothy said. "She may not be the same person anymore, Frannie. Are you prepared for that?"

Frannie shot her response back at him. "She and the owner of Le Jardin, Henri de Mourdant, are the reasons I survived that autumn when my good name was slandered."

Timothy halted. "I know I failed you then. I've considered how we might be married now had I come to you immediately."

Frannie shook her head and began walking again. "I didn't want you to save me. I wanted to vindicate myself, or at least to defy Stewart Stringham's power to determine my destiny. Le Jardin and Jenny made me strong again, and I'm grateful to be able to repay the favor."

Timothy felt the sting of her rebuke.

Frannie glanced at him. "I'm sorry for being so sharp," she

said. "My nerves are raw, I suppose. I'm angry, and I'm—I'm steeled for a fight. I'm sorry you're the unfortunate recipient."

Daring rejection, Timothy reached out and took hold of her arm. "We've never been able to recapture what we had that spring, have we?"

Frannie took on a wistful look. "It was a magical spring. After all the horrible things that transpired with Frederick Stringham and Dupree, I needed to feel that I was still capable of loving and trusting someone again. You did that for me, and I'll never forget that."

"Jed and I wanted to kill them both for what they did to you."

Frannie gazed off blankly. "When a young woman survives a kidnapping attempt only to have her fiancé break their engagement and publicly charge her with impropriety, she should hope to find solace in her own home, but true to form, my mother's plan was to hide me away in Europe until the gossip blew over." She brought her eyes to meet Timothy's. "I cherish the pearls you gave me when you met our ship upon our return home."

Timothy brought his cheek to hers. "As I recall, when I dropped you off at Mrs. Murdock's school I also kissed you and asked you to consider building a future with me."

Frannie took a step back. "I thought my life was perfect. But an hour later, as you headed to New York for law school, the filthy rumors circulated, and it was recommended that I withdraw from school to quell the chatter. It didn't matter that I was innocent. I became an outcast, wondering if those promises we discussed were still possible.

"I spent hours walking around Philadelphia, afraid to go home and face my parents' embarrassment, and unwilling to become a recluse here at the Willows. And then there was my worry over how you and your family would react. That's when I found Le Jardin. Henri treated me like a daughter, and Jenny was my dearest friend. What would I have done without her?"

Timothy gently took Frannie's shoulders, forcing her to face him squarely. "But Le Jardin is gone now, Frannie. Henri is out west, and the other singers are building new lives. Perhaps it's time for you to let go of the past and embrace something real."

"This isn't about Jenny. This is about Arthur! You think I should accept that he will die?"

"I don't want to see you pining your life away for an unrealistic dream."

Frannie turned abruptly from him. "I love Arthur, Timothy. I'm sorry if my saying so hurts you, but it happened completely by accident. And yes, he may die, but the critical element we lack will not miraculously appear if he does."

Timothy's shoulders rounded. "Would you prefer being alone to being with me?"

"Am I truly your first love? If you were honest with yourself you'd admit that Arthur did not come between us. Washington did. You love the workings of the government. America is your first love, and you need a woman who loves and understands it equally."

Frannie strode away and Timothy joined her stride for stride until they reached the river. They paused there silently for a while. Timothy felt his throat becoming thick with emotion, and he wished he had never raised the topic of their relationship this day.

"Couldn't you learn to love my world, Frannie?"

Frannie moved to him, slipping beneath his arm and laying her head on his shoulder. "I don't belong there, Timothy. I'm an attraction, an entertainer who amuses them." She lifted her head to softly kiss his cheek. "As you once put it yourself, I'm the 'wild woman of the Willows.'"

He kissed her head, lingering there. His voice was husky as he confessed, "I don't think I can love my world without the wild woman in it."

Frannie turned to face him. She placed her hands on his shoulders and looked him in the eyes. "Yes, you can, my friend. And you must."

CHAPTER 6

On board the HMS Tonnant, *Vice Admiral Cochrane's flagship*

Major General Robert Ross grappled with his indecision as he watched the bulk of the British fleet prepare to depart the Patuxent River, the nest from which they had launched their daring blitz across Maryland to take Washington City. His superior, Vice Admiral Cochrane, commander in chief of the North American Station, was dividing the fleet, sending some ships to Tangier Island in the Chesapeake Bay to re-establish Fort Albion, their temporary base, while Cochrane led another portion of the fleet up the Potomac to confuse the Americans, who expected the British to make a run on Baltimore.

Ross's naval equal, Admiral George Cockburn, was salivating to conquer Baltimore, but Ross had voted against that move. Fort McHenry's fortifications and strategic positioning on a peninsula jutting out into the Patapsco River made it nearly impenetrable. And what of the Americans—would they rally? Ross felt it was too great a risk. A loss at Baltimore would diminish the victory at Washington, a victory that had cost so much young British blood.

Ross had sent his attaché, Captain Smith, back to London to assure the Admiralty that he would not march his men on Baltimore. So, while the rest of the fleet created a feign and prepared for their next encounter, Ross had ordered his brave men, decorated veterans of the Napoleonic Wars, to roost in the Patuxent to wait and watch against a rear attack. He was so sure of his position four days ago, but now doubts plagued him.

As the fleet began pulling up anchors, longing for the exhilaration of battle swept through the forty-eight-year-old hero's heart. Ross loved his men as they loved him. They would go to battle and thank him for the honor. He had seen it many times, most recently at the bloodbath of Bladensburg. Though many of their fellow soldiers were cut down by enemy fire, his men kept running toward the American line, willing to die to gain a single yard's advance. The Americans had feared them, their lines breaking at the very sight of young British courage, and in the end Ross's men had won the ultimate prize for Britain—they had captured the American capital.

Like a thoroughbred in the gate, he felt nervous, anxious, hungry. Had Cockburn simply made his case for a Baltimore victory so compelling that Ross was hungering for it as well?

Ross leaned over the table and stared down at the battle map again. His finger tapped on the pentagon that represented the nearly impenetrable Fort McHenry. Along the shorelines across from the fort sat artillery batteries that created a deadly crossfire for enemy ships. Baltimore was nearly invulnerable to a naval assault, but ground options were no better. The fort's five corners placed sharpshooters at varying angles, catching intruders in a crossfire as well. No, Baltimore would not be an easy sweep like Washington. But could it be done?

Cockburn had proposed a two-pronged surprise attack that would overwhelm the city's defenses. While the fleet pounded the fort from beyond the reach of McHenry's artillery, Ross and Cockburn could land their men on another peninsula a few miles east of the city—at North Point—and march them to Baltimore.

The strategy was sound, but there were incalculable variables. How many Americans would rally to the city? There was an even more unanswerable question. This time, would the American forces hold their lines in the heat of battle, or would they break in fear and run as they had before? Cockburn believed they would fold once again. Was he right, or had Britain aroused some sleeping patriotism in these Americans?

CHAPTER 7

Tuesday, August 30, 1814
Fort McHenry in Baltimore, Maryland

The horses Abel and his son Caleb secured from the Willows had been conscripted to carry supplies Hannah and Frannie had sent along with the Pennsylvania militia, leaving Abel and Caleb to walk their way to Baltimore with the rest of the men. Abel noticed the sideways glances that accompanied whispered conversations whenever new people met him. Yes, he was a very large man—six feet eight inches of solid brown brawn—but he knew it wasn't just his size that captivated these men. It was the *other* thing that brought him notoriety.

Abel learned early that size and strength are both a blessing and a curse to a man born into slavery. Such a man is able to lift and tote twice what other men can, but then again, that becomes exactly what an overseer expects from the big slave. Not the big *man*. The big *slave*.

The master and overseer fear the slave, so they double the guard and come down quick with the lash. But they need that slave, so they're slow to cause harm that would disable. Abel's Achilles heel was always his parents. Anytime his temper would flare, the overseer, or his master, Stewart Stringham, would threaten to sell his mother away, or harm his father, who was a big man himself before the water wheel at the White Oak mill ground him down into a broken memory of who he had once been. Abel had only been about ten years old that horrible day. His anger festered as he watched his brilliant father bend and scrape before dimwitted white overseers because they were free and they held a whip or a gun. But Abel rarely spoke after that, keeping all the learning his father was secretly passing on to him hidden inside.

Abel avoided love and marriage until he was nearly thirty, knowing the object of his affection would also become a pawn to keep him in check. Her name was Lily. She was a sweet woman, and Abel became a new man—kowtowing like his father, understanding the courage it took to submit one's will to protect one's family. Lily died bringing their fourth child, little Helen, into the world. The overseer then began doubling Abel's work, threatening to sell off Abel's children if he didn't comply. He hated his life. He hated whites. He longed for freedom and plotted his family's escape. Death would be better than slavery, he figured. And then came the miracle of his redemption. That was what those men were whispering about.

Temperatures were sweltering as they marched into Baltimore, making Abel doubly glad he and Caleb had their hair cut close to the scalp the previous week. Abel's large brown eyes stung from salty perspiration, so he pulled out Bitty's red bandana and lifted his sweat-soaked farm hat to wipe his head and brow. Waving the floppy old hat back and forth a few times moved the dead air some; he was grateful for any semblance of a breeze.

He glanced at his son. Caleb was a smaller version of his father, possessing the smaller features and rich brown coloring passed down from Abel's father, Jerome's, Caribbean heritage. Abel's mother, Sarah, was a darker woman, and from her African descent the pair inherited thicker lips and large brown eyes. The story was famous along the river, and combined with Abel's size and unique features, it drew him attention wherever he went. And so it was today.

A group of five young Negroes kept glancing back at Abel and whispering. Abel recognized the sixth and only other man of color in the group. A black-skinned man of medium build, Titus had spent a dangerous night at the Willows almost a year back. The man probably didn't know Abel had seen him, or how closely their fortunes were tied.

Wagons kept spilling out of Baltimore, the clatter of their wheels on the brick streets the primary sign of life as her remaining citizens cowered in their homes. Abel was appalled by the ignominious cowardice of a people blessed with the freedom he was only beginning to taste. He knew he would gladly die to preserve such liberties for his own children. It was why he had torn his son from Bitty's arms, bringing him along—so Caleb would know the sweetness of fighting for a better life, a better world. And so many of these privileged people who already had what he yearned for were willing to surrender without a fight. How could they?

Baltimore was the third largest city in the nation, an important port where the famed clipper ships were built. It was these swift vessels, and the scores of privateers that launched from this port, that made Baltimore a British target. Defending the port was critical to the nation's interests. Abel had read that in the broadsheets Hannah had given him, along with a dozen new books he would have to wait to read until he returned home.

As the group marched past Federal Hill and down the Old Fort Road, he saw it, poised against the setting sun—the magnificent new flag Major George Armistead had commissioned for Fort McHenry. The snap of the fabric carried on the Patapsco River's cooler evening breeze, and even from afar, the flag imbued the men with renewed vigor and they stepped up their pace.

It was nearly dark when they finally arrived at the star-shaped fort and found a spot of empty shoreline to set up camp. Tents, company flags, and bodies dressed in a variety of uniform pieces and civilian attire seemed to spread as far as Abel could see in the limited light.

At first light he inquired about the intake process. No recruitment officers were on hand to receive him, so he returned to camp and found Caleb sitting by the fire. Father and son pitched in to prepare a rudimentary breakfast of oatmeal and biscuits. As they ate, Abel noticed how quiet his son was this morning. And he couldn't ignore the wary look in the boy's eyes, and how close Caleb sat to him as they ate their breakfast with the other six Negro men.

"Are you disappointed because we can't sleep inside the fort?" Abel asked. "It can't be helped, you know. There were already one hundred regulars assigned to the fort before the war commenced. Since the attack on Washington, one thousand new troops have arrived from all over Maryland, Virginia, and Pennsylvania. I heard Sergeant McCoy say the total number of soldiers surrounding the city might reach near thirty thousand. Can you imagine that, Caleb?"

After a momentary flicker of enthusiasm, the light in the boy's eyes dimmed. Abel drew his muscular arm around his son, who was tall for twelve but not nearly as large as his father was at that age. He playfully jostled Caleb until the lad could no longer withhold his smile. For a brief moment he snuggled close to his father's chest, and then in the next, he withdrew once more.

"What's the matter, Caleb?"

"I want to go home to the Willows."

"The time comes when every man has to leave the nest and test his own wings."

Abel noticed the way Caleb's eyes darted to where the other six Negroes sat eating their food. Titus sat apart from the group, but the other five sat in a cluster, stealing glances at Abel and Caleb from time to time.

"How about taking a walk down by the river with me?" Abel asked his son.

Relief filled Caleb's eyes. He stood quickly, choosing a path that took him far from the six men, and Abel followed.

Once they were at the river's edge, Abel picked up a flat rock and skipped it across the water. "The cooks here can't match Bitty Mama's cooking, can they?"

Caleb's hands slipped to his sides as he stared out at the water. "I heard those men talking about you. They said you were famous—the highest-priced . . . you know . . . the most expensive slave ever bought along the river."

The reference to his past stung Abel. It was an onerous way for a man to achieve fame. Two years ago, Jed Pearson had approached Stewart Stringham, the brutal owner of Abel's entire family, asking to buy them all. The master of White Oak saw it as an opportunity to make himself a tidy profit and a legend in one day. He had named an absurdly high price, which Jed ultimately paid—all because Bitty asked him to.

Abel nudged the boy lovingly. "You know the story. Why did hearing it bother you?"

Caleb shrugged and lowered his head. "I remember how it was at White Oak. I expected some meanness from the whites, but not from them."

Abel wrestled his anger down. "Go on."

Caleb swallowed hard. "They said you were the highest-priced nigger in the state, and that free or not, you were still just a nigger and nothing more."

Abel hated that word. He had hoped his children would be spared from hearing it once they moved to the Willows, but here it was. He considered how to answer while he worked his tight jaw, knowing his response would shape his son's view of himself, and of his father.

Finally, Abel placed his hands on his son's shoulders and said, "Those men must be very afraid."

"What?"

"A brave man—I mean a *really* brave man—accepts people for who they are. He doesn't need to bring a man down to make himself feel better. So these men must be very afraid."

Caleb appeared to ponder that idea. "Of us? Because you're six feet eight inches tall?"

Abel smiled. "Maybe they're afraid of us, but more likely they're just plain afraid."

"But aren't they free too?"

"Some are, but some are likely runaways hiding from their masters, or men hoping they can join the army and earn enough money to buy their freedom, or their children's freedom. That's pretty sad. I suppose living on the Willows makes us forget how blessed we are. What does the good book say? 'For unto whomsoever much is given, of him shall much be required.'"

Caleb eyed the men with sadness in his eyes. "They're still mean."

"I know. Do you remember that line your grandfather used to spout off about fear—'Cowards die many times before their deaths'?"

"From Shakespeare?"

"That's right. Don't let them make you afraid, Caleb. When people are cruel to you, you need to dig down deep and remember who you are—that you are a bright, young, free man who is being educated. You can read and write, and even read some in Latin. Imagine that! And even if you have to hide those gifts for now, no law can take what you've learned from you. And you're a landowner, Caleb! Maybe it's just a small parcel, but it's real, and it's ours. So when men are hard on you or mean to you, you just square these strong shoulders and remember that you're making a better way in this world for Eli, and Little Grandy, and Helen. If you can remember that, there's nothing these men can say to you that will make you afraid."

Caleb's eyes shone. "Yes sir, Papa."

Abel pulled Caleb close and hugged him tightly. "You're a good boy, Caleb. I'm proud of you, Son. Papa's always proud of you. You know that, right?"

Caleb smiled. "Yes, sir."

"Now you run off and help the ladies with the dishes, all right?"

Caleb ran off as he was told, while Abel set a course back to the fire and over to where the five men still sat. The kettle of oatmeal was nearly empty, but Abel placed a biscuit on his plate and scraped the spoon around and around the kettle with slow deliberateness. He shifted into fieldspeak, the casual dialect most common to slaves, figuring it wisest to blend in.

"It's nearly gone. Any of you want more?" he asked. The men waved him off, urging him to finish off the mush. Again, he slowly scraped the spoon around and around the kettle, getting the men's attention. He gathered the oatmeal into the spoon and slowly tapped the utensil against his plate over and over like a gavel on a table. "I hear you've met my son."

"Uh, Caleb?" inquired one overly friendly man. "Yes, yes, a fine boy."

"Fine boy," another man repeated.

Abel kept tapping his plate. "There's something about a man's son . . . How does that saying go?" Abel first had to compose a saying. "Oh, yes. The friend of a man's son is the man's friend too. Ever heard that saying?"

After a long silence, one of the five spoke. "Yes, yes."

"That's a good ole sayin'," another put in.

"I think so," Abel replied. He stuffed the entire biscuit into his huge mouth with ease, then gave the men a wink. They sat as still as stone. "Allow me," he added as he collected all their plates and utensils and headed for the washtubs. "Now you gentlemen have a good day."

He experienced a twinge of guilt over how good it felt to cow those five, but not enough to remove the broad smile from his face.

"Abel?"

He turned and recognized the man calling to him with his hand outstretched. "Hello, Abel. Do you remember me—Dr. Randolph Foster? I'm a member of Jed's militia group."

Abel walked over to Foster and reluctantly shook his hand. "Yes, sir. I remember you."

The doctor's chin dropped. "The memory is no doubt an unfavorable one. I failed you last spring, Abel. You offered to risk your life and go into battle with us, and when members of our militia company refused to fight by your side I advised Jed to have you leave us."

Abel needed no reminder. It was the sting of that day—the idea that his freedom had to remain a secret, and the reality that his color would always trump his character in most men's eyes—that inspired him to make a rash decision a leave his family to join the military one day.

"I was as concerned for your safety as I was about keeping the group unified. I feared you were at greater risk from the American soldiers than from the British marauders."

"I hold no ill feelings toward you."

"I appreciate that, Abel."

Abel couldn't deny that Foster sounded sincere.

"I'm leading the Patuxent militia now. Since Washington, the group has become considerably more hospitable. When I heard you were here I saw an opportunity to make up for my previous failing. I'd like to invite you join our company."

"I surely appreciate the gesture, Dr. Foster, but I intend to enlist in the regular army."

"The regular army? Are you prepared to enlist for two years, Abel? You won't be able to walk away when the battle is over. You do understand that, don't you?"

"Of course I do." Abel noted the arrogance in his own reply. "No disrespect intended, Dr. Foster, but I'm a free man now. I shouldn't need to be invited to protect what's also mine. Joining up is my right, and I like the sound of that."

"Indeed you should, Abel. Well said. Well said."

Abel became more contrite. "I'm anxious to receive a soldier's pay—eight dollars a month." He savored the words.

"And the fifty-dollar enlistment bonus."

"Fifty dollars? For enlisting?"

Dr. Foster's eyes darted to the ground. "That's assuming they accept you." He stared off at the other men of color. "The recruitment officers will be checking for papers. I know you have yours, but you should warn your friends that runaways will be turned over to the law."

"You don't think they'll accept me, do you?"

Dr. Foster shifted his feet and stepped closer. "There are some freemen in the militias, and Commodore Barney had a few amongst his flotillamen, but generally speaking, it's harder for a Negro man to become a regular. And what will you do about your son?"

"Caleb? He's taller than half of the men, and a fine shot."

"None of that will matter if you are deployed elsewhere. The military requires recruits to be sixteen years of age."

The news took Abel by surprise.

"Let me help you while Jed is, well, while he's away. I'd be pleased to make a few introductions in your behalf. I know Judge Nicholson. He raised and trained an artillery company with his own money. He's the second-in-command here at the fort, under the major. And his Baltimore Fencibles are an admirable group. They're an elite volunteer group, but it could be the first step to your becoming a regular. I might even be able to get Caleb a paying job as a cook."

Pride caused Abel to hesitate. This was something he wanted to do on his own, to prove that being free was more than a piece of paper. "I came here to prove that I'm an American man the same as any other. I came to make my own way. Thank you kindly, Dr. Foster."

As Abel headed on toward the washtubs, he heard Dr. Foster's disappointed voice. "We all need help sometimes, Abel. It's not an issue of color. It's an issue of humanity."

Abel slowed his stride, remembering his earlier words to Caleb about making a better way in this world for Eli and Grandy and Helen. He turned back and saw the frustration etched on the physician's face. "All right. I accept your offer. Thank you."

Abel's dream of enlisting was temporarily delayed when Dr. Foster learned that his friend, Judge Nicholson, captain of the Baltimore Fencibles, was away from the fort, reportedly bedridden after rising from his sickbed in New York to make a breakneck return to Baltimore. Still, Abel's time in the fort had been fascinating. Since no one knew he could read, he was paraded past bulletins, broadsheets, maps, battle plans, and one troubling document.

The other six men of color in Abel's group were drilling with the militia, with Caleb marching beside them, when Abel returned to the camp. He watched the impressive drills, hungering more than ever to enlist in the regulars. When the drilling ended the six other men joined Abel by the fire, where he had a pot of soup brewing.

"We took good care of Caleb while you was gone, Abel," piped up the man named Smith. "Tell your pa, Caleb. We let you march right there beside us, didn't we?"

Caleb beamed at his father. "Sergeant McCoy called me Private Caleb."

Abel shot the men a knowing smile. "That's just fine, Son."

The older man of the group, a fellow named Jim, sidled up to Abel. "Are you joinin' up with Captain Foster's company?"

Abel stirred the soup. "Nope."

"We saw you talkin' to him," added Chester, Jim's son.

"We did some talking," Abel admitted as he continued to stir the soup. "I have a warning which I'm passing along. The officers will be checking for freedom papers, and they have a list of runaways. Any runaways they find will be turned over to the law."

Jim and Chester responded matter-of-factly to the news, but the other four men, Titus included, were visibly shaken.

"Sergeant McCoy will vouch for us," insisted one of the men.

"Fine then," Abel said nonchalantly. "Soup's ready."

"Will they be rootin' through the militias checkin' papers too?" asked another man.

"Where are you from? The list seemed to mostly have the names of local runaways."

Abel watched Titus's reaction from the corner of his eye and added, "If I were a local on the run, I'd pull out nice and quiet like."

Jim and Chester scooped up large bowls of soup and grabbed two biscuits each, then settled down to eat with their backs against their packs. Titus filled his bowl as well, broke two biscuits into it, and settled on a log to stare out at the river. The other three characters stuffed biscuits into their bags, tipped their hats, and carefully moved on, each taking a separate route.

"We met up with them in Bladensburg," Jim explained once the men were gone. "They said they were part of a company out of Harrisburg, Pennsylvania. I don't think Sergeant McCoy believed them, but he's a good sort. I hope they make it over the line without gettin' caught."

"Abel, would you mind helping me move another timber near the fire?" Titus suddenly asked.

Abel rose and the two men walked a distance away from the others. Titus could almost fit under Abel's armpit, but he had a powerful spirit about him.

"I know you're a runaway from White Oak," Abel said. "You'd do well to move along."

Titus pulled on his military suspenders. "I'm no runaway. I've got papers."

"Forged by Frederick Stringham, the son of your master. I was awake that night last October when you arrived at the Willows with your family and Frederick Stringham's wife. I heard the story—how Frederick Stringham signed freedom papers over to you in exchange for you getting his wife off White Oak land before the mercenaries arrived. Jed told you then they weren't legal. That's why he led you away to Philadelphia. Why did you come back?"

Slumping on the timber, Titus slid his hat over his face and down to his chest, where it came to rest. "Same as you, I s'pose. Didn't you come to break those invisible ropes that still bind you? I'll get ten acres of land in western Pennsylvania after the war is over. Ten acres of my own soil to grow my own crops and build my wife a home. That dream was worth any risk."

The story hit too close to Abel's heart. "Stringham must have purchased you after Jed Pearson brought my family to the Willows."

"Three men and my entire family was purchased to replace you 'n' yours. Since we were among the newest slaves, Frederick Stringham figured his father might not notice us bein' gone, so we was chosen to smuggle his missus to the Willows."

Abel felt a swell of inexplicable guilt. "Let me see your papers."

Titus's brow furrowed as he studied Abel. "Then what they said is true. You can read."

"What else did they say?"

"Just that you were probably lucky enough to get learnin' to boot."

Abel didn't reply. The disparity between him and the group was so painful he tried not to think about it. Yes, he was lucky, very lucky. His father attributed all such fortune to God, calling the recipients blessed. And those blessed were required to bless others in return.

Titus unbuttoned his military shirt, revealing a leather pouch that hung from a cord around his neck. From the pouch he retrieved the sacred freedom document, which he handed to Abel. Seconds passed while Abel read. Then he began to chuckle.

"I hope it's good news that's making you laugh," Titus said.

"A thread of divine justice seems to be at work here, Titus. I think this paper might be legal! A fire destroyed most of White Oak last month. Stewart Stringham and his wife were both killed. Frederick Stringham owns the entire estate now."

"And that's Frederick's signature on the paper!"

"There's one problem, though—the date. It's signed before Stewart Stringham died."

Titus rose from the timber and began to pace, his fret and worry evident. Turning his back to Abel, he walked to the river, dipped his finger in, and poked on his paper. Studying the result, he waved the paper in the air and then returned and sat down, displaying the paper. The date was gone, replaced by an illegible gray smear.

"I'm not sure that was a wise solution," Abel said.

"It's the only solution I got."

The next morning Dr. Foster came to find Abel, with a Private Ribaldi in tow. "Judge Nicholson is here and he'll see you now. Private Ribaldi will escort you."

A swarm of butterflies seemed to fill Abel's mighty chest. He had purposely marred his eloquent tongue to fit in with the ranks. Now he wondered what course to take with the captain. He stood and dusted himself off, looking to Dr. Foster for approval.

"You look just fine, Abel. Now hurry on."

Private Ribaldi had a thick Italian accent, or so Abel guessed. Ribaldi narrated their walk into the fort as they crossed the bridge that spanned the fort's moat, under the shadow of Fort McHenry's first defense, the story-high, triangular ravelin that faced the Patapsco. Cannons and cannoneers stood at the ready, with kegs of powder and pyramids of balls stacked nearby.

They moved on through the sally port, or entrance to the fort. After saluting, Ribaldi led on through to the interior, which proved to be much smaller than Abel imagined. Directly before them stood the mast that held the massive flag. Abel stopped and looked straight up to admire the sight. Before them spread the pentagonal parade grounds. The enlisted men's barracks, two long, two-story brick buildings, stood to Abel's left. A similar but smaller building, the junior officer's barracks, lay directly across from the sally port. A round-roofed building was situated between the junior officer's barracks and those where the commanding officer, Major Armistead, resided with his family.

Ribaldi led on across the bustling parade ground to the junior officer's barracks and saluted the guard, who opened the door and reported Abel's arrival before ushering him in.

Captain Nicholson still showed evidence of his illness. His color was wan and his large eyes drooped with fatigue. His brown hair and bushy sideburns had a natural wave, and when brushed forward, the hair framed his delicately featured face, making him appear much too young to be a judge or a captain. But dressed in his officer's uniform, he cut a sterling picture of quiet authority.

Nicholson was visibly taken aback by Abel's size, breaking into a delighted chuckle. The captain greeted the former slave and then said, "Dr. Foster tells me you'd like to join my artillery company. Is that true?"

Having decided not to hide who or what he really was, Abel straightened his wide shoulders and replied, "I wish to be a regular, sir—with pay and a signing bonus and all that's due an American soldier. I'm here to make a better life for my family."

Nicholson studied the man before him. "When I heard you were tall and strong, I selfishly wanted you for your brawn. I need strong men who can lift balls for hours without failing. But you're much more than you appear on first glance. You're a remarkable man, Abel."

At first, Abel liked the sound of that, but it haunted him as well. "Not so remarkable, sir. I believe most men want to improve life for their families."

"Yes, they do. And you've done that for your family today. Show me your papers, and if everything is in order, I'll see that you'll be a regular soldier before suppertime. But I'll ask Major Armistead to assign you to serve alongside my volunteers."

Abel proudly handed over his papers. "And my boy, Caleb. Dr. Foster said there might be work for him as well."

"One of the junior officers' wives runs the laundry and kitchen. I could employ him there, but it's hard work. I think she pays her helpers ten cents a day plus their meals."

Abel did the math and marveled at the nest egg they could raise for their family. "That would be fine, sir. Just fine."

"Everything seems to be in order here." Nicholson extended his hand to Abel. "Welcome to the army of the United States of America, Abel. Get your son and we'll swear you in right away. I'm sure we don't have any uniforms to fit a man of your stature, so you'll need to see Mrs. Wainwright in the building behind the fort. She'll measure you and have a uniform for you in just a few days."

Overwhelmed by the flood of good fortune, Abel dared to hope for even more. "Captain Nicholson, sir, the Pennsylvania Militia gives a bonus of land to their volunteers. Is there a provision of land for regulars?"

"Yes, Abel. Soldiers will get a deed for western land in return for their service."

"Then I know one other man who'd like to improve things for his family, too."

Nicholson smiled. "Does he also have his freedom papers?

Abel swallowed hard. "He showed them to me this morning."

"Very well. Bring him by when you return."

Minor subterfuge solved the issue of the missing date on Titus's papers. When he presented them to Captain Nicholson's aide, he wiped his fingers across his sweaty brow and held the paper in his wet hand, directly over the smeared spot. The aide found the condition of the paper so distasteful that he barely handled the document, giving it less than the normal scrutiny. By 4:00 PM on Wednesday, August 31, 1814, Captain Joseph Hopper Nicholson swore in America's two newest soldiers, Abel and Titus, as Caleb beamed from behind.

CHAPTER 8

Thursday, September 1, 1814
Somewhere off the Atlantic Coast of America

Jed's wounds festered in the filth, his shackles adding new agony to his burned flesh. His fever rose and abated, the only measure of the monotonous passing of time. He was foul and sick, his hair and beard rank. Fighting the urge to surrender to the sweet release of death, he gratefully accepted the scant rations delivered twice a day. His only visitors now were those who came to torment him, until even the delivery of his rations was more about inflicting misery upon him than delivering his food.

He wondered if Arthur was still alive and, if so, where he might be. Was he still in America? Had he lived long enough to receive care from the British military's surgeons? Thoughts of Arthur turned Jed's thoughts to Frannie and her grief. It was all too much to bear.

He tried to focus on happier things. After all, a child was coming sometime after the New Year, and no matter what befell him, he would be able to keep the spirit of the promise he had made to Hannah—that she would never be alone.

To pass the time and deflect his thoughts from his misery, Jed played a game, scrambling his features with Hannah's, creating a face for the anticipated little one. He could envision Hannah running across the meadow holding the hand of a little dark-haired boy or girl with his eyes or Hannah's, with his wavy tousles or Hannah's straight locks. But he could never place himself in the image, and that frightened him more than he dared admit.

He planned for the coming planting season, mentally distributing the various crops across the Willow's vast acreage, and holding conversations with Markus, Jack, and Abel as if they were actually present. On day three, his captors caught him in such a conversation. Calling their friends, they sat on the steps jeering at Jed as if he were a loon. Jed played along, knowing that as long as they were laughing at him, he was at least human in their eyes.

But most of Jed's conversations were passed following Jerome's advice, talking to God. The first few were conversations of contrition. Bitterness and anger made a brief return after an especially egregious visit from those delivering his meal. The stench in the hold had become so onerous from the animals' waste and his own that few men cared to venture below. Jed thanked God for the cool water surrounding the ship's belly, moderating the hold's temperature, and for the stench that kept his tormentors at bay, affording him a chance to heal.

Once the pleasure of tormenting him had lost its novelty, the task of bringing his food passed to a rail of a lad, a sailing apprentice, Jed supposed, with wide brown eyes and a dirty face and hands. Joy filled Jed's heart as the boy lifted the hatch, allowing that first sliver of life-affirming sunlight in from the windows that lit the middle deck where the crew was berthed. A burst of sweet breeze rushed in as well, stirring the dead air and imbuing hope.

Named Ethan, the lad was an orphan from Liverpool, apprenticed through the benevolence of an officer. Ethan dreamed of someday captaining a British warship, but he was more willing than bright, making that prospect unlikely. Where the rest of the crew found him a nuisance, Jed found him a blessing, engaging him in conversation to extend each meal delivery a moment longer.

In return, Ethan had begun to bring Jed some little extras—an extra cup of clean water, a tiny stub of soap, two strips of clean bandage, a biscuit. These kindnesses exceeded any other Jed had ever received, particularly since he knew the risk the lad took to smuggle them in.

Jed heard a scuffle and then a loud cheer above him in the crew quarters. Hours had passed since he had last seen Ethan and he waited, hoping the lad would share the cause of the celebration. He knew it would make for a good story.

Jed was asleep when the hatch opened. The light cut across his bearded face, drawing an instant smile. He never spoke first in the event another sailor entered, but it was Ethan's two bare feet that descended the steps. Jed watched to see if others followed, but seeing none, he sat up anxiously and waited to see the boy's face. There was something odd about it this day. Even though Ethan was cloaked in shadows with the sun's light behind him, Jed could see a blackened eye and a bruised and swollen cheek. The boy's lips were split and bleeding, and when he spoke, a gruesome gap appeared where his front teeth had been.

Jed's limbs went slack and his breathing stalled as he took in the sight, remembering the ruckus above his head earlier. He instantly felt sick. "What happened to you, Ethan? Who did this?" Then he caught sight of a bloody bandage wrapped around Ethan's left hand.

"Tell 'im, boy!" ordered a harsh voice from above the hatch.

Ethan's eyes were cast down, never meeting Jed's. "I can't come ta see you anymore. No one will. They'll toss your rations down in a sack tied to a rope twice a day. If it comes back up with your food still in it, they'll assume you're dead." He sniffed and drew his good hand across his swollen nose, leaving a red streak on his wrist.

"Tell 'im the rest, boy!"

"I took—"

"You stole!"

Ethan shuddered and drew his wounded hand to his breast. "I stole a stick of jerky to bring to you. I got caught and they cut off one of my fingers to mark me as a thief. If I try to see you again, they said they'll hold a trial and toss me overboard for treason."

Unable to control the trembling that overtook him, Jed struggled to mutter, "I'm s–s–sorry, Ethan. I'm s–s–so sorry." A hand reached down, grabbed Ethan's arm, and jerked the lad up the ladder, then slammed the hatch shut with a bang.

Jed spread his tethered arms and screamed through the darkness, "Why? Where is honor? Where is mercy?" Then he folded into a ball and sobbed for the child.

The gnaw of hunger woke him, but hours passed before the hatch opened, lowering a sack containing a dry crust of bread and a cask of water. That was all. Now Jed understood. He was in exile, complete exile. No human contact for the remainder of the voyage. He would fester in his filth, devoid of another voice or face until the journey's end, if he survived that long.

He scraped his cuff against the wood. Day six . . .

Friday, September 2, 1814
London, England

Juan Arroyo Corvas rose from his knees and tucked the crucifix back into his silk shirt before leaving the chapel. He stopped to enjoy a few strains of music lilting from the choir near the high altar. The priest nodded to him, extending a dish for contributions for the poor, and Juan dropped in the four gold doubloons he had prepared to offer. The priest honored the Spaniard's gift with a low bow. He then attempted to guide the wealthy benefactor to the exit, but Juan bowed reverently and declined the offer. He knew St. Paul's well, as the creditor had sent him here many times to attend to his unseemly business.

It was difficult to believe that nearly ten years had passed since Juan first entered St. Paul's. That is when the sordid business began that brought him here today, penitent and seeking to cleanse his soul. This was the place he had been sent to deliver messages to men who, like his father, had become indebted to the creditor. Juan had inherited his father's debt upon his death, and the terms of repayment? Favors for favor. Hideous, illegal, immoral favors, and though Juan had longed to walk away in the beginning, eventually he too had allowed greed to draw him back in.

Amado stood in the street tending two white Andalusian stallions. The magnificent Spanish steeds and the handsome Spanish lad with his onyx eyes and coal black hair drew an attentive crowd. "Did you get your answers, Cousin?" he called out to Juan with his thick Spanish accent. "These two are getting very nervous."

"Yes. I now have a plan. Let's pack rations for a week or two and be on our way."

"And where are we going?"

"To see a man named Señor Ramsey. He lives on a manor in the countryside, about an hour's ride from the city."

"Then why do we need so many rations?"

"You will soon understand."

As expected, Amado pressed his father's favorite cousin for an explanation of their journey. "Is this Stephen Ramsey a wealthy man, Cousin?"

"Yes," Juan answered. "A very wealthy and powerful man."

"And what does this powerful man do? Is he in Britain's Parliament?"

"No. This man *owns* many of the men of Parliament." Juan smiled sadly. It was an unfortunate truth, but one that would occupy his young cousin for a while. They exited the city and Juan turned down the road that led to Stephen Ramsey's estate. He had been to Ramsey's home many times before discovering he was the demon creditor. Once the secret was exposed, Juan ceased to fear him, and that somehow lessened Ramsey's power over him. Oddly enough, soon thereafter, Ramsey had himself sought redemption, and life improved—until two weeks ago.

Amado pulled his horse up short, and Juan knew his sixteen-year-old cousin had figured out the secret. "This is the man who owned you, isn't he?" Amado asked with fear in his voice.

Juan continued to ride, forcing the young man to hurry to catch up to him. "Yes, but you do not need to fear him. This time he has not summoned me. I am going there to save him."

"Save him?"

"And to ask for his forgiveness."

"After all he has done to you, why should you ask his forgiveness for anything?"

The answer was simple, and yet very complex for a boy like Amado to understand. "Despite all the wealth and power this man amassed through his wickedness, he had one treasure he adored above all his others—one good son, named Arthur, who loved God and went about doing good to everyone. He even became a soldier to restore dignity to the family's name."

"And did he?"

"Yes. I've talked to officers of British ships as they sail into Liverpool, and everyone who knows him speaks only good about Lieutenant Arthur Ramsey. But sometimes, doing good brings more enemies upon a man than doing evil. Such was the case for Arthur.

"A wicked man from my past, named Jervis, served as a mercenary in America, in a place called Maryland. He was hired by a man named Dupree to murder many people, and Arthur was the spy who foiled the plan. Now Jervis has a vendetta against Arthur Ramsey. Two weeks ago, I accidentally provided Jervis with information that will lead him to Arthur's home. We must warn Mr. Ramsey. That is why we are traveling there."

It was late afternoon when the pair arrived at Ramsey's sprawling property. Juan noticed the many changes—bright curtains in the windows, flowers growing in the garden, balls and wooden toys scattered along the flagstone path. Where once it had appeared dark and cold, it now looked like a home for a family.

Juan instructed Amado to wait with the horses. He approached the door and banged on it with the knocker. Juan was surprised to be greeted by a butler instead of the housekeeper, Mrs. McGowan, who had always answered the door in the past.

The man studied Juan from the plume of his hat to the finely polished leather of his boots. Obviously pleased with what he saw, the butler said, "Yes, sir. How may I help you?"

"I've come to see Mr. Ramsey on a matter of great urgency."

"I'm very sorry, sir. The master is out."

A cockney woman's voice called from the parlor. "Mr. Smythe, is someone callin' for Steph—I mean Mr. Ramsey?"

"Yes, Mum," the butler answered to the voice. "I've told him the master is away."

The woman who approached the door was lovely, thirtyish, slightly plump, and elegantly dressed in a white lace frock. Her face was familiar, but it required moments before Juan identified her. "Mrs. McGowan? H–h–hello, madam. Please, forgive me. You look . . ."

"Different? I know. Must come as a bit of a shock to ya. My mind's still reelin' from it all, but Mr. Ramsey wants somethin' better for me. 'E's been a gem ta me an' my boys."

"I hear he is away. I must get in touch with him quickly."

"I'm sorry. 'E left three days ago and 'e won't be 'ome for several weeks."

"The information I have regards his son. Have you received any word from him?"

"From Arthur? No. Not a card or a letter in weeks. But perhaps I can 'elp you deliver your news to Mr. Ramsey. To be honest, Stephen and I are ta be wed in a fortnight. We were to've been wed tomorrow were it not for some sudden trouble with 'is shippin' business."

Juan bowed. "Congratulations to you both, madam, but my business with Mr. Ramsey concerns a very delicate matter. I would prefer to return and speak to him directly."

"Suit yourself. Good day, Mr. Corvas."

She began to close the door when Juan interjected, "You said he went away because of shipping business? May I ask how this came to his attention so suddenly?"

"A courier came with reports about a theft off one of 'is ships in the Liverpool harbor."

"Has a sailor named Jervis been here to see Mr. Ramsey?"

Again the woman's brow wrinkled in thought. "No, no one named Jervis. The only comp'ny I've had was a man named Porter. A nice farming gent, said he rented land from Mr. Ramsey."

Juan was relieved. He had at least beaten Jervis here, and hopefully he still had time to warn Arthur. He bid the woman goodbye and walked away toward his cousin.

"I must go away for a week, perhaps two. I need you to remain here, Amado." The boy began to protest but Juan interrupted him. "You must be my eyes and ears. Watch who comes and who goes. Record every detail, and bring me word as soon as Mr. Ramsey returns."

"And what will you be doing, Cousin?"

"I have business in Liverpool."

CHAPTER 9

Friday, September 2, 1814
Georgetown, District of Columbia

Francis Scott Key had read the letter from General John Mason three times. The instructions were not unexpected, but a sudden coldness crept into Frank's heart each time he considered the quest upon which he was about to embark. He went to the window hoping to see Polly and the children coming up the walk from the park, but there was still no sign of them. *Mr. West will find them,* he told himself.

He entered his office seeking solace and found his Bible on his desk, still opened to the book of Jonah, the tale of another man reticent to go where he was called. Key's eyes scanned a few verses, but his mind was occupied by the incomprehensible twist of fate drawing him deeper and deeper into the very conflict he had once opposed. There was no longer any vacillation about the war. He had been at Bladensburg. His nation was at dire risk, and he was fully engaged in the fight.

He thought about his good, brave friend, Dr. William Beanes. According to Mr. West, the sixty-year-old physician had been dragged from his bed in the middle of night, placed backwards on a mule with his feet tied beneath the animal's belly, and paraded from Upper Marlboro to Benedict. The humiliation of it incensed the normally mellow Key. Such behavior wasn't justice. It was torture, and all because Beanes, whom the British took a liking to on their march into Washington, dared arrest British stragglers passing through his village after their victorious march from the smoldering city of Washington.

Key feared for his friend. William had been born in Scotland, and British Major General Robert Ross threatened to try him as a British traitor. Mr. West had come to Georgetown seeking Timothy Shepard's help, and Timothy had led him to Key.

He moved to the piano, hoping to find a measure of comfort there. His hands began running through the chorus of a hymn he was composing. The lyrics candidly expressed his witness of Christ, reminding him of his ongoing wrestle over whether or not to enter the Episcopalian ministry. The request had come in April—an invitation to move to Baltimore and serve as the associate rector of St. Paul's Parish. Now Key the lawyer would be going to Baltimore for a very different purpose.

The disarray in the family's brick town home would have to remain, testifying to the panicked exodus he and his brother-in-law, Roger Taney, had arranged for Polly and the children. Clothes and toys would hastily be gathered before Roger Taney ferried the family north to Key's parents' farm, Terra Rubra, near Fredericktown. Polly had already vowed she would not go, but Key knew he must convince her.

Key caressed a wooden horse that belonged to John Ross. One of baby Edward's knitted blankets lay crumpled on a chair. When Key picked it up and pressed it to his face, the scent of talc and lavender soap made his heart ache. A thousand *what-ifs* and questions invaded his peace. *Polly knows with certainty that I love her, doesn't she?* He could only hope he had told her and shown her enough to carry her through what might come. There was no more time. What they had already said and shared would need to be enough.

And the children. Frank had only dreamed of so great a family when he fell in love with Mary "Polly" Lloyd. They hoped to fill the house to overflowing in the coming years, but would that dream be realized? And would the six children with whom he had already been blessed remember Papa's face, his piggyback rides to bed, the gentle touch of his lips on their ears as he shared whispered *I love you*'s each night? Elizabeth, Maria, Francis Jr., and John Scott likely would. From five to eleven years of age, they were old enough to have stored sufficient memories. But little Anna and baby Edward—would Papa be but a memory to them if things went awry with the British?

Key knew such thinking would not serve him well, so he headed upstairs to place his trust in the one sure Rock of his faith. While climbing the stairs he asked for forgiveness for his fear. Then, as he knelt beside his bed, a rush of peace washed the darkness away, leaving trust in its wake. God's will would be done, and he would serve as the best vessel he could.

The sound of carriage wheels on the brick road brought Key to his feet. He ran to the window, but before he reached the curtains he heard the door groan against its wooden jam, and then the hurried tap of Polly's feet on the wooden floors as she searched for him. "Frank! Frank!"

He rushed downstairs, sweeping his wife into his arms. "Hello, darling." His voice remained even despite the urgency he felt.

"Frank?" Polly asked warily as she pulled back to study his face. "Why did you send Mr. West to find me? Something else is amiss now, isn't it?"

He caught the flutter in her voice that generally preceded her tears. "Don't fret, my darling." He kissed her soundly, suddenly regretting all the missed opportunities when a cursory peck had been substituted. "I do most assuredly love you, Polly. I hope you know that."

"Frank, please. You're avoidance is scaring me to death."

"I need you to pack some things for you and the children. Roger is taking you all to Terra Rubra tomorrow."

Polly untied her hat and set it down firmly. "So Roger's visit here was not merely social. You two have intended to wear away at me until I consent to leave you. Well, we'll send the children, but I am not leaving."

"The British are still in the Potomac. You will all be safer in Fredericktown."

"And what of you?"

Frank Key's hand raked through his curly brown hair as he wondered how many details to disclose. "President Madison has agreed to our mission to free Dr. Beanes. He sent a sealed letter to General John Mason, the United States commissioner general of prisoners, in our behalf, and General Mason's orders to me have arrived this hour."

"What do they require of you?"

Frank saw the uncertainty in her eyes. There was sufficient cause. Ten days ago, he and Polly had secreted their children to Fredericktown to protect them from a British attack. Then he had hidden his brave wife in the home of a friend, fearing she and their home could be in jeopardy if the city fell. In a seemingly bizarre reversal of principles, he had found himself—the peacemaker and early opponent of the war—on the battlefield during the Battle of Bladensburg. But he was where he had wanted to be. After the atrocities at Hampton and Havre de Grace, after the relentless torching of towns and homes along the Patuxent, he had joined the Washington militia. His will to defend his nation was as steeled as any other. But how much should he tell Polly?

"I'm to meet a Colonel Skinner, the prisoner exchange agent, in Baltimore in two days."

"How safe will you be during this mission?"

Frank had never lied to Polly, and he saw no good in doing it now. He led her to the settee. "Come sit with me," he said, sitting by her side. "Once the colonel and I connect, we are to secure a cartel ship that will sail us to the British fleet, anchored near Tangier Island." Polly's face went ashen.

"Don't fear, my darling," Frank said. "I'll have a wise government escort and a skilled ship's captain."

"But three or four men, no matter how brave, have no chance against the British military, particularly after all we've seen and heard this past week. They could kill you all, or capture you as well as Dr. Beanes. How will that serve to do anyone good?"

She folded over, clearly bereft of courage, and wet Frank's lap with her tears. He gently raised her up to rest against him, continuing his efforts to console her.

"There, there, Polly. Don't be afraid. General Mason has already sent a letter on to British Major General Ross informing him of our arrival. It details our government's—the president's—concerns in the strongest language. They will know exactly why we are coming long before we arrive, and we are bringing along signed letters from wounded British soldiers, attesting to the fine treatment they are receiving in our care. So you see? We are well prepared to physically facilitate Dr. Beanes's release."

"In my thinking they'll just be more angry when you arrive."

"Faith, Polly. I have worked through similar fears, but now I believe we must have faith, trusting that God has reproved us sufficiently, and that He will now bare His mighty arm to preserve us and our nation. Time is short. Where is Mr. West?"

Polly's arms were wrapped tightly around her waist. "I suppose he is still with the rig. His plans are to return home to Upper Marlboro today. The children are outside playing with their Uncle Roger, believing he has come here to play."

"Let them think so for now. Begin packing while I attend to a few details here."

Frank quickly dashed off a brief note to Timothy Shepard. After folding it, he used a candle to light the wick of a stick of sealing wax and watched as it dripped over the fold. Then he sought out Mr. West.

"When will you be leaving for Baltimore?" West asked.

"First I need to help my family pack and prepare to send them on their way north. Then I'll hasten on to Baltimore in time to meet Colonel Skinner Sunday morning."

West offered Key his hand. "Thank you for helping us, Mr. Key. Today's broadsheet indicates the other men taken from our village have been released and returned home. Dr. Beanes is the only one they've set their minds on keeping."

"We'll do our best to see that William is also returned safely home. May I ask a favor, sir? The militia is posted just down the block. Take this letter to them and tell them I require a courier to deliver it to the Willows farm on the Patuxent River Road by tomorrow."

"I'll see to it."

The two men shook hands in farewell, in essence passing the baton in the race to save Dr. Beanes's life, hoping this exercise of diplomatic muscle would prove the continuity and integrity of the United States government as well.

That evening the Keys mounted the stairs together, Frank's arm wrapped around Polly's slim waist. One by one, he and Polly opened doors where curly-headed children slept. He pressed his lips to their ears and whispered, "I love you," placing kisses on each tousled head.

After five hours sleep, he bade Polly not to rise as he slipped from the bed, but as soon as he knelt to pray he felt her small form slide down beside him. After the prayer, he quickly dressed and left with only his small carpetbag in tow. The morning air was cool. *Good weather for a hard ride.* Soon, Frank mounted his horse and exited the barn, his heart light and hopeful. When he allowed himself one final sweep of the house to hold in his memory, he saw two windows filled with faces he loved more than life itself. Roger Taney, his sister's husband, was sober as he offered his friend a wave. In another window he saw Polly with little Edward in her arms. Her face was worried, but brighter now. *She feels it too,* Frank thought.

He pushed his horse hard on the Baltimore Road. Reaching the city around noon, he checked into the Indian Queen Hotel to rendezvous with John Skinner, arriving early enough to bathe and dress. Around 2:00 PM, he heard a knock on the door. Colonel John Skinner had arrived. Key handed him his set of documents and orders from General Mason, and now their mission was about to begin.

CHAPTER 10

Saturday, September 3, 1814
The Willows

The first leaves were beginning to yellow as if the heat had simply burned the life right out of them. Markus sat on the front porch of his small home, unable to enjoy autumn's opening act. He always considered himself a seaman first, and he had simply fallen into farming when Jed pulled him from his tobacco barge to be the Willows' farm manager. But he was a farmer now as well, with a farm that needed attention—and no time to attend to it.

They had both been just kids when they met. Jed was heading back to Philadelphia to finish his studies at the University of Pennsylvania, and Markus provided the white skin the vendors required to do business with the farm, which was actually run by Jack and Bitty with an occasional visit from Jed's more city-suited father.

Markus learned the farming business quickly, and though he was only two years older than Jed, the pair had become a savvy business team who respected and recognized the wisdom of their darker-skinned partners. Everything was peaceful and perfect on the Willows for a time.

The war changed the lives of everyone along the Patuxent. Markus had returned to Hampton, Virginia, to raise his father's old ship, the *Irish Lass,* and he ended up finding a flesh-and-blood

Irish lass to love. Instinctively, he reached into his pocket to touch the watch fob made from her braided red hair. Each thought of her sent his hand reaching for a quick brush of the only earthly reminder he had of her. Her name was Lyra, and their time together had been too brief, though he knew a lifetime together would have been too little. She was simply that kind of woman.

When the British had set their French assassins loose on Hampton, sweet, blind Lyra leapt into a rapid-flowing creek to escape her lascivious attackers. Markus had raced from a battle to save her from the renegades, but he was moments too late . . . moments too late.

Commodore Barney's call to serve with the Chesapeake Flotilla—a ragtag fleet of heavily armed barges—had given Markus a purpose after Lyra's death. At first, his only goals were to kill as many British as he could and to die in the process. Then one day, as he stood on the deck of his ship, he realized how desperately he missed the feel of solid ground under his feet, and the smell of rich soil. He realized he longed for home—for the Willows. He had become a farmer who was dreaming of life again. And then he met Arthur, one of the most honorable men he had ever known. He came to understand that most men share the same dream, despite the color of their uniform.

The view from Markus's beloved porch revealed an endless sea of charred fields that needed to be plowed and repairs that needed to be made, but Samuel vetoed his every move. Markus protested but was secretly glad for a reason to rest. His side hurt like the dickens, but he knew he'd soon be called to captain Mr. Key's vessel. If all went well, that assignment would be quickly concluded, but Markus knew he would have a hard time returning to the Willows as long as his flotilla brothers were manning the artillery batteries, back in harm's way, without him.

Samuel wandered over from the main house and Markus pulled himself from his worrying. "How are they?" he asked as Samuel sat down.

"Hannah's doing fine, but that baby could come late October."

"So soon? And the poor thing doesn't even have a proper cradle. Jed was plannin' ta build one." Markus sighed "And Frannie?"

Samuel's eyebrows rose. "She's in love with a ghost."

"You don't think Arthur'll make it?"

"I know only a handful of surgeons who could address such injuries to the abdomen. Still, a school of medicine in Norway is pioneering some remarkable work. If his military surgeons were trained there, then he might have a chance." He sighed aloud. "And Frannie will hold on to an improbable hope, leaving her and Timothy in an impossible situation."

"Poor Timothy does look like a dog who's lost 'is favorite bone."

"Don't let Frannie hear you say that." Samuel chuckled.

"Maybe you ought ta tell 'er I said it. I'd love ta see some of 'er old spit return."

"As curious a waif as Mrs. Tyler is, her arrival has been beneficial for both Frannie and Hannah. Having someone to fuss over deflects their attentions off their own worries."

"How's she gettin' on?"

"I have no balms or powders for what ails her." Samuel scowled and pointed past the main house to the meadow. "He's the only one available who might."

The Reverend Charles Myers came into view, beating his hat against his pants leg to dust it off. He replaced it and climbed the porch of the main house, knocking so soundly on the door that the men could hear it from where they sat. A few moments later he emerged with Jenny Tyler on his arm, dressed simply but nonetheless looking beautiful and frail.

"What's that about?" Markus asked in irritation. "He looks like a dandy comin' courtin'."

"I sent for him. I think the reverend may be able to help Mrs. Tyler in ways I cannot. He's a good listener. Hannah thinks that's why the children love him so. His patience for their questions is never-ending. I hope he is equally skilled with people who don't want to talk at all."

Jenny turned toward Markus's house, making momentary eye contact with him. Her melancholy pained him, and, as if noting the sorrow her gaze stirred, she turned back away.

"I just hope he remembers she's a married woman," Markus said with a frown.

"Married to what?" Samuel muttered softly.

Markus became pensive as he watched the reverend and Jenny disappear over the hill toward the meadow where the church was being built. The children's laughter drifted by as they played, and Markus's face brightened as an idea came to him.

"I just remembered that Jed sent some beautiful oak logs ta Baltimore ta be planed. I'll have to swing by that mill and pick them up after my business with Mr. Key is concluded. Maybe I can get that cradle built before the wee bairn arrives. Yes, sir!" He slapped his knee.

"That's the happiest I've heard you sound since we met up," Samuel said. "I wish I could stay and deliver this baby, or take Hannah to Baltimore with me, but the truth is, Bitty's as wise a midwife as I've seen, and Hannah's likely far safer here than in Baltimore right now."

"Jed's plans were solid. 'E had the stock moved to deeper pastures and the hogsheads of tobacco stored in sheds in the far corners of the property. They'll fetch a pretty penny once the markets get goin' again. And Bitty had the women bottle and dry everything they could, so even though there won't be much of a harvest this year, they'll have food and money enough until spring. And there's always fish in the river and game to be shot."

"Has Timothy ever been hunting or baited a hook?" Samuel asked with a laugh.

"I'm not countin' on our silver-spooned friend to do anythin' but keep these women safe." Markus shook his head. "Royal and

Sookie can keep the larder full. They'll all do just fine."

"Sounds as if you're planning on being away for a while."

"I've been thinkin', and I agree that endin' this war quickly is what'll serve everyone's interests best. I'll see how long Timothy can stay on. That's how long I'll be away."

They heard the sound before they saw it—the pounding staccato of a horse's hoofs on River Road. A dust cloud was the next sign that a rider was nearing, and then the horse broke around the corner, headed for the Willows.

Markus was already on his feet and moving off the porch, with Samuel following behind at a brisk trot. They met the uniformed rider at the Willows' porch, where Timothy Shepard already stood, dressed more like a banker than a farmer.

"Mr. Shepard?" the rider asked from his saddle.

"I am. Are you sent from Mr. Key?"

"I am, sir." He handed Timothy a letter bearing a government seal.

Before Timothy began to read, the breathless young soldier turned his horse to depart. "Wait!" Timothy called. "Are you not to await my reply?"

"No, sir. My orders are to hasten to Fort McHenry."

"Why? Is there news of the British fleet's movements?"

The young soldier drew back, his brow furrowed with disbelief. "Haven't you heard, sir? The fleet divided. Half their ships sailed up the Potomac. Once Fort Warburton was abandoned, those British ships sailed right into Alexandria as if they'd been invited. They've sacked her—lowered her flag, cleaned out the warehouses, taken the merchandise on the docks and anything that ever floated. The fleet was heading away from Alexandria when I rode out a few hours ago, but some fearsome commander named Captain Rodgers arrived from Philadelphia and he's sworn to harass them all the way down the Potomac. He even threatened to fire his guns on Alexandria itself if they didn't raise the Stars and Stripes again."

"I heard about this the other day. You said the fleet divided. Where is the other half now?" Markus asked.

"Near Tangier Island. Only a gunship and the troop transports are left in the Patuxent."

Markus began to smile. "If Ross's ground troops are still here, he may have decided against marching them to Baltimore. And if the British try to take the city by water, they'll fail. McHenry and the batteries completely control the waterway to Baltimore."

The soldier frowned and shifted uncomfortably in his saddle. "Volunteers are swarming in by the hundreds now, but none of that may matter, sir. Have you not read a recent paper? New York and New England may be the next to be conquered! Britain has a fleet of ships and ten thousand troops gathered near Lake Champlain. People are saying that if we lose there, the whole Union may dissolve! That's why I've got to hurry. Good day, sirs." He gave his horse a firm kick and the two thundered up the River Road toward Baltimore.

Timothy finally began to read his letter. His face become increasingly taciturn until, unable to bear it any longer, Markus burst in. "Good heavens, Timothy! What's it say?"

Timothy handed the note to Markus. "If you're willing to go you must leave within the hour. Mr. Key has made alternative arrangements in the event you don't arrive, but I'd feel better with you at the helm. The importance of this mission seems greater than ever. We need to send a clear message that this union still stands and that President Madison is at its head."

Hannah, Frannie, and Bitty hurried out of the house, wiping their hands on their aprons. "What is it, Timothy?" Frannie asked.

Timothy's eyes were riveted on Markus. "If you're going, you'll need to leave for Baltimore quickly. What have you decided?"

"You're committed to stay here and look over things while I'm away?"

"I've told you, you have my word."

"And if things get complicated in Baltimore, how long can you stay?"

"I'll stay until you return, but you needn't worry. Frank Key's letter expressly indicates that he must sail tomorrow for the fleet. Figure a day's voyage to rendezvous and deliver the letters to Major General Ross, and another day's sail back to the harbor, with a day's ride to return here. You should be home by Tuesday, Wednesday at the latest."

"And if I'm not?" Markus pressed.

Timothy nodded. "I'll be here."

Samuel had remained very quiet. Now he looked at Hannah. "I think I'll be joining Markus. These numbers will overwhelm the city. Doctors will be in short supply compared to the need. I feel I must return as well."

It was suppertime when Markus and Samuel arrived in Baltimore. Portly Samuel always did his best to dress like a professional in his dark suit and white shirt, though he always looked rumpled, sweaty, and fatigued. Markus looked more rested than he'd been in days and wore clean civilian clothes—dark cotton pants and a blue, button-front work shirt with the sleeves rolled up—since nothing wearable remained from his lax naval uniform. His red beard covered the lower portion of his face, and with his nearly shoulder-length hair, which he tied in back, he looked more like a pirate than an officer. Adding to the effect was a scabbed-over cut that ran along his brow, and various cuts and scars on his hands and arms, remnants from the flotilla's encounter with the British at St. Leonard's Creek. He favored his right shoulder, still tender from a bayonet cut at Bladensburg, and his side ached where he'd been shot. Regardless, the nervous energy enveloping the port city made him hunger to get back into the fight.

Wagons continued to exit the city, but the sea of musket-toting volunteers coursing in now far outnumbered them. A boy stood on the corner handing out broadsheets announcing the day's meeting of the Committee of Vigilance and Safety, chaired by the city's mayor, Edward Johnson. Members were to watch for "spies and deserters," the paper said. Signs posted in storefronts announced the need for volunteers with shovels and wheelbarrows, willing to assist in building up the city's defensive barriers. Women and children manned most of the stores, since the majority of local men had joined the ranks of volunteers.

Markus and Samuel were famished and tired, and food was the next order of business.

"Where's the Indian Queen Hotel, Samuel?" Markus asked. "That's where I'm ta meet Mr. Key and Colonel Skinner."

"On Baltimore Street, about two blocks north of the harbor. They have a fine restaurant where we can grab some supper."

The pair stabled their horses and waited for an hour to be seated, owing to the flood of people in town. They finally left and settled for meat pies a woman sold in front of her home, capitalizing on the hungry crowd. They sat on the woman's stoop, eating and reading the broadsheet when a notice caught Samuel's eye.

"It's as I thought. The hospitals are besieged with the sick and injured."

"No one's even fired a shot 'ere yet," Markus said.

"No, but some wounded are still straggling in from Washington, and the sheer numbers of people here create their own problems. The hospital is calling all available medical personnel in." Samuel wolfed down his last bite. "I'd best hurry to the hotel and gather my things."

It was nearing dusk. Watch fires already burned in the streets to discourage looting and to make patrols more effective. Samuel mounted his horse and offered a hand of parting to Markus.

"Good luck to you. Stop by the hospital and get word to me before you head back to the Willows, will you? Let's pray this all ends quickly and in our favor. Godspeed, friend."

"And to you, Samuel."

Markus entered the hotel and checked with the desk clerk to see if Mr. Key had arrived. Two men approached him from behind. One asked, "Are you Captain O'Malley?"

His eyes darted from one man to the other. "I am. Are you Mr. Key?"

The taller of the two men smiled warmly. "Please, call me Frank." He extended his hand. "This is Colonel John Skinner, the prisoner exchange agent."

Markus smiled and offered his own hand to each of the gentlemen. "It's a pleasure ta meet ya both. And the name's Markus."

"The pleasure is all ours," Skinner said. "The daring of the flotillamen has been a large part of the swell of patriotism we see here in Baltimore. Your company made us all very proud. I'd be delighted if you'd share some good stories from your campaign on our trip."

Markus's discomfort over the praise brought Frank Key to his rescue.

"Have you eaten, Captain?" Key asked.

"Just finished."

Key turned to Skinner. "Then shall we attend to showing Captain O'Malley his ship?"

Skinner blushed. "Captain O'Malley, I commissioned a vessel and a crew last evening. Do you have a proper uniform? This diplomatic mission must represent the president well."

A flustered Markus frowned. "Mine was a mite ragged after Washington, and I've had no time to get another."

"My brother-in-law, Captain Nicholson, is the commander of the Baltimore Fencibles at Fort McHenry," Key said. "I'm sure he'll have some Sea Fencibles' uniforms at the fort."

Skinner agreed and the three men walked toward the docks to make a final inspection of their ship. On the way, they passed a flyer nailed to a pole, and Markus slowed to study it. With the heading "Entertainment," it featured the image of a beautiful, voluptuous singer named Genevieve, whose long, golden hair flowed over her bare shoulders to meet the low-cut bodice of a blue gown. She was drawn in an enticing way, with what Markus considered "come-hither" eyes and a pouty mouth intended to make men swoon. It was no wonder the proprietor of the theater had plastered the streets near the port with the fliers. These sailors would likely fill the theater at the chance to see such a woman. Markus noted the date—that very evening—and thought even he might catch the show if they arrived back in time. As they neared the port he noticed most of the fliers were torn down, smeared with mud or desecrated in diverse ways. It was clear someone was angry over Miss Genevieve's arrival.

They reached the dock where a packet ship, aptly named *President,* was moored. Markus jumped aboard and began inspecting the vessel. The white flag of truce was folded and ready to be raised, and every other aspect of the ship was unimposing and reflective of their mission of peace. Markus expected that, but other things disturbed him. "It's only got one gun and two balls!"

"This ship is now a cartel ship dedicated to the exchange of communications and the movement of prisoners," Skinner explained. "There are very specific requirements that must be met for such a vessel under the Articles of War. It must contain no cargo, no ammunitions, and no implements of war. One gun is all we're allowed, for signaling purposes only."

Markus scowled at the crew. "And you've got nine crewmen aboard, eight lieutenants and one of them wearin' captain's bars. So why am I 'ere? If you're not even carryin' a weapon ta defend yourself and you've already got a crew, why do ya need me?"

Key stepped forward. "We have no idea what we might face, Captain. It will be a comfort to have a man along who has already won the favor of the British."

Skinner cocked his head to the side and smiled. "We know you're a fine ship's captain, but the importance of your battle skills is negligible since we are clearly at the British fleet's mercy. However, flotillamen are amongst the only Americans the British respect right now. Major General Ross and Admiral Cockburn both said as much to Commodore Barney after Bladensburg. Therefore, your presence may be very important if negotiations stall."

"So, I'm a trump card. A guest."

"More or less. Does that offend you?"

Markus stared at Skinner, considering the question, then shrugged. "I've already let them shoot at me plenty. I suppose it won't hurt me none to smile pretty for 'em for a change."

"Good man," Skinner said as he thumped Markus on the back. "Good man, indeed. Captain John Ferguson is the *President*'s regular captain. He sails her between Norfolk and Baltimore. His first mate is Lieutenant James Grammatt."

Markus flashed the man a warm smile and asked, "So you're from Norfolk, are ya?"

Captain Ferguson extended his hand and gave Markus's a hearty shake. "I hear you're from Hampton, Captain O'Malley, and a flotillaman to boot. It's an honor to sail with you, sir."

Lieutenant Grammatt offered his own hand, but Markus quickly quelled the praise. "I'm no hero, boys. I was just blessed to follow a good commander, Commodore Barney. Now, if you're lookin' for real entertainment, I'd suggest ya go buy a ticket for that girly show posted around the waterfront."

The men's faces scowled at the reference. "That tart! She's a traitor! She entertained the British troops the night the capital burned. She's not welcome here."

"Is she an American?" Markus wondered.

"Yes, that's the pity of it. Word is, the British stuffed her purse with trinkets and jewelry stolen from the president's own house before they burned it. That was her payment for singing for them. She's a vulture who got fat picking the bones of our nation's misery. The proprietor of the Baltimore Theater invited her weeks ago, to boost morale, but when word reached Baltimore about her treachery in Washington, he posted a big Show Cancelled sign."

Markus regretted he had ever had a notion to go himself. "That's a sad tale, to be sure. Well, first light then, men. We'll show the British some good American spine tomorrow, won't we?"

The mood was light and optimistic as Markus, Key, and Skinner parted company with the sailors. Skinner looked to his companions and asked, "Gentleman, shall we now hurry on to Fort McHenry?"

CHAPTER 11

Saturday, September 3, 1814, 7:00 PM
Fort McHenry

Major George Armistead saw the line of vendors tenaciously waiting in the parade grounds to be paid for their deliveries—crates of eggs; sacks of flour, sugar, and salt; and animals penned outside the stockade. The cooks and laundresses were also in a dither. Armistead had no money with which to pay them, and no assurance if or when more funds were coming.

The major leaned back in his chair and rubbed his fingers deep into his eyes. He had no time for this! With the enemy in the bay again, an attack on Baltimore was possible with only a day's notice. And instead of reviewing his troops, he was literally counting chickens to be sure his troops were fed the next day.

The private knocked on the door as he opened it. "Captain Nicholson's almost here, sir!"

The question was whether or not Nicholson had been successful in arranging temporary funding for the troops. "I want to see him as soon as he arrives. Let no one else delay him, understood?"

"Yes, sir!" the private said as he closed the door.

Moments later, it opened again. This time Captain Nicholson entered, red-faced and puffing in exasperation, with a leather satchel in tow.

"Did you get the money?" Armistead asked.

Nicholson pulled a bundle of bills from the satchel and laid them before the major. "The bankers were most cooperative when they realized they could either temporarily fund the troops or come and fight in their place."

"An army filled with bankers!" The major huffed, making his brown curls dance along his high forehead. "In all seriousness, Joseph, this situation is very bad for morale."

"With what's happened in Washington, I suppose we're fortunate the government stands at all. At least we're fine for another month or so."

"Only because my second-in-command is a local judge from a well-connected family. I'm just a Virginian who came from Fort Niagara. I doubt they'd have agreed were I to have asked."

"After hearing how Captain Beall abandoned Fort Warburton, everyone in Baltimore is grateful he was sent there and you were brought here to Baltimore to replace him."

Armistead's head dipped modestly. "Thank you." He stood and took his coat from the rack. "I suppose I should see to getting our merchants paid."

"I can see to that."

With a gentle wave, Armistead dismissed the suggestion. "I want to mill about the men anyway. Tell me, how are our newest recruits adjusting to army life?"

"Abel and Titus? They're a quiet pair. We finally have Abel's uniform tailored to fit properly." Nicholson chuckled. "No one's buttons or boots shine more. And he's too large for a bunk, so he, Titus, and Caleb have chosen to sleep in a tent beside the barracks. It might actually be wise."

"Why? Aren't the other men accepting them into their ranks?"

"Two-thirds of our enlistees are recent immigrants, so most are tolerant. Only a few of the men take serious issue with the former slaves being here—Emerson Hildebrand and Roscoe Skully."

Major Armistead's eyes narrowed. "The little blueblood and his thug."

"I think I can handle them, sir."

"See that you do. If things work out, then I'm not opposed to integrating the troops. But I don't want discord in the ranks over a social experiment."

"It's more than that, sir. The cook says Abel's son, Caleb, is a huge help, and when he's not running errands for her, he drills alongside his father's company. I daresay we cannot imagine what being a soldier means to these men and their families."

"I'm sure. Still, we need these men to fight the enemy, not one another."

Abel was sitting alone on the bunk assigned to him and Titus. He never slept in it but it made a good seat when he polished his boots, as he was doing when Caleb strode in. He saw the fatigue in his son's eyes, but there was something else there as well—pride—and Abel knew he had made the right decision in bringing him along to the fort.

Caleb sat down beside his father, staring at every detail of the sparse accommodations his father and fifteen other men shared. "You're a real soldier now," he said in apparent awe.

"Life will be different for us after this, Caleb. We're doing just what we set out to do. We're making a better life for the others, aren't we?"

Caleb nodded and smiled as he continued to study the barracks. Four stacks of two bunks each filled the south end of the room. Two men shared each bunk, which consisted of nothing more than a board bottom with a thin mattress thrown over the top. The sergeant had a separate bunk in the corner. Two circular gun racks stood in the middle of the room, with slots to hold eight soldiers' muskets. A shelf ran along the wall at shoulder height, providing storage for the soldiers' uniforms, their hats, and the backpacks that stored their ammunition, their utensils, and everything else they owned.

"See how the trim on these wooden walls is painted yellow?" Abel asked. "That means we're an artillery company. When we see that stripe, we're reminded of who and what we are."

Caleb's eyes widened as he reached up to touch the golden buttons on his father's suspenders. It was a proud moment shared between father and son, until Emerson Hildebrand, Roscoe Skully, and several other members of the company entered.

So new to America that their English was very weak, three other soldiers eyed Abel nervously and quickly exited the barracks. Two others, Belisi and Stoddard, sat on their bunks as if waiting for a show to begin. Abel stopped shining his boot as every muscle in his body tensed.

Hildebrand placed his dirty foot on Abel's bunk. "What are you doing in here, boy?"

Skully snickered. "Yeah! Get outside in your tent. Dogs aren't allowed inside."

After another round of snickering Abel whispered to Caleb, "Get out. Get out now."

Caleb began to tremble, drawing Hildebrand's attention.

"Look at this scared little pup. What's the matter, boy? You don't want to be in here? Tell your papa. Look him in the eye and tell him you don't want to be a soldier puppy no more."

Abel raised his eyebrow and gave Caleb an almost imperceptible nod, and the boy bolted for the door, scrambling between the men as their laughter followed.

The muscles and sinews on Abel's arms bulged as he forced himself to return to shining his boot again. Hildebrand bent low until his blond curls brushed Abel's cheek. "You like polishing boots, eh boy? Then polish mine."

The rhythm of polishing his own boot remained unchanged as Abel attempted to ignore the man.

Now Skully plopped his foot down beside Abel. "Did you hear Private Hildebrand, darkie?" When Abel still didn't reply, Skully added, "I s'pose he's deaf, Emerson."

"Or stupid!"

Abel felt his temper roil until it was all he could do to keep from shaking. He knew he was moments from losing his restraint and doing something he had always dreamed of doing—hitting an abusive white man—but free or not, there would be no salvation for a Negro who crossed that mark. The pride of a moment ago slipped away like water through his fingers.

Be calm, Abel. Be smart . . . He heard the advice of his father, whispered to him so many times on White Oak when Abel felt death would be better than slavery. Now he was free, with papers and a uniform in the United States Army, yet nothing seemed any different.

Hildebrand lifted his foot and kicked Abel's boot out of his hands, placing his own booted foot in the big man's lap. "Clean my boot, boy, with your tongue."

The room fell silent as if everyone in the room knew Hildebrand had pushed Abel too far. With a quick move of his hand, Abel knocked Hildebrand's foot away, sending him stumbling into Skully's arms. Abel rose to his full height, his head nearly touching the ceiling. He willed his arms to his side, with club-sized fists clenched so tightly he could hear his knuckles crack. Hildebrand and Skully cowered before Abel as he glowered down at them.

Voices from outside caught all the men's attention. Everyone knew Major Armistead's intolerance for fighting among the ranks, so the soldiers straightened, glaring at one another.

The door opened and in walked Sergeant Carpenter, Major Armistead, Markus, and Caleb. The sergeant's face reflected pure fury, while the major's rigid carriage spoke of worry. His glance moved from Abel, to Hildebrand and Skully, to their audience, and then back again as the five men snapped to an irreverent attention. Markus stood behind, his own body tense.

"Do we have a problem here, gentlemen?" Carpenter asked coolly.

An uncomfortable silence ensued as Hildebrand and Abel stared one another down.

"No, sir, Sergeant," Hildebrand finally said. "Just enjoying a little recreation."

"A little recreation . . ." Carpenter grumbled. "Well, allow me to provide some of that recreation. The five of you are to rise an hour before reveille every morning this week. You draw all the cook's water. And I think the officers would enjoy a nice bath every night. So you'll be drawing water every evening as well. Is that clear?"

"Yes, sir," they replied in unison.

"At ease! Abel, the major would like a word with you. The rest of you pups? Outside!"

Abel knew the reference to "pups" could only have come from Caleb's report of the event, and that caused him to worry for his son. Hildebrand and Skully gave Abel one final, cautious sneer. Before slipping through the door they shot Caleb a threatening glare that made the boy shrink. Abel knew Markus caught it as well by the way he followed closely behind the boy with his hand on his shoulder.

Major Armistead extended his hand to Abel. "Hello, Abel, I'm Major Armistead. Captain Nicholson has given me a glowing report about you and Titus. I'd hoped your time here would be a chance for you to embrace that new life you spoke to him about, but it appears some men are unwilling to afford you that chance. And I can't have tension amongst the troops."

Abel saw his new life begin to slip away. He saw it in the way he naturally compressed his body to appear less imposing, felt it in the fearful thump of his mighty heart, heard it in the slurring of his educated tongue, the urge to placate, to please, to grovel. He reverted into the old pattern so easily—anger, then fear for a loved one, then obeisance. He wondered if it was this way for every man, not just men of a darker color. He didn't know. All he knew was that he was not yet ready to let go of this opportunity. "There won't be any more trouble, Major. I promise."

Major Armistead searched his face for several seconds. "All right, Abel. We'll give it a little longer."

Once the room emptied, Abel slumped on the bunk and felt his body go limp. After a few minutes, he strode outside to where a large fire was glowing. Caleb and Markus were seated on one side. Hildebrand and Skully were seated on the other, fearfully watching Abel's approach. Abel knew immediately who was responsible for the change in their demeanor.

As Markus approached, arms stretched wide, Abel smiled and shook his head.

"You and Jed! You both shoulda joined the navy, Abel. I've met too many soldiers with a burr in their bonnet. You'd best watch your back, my friend."

"I'm tempted to send Caleb back home, but you're not headed there, are you, Markus?"

"I've been asked ta sail on a cartel ship as part of a delegation tryin' to save Frannie's friend, Dr. Beanes. We sail tomorrow ta rendezvous with the British fleet, but I'll come for Caleb on my way back if you'd like."

Abel looked at Caleb, who was enjoying the company of Captain Nicholson, Francis Scott Key, and Colonel Skinner. "It's wrong that men can take this away from him."

Markus patted Abel's arm. "Then wait a bit and just see how things work out. I have a feelin' it might all die down."

"You do, do you? Tell me, what did you say to those two to take the spit out of them?"

Markus turned sheepish. "Just a wee bit of a lie. I made sure they overheard me tellin' Caleb that we're so relieved back on the Willows over the news that the last man you tangled with is now expected to walk again."

A laugh broke from Abel, and suddenly he missed the Willows more than ever. Markus seemed to sense it. From within his jacket he pulled a stack of letters. "Bitty and the children sent these along." He reached into his satchel and retrieved a bundle wrapped in fabric. "She also sent along a bit of her home cookin'."

Abel gratefully took the proffered items, and the pair wandered over to the fire. Caleb lay on his back looking up at the flag.

"It's a thing of beauty, isn't it Caleb?" Markus asked.

"It looks like it's touching the stars."

The comment transformed Major Armistead's stern countenance. "It does, doesn't it? That pole is nearly ninety feet tall, Caleb, and the flag itself is thirty feet by forty-two feet. That's almost three times as tall as your father, and he could stretch six times along its width. And see those stars? How big do you think each one is?"

Caleb moved his hands to form a wide circle.

"Even bigger than that. Each star is two feet across." The major imitated the size himself. "The flying of such a large garrison flag requires great care. We never fly it in bad weather. We fly the smaller, lighter storm flag at such times. When the large garrison flag gets wet, its weight greatly increases, and if flown in high winds it would become like a sail. Either could cause it to snap its pole and fall. We never want our flag to come down. Do you know why?"

"Because no one will know whose fort it is!"

"That's right. As long as the Stars and Stripes are flying, everyone for miles around will feel safe and know we are in control of Fort McHenry."

"It must be the biggest flag and the longest pole on the whole earth," Caleb replied.

Major Armistead smiled. "There are many bigger."

Caleb's mouth fell agape.

The major continued, "My original request was for this one to be even larger. I told my superior, Major General Smith, that the men of Fort McHenry were ready to defend Baltimore but they had no suitable ensign to display over their star fort. I asked Mrs.

Pickersgill to sew a flag so large that the British would have no difficulty seeing it from a distance. I think this flag will do quite nicely."

"Who is Mrs. Pickersgill?"

"Mary Pickersgill is the woman who sewed this flag, Caleb. Actually, it was she and her daughter, a young girl just about your age, who sewed it, with a little help from a niece. And you might find this interesting, Caleb. Another of Mrs. Pickersgill's helpers was a young Negro girl, an indentured servant named Grace Wisher."

The look of wonder returned to Caleb's face and he turned around to look at his father.

"Mrs. Pickersgill's mother also helped. She once sewed flags for General Washington."

"George Washington?" Caleb sat up now, clearly impressed.

Armistead smiled. "Sergeant, tell Caleb the story of the night you first saw the flag."

"Me, sir? Oh, it was a quite a night." The officer moved in close and sat on a crate, eye level with Caleb. "You see, I was navigating my horse along East Pratt, glancing down each side street and alley, scanning for spies or traitors, when I saw a glow radiating from Clagett's Brewery well after closing." His voice filled with mystery. "And then I noticed movement along an alleyway. I saw in shadow a lone, slim figure hefting something through the darkness toward the brewery's malt house. I shouted, 'Who goes there?' but the figure clutched the burden closer and began to run toward the malt house.

"I urged my horse into a gallop and shouted again, 'Halt right where you are!' but the person just kept running. My horse quickly bore down upon the intruder, but who do you think it was?"

Caleb shook his head.

"It was a frightened wisp of a girl!"

"A girl?" Caleb said incredulously.

"A girl. Of course at the time I didn't know if she was a thief or a spy or a runaway, but as I studied her, I noticed her eyes were rimmed with fatigue, and that clutched in her arms were bundles of fabric. "I asked her, 'What mischief are you up to, child? I daresay your father will be appalled when he hears that his daughter is running the streets at such an unseemly hour.' But her answer tore at my heart. She told me her father was dead, but that her mother and grandmother both knew where she was, because it was they who had sent her on her errand—to fetch the binding and the remaining stars for the flags."

"This flag?"

"The very same, and the smaller storm flag, too. Except I didn't know anything about them at the time, so I thought her story was pure malarkey! Then she explained that she and the other women of her family were sewing the flags for Fort McHenry."

Carpenter's face grew wistful. "Her name was Caroline Pickersgill and she was only thirteen," he said, emphasizing her age. "I began to help her carry the stars when her mother arrived, worried at Caroline's delay. After making our introductions, she invited me in for the privilege of a look.

"I followed the women into the malt house of the brewery, where red and white stripes sprawled across the wooden floor from a gigantic blue square. An older woman was stitching a white star to the field of blue, while two other young girls were stitching a red stripe to a white one. My first thoughts were the same as yours, Caleb. Spread there, on the floor, it looked to be the biggest flag on the entire earth, and that's what I told Mrs. Pickersgill.

"She laughed and taught me a good deal about flags that night. For example, guess how much fabric it took to make this flag?"

Caleb shrugged.

"Four hundred yards of prime English woolen bunting," Carpenter said.

"Four hundred yards?"

Carpenter pointed to the flag. "Two strips of fabric had to first be sewn together to form each of the flag's fifteen stripes. They needed a very long and open floor to lay those huge pieces out, and the brewery afforded them the only convenient location. After the men would leave work, the ladies would sweep the malt house floor very clean. Then they would lay out the completed portion, working on their hands and knees until midnight most nights, so they could sew each of the additional pieces together. When I arrived, they were beginning to stitch the cotton stars in place."

"They were almost finished?"

"No, there was still more to be done. Those stars are especially complicated, because they aren't just sewn in. They peek through a cutout on the reverse side. The technique has some fancy name, but it was very delicate work, and the woman I saw doing it was little Caroline's grandmother, Mrs. Rebecca Young of Philadelphia, who once sewed flags and uniforms for General Washington and the forces of the Continental Army. She was an older lady of about sixty years, kneeling over a field of indigo blue as she sewed around the cutout where a large white star peeked through."

The sergeant's eyes began to glisten. "I offered the dear lady my hand to help her stand, but even assisted, she was so stiff she could scarcely rise, and yet there she was, on her knees, sewing that grand flag."

Carpenter's voice broke. "I bent to kiss that dear old woman's wrinkled hand and told her how my father once marched with General Washington to defend our liberty, perhaps beneath one of her flags. And there she was, helping sew a flag to rally us in defense of our liberty once more. So I can hardly look at that flag without my heart swelling in my breast."

Major Armistead placed a supportive hand on the sergeant's shoulder. "Since the fall of Washington, I believe our feelings are more tender about such things. I well remember the day Mrs. Pickersgill and Caroline delivered the flag—August 19th of the last year. It was a proud day as we ran her up the pole for the first time, watching her wave defiantly, as if we were shaking our fists at the British for the atrocities in Hampton, and now for those at Washington."

The major turned his attentions to the troops, his impassioned eyes meeting theirs. "Those fine ladies still live within this city, gentlemen. They've provided us with a worthy ensign of this fine nation. Now we must do our part to assure that it continues to fly. There can be no disharmony between us. We must not let pettiness distract us from our duty. When you feel weary or disgruntled, or you lose hope, I want you to remember Sergeant Carpenter's story, and the service the Pickersgill women have rendered, and then carry on with honor. Remember that."

A quiet ripple of assent moved through the crowd. Abel recognized the personal message conveyed in the major's speech about unity and honor. He saw the major's eyes scan his face and the faces of Hildebrand and Skully, warning the three men to forget the evening's events. He also saw how the mention of Hampton no longer broke Markus. Instead, the Irishman seemed emboldened by the remembrance, and Abel understood both points. While some things must be put away, some things must never be forgotten.

The bugler blew reveille and the fort's chaplain offered a prayer. In the militia camps scattered along the forts perimeter, each unit was likely doing the same. The wind picked up, evidenced by the snapping of the flag's fabric and the thump of the hoist against the wooden pole. Markus scanned the cloud-studded sky, spit into his hand, and lifted it to check the wind.

"A storm's blowing in," Captain Nicholson noted.

"Aye. From the south, most likely the fringe of a hurricane in the Caribbean. It's that time o' year."

"Men, lower the garrison flag and run up the storm flag," Major Armistead ordered.

As men scrambled to obey, others moved onto their bunks, while those preparing to travel said their goodbyes. Abel noticed the final moments shared between Mr. Key and his brother-in-law, Captain Nicholson. "Mr. Key looks worried," Abel said.

Markus glanced at Key and then quickly looked away. "'E's the father of a large family. He's got a lot ta lose if the British get their dander up."

"And you?"

"I'm an old Irish alley cat, Abel. I got nothing much to live for, no one but my friends to miss me, and yet try as 'e may, the devil can't catch a good enough hold o' me to keep me dead. Now you, my friend, mind my warnin' and watch your back. I saw the looks that lieutenant had in his eyes before 'e tried to get Jed killed in that bridge explosion. Your two bunkmates got that same look. The major quelled things for the night, but watch yourself and your son come tomorrow."

Titus wandered over, preparing for bed. Abel introduced him to Markus.

"Well, nice meetin' ya, Captain. I'm turning in, Abel. You should too. I hear you got water duty for a spell." Titus slapped Abel on the shoulder. "Must've been one dust-up! For once, I'm glad I had kitchen duty." Titus walked away, chuckling to himself.

"The word's gettin' out," Markus said. "Do you still want me to swing by for the boy when I get back?"

Abel gave the idea some thought. "I can't say whether or not I'll send him home, but I'd appreciate it if you'd come by and check on us."

★ ★ ★ ★ ★

The men parted and Markus strolled over to where Mr. Skinner anxiously waited with the horses. "We've got to get moving or we'll be spending half an hour riding in the rain!"

Just then, Mr. Key arrived with Captain Nicholson.

"Good luck to you all," Nicholson said. "Frank, don't worry about Polly or the children. If you're not back here in four days, I'll send a courier to check on everyone."

The men locked eyes, both knowing that the need for a courier would portend bad news for one or all of them.

Markus, Key, and Skinner were soaked when they returned to the Indian Queen Hotel. Markus called for a bath though it was nearly 10:00, and the men agreed they'd meet at 7:00 in the morning.

The Irishman grumbled as he peeled wet layers of cotton away from his various wounds and bandages, which were also wet now. Catching a glimpse of himself in the mirror, he considered what a sorry sight he was. His hair was loose and stringy and his beard dripped water on his chest, which itself was so scarred and discolored he almost felt glad no woman would likely ever see him without a shirt again. He was twenty-six years old and looked like he was near ready for the grave. Then he considered what he had said to Abel about the devil not being able to keep him dead, and he knew that from the look of him, his statement might have been a bit premature.

Worried over the condition of his new Sea Fencibles' uniform, Markus pulled out the blue pants and coat. Fortunately, they had remained dry in his saddlebags. He folded the items carefully and placed them in the highboy, then tore through his bag to find dry underclothing while he waited on the hot water. In the process, he noticed a letter flutter to the floor.

The plain paper looked like the sheets Hannah kept in the kitchen for scribbling notes and lists on. The handwriting was unfamiliar to him—delicate but somewhat sloppy, as if it had either been rushed or written by an untrained hand. Markus sat on the edge of his bed and unfolded the paper, noting that there was but a single paragraph. He scanned to the bottom to note the sender's name—Mrs. Jeremiah Tyler.

A nervous wave rushed over him, causing his arms to prickle. Markus dismissed it as a chill resulting from his wet condition, and he began to read.

Dear Mr. O'Malley,

I expect I'll be gone when you return. Now that I am strong and well, I will move along to trouble my dear friends no longer. I wanted to thank you for your kindness and courage on the day we met. I'm sorry you have already paid so great a price for my mistakes and follies. You and Dr. Renfro have shown me more gentlemanly courtesy and concern than I have known in a great while, and I will not forget it. Sometimes we can experience more happiness in a moment than we've known in a long lifetime. Think on that when you miss your dear wife. Please be safe. I pray I've caused you no lasting ill.

With kindness,
Jenny Tyler

A new coldness settled into Markus. She would be gone—the pretty little lady with the sad eyes would not be at the Willows when he returned. Somehow, despite the few words they had actually shared, that notion saddened him.

He wondered how she knew so much about him, about Lyra, when she had barely spent a few waking moments near him. And then he thought back to the day he and Samuel came upon her, how Samuel and he had been talking about Jed and the war—about Lyra and about Markus's ache for her. He had held her in his arms for a time. Had she also been awake then? Evidently so, at least for a portion of the time. The letter began to make sense to him now.

Markus wondered what manner of man had hurt her so and broken her spirit. The thought made him want to lash out at someone or something, but he felt himself reverting back to the angry man he had become after Lyra's death, so he reined his anger in. He knew there were a great many ways for a person to be broken. His hurts were primarily on the outside now, and soothed by time and care, they would heal, leaving only the shadow of a scar. But he had known the kind of dark hurt that festered inside, the kind Mrs. Tyler currently knew.

He noted others of her words to him—*"kindness and courage . . . gentlemanly courtesy and concern."* Were those words really intended for him? They seemed meant for another man. Turning back to the mirror, Markus drew his fingers through his tangled hair and wondered if, when the war was finally over, he could learn to be a real gentleman, maybe even find a woman who could love him once more.

A knock sounded. His water had arrived. Markus thanked the concierge and asked him to send up a pair of scissors and a shaving kit as well. After all, tomorrow he'd be sailing under direct orders from the president of the United States of America, and he wanted to look his best.

CHAPTER 12

Monday, September 5, 1814
The Willows

Jenny Potter Tyler knew she must leave the Willows. The sweet Irishman who had been so kind to her would hate her once he knew. She knew his kind—proud and brave, a line-in-the-sand kind of man where everything was either black or white. And her life was mostly gray.

She changed from Frannie's borrowed nightgown back into her blue satin dress. The costume looked ridiculously out of place during the day, and more so here on the Willows, where everyone wore simple work clothes most of the time.

Jenny had no firm plans. The last one had failed miserably, so it didn't much matter. She had the ruby ring and the fifty dollars sewn into her clothes. There was also the diamond-studded stickpin she concealed in her hair. She would sell that first and be glad to see it gone. She would start on the River Road away from Calverton and hope someone offered her a ride. Maybe a boat would pick her up at the next dock. It really didn't matter. The only destination left to her was "away."

After quickly scribbling a brief note to Frannie, Jenny slipped down the hallway and out the front door. The sun had not yet risen, but the moon lit her way. As she walked in the wet, dewy grass she was unaware of the pair of eyes watching her departure.

When she reached the road, she headed north. The sun was beginning to rise over the farmland, reminding her of her childhood in Cutter Springs, Pennsylvania. Farm life was hard, but there were many good memories, like playing in the creek with her younger brother, warm milk every morning, fresh peas from the garden, the innocence of a new lamb. Things changed after her mother died. Her father and she would drive the wagon into the city to sell their produce, while her brother worked the farm. It was there in Philadelphia, singing to entertain herself on market day, that Henri had discovered her. He invited her to join the chanteuses of Le Jardin and her life began to change. She saved nearly a thousand dollars with the intentions of buying a little grocery where her father could sell his wares. It would mean a decent life even if she never wed, and a wonderful dowry if she did. And then the war came, and all her plans went to ruin.

She turned at the sound of a wagon approaching from behind, driven by a thin young man with a plump young woman in the wagon seat. Jenny waved and they pulled alongside her.

The driver's face was green in places where bruises were healing. He scowled as he scrutinized her. "Do you need help? Did your wagon break down?"

"No, sir." She raised her skirt above her ankles. "These two feet are all I have."

"What on earth are you doing out here dressed like that at this hour?" His wife touched his arm and whispered a call for kindness, to which he replied, "Well, you can't be too careful, Penelope. There are traitors and refugees roaming the countryside. Where are you headed?"

The woman's soft, sad eyes made Jenny feel safe despite the man's critical glare. Jenny was glad the later questions freed her from having to answer the first. "I was staying with Frannie Pearson at the Willows, but they suffered a fire and now they have so many people crammed into the main house. I felt it was best to move along."

The man's face softened and then he became stoic. "Yes, we know all about the fire."

Without a word he extended his hand and helped Jenny climb up. Once she was seated beside him he faced forward and rattled off, "Frederick Stringham's my name. This is my wife."

The woman offered her hand. "Hello. I'm Penelope."

Stringham quickly cut back in. "I own the White Oak Plantation, the estate that borders the Willows. The same fire that damaged the Willows completely destroyed the main house and barn on my farm because I was there, saving the Pearsons' place instead of protecting mine."

Penelope gently touched his arm. "But we're rebuilding." She glanced at Jenny. "Mr. Stringham was very courageous that day. He took quite a beating from the mercenaries who set those fires, and yet he came to the Pearsons to protect me because I was there."

"Yes, and what did my courage get me? They've still got a barn . . . and a house."

Penelope's head immediately dropped forward as if she were shamed by the statement.

"Have the Pearsons completed their repairs?" he asked Jenny.

"Uh . . . um . . . no. I—I don't think so."

It was the first time Frederick Stringham had smiled since their meeting. Something about him reminded Jenny of two men she knew—her husband, and the man she hired in Washington to help her escape from the city. Frederick Stringham possessed a certain lean handsomeness, but his eyes were cold and angry, not like the warm eyes of her rescuers—Mr. O'Malley and Dr. Renfro. And like her own husband, Stringham regarded his wife with little interest. Suddenly, she wished she were walking again.

"How far are you headed?" Stringham asked. "I can take you as far as Baltimore."

"Baltimore?" She gave that destination some thought. It was not a place she could count on being made welcome, but she would figure out a way to make that option work. It would be a long ride with ornery company, but at least Stringham wasn't leering at her or groping her. There was some comfort in his narcissism. "Yes, Baltimore will be fine."

Breakfast was long past when Frannie finally went to check on Jenny and found her gone. The brief note distressed her.

Dear Frannie,

Thank you for taking me in, but I must go. Please forgive me and pray for better days for us all.

Jenny

Frannie flew down the stairs and straight to Markus's house to find Timothy sitting in his suit, reading a book. "Did you say something to Jenny to make her want to leave?"

The question visibly wounded the man. "I would never!"

"She's gone! She left early this morning with no explanation other than this." Frannie handed him the note. "You were so concerned about her impact on me. I just wondered if . . ." The hurt in his eyes cooled her fire. "I'm sorry, Timothy, but why would she have left this way?"

"She's evidently a very troubled young woman, Francis. The real question is how you could ever accuse me of such a thing. What of the great trust you claim to have in me?"

Frannie slid down into a nearby chair. "I'm sorry. It's just such a sorrow to me. She came when I sorely needed a distraction. I miss her already."

"Do you want me to ride the River Road and search for her?"

Frannie bit her lip as she considered the suggestion. "No, I suppose not. Clearly she wanted to leave. But why, Timothy?"

"Too many things don't add up with your friend, Frannie. Why was she traveling, dressed in a costume designed for the stage? And why is she so emaciated and work-worn while wearing a ruby ring? The man who was with her was cause enough to worry about the company she kept. I fear she may be in serious trouble—the kind you don't need right now."

Hannah strolled over. "Frannie, is everything all right? I saw you race out the door."

Frannie looked to Timothy for support. "Jenny's gone. She stole away sometime before first light, leaving only a brief apology. It's all so strange."

Hannah tapped her lips in thought. "Reverend Myers has been spending a considerable amount of time with her. Perhaps he knows something more. He's in the kitchen with Bitty."

As they headed for the main house, Hannah tugged at a strand of her dark hair, an action Frannie recognized as a sign of distress.

"What's troubling you, Hannah?"

Hannah looked at her and halted. "I saw Jenny leave this morning."

"What? And you didn't try to stop here."

"Hear me out, Frannie. Jenny's departure may be a blessing in disguise. I think there's a warrant out for her arrest."

"Where would you get such an idea?"

"When the soldiers left here a sheriff's dispatch was left behind. 'Wanted' was printed across the top in bold letters, and the image was of a beautiful woman in a blue dress. I didn't make the connection when Jenny arrived. She was so distressed, looking nothing like the image on the paper, but that woman was also a singer, and once Jenny was cleaned and rested, I noticed the similarities. The woman's name was Genevieve."

Frannie turned white. "Jenny's stage name was Genevieve."

140

"There were several charges listed below the image—thievery, assault, abandonment, and treason. She's in very serious trouble, Frannie."

They reached the kitchen, where the reverend was seated next to Bitty, helping her with her penmanship. He quickly rose as Hannah, Timothy, and Frannie entered.

"What are you two doing?" Hannah asked nervously.

Bitty responded with uncharacteristic shyness. "He said it was all right. He said we didn't need to keep our readin' and writin' a secret anymore."

The reverend quickly rose and bowed slightly. "I've known since the first day I arrived. The children run about the yard reading everything—the lettering on seed bags, the names of the liniments and tonics in the barn. Even the tiniest ones draw their letters in the dirt. You've no need to worry, Mrs. Pearson. It's not illegal in Maryland for freedmen to read and write."

"Legalities aside, there are ample risks from the narrow-minded, Reverend. Jack and Abel found that out when men in Calverton realized they could read the handbills in a store."

Timothy laid a hand on Hannah's shoulder. "I think it's fine, Hannah."

Hannah remained on edge. While Frannie scooped up Bitty's toddler from the floor, Hannah moved behind Bitty and gave the tiny woman a hug. "Is that a letter from Abel?"

Bitty turned around and beamed. "Yes, it is. And it's good news, too! Abel is gettin' a deed to land out west somewhere, and aside from his pay of eight dollars a month, he's gettin' a fifty-dollar signin' bonus!"

"Bitty, that's wonderful!"

"And Caleb's found work too, as a cook, so he's gettin' paid too."

Frannie's face clouded. "Are you leaving the Willows, Bitty?"

Bitty gently slapped Frannie's hand. "Of course not, darlin'. We own land right here too, don't we? But now we got a stake for the children if they want to homestead. We got choices and opportunities aplenty! And one little secret I'm not obliged to share just yet."

"Bitty!" Hannah teased. "You can't say such a thing and leave us tortured."

Bitty clutched her papers close to her shoulder, taunting the women by pulling far away. "Uh, uh, uh! It's just a little over-the-fence chatter from White Oak's slaves. You'll find out soon enough." She wagged a finger at the reverend. "And don't you go tellin' them!"

Reverend Myers raised his hands in surrender. "I'm bound by a vow of silence."

"You best be!" Bitty said comically as she took her things and headed for the room she and the children shared upstairs while they waited for their cabin to be rebuilt.

"I hope I've laid your fears to rest, Mrs. Pearson. Good morning, Miss Pearson, Mr. Shepard." The reverend pulled out a chair for Hannah and she sat.

"Thank you," Hannah replied as she studied the man. He was an anomaly to her. His baby face and hands indicated that he was young, perhaps close to her own age of twenty, and raised without knowing hard work. His eyes were wise and sober, and she had seen the maturity with which he handled the residents' concerns. He was a blessing to them, she had to admit, serving as their daily counselor as well as their spiritual advisor. And yet he was, admittedly, a novice without any formal ministerial training. She wondered how someone so young could be so wise.

The reverend shrank under her scrutiny, causing Hannah to look away. He cleared his throat and said, "I've got some good news to share. We're placing the last of the roofing timbers on the chapel today. We should be able to move the women and children back to the meadows by week's end if they don't mind living there until the cabins are finished."

"Oh, that's wonderful!" Frannie said. "Is that Bitty's secret?"

The reverend smiled wryly and shook his head. "No, no, no . . ."

Hannah cut back in. "Reverend Myers, were you aware that Jenny Tyler left?"

His head turned abruptly at the news. "That's odd. She made plans to meet with me today."

"I want to show you something." Hannah stood and went to the drawer where she kept her writing paper. She opened it and turned in distress. "Frannie, the sheriff's notice is missing."

"Oh, no. It's my fault," Frannie exclaimed. "Jenny wanted to thank Markus for his kindness before he left, and I directed her to that drawer for a piece of writing paper."

"I'm afraid I don't understand," the reverend said.

"Mrs. Tyler is being sought by the law." Frannie sighed. "She must have seen the notice and realized we were aware of her troubles."

His face reflected sadness more than surprise.

"You already knew, didn't you, Reverend? Did she tell you?"

"She told me very little. What I do know is that her last concern is herself, so I assume she left to spare you all any trouble her presence might cause."

Frannie placed her hand on Timothy's.

"I'll saddle two horses," he said, then hurried off.

Frannie also went to change, leaving Hannah and the reverend alone. The situation was immediately awkward.

"You've done a wonderful job on the chapel," Hannah said. "It rose so quickly."

The reverend smiled. "It was a Willows success. Everyone pitched in. I've been impressed by the freedmen's hunger for a chapel. Since the first wall was raised, they've come in there to sit and sing." He chuckled. "Jerome left deep spiritual roots here."

"He was a remarkable man."

"The people here consider you quite remarkable, too. They've told me about your gift—your powerful intuitions. Do you believe it's the Lord speaking to you personally?"

Hannah stood abruptly. "I'm not crazy, if that's what you're asking me!"

"Of course not," the reverend said apologetically. "Please, I didn't mean to upset you. I truly want to understand. Sit a moment longer and tell me only what you'd like to share."

Hannah sat tentatively and eyed the young man with skepticism. "I cannot give you a demonstration, if that's what you want. I can't control it, nor can I explain it. I only know that I receive strong . . . well . . . impressions. Sometimes it's merely an idea, a thought. Sometimes it's more visual."

"And what are these impressions about?"

"About people I love." She gave that some thought and realized something she hadn't considered before. "But they're often more specific than that. They almost always involve my husband, Jed. Perhaps it's because he has always been my protector—my champion." Hannah felt her eyes begin to mist and she dabbed at them. "Even when I was young, when I was sad or lonely or afraid, I could think about Jed and picture him in my mind, and peace would wash over me. As I grew, the impressions became stronger, providing me with answers and guidance. They saved my life a few years ago, but still, Jed was almost always part of that answer."

The reverend looked away shyly. "It's clear how devoted you two are to each other."

Hannah felt her mind drift to Jed. A momentary smile graced her lips as the memory brought him near. "I cannot feel whole without him. It is as if half of my soul is in him, and half of his is with me, occupying the emptiness but not quite filling it."

"God is love, and where great love exists, His Spirit may well come. Perhaps that's why the Spirit whispers to you of your husband."

"You believe in such things?"

"I believe God can manifest His love to us in many ways."

"No, most people think you are crazed or devil-possessed if you ascribe to such beliefs."

"Not all. Some ministers believe a new day of religious awakening is dawning."

Hannah curiosity was piqued. "What kind of awakening?"

"Our independence from Europe has affected our religiosity as well as our politics. Since our great Revolution, we've had no kings acting as God's mouthpiece, filtering His word. A second Great Awakening is sweeping across the land, with American religionists asking God to reveal Himself to them without a king as their conduit. Some remain rigid, controlling man's access to God like gatekeepers, but some believe God desires for us to ponder His word individually, and that we each are entitled to receive a portion of His Spirit personally."

"Another minister, a friend named Emmett Schultz, once told me this, but I appreciate being reminded of it. And you think it could explain how I have this peace about Jed's situation?"

"As I said, Hannah, marriage is ordained of God. Who deserves a portion of God's Spirit more than two who faithfully honor His covenant?"

CHAPTER 13

Monday, September 5, 1814
Off the Atlantic Coast

As close as Jed could reckon, a week had passed—seven marks on the ship's hull—though time no longer had meaning to him. Night and day were futile, insignificance references. His putrid body felt foreign to him, and, fearing his mind was decaying as rapidly as his stamina, he began reciting any passages he could recall to the stock awaiting slaughter to feed the crew.

As promised, twice a day the hatch opened and the rope-tied sack, the newest element in the crew's sport, was lowered. Sometimes actual food of varying amounts and decay would be in the sack. Sometimes it would be a rat, or worse. Jed learned not to let his hopes rise when that longed-for sliver of light first broke from the hatch, nor to allow his hunger to rule his mood, though lack of food wearied him not only physically but mentally as well.

Each day, he vowed not to let his captors break him. And he prayed, releasing his anger, fully submitting to Jerome's otherworldly advice to surrender his will to God. As time passed, Jed began to notice a number of tiny blessings.

His hearing became acute as he strained to catch any human conversation that filtered through the deck. At first he would only catch a word here and there, but voices soon became familiar

146

to him. One of the most talkative crewmen was also one of the loudest, complaining each night about some unpleasant task. Three times a day, the words "lieutenant" and "sick" and "dying" filtered through the deck floor, grumbled amid a string of epithets and curse words, until Jed felt certain he had heard the name Ramsey among the vile stream. *Ramsey?*

Jed scrambled to stand. Drawing as close to the deck as possible, he stretched and listened intently but didn't hear the name again. Finally, he sat down and fell asleep, missing most of the afternoon's tirade, but during the evening hour he clearly heard the name Ramsey again. *Arthur is here?* It made sense. Markus had said Arthur had made it to the fleet alive, and if so, wouldn't he have been placed on a ship for England to receive medical treatment? Jed remembered Captain Smith saying the *Iphigenia* was the ship being rushed back to England with the report of Washington's defeat. It seemed perfectly logical to Jed, but could it be? He dared not get his hopes up, but when he heard the name Lieutenant Ramsey, his heart leapt. *Arthur is still alive!*

Jed imagined scenarios where Arthur would become aware of the American prisoner in the hold named Pearson, and effect some salvation for him. He didn't mind that the sack came down containing only potato peels that night, or that the increased rocking of the ship and splash of the waves made eavesdropping through the decks more difficult.

Later, the sea got rough, tossing the animals about. Jed heard a report of a hurricane and felt it punishing the ship. Tethered to the wall, he pounded back and forth with every violent lurch, agitating wounds that had just begun to heal. Filthy water sloshed onto him, soaking him to the bone. Sheep and cattle scrambled to hold their footing, bleating in fear, and fowl squawked in toppling cages. Jed heard the crash of barrels, the scramble of feet, and shouting voices above him for hours. As if he had been utterly forgotten, no food or water was sent down for two days.

147

His thirst was rabid, causing him to consider dipping from the fetid sewage. Bruised in body and broken in spirit, he raised his eyes heavenward and cried out, "What more, Lord?"

Soon, Jerome's soothing voice returned. *"Trust the Lord, Jed. He hasn't forgotten you. He's giving you an opportunity here."*

"I'm running low on faith, Jerome," Jed cried softly as he crumpled against the hull. Again he trusted and again he prayed. "Please . . . please, Lord . . . help me." And then the sea stilled.

Despite the melee above, Jed fell into a fitful rest. The next morning two men came and dragged his battered body from the hold, tossing him onto the littered deck above. Jed sucked deeply, drawing down huge, hungry gulps of fresh sea air as he surveyed the damage. The largest of the ship's masts lay across the deck. Large portions of the railing were missing, and the entire deck was littered with splintered wood and purloined cargo from towns in Maryland and Virginia.

A British officer named Sneed pounded over. Jed recognized him from his imprisonment in Washington. "You claimed to be a farmer," Sneed began. "The smithy and his mate were both washed overboard with a trunk full of parts. Do you have experience forging metal?"

Relishing the freedom to move his limbs again, Jed rolled his shoulders and neck and then stretched his back, filling every inch of his lungs with the sweet, crisp air as if to store it up.

Sneed grabbed him by the collar. "Can you make iron pins? Can you mend something like this?" He held up a piece of twisted metal that was evidently essential to the ship.

Jed's heart began to race as he saw an opportunity to bargain. He took the item in his filthy hands, turning it over and over, trying to conceal his nervous excitement. "With the proper tools and a forge? Perhaps."

The Brit tightened his grip on Jed's collar, wrenching his neck at an awkward angle. "This ship sustained damage that must be repaired if we are to survive this voyage, Pearson. Your life hangs in the balance as well as ours!"

Jed grinned at the man. "I'm headed for Dartmoor. I'd say you care more about living than I."

"Men survive Dartmoor, fool, but it's certain death if this ship sinks or if we float around until we die of thirst!"

Captain Smith burst through a cabin door and hurried over. "Can he make the repairs?"

The first officer sent Jed crashing to the deck with an angry shove, then drew back his own fist. "He can do it and he will do it, or he'll die here on the spot."

"Mr. Sneed! I don't see the wisdom in threatening to kill the man whose help we need."

Sneed straightened and then sneered at Jed with his lips curled back, exposing his few remaining brown teeth. "I don't trust this filthy scoundrel."

Smith's face went red. "You idiot. We need his help."

"He's a lying, murderous coward!"

"We don't even know if he was the shooter."

Deathly silence followed the collective gasp of the men. Smith scanned the crew. "It's true. We don't know if Pearson was our shooter. Reports came in about another gunman, a barber, but we were unable to capture him to verify the story." Smith's guilty gaze now fell on Jed. "Such a violation of international law could not go unpunished, but without an eyewitness, and with no time for a trial, returning you to England was the only recourse."

Jed's chest heaved in anger as his arms spread wide. "You have kidnapped me to have a scapegoat? Does the truth not matter?"

"Does honor matter, Mr. Pearson?" Smith shouted back. "Or does your nation support the random murder of young men whose only crime was the fact that they carried a flag of truce?"

"I condemn the action as well, but how will consigning me to Dartmoor serve your cause? I didn't fire those shots! Can I expect justice and fairness at this so-called trial?"

"You must understand that those shots changed everything, Mr. Pearson. Admiral Cockburn and General Ross rode into Washington under a flag of peace to hold a parlay and lay the city under contribution. A fee was all they required as proof that Washington had submitted, but you, or one of your countrymen, murdered members of that delegation, very nearly assassinating Major General Ross himself. That is why your capital was burned— out of retaliation. So if you want to blame someone for the fall of Washington City, look at your own ignorant citizenry!"

Jed's chest continued to heave in fury. "You expect an innocent individual to answer for the ignorance of a city?"

Smith's eyes closed halfway, matching the downturn in his mouth. "An event of this magnitude cannot be left unresolved. Someone must answer for it, and I regret to say that as things now stand, you will, most certainly, be found guilty and sent to Dartmoor."

Smith offered Jed his hand to raise him to his feet. It dangled there for several seconds as Jed's previous optimism evaporated. He shot Smith a black look that proclaimed his hatred and disdain, but the officer's compassion was evident as he continued to reach his hand to the prisoner. At last Jed took it, allowing Smith to pull him to his feet.

"I'm sorry if you truly are innocent, but I can improve your situation. I've told you who and what I am, Mr. Pearson. The necessity of my safe arrival in London is important to both our nations. The reports I carry will impact peace negotiations and decide the end of this war. You have a stake in this conflict's rapid conclusion. We've also lost half of our water barrels in the storm, placing all of us in danger of dying of thirst. I therefore would be willing to provide certain . . . assurances, let us say, in return for your service."

"What sort of assurances?" Jed growled.

"I cannot commute the imposed sentence, but I could make certain arrangements in your behalf. We've been blown off course. There is an atoll off the starboard bow we're attempting to reach. Once we reach it, help shore up this vessel enough to get me to Bermuda where I can catch another ship, and I'll seek an alternative placement for you to serve out your sentence."

Jed scanned the vast expanse of endless sea, wondering what other option he had. He was a captive, wholly at their mercy, and though things were not as improved as he had momentarily hoped, they were better than they had been before the conversation began. He knew he would do anything—anything!—to improve his chances of survival so he could return to Hannah. As he thought of his prayer, a pleasant thought came to his mind. "I believe you have an injured officer on board—a Lieutenant Ramsey?"

"Why yes. Yes, we do."

"He showed mercy and honor to my friends at Hampton, and he aided Commodore Barney at Bladensburg. Allow me to repay him for his kindness. Situate me near him and allow me to serve as his personal steward." Jed raised an eyebrow at Captain Smith. "And whether he lives or dies, whether I'm found guilty or not, guarantee that I won't be sent to Dartmoor."

"I told you I cannot commute your sentence."

Jed grasped Smith's hand and bore his eyes into the Brit's. "I ask only for mercy in return for my help. Promise me, on your honor. I've seen how enemies become friends when respect has been earned. Prepare a document explaining how I assisted in saving your crew and about my service to Lieutenant Ramsey. Describe how you guaranteed me these arrangements, and I will make the attempt to forge whatever you need."

"You are asking a great deal. I cannot assure where you serve your sentence."

"Do the best you can. Tell them everything you've said here— about the barber, about my possible innocence, and about how I helped save this ship. I beg you to mediate in my behalf."

Captain Smith's fingers rubbed across his lips as he studied Jed's face, considering the notion. "I doubt you are a man accustomed to begging for anything. All right, I'll do my best."

Jed eyed the man. "Your very best?"

"You have my word as an officer, and you'll have my written guarantee as well."

A lump formed in Jed's tight throat. As the relief became real to him, his body shook and his knees quivered, nearly buckling him. Smith rushed in to bolster Jed, despite his filth, despite his rank odor. The officer turned to the crew and announced, "Lieutenant Pearson is now under my personal protection. Harm him, and you'll answer personally to me. Is that clear?"

A discontented silence came from the crew, and Jed remembered one other captive soul on the ship. "And one more thing," he said. "Make Ethan my assistant. Make me sovereign over him and place him under your protection as well."

Smith sighed, clearly at his limit. "Very well." He called out to three sailors. "Unshackle him, clean him up, and bring him a set of proper clothes and some gear. Then stow his things in Lieutenant Ramsey's quarters."

A sailor carried a set of keys to Jed and began unlocking his shackles and manacles. Once Jed was freed, he dropped to his knees and closed his eyes in gratitude.

"I don't know how long this lull will continue," Smith told Jed. "Get your supplies loaded. As soon as we can launch a boat, row to the atoll and make your preparations. I'll bring the signed document to you within the hour."

"Not a moment more, sir. I'll hold you to your word."

Smith smiled and nodded. "I'd wager that your education was not merely in agriculture, was it, Lieutenant? I hope you're as good at the needed task as you are at negotiations. We'll soon see. Seaman Roust will take you to Lieutenant Ramsey's quarters to clean up and change."

As Jed followed the young, lanky sailor, he closed his eyes and heard Jerome's promise once more. *"He hasn't forgotten you, Jed. He's giving you an opportunity here. Trust the Lord."*

I do, Jerome. I do. Thank you, Lord.

Roust opened the door and stepped aside. A foul odor rolled out and he smirked. "I'm glad to see you freed if it means I don't have to deal wif the drippy lieutenant no more."

Jed recognized his voice immediately. This was the loud, grousing sailor who complained about caring for Arthur. The air was indeed malodorous, but it was easily tolerable after the cesspool Jed had been living in.

He entered the room, barely recognizing Arthur, whose boyish face was pale and drawn in pain. The brown curls that once framed his youthful, kindly face were unkempt and matted with sweat. He was naked, clothed only in bandages that swathed his torso and arms, and covered by a thin blanket that was pulled up across his abdomen, concealing the source of the large lump that extended across his vitals and to his groin.

"What is the nature of his injuries?"

Roust began to snicker. "'E's like a baby, 'e is. And now you've got the pleasant task of wipin' 'is bum and changin' 'is dressings three times a day, and that includes washin' those stinkin' bandages to the surgeons' satisfaction."

"Must you speak that way about him? Did you know him before he was injured? He's a fine officer, and among the gentlest and best of men."

The reproof subdued Roust. "How do you know so much about one of our officers?"

Jed could say volumes about Arthur, things that would likely get the valiant theologian tried for aiding and abetting the enemy. So Jed drew from Arthur's meritorious experience in Virginia, where he and Markus had first become acquainted. "Lieutenant Ramsey was very good to some friends of mine after the Chasseurs attacked them in Hampton, Virginia."

Roust grunted in reply. "There's work clothes in the trunk.

You'll likely need to change yourself after cleanin' 'im up, so prepare for lots of scrubbin', Yank." And then he left.

Jed drew near his friend and spoke to him. "Arthur? Arthur?"

Arthur's eyes opened slightly and a hint of a smile tugged at his lips and then faded. Tears sprang to Jed's eyes over that small gesture. "Arthur, it's Jed. I'm here. I'm going to care for you from now on." The smile reappeared, and then Arthur fell back to sleep.

Jed knew his life had spun completely around in the matter of an hour. He had air to breathe, soap and water and clean clothes, and now a friend. More than that, his hope was nearly tangible now. Overwhelmed, he knelt by Arthur's bedside and prayed, wetting Arthur's blanket with his tears.

CHAPTER 14

Monday, September 5, 1814
On board the HMS Royal Oak, *anchored in the Patuxent River near Benedict, Maryland*

Ross had written and rewritten the report of the assault on Washington ad nauseam, spending more time drumming his fingers on the desk than composing. He heard voices raise and turned his attentions to the bow of the ship, where four of his men sat playing a card game called poker that was spreading through the troops, having been taught to them by an American spy they had contracted.

Two of the men now stood, and then the yelling escalated to pointing, and finally to one soldier soundly landing a right hook to the jaw of another, who tumbled backwards into the river. That was the last straw for their commander.

"Wainwright!" Ross shouted. The aide shot to attention and hurried over. "Throw those men in the brig! Then assemble the officers in one hour."

Wainwright complied quickly, leaving Ross one hour to make a potentially devastating decision—whether to go to Baltimore or not. He had been so clear, so determined not to go, but things were unraveling before his eyes and he needed to revisit the decision. He scanned the transport ships filled with his men—some of the best and bravest warriors of Britain, the men who tamed Napoleon—

whose discipline had decayed before his eyes.

Ross's objections to going were good ones. The impact of the British's historic, sweeping victory at Washington could be diminished by anything less than an equally decisive win at Baltimore, which he did not believe could happen. Reconnaissance teams had seen the steady flow of American volunteers moving northeast, dressed in every possible variation of attire. They were coming, and Baltimore swelled with their numbers.

He looked at his men again. They would be the ones to march directly into the hornets' nest and face Major General Samuel Smith's burgeoning Baltimore defenses. Ross had already seen so many good men die, and he had no stomach for a fight with such an anticlimactic purpose and an unlikely yield. Yet here they were, languishing in the Patuxent while Cockburn attempted to wear away at Vice Admiral Cochrane's reluctance. Ross wondered if Cockburn would try to land his own men and take this city alone. He cringed at the thought.

Wainwright soon reappeared. "The officers are all assembled on the *Royal Oak* as you ordered. What will you tell them?"

Major General Ross clasped his hands together, working his knuckles as he silently prayed for some confirmation. He had never felt so conflicted or so unsure. Cockburn had been right about the ease with which Washington was taken. Baltimore was better armed, but were these Americans any more ready? Perhaps they really had no idea about war and warring. Perhaps all their great warriors had died with General Washington.

Ross's internal struggle continued as Wainwright stood waiting for his commander's answer. *Maybe it's true,* Ross thought. *Maybe they have no strategy in Baltimore, either. Preparations mean little without the leadership to direct their use.*

He looked at his detailed report of the marvelous Washington campaign, and he made his decision. "Ensign, order the officers to begin preparations to move our expeditionary forces tomorrow. We're sailing to Tangier Island to join the rest of the fleet."

"And Baltimore, sir?"

He knew where his vote now lay.

The departure from Baltimore was uneventful for the little American diplomatic crew. That evening, they anchored at the base of the Patapsco River, near the mouth of Chesapeake Bay, some twenty miles from the city.

Markus was pleased with the small ship, and Captain Ferguson was first rate. When evening rolled around, the seamen bunked on deck while Markus, Key, and Skinner went below. Skinner set about making an entry to a letter he was preparing for General Mason:

Monday, the 5th of September

Dear General Mason,

I am writing to you from our cartel ship in the Patapsco River. It will please you to know that Mr. Key reached here yesterday morning and handed me your instructions, and dispatches for Admiral Cochrane and Major General Ross. The testimonials from the wounded British soldiers, attesting to the quality of their care in American hands, will be very helpful indeed. Thank you.

We are now on our way and expect to find them in the Patuxent, and hope to be back on Wednesday night.

Yours,
John Skinner

P.S. To get Doctor Beanes upon giving a receipt under the circumstances is as much as I expect, if not more. Making allowances for the opinion and feelings of an enemy, they will no doubt consider him as having waived all "benefit of exception from the general rule of combatant persons." The best, however, shall be done with the ardent desire to accomplish your views and wishes.

"Your face looks a bit pinched, Colonel," Markus said.

John Skinner smiled. "I'm writing a letter to General Mason—part of my report on this mission."

"Seems ta me that you don't feel too good about our chances of freein' Dr. Beanes."

Skinner looked to Mr. Key. "General Mason's dispatch to Major General Ross contains our version of the events surrounding the arrest of Dr. Beanes, but I'm certain there must be more to the story. I can't believe the British would take a civilian without some justification."

"Does pride count as justification?" Markus asked. "I was there in Upper Marlborough when Dr. Beanes was taken. After the devils sacked Washington, Francis Pearson and I carried a wounded British soldier there so Dr. Beanes could treat 'im. The bulk of the army passed through a day later without any trouble. Dr. Beanes was worried about 'is citizens, so 'e sent everyone into the woods to hide. 'E told us 'e'd be 'congenial and keep the soldiers content so they'd pass without malice,' and they did, the next mornin', with my best friend tucked inta their wagons, falsely accused of firin' on their peace delegation."

Markus was all riled up now, his anger exaggerating his mild Irish lilt to a full brogue. "Then three British stragglers came through the followin' day, and Dr. Beanes and a few of the townsmen arrested them for fear they'd come ta loot the town, or worse. One of the hooligans escaped and ran back ta 'is company.

That night a detachment arrived and dragged Dr. Beanes and a few of 'is friends off, scarcely lettin' the poor man dress. They hefted 'im up and tied 'im on a mule and made a spectacle of' im, paradin' 'im amongst the ranks like a fool. We were so worried about the women and the children that we were afraid to respond."

Skinner nodded as if some great truth had been divulged. "Beanes is a Scotsman by birth, with a trace of his mother tongue, am I right?"

Key and Markus nodded, and Key said, "Yes, he still has a fairly prominent brogue."

"His congeniality was likely interpreted as brotherhood, or British loyalty. Perhaps that's even why he decided to be the one to stay behind and 'make the soldiers content,' because he understood that they would be inclined toward another Briton. Sadly, that's why they're holding him for treason. They now consider him a British traitor, and will, no doubt, consider him as having waived all 'benefit of exception from the general rule of combatant persons.'"

"What are you sayin'?"

Mr. Key seemed sorely distressed by Colonel's Skinner's analysis. "He means the British regard Dr. Beanes as a Briton, so they could actually try him for treason."

Skinner leaned back and sighed. "I don't know if we will be successful in freeing him, but I believe our best hope is this stack of letters from the British wounded."

"Blast the devils for comin' 'ere in the first place. And blast them that give 'em aid."

Skinner stared curiously at Markus. "Didn't you aid that wounded British soldier?"

The comment brought Markus up short. He had become so close to Arthur that he didn't even think of him as he thought of Ross's other soldiers. "'E saved members of my family in Hampton, and I figured I owed 'im a fightin' chance. But that woman the crew was talkin' about—that singer who entertained the troops the night they burned Washington City?" He snarled. "We were racin' from one end of the city to the other, destroyin' the Arsenal and the navy yard to keep the ships and munitions from fallin' into their hands. And while we're riskin' our necks ta stop 'em, she's out there singin' to 'em. I'd like to ship 'er ta England with the rest of 'em."

"Save some of that fire, Captain O'Malley," Frank Key said. "We may need it when we meet the British."

Admiral Cockburn received the news from the reconnaissance ship with exultation. Ross and his portion of the British fleet were moving down the Patuxent and heading for the fleet's Fort Albion on Tangier Island! Cockburn hurriedly dressed in full uniform and ordered a ship to ferry him to Vice Admiral Cochrane's flagship, the HMS *Tonnant,* where the vice admiral, the commander in chief of the North American Station, was situated. The timing would be critical, but he felt the rush of triumph course through his veins.

Like Major General Ross, Vice Admiral Cochrane feared that a loss in Baltimore would dilute the British victory in Washington, but Cockburn saw only more victory and glory for the Crown—and for those who brought the victory to the Crown. He had increased his fortune substantially in America, filling his ships with the finest goods the young, resource-rich nation had produced, and the best goods plundered from American homes and businesses. He had sent ships home with holds packed to the joists with tobacco, a commodity that traded well in the European markets. He could scarcely imagine what treasures a bustling port city like Baltimore held, but he wanted something else from this place.

Baltimore was the home of the sleek and deadly Baltimore clipper ship. These lightly armed private ships had been legally militarized to sail under government-issued letters of marque, but they were lightning-quick and legendary. Cockburn had not personally encountered one of these topsail schooners, but their beauty and speed made sailors swoon. Capturing one would be lovely, but destroying the shipyards that created them would satisfy him even more.

Now he needed to move Vice Admiral Cochrane from his current battle opinion. On the sea, Admiral George Cockburn was the second-in-command only to Vice Admiral Cochrane, but in a land-sea operation like the American campaign, Major General Robert Ross outranked him. Therefore, Cockburn would need Ross's support. Cockburn wasn't overly concerned. He had convinced Ross to attack Washington City, and he felt confident he could convince him to go on to Baltimore.

Ross's loyalty to his men was the problem. His devotion made him overly cautious and limited his daring. He thought too much on casualty estimates and individual losses, and he mourned each loss too personally. It was a dreadful weakness a military man could not afford. *After all,* Cockburn thought, *how can a surgeon remove an abscess if he constantly frets over each cut?*

No matter. Cockburn had timed everything carefully. If the winds held, he could estimate the ships' arrival within an hour. He would ply Cochrane and open his eyes to the possibilities of an assault on the city by praising Ross's soldiers for their unparalleled excellence, noting how Cochrane himself had showered laurels upon their leader. Never again might such celebrated warriors combine in a single operation. It was historic, and the Americans' fear was on the Britons' side. Yes, this was the time and the place to strike a second blow at America, and little by little, brick by brick, Cockburn would make his case for a run on Baltimore.

Before disembarking the sloop and embarking the *Tonnant,* Admiral Cockburn adjusted his epaulettes and straightened each button so the embossed images were precisely straight. He turned to the captain of the vessel and ordered, "Stay moored nearby. Send a messenger to me the moment Ross's ships break the horizon. I'll be in Admiral Cochrane's quarters."

Admiral Cockburn watched the clock carefully as he sat with Admiral Cochrane. He could feel the admiral's reluctance waver. What man of war could walk away from such a moment on so grand a stage? The Chesapeake campaign had been the prelude, Washington was the army's main performance, but Baltimore would make a perfect naval denouement.

He spoke casually to Cochrane of the excitement the sea campaigns along the northern theater were generating. Cockburn hoped to appeal to the admiral's hunger for victory. They knew the Great Lakes were churning from the artillery being delivered in those battles. News of the severing of New York and New England from their neighbors was expected any day, and Cockburn could see Cochrane weighing each word, vacillating in his resolve. Cockburn made his play.

"It is my opinion that Baltimore is no more ready than Washington was," he said.

"Fort McHenry is daunting. Its location makes entering the Patapsco nearly impossible."

"We must eliminate that threat first with a complete barrage—send the soldiers fleeing from their posts or destroy the guns altogether."

Cochrane eyed his colleague carefully. "I do not think so, George. We've done too well to let this little fort upend us. It's New Orleans that we need. Let's not give the Americans the chance for a victory that would revive their dampened spirits. No, I think we'll pass on Baltimore and have you sail your squadron to Bermuda to prepare for our assault on New Orleans."

Cockburn was nearly rendered speechless. "Are you certain, sir? General Ross will be rendezvousing with us shortly. Perhaps we should—"

"Quite certain, Admiral. General Ross and I are of the same opinion. Your ships are well stocked and ready for departure. You may leave immediately."

As Cockburn sailed down the Potomac, headed south to the Chesapeake's entrance to the Atlantic, Ross was heading out of the Patuxent, where he met Admiral Cochrane's portion of the fleet. Ross boarded the HMS *Tonnant* to present his report of the mood along the Patuxent. He entered Admiral Cochrane's cabin and immediately felt the power of his superior's post. The walls were adorned with commendations from the Admiralty, and while he was not the dandy Cockburn was, Vice Admiral Cochrane looked almost regal in his uniform, exuding the authority that flowed down the chain of command. Ross appeared plain when compared to his colleagues. His uniform bore the necessary adornments and nothing more. His neck was still raw from his wound at Orthes, and he preferred simplicity and comfort to pomp and show.

He was greeted by the vice admiral, whose hand was outstretched. "Good to see you, Robert. I assume things were quiet along the Patuxent?"

"Completely, sir, although reconnaissance teams reported a great deal of movement along the roads, particularly heading northeast to Baltimore."

"And a great deal of movement away from the city as well, if my own spies are correct."

"Very true. And how is the traffic on the Potomac?"

"We move fairly unmolested. A few random shots fired from the shore, but nothing of consequence. There is greater activity north."

"Are you still of the opinion that Baltimore cannot be taken by water alone?" Ross asked.

"It would require a perfectly timed offensive from land and sea. George Cockburn was frustrated this afternoon by my decision not to proceed. I know you agree with me on this." The comment sounded like a question.

"I was determined to avoid a run on that city."

"And now, Robert?"

"I must admit I am conflicted on the matter. I still cannot say whether Baltimore is a wise target, but sitting here in these waters weakens my men."

"We have a satisfactory base set up on Tangier Island in the Virginia portion of the bay. You can drill them there while we decide when and where to take the rest of the fleet."

"It's more than that," Ross said. "I go round and round about Baltimore. George Cockburn was correct about Washington. It's no secret that we do not care for one another personally, but I do respect his military savvy, and he has the complete loyalty of his crew."

Cochrane sat in his chair and leaned back. "But he and his men have earned a rather despicable reputation after Hampton and a few other campaigns."

"I condemn his actions in Hampton, but we cannot deny that Admiral Cockburn's raids did soften up the Chesapeake by filling the locals with dread before the first boot landed."

Cochrane placed his hands on his desk, clasping and unclasping them. "You're right . . . It's true."

Ross nodded. "I've gone round and round about my decision and I'm still convinced that a landing near Fort McHenry would be suicide, but I'm of the opinion that one of our previously discussed options has merit. An approach from further east might prove favorable. "

"A variation on Admiral Cockburn's plan."

"Yes. It would, of course, still require very precise timing. The land offensive would need the full support of the navy to pound McHenry until the fort's guns go silent."

164

Cochrane smiled. "George as much as said the exact same thing a few hours ago, but I was so certain you could not be swayed that I sent him to Bermuda to prepare for New Orleans."

Ross looked the admiral in the eye and smiled. "I was too hasty in rejecting the proposition. We were so unopposed in Washington that it felt like a gift. I couldn't believe we could be so fortunate twice, but there is no question as to who has the superior forces. It may simply be a matter of employing them well."

"So are we resigned to go?"

"I believe we are," Ross replied.

Admiral Cochrane let out a hearty laugh. "Then I need to send a cutter to catch George Cockburn and his squadron to bring them back before they reach the Atlantic!"

CHAPTER 15

Wednesday, September 7, 1814
Tangier Island in the Chesapeake Bay

Markus felt like a fifth wheel as Captain Ferguson sailed the sloop, her white flag fluttering in the wind, down the middle of the bay, watching for any sign of the British fleet. They were all on edge, searching the bay for a second day when they expected to have completed their negotiations and be sailing home by now. Where was the fleet?

Frank Key occupied himself by reading from the Bible again, but his eyes lingered on the same spot for too long, an indication that his mind was somewhere else, most likely on his family. Markus noted the drawn appearance of his face, which bore the unmistakable etch of longing. He understood. Key was a family man, and from what Markus knew, he had a large, beautiful family, and a wife he adored and may not see again if things went poorly. No one knew exactly how the British would respond to the request to release Dr. Beanes.

John Skinner was altogether a different matter. Markus felt the man was born to government work, as Timothy was. No matter if they sailed a thousand days, Markus had a suspicion Skinner would always have one more letter to write or another report to prepare.

As for himself, Markus had faced death too many times to fear much in this life, so he did what came most naturally to him—he worried about Jed, about Hannah, about Frannie and Timothy, and about Mrs. Tyler, whose husband he'd like to throttle. Markus fretted over the pittance of a harvest they'd have, and that leaky roof on the main house, and about the new bairn coming soon. And then he realized he hadn't thought about Lyra this day, and it saddened him.

As they neared Annapolis, a British frigate appeared from within the confines of a tributary. The bigger ship signaled for them to pull up in preparation to be boarded, and John Skinner glanced nervously at Key, knowing the moment of truth was at hand.

Four British sailors climbed aboard their boat, inspecting it thoroughly. With a signal to their crew that the American vessel had passed their check, permission was granted for Skinner and Key to board the British ship. John Skinner requested to speak to the vessel's captain, who seemed pleased to have the delegates aboard. "I'm Colonel John Skinner, the United States prisoner exchange agent. I also have Mr. Francis Scott Key with me. We've come to speak with General Ross about the release of a prisoner, a Dr. William Beanes, and we do so representing the United States commissioner general of prisoners, with the full authority of President James Madison."

"General Ross is still in the Patuxent as far as I know. We'll take you there to meet him."

"And what of our ship and crew?" Key asked.

"They'll be led to Tangier Island to wait for the fleet's return."

Markus bullied up to the officer. "Oh, no! We're not goin' ta be separated!"

"Is that an Irish accent I hear?" the Brit asked with a threat in his voice.

"It most certainly is! I'm Irish-Virginian, born in Hampton, Virginia. There was an entire family of us lived there 'til some of yours cut us down. Do you remember Hampton?"

The Briton backed down and issued the order to sail the ship to Tangier Island. Markus's face was taut as he looked up to the deck of the British frigate where John Skinner and Francis Key stood. They too were not pleased about being separated, but having no choice, Key and Skinner agreed to the terms, and Markus worried about the fate of the pair as the *President* began sailing away to Tangier.

The frigate sailed for over an hour and then the white billows of sails appeared on the horizon, growing larger with every minute. The two Americans grew uneasy as the HMS *Tonnant* drew near, her cannon doors open, exposing the massive guns that held their city's fate.

John Skinner and Francis Key were transferred onto the *Tonnant,* where they were received with all military courtesy by a detail of lower-level officers. Skinner again provided his formal introduction.

"I understand you wish to speak to Major General Ross about a matter involving a prisoner," the aide said.

"That is correct."

"I am sorry to say that the general is previously occupied at the moment. I'm sure you understand. Since we had no idea you were coming it will take some time to rearrange his schedule. But, in the meantime, we are instructed to make you comfortable. If you'll follow me."

Skinner and Key were escorted to a small stateroom that was opulent by American military standards. "Fresh water and towels are here if you care to freshen up. Someone will call for you when dinner is served, if not before." He closed the doors, leaving the two befuddled Americans alone. Skinner drafted some discussion points for the meeting, while Key prayed and paced. Sometime later, the aide returned. "The general will see you now."

The aide led them to a large wooden door that opened to an office where three men stood. Skinner instantly recognized Ross and Cockburn from previous negotiations he had conducted. General Ross took two large strides toward them, causing his brown curls to dance around his head. Extending his hand, he said, "Colonel Skinner, so good to see you, sir."

"And you, General Ross. So good to see you as well. Admiral Cochrane, may I present Mr. Francis Scott Key?" All the men shook hands.

Key bowed and Skinner cleared his throat. "Gentlemen, the reason for our intrusion is contained in this letter from General John Mason, the United—"

"Yes, yes, yes," Cockburn interrupted with a rude swish of his hand.

Skinner withdrew General Mason's letter to Ross from the packet and handed it to him.

As the general read, his face flushed and his eyes began to bulge. "Your general is calling Beanes a 'non-combatant character'? And he's accusing me of departing from the uses of civilized warfare? Let me assure you, Colonel, Dr. Beanes's behavior was vile, and I for one intend to hold him accountable!"

Admiral Cochrane entered the conversation. "From what I've been told, Dr. Beanes is guilty of treasonous behavior meriting the most severe punishment."

Skinner handed over the pouch of letters from the British wounded who were being nursed back to health in American facilities. "Your wounded are receiving excellent care in the states. Dr. Beanes himself treated some of them. Please read the letters. You'll note that they describe their care as 'humane and kind.' All we are asking is that a portion of the mercy we are showing to your wounded be shown to Dr. Beanes."

Frank Key stepped up. "He is nearing sixty-five, General. He is a much beloved man of good standing in his community and a man known for his humanity, generosity, and honesty."

"Yet a man who murdered a British soldier!" Cockburn countered.

"Not so, sir," Skinner replied. "The only British casualty was a soldier ailing from wounds which were too grievous to be addressed." Skinner noted that General Ross was reading the British soldiers' letters with great intent. The agent silently prayed that the general was indeed as good a man as his reputation claimed, and that the letters had reached that goodness.

Ross shook the stack of letters. "How is their morale?"

"They long to be returned to the fleet, but they are still too weak to be moved."

Ross looked from Admiral Cochrane to Skinner. "Let me peruse these before dinner. Gentlemen, I look forward to seeing you both then."

Ross left and his aide escorted Skinner and Key back to their room.

"Did you accomplish what you needed to during that meeting?" Key asked.

"I cannot even venture a guess."

Silence seemed to be the primary item served up at dinner. It was an awkward hour during which some lovely dishes were passed to men who ate with only an occasional sound. Admiral Codrington, captain of the fleet, joined the silent group. Skinner noticed Key adjusting his collar a few times, obviously discomfited by the mood in the room. However, Colonel Skinner was no novice at the negotiating table. He knew the silence was likely a strategy to make the Americans squirm, and assuming he was right, he ate heartily to repel it, encouraging Key to do the same. Little did he know how much further the British would push the game.

Oddly, no mention of Beanes was made, though he was the sole reason the two Americans had come. Francis Key shot worried glances at Skinner throughout the meal, probably wondering when he would raise the issue again. But Skinner knew the game well and held his tongue, enjoying his meal as long as his hosts.

At the meal's conclusion, Ross leaned back and glanced at Admiral Cochrane, who nodded while clearly trying to hold back the smirk playing on his lips.

"Your government objects to our treatment of Dr. Beanes," began Ross. "In my opinion, Dr. Beanes is fortunate that a few nights in the brig is all we've subjected him to. I do not think he is as honest as you've portrayed him, Mr. Key. He deceived us, feigning friendship to achieve our confidence, then fell violently on men who came to him, assuming he was their friend. It's a dishonorable ploy for which I have no respect. In my opinion, he's lucky to have not been shot or hung by now."

The three admirals all nodded their assent. Key began to rebut, but when Skinner shot him a wary glance, the attorney in Key seemed to understand the game as well. He folded his napkin with deliberateness and leaned back in his chair. Skinner watched Cockburn pick at his nails, and he did the same. *Tit for tat.* Skinner smiled. Things were going their way.

"But owing to the heartfelt letters of my noble wounded, I will consider your request for Beanes's release. It is not because I believe he is innocent, which I clearly do not. However, I do feel a certain . . . obligation to release him as a response to the goodness and mercy shown by the Americans who have treated my men."

Skinner nodded, showing only a trace of the relief he felt.

"Join me in Admiral Cochrane's office and we'll make the arrangements, shall we?"

"That's very gracious of you, General," Skinner said as he and the other men rose. Skinner offered his hand to Ross, who left it there for a moment before receiving it into his own. The pompous gesture didn't unnerve Skinner. Ross and the Britons controlled the game, and their offer to release Beanes was far more benevolent than Skinner had expected.

Once the pair had entered Cochrane's office, Ross sat behind the admiral's desk and began composing a letter to General Mason that made it clear Beanes's arrest was warranted and that his release was a broad act of mercy.

> *Dr. Beanes having acted hostilely toward certain soldiers of the British army under my command, by making them prisoners when proceeding to join the army, & having attempted to justify his conduct when I spoke to him on the subject, I conceived myself authorized & called upon to cause his being detained as a prisoner. Mr. Skinner, to whom I have imparted the circumstances, will detail them more fully.*
>
> *The friendly treatment, however, experienced by the wounded officers and men of the British Army left at Bladensburg, enables me to meet your wishes regarding that gentleman. I shall accordingly give directions for his being released, not from an opinion that his detention is not justified, but purely in proof of the obligation which I feel for the attention with which the wounded have been treated. . . .*

When the ink was dry, Ross handed the letter to Colonel Skinner for delivery.

"Tomorrow the fleet will set sail for Tangier Island. We'll turn Dr. Beanes over to you when we arrive. Tonight, please be our guest on board the *Tonnant*. We'll see you and Mr. Key in the morning.

The Americans awoke early on Thursday, September 8, anxious to reach Tangier Island, get Beanes aboard the *President,* and make a hurried return to Baltimore. They hoped the feat would be accomplished that simply, and that all was well with Markus and the crew, but they were unable to ignore the bustle of activity all around them as they moved about on the deck.

Officers on board the scattered ships of the fleet communicated with one another by signal flags, and the two Americans watched as the intricately ordered procession began. "It's really quite astounding, isn't it?" Skinner said. "It's beautiful, like a living organism."

Key's attention seemed riveted on the fearsome number of ships. "I see only a beast that may devour Baltimore. Do you believe they would treat us as guests and allow us to move freely upon their ship, if they intended to attack the city? They couldn't be that cold, could they?"

Skinner didn't reply.

The fleet reached Tangier Island late in the day, and the same group of gentlemen assembled the previous evening were again seated at dinner. This time the conversation ran freely, and the evening's tone was almost giddy. Skinner found the mood unnerving.

"Will we be making land tonight?" Key asked. "I'm anxious to see Dr. Beanes."

Admiral Cochrane cut another bite of roast beef and dangled it from his fork as he spoke. "Dr. Beanes has been moved to the *Surprise,* as you two will be. I have officers I must bring aboard the *Tonnant* so we can make final preparations, and they will need your quarters. You'll be quite comfortable aboard the *Surprise.* My own son, Sir Thomas, is the commander."

Key and Skinner looked warily at one another. "Excuse me, Admiral Cochrane," Skinner began, "but I assumed we would be sleeping on our own ship tonight."

"I'm afraid there's been a change—"

A courier appeared at the door.

"Excuse me, Admiral. The supplies are nearly loaded."

"Excellent. And the munitions?"

"The Congreve rockets are loaded onto the *Erebus.* The remaining munitions are being distributed among all the ships as we speak."

Key's and Skinner's eyes searched the faces of the men at the table.

"Very good. Tell the men to be prepared to load at first light."

Cockburn eyed his superior. "The men are very excited about their next deployment."

"I hope they perform their duties as well in Baltimore as they have in Washington."

Key's panicked gaze shot from one of his hosts to another. "Do you mean to say you are going to attack Baltimore?"

"We are indeed, Mr. Key," Cochrane replied coolly.

Skinner dropped his fork with a loud bang that drew all eyes to him. "What are your intentions there? A diplomatic apology? To demand tribute? What?"

"Our plan, Mr. Skinner, is to burn the city, or at least selected portions of it."

"You can't mean that!" Skinner cried.

Cochrane leaned forward as if he were schooling small children. "This is a war, and your people are preparing to come against us. We must quell their determination to do so."

Key's gentle hands curled into fists, and he looked as if he might vomit. "Baltimore is not an abandoned city as Washington was! There are women and children there! I have family there!"

Cochrane chewed nonchalantly on his beef. "Then I'd advise them to leave immediately."

"And will your men go ashore?" Skinner asked thinly.

Cockburn fielded the question. "Baltimore is what, your third-largest city? I daresay there should be some amusements there

174

to entertain the men. It's been so long since they've enjoyed the comforts a city affords."

Skinner sensed a thread of lewd intent in Cockburn's quest for "entertainment." Was it for show? He couldn't be sure. The game was part of the strategy of war. He knew that. Fear, intimidation, shock and awe—it was as old as war itself. He thought of Joshua's army surrounding Jericho with their marching and horn-blowing, and the Assyrians who instilled fear in their guests by staking heads outside their cities' walls. And what of the Romans' public crucifixions? They were done as much to subdue a people as they were to punish individual criminals. Key's expression assured Skinner that he too was consumed by the same fears, and Skinner silently prayed that this game was only such and nothing more.

"Is this to be another Hampton?" Key challenged.

Skinner and Key had recently discussed the horror inflicted upon the women of Hampton, Virginia, when Cockburn's men went ashore to plunder and subdue that place.

Cockburn's eyes burned at what he must have considered Key's impertinence.

Admiral Cochrane laid his utensils aside and wiped his mouth with great deliberateness. Leaning back against his chair, he looked at Cockburn. "Yes, George, you really must rein your lads in. Some show of self-discipline is requested. Are we clear on this matter?"

George Cockburn relaxed his posture and smirked. "I'll have a word with them."

"How can you do this?" Key's head fell heavily into his hands.

Skinner searched each of the Britons' faces for some show of mercy, but there was none.

General Ross finally spoke up. "Gentlemen, shall we try to maintain some decorum?"

Skinner stood shakily and laid his napkin on the table. "Neither Mr. Key nor I are feeling well. If you'll excuse us, we'd like to retire for the night."

"Of course." Ross signaled to a steward. "Call for an escort."

Moments later a sailor arrived and escorted Skinner and Key to the *Surprise.*

"Do you think they'll do what they implied?" Key asked.

Skinner glanced north toward Baltimore. "I sincerely wish I knew."

Something was very wrong. Key and Skinner were too long delayed, and Markus had a terrifying feeling he knew why. He had overheard the four British guards announcing each portion of the fleet as it arrived yesterday—Ross's transports from the Patuxent; Cochrane's squadron returning from pillaging Alexandria, Virginia; and the most surprising arrivals of the day, Cockburn's squadron, who had returned after leaving for Bermuda in a snit when the admiral's plans to attack Baltimore were denied. *So he's back, is he?* mused Markus. It all added up now—the string of small boats resupplying the rest of the fleet, Cockburn's return, the packing and loading of tents, and the transfer of men from Fort Albion onto ships. *They're gonna make a run on Baltimore!*

Markus considered his pitiable, defenseless state. He had nothing with which to effect an escape. Armed guards were assigned to the little cartel ship to keep the American crew in line, and even if they could overwhelm one, could they overwhelm all four without a single gun being fired to warn the fleet? He didn't think so.

Captain Ferguson and his crew went below to bunk down for the night, with two of the guards following behind. The older of the two left above sat in the rear of the ship, laying his musket across his lap. In a few minutes his snores assured Markus that he was asleep. The remaining guard was nineteen or so years old, and fresh. Markus decided to get right to the point.

"You're readyin' ta sail to Baltimore, aren't ya?"

176

The sailor's eyes grew wide and he raised his gun. "Who told you that?"

"I've got eyes, lad. You're readyin' for a battle. Baltimore's the logical conclusion."

The sailor said no more.

"Were you at Hampton, Son? Terrible things happened there."

The lad eyed him cautiously.

"Your troops murdered an old man while shooting at a stray dog. They shot his old wife and left her for dead whilst they chased down her granddaughter and raped the poor thing."

"That's not true!"

Markus felt the boy's horror and replied softly, "Aye, it is, Son. They headed to a farm, stripped an old man down, and tortured him with their bayonets because they found a woman's nightcap in the home and he wouldn't tell them where the women and children were hidden."

"You're lying," the lad said. "We would never do that!"

"Have you been in battle yet, Son?"

The boy hesitated. "No. I've never landed."

"Haven't you heard the stories about how your comrades found those women and children hidin' under a porch? How one of them was pretty and blind, and they made sport of passin' 'er around their group, grabbin' at 'er and dishonorin' 'er until she finally managed ta break through their line? She ran and ran as far and as fast as she could ta get away from 'em, but they were chasin' 'er and she ran smack into a post and broke 'er shoulder. But she kept runnin' on until she heard the sound of the creek. She thought if she could just make it there she could float away to safety. She thought she heard the sound of her husband callin' out for 'er, tryin' ta save 'er. She turned to listen just for a second, but she was already rabid with fear, and she leapt inta the water, only she couldn't swim with that broken shoulder."

177

The lad was frozen in horror, and Markus realized that his own eyes were moist.

"She washed up on the shoals and died within the hour. She opened her eyes only once. 'Er husband hoped she knew 'e was there. Her name was Lyra, Son." Markus pulled out the watch fob made of Lyra's red hair. "She was my wife."

"No, I don't believe you! We're men of honor. It was the French Chasseurs!"

"So you have heard the tales."

"Just exaggerated fish tales men share at sea."

"Is that what they call it? Is that what they tell you about their plans for Baltimore?"

The lad suddenly looked much too young for his uniform. "We're taking the fort, and then we're subduing the people. We didn't hurt citizens in Washington, did we?"

"That city was abandoned, but Baltimore isn't. Let me slip over the side and swim away to warn the women and children, Son. You can take the fort and have the guns. Let me just warn them to evacuate their women and their wee bairns."

The boy looked at Markus sideways, obviously dumbfounded by the request, but he hadn't shot him yet, so Markus considered it a good sign.

"No one will know, boy. I'll slip away so quiet they'll think it happened in the dead of night. You'll do a great good, and no one will know."

"No one will know what?" a voice called from the rear of the ship. "Is he fillin' your head full of lies, boy?"

"I didn't believe any of it," the young guard said nervously as the second guard approached.

"And why should you let him spoil our fun? Baltimore's a big city, not like that swamp they call a capital. After we make those Yanks run from Fort McHenry, we're going into that big city to take a hot bath and see the sights. Do you still have that advertisement I gave you?"

The boy produced one of Genevieve's handbills. "She's the prettiest thing I ever saw."

"She sat right here on my lap in Washington and gave me one of the sweetest kisses I ever had. We'll find us a good show here in Baltimore, too. Now go below and get yourself situated for the night, all right? Me and the captain will have us a little chat."

The boy did as he was ordered and Markus braced for a beating, or worse. The bulky Brit came nose to nose with him, but the emotion present in his eyes was not anger so much as fear.

"I would have expected better of you, Captain. What do you think would have happened to him if you'd have gotten away on his watch and jeopardized this mission? Admiral Cockburn's harder on his own than he is on the enemy. Have you seen men whipped to death for dereliction? Well, I have, and that's the terrible fate you nearly consigned that lad to. Or were you fine with getting him killed so you could save others? Is that it? You're one of the flotilla heroes who's won the praise of our commanders, but when you talk about honor and the horrors of war, don't forget how thin the line is between the two, Captain O'Malley."

CHAPTER 16

Thursday, September 8, 1814
Melville Island Prison, Halifax, Nova Scotia

Major Dudley Snowden strained to hear the frail voice among the labored sounds of Melville Island's tightly hammocked sleeping prisoners, squeezed into crowded cells. He disturbed his neighbor as he sat up to catch a repeat of the voice. "Did someone call for me?"

The wisp of sound returned. "I'm not doin' well, Major."

Dudley recognized the voice as that of a young sailor named Martin. The faint cry was followed by racking sounds of coughing. Dudley knew from the rattle in the young soldier's lungs that he probably wouldn't see the morning light break.

"Could you read me those verses, sir?" the dying lad asked.

Dudley knew which verses he wanted to hear. They were the ones the group had begun debating in the yard the last day they were allowed outside while the guards cleared the cells of the dead. Dudley had opened his tattered Bible as he did every day, but the excessive number of dead souls being carried from the prison to the nearby Deadman's Island gravesite chilled even the sternest doubter, and the group had huddled close to hear the promises of heaven.

A tiny shaft of light filtered through the window in the stone wall. It was why he chose this spot, knowing that any sliver of visible light would eventually pass through the aperture. He pulled the volume from within his threadbare jacket and thumbed to 1 Corinthians 15. He touched the seventeen names scrawled around the edges of the ragged pages—those belonging to spiritual doubters who had never been baptized and who, now fearing both the likelihood of death and the consequences of their procrastination, had begged Dudley to determine if the promises described on the pages were true, and if so, committed Dudley to see that the neglected ordinance was performed in their behalf. Again he heard the voice.

"Martin? I have my Bible open."

"To the Resurrection page, sir?"

Dudley managed a trembling smile, grateful that this lad's baptism and testimony of Christ offered him so much peace in his final hours. "Yes, Son."

As soon as Dudley finished the fourth verse, two other voices asked, "Could you read the last two again, Major?"

Through moist eyes he repeated the verses: "'For I delivered unto you first of all that which I also received, how that Christ died for our sins according to the scriptures; And that he was buried, and that he rose again the third day according to the scriptures.'"

Apparently comforted by the familiar phrases, the men settled down, listening in silence until Dudley neared verse 29. Out of habit, he slowed as he read, "'Else what shall they do which are baptized for the dead, if the dead rise not at all? why are they then baptized for the dead?'"

"You'll see about gettin' us baptized, right, Major?" a man asked. "It's the one thing the Lord asked of me in this life. I didn't think much on it before, but I think on it a lot now."

A second man agreed. "You're the closest thing we got to a preacher here, Major. We all keep praying to God, tellin' the Lord that if only one of us leaves here alive, please let it be you, 'cause if you say you'll try to save us, then you will. You, Major, you must survive."

You must survive. A similar charge had been given to him by Red Jacket, an Iroquois chief he had met along the long march to Montreal after the fall of Fort Detroit. Suffering himself, and having just forfeited his blanket to a sick boy, Dudley felt sure he would die before morning. Then Red Jacket came and handed him his own blanket with a turtle pattern woven in.

"You must not die, Snow-den." Red Jacket circled his arms over his head and brought his mournful eyes to meet Dudley's. "The great Turtle, Mother Earth, struggles."

"The war?"

"Yes. Too much war." He stood abruptly and brought his fists together. "You must make peace, make balance."

"But how?" Dudley asked tentatively. "I am but one man, and a prisoner."

Red Jacket thumped his fist to his chest. "Listen. You will hear what to do."

Dudley pulled the blanket more tightly around him. So badly soiled now that he could barely see the intricate weaving, the blanket was no less dear to him. He fingered the fringe and wondered if the spiritual function he served for these prisoners would fulfill Red Jacket's charge for him, or if something more would be required.

Dudley smiled at the incongruity of it all—how the burden he bore somehow actually freed him because he somehow knew he would *not* die here, that he would outlive Melville Island because he did have a work to do.

"I've never heard a minister address the topic of baptism of the dead, though I do promise to look into it. But if anyone else finds it they must tell the others so we can attend to our fallen brothers. Agreed?"

"Aye," they answered, sounding more hopeful than before.

Dudley smiled at the rising confidence in their voices—how they seemed buoyed up from simply hearing that he believed they might survive.

"But you are a believer of the word, are you not sir?" a frail, older man called out. "You do believe that if God placed such a thing in the Bible it surely must be possible, don't you?"

Dudley knew his beloved sister-in-law, Hannah, would have ventured off on one of her spiritual leaps, attributing the silence on this point of doctrine in the Bible as something other than the incongruity of God. His wife, Beatrice, was beginning to think similarly, the result of Hannah's influence as well as that of Beatrice's hosts, the Stephen Mack family. Dudley wasn't surprised by the effect the Macks were having on his wife. The few candid moments he had spent discussing religion with Captain Mack at Fort Detroit had opened his own spiritual eyes

Dudley peered through the darkness at the questioner and replied, "I do, friend. The question is where and when such miracles will be made available to men. But if we believe and seek, I trust that God will reverence our earnest desires."

A British guard named Dewitt came to the cell area carrying something under his jacket. Despite the men's practice of electing a president for the week, Dewitt recognized Dudley as the one stable leader of the Americans. In truth, Dudley was the highest-ranking officer in the prison, having forfeited his privilege to be sent home in a prisoner exchange to allow a very ill enlisted man to go home in his stead. It was the search for redemption, not benevolence alone, that had prompted Dudley's choice. He reverently touched his Bible, given to him by a Canadian woman, Laura Peddicord, whose compassion on the American prisoners and friendship with Dudley had placed her in harm's way. Though there had been no word regarding her fate, her father's death during the American sacking of York had been confirmed, and so, seeking penance, Dudley had forfeited his opportunity for freedom, asking instead to be transferred to Halifax, Nova Scotia's dreaded Melville Island, with his men.

"Major Snowden," the British guard whispered. "I was able ta salvage two extra loaves of bread after the guards' supper."

He pulled the precious rations out, waiting for Dudley's instructions.

"Thank you, Sergeant. Who needs the bread the most, friends?" Dudley asked the men. For several moments not a sound was uttered, and then residents from the different cells began naming men in their group who were the weakest, and with a nod from the current week's president, a soldier named Mathers, Dudley asked the guard to distribute hunks of the precious loaves as designated. When the last morsel was dispersed, the guard sat by the barred doors and entered the conversation.

"I see you're readin' from the good book, Major. The same chapters in Corinthians?"

Dudley nodded. "The very same."

The Briton nodded in reply. "I've been listenin' in ta your Bible discussions. Ended up readin' a little myself. Funny how I never noticed those verses before. Never heard a vicar speak on 'em either, nor some of the others in that chapter, like the ones about the stars and such."

Dudley shifted the Bible to catch a shaft of light and read:

There are also celestial bodies, and bodies terrestrial: but the glory of the celestial is one, and the glory of the terrestrial is another.

There is one glory of the sun, and another glory of the moon, and another glory of the stars: for one star differeth from another star in glory.

So also is the resurrection of the dead. It is sown in corruption; it is raised in incorruption:

It is sown in dishonour; it is raised in glory: it is sown in weakness; it is raised in power:

It is sown a natural body; it is raised a spiritual body. . . .

Again the British man simply nodded in silence until he gave voice to his thoughts. "I don't know what it means, leastwise not all of it."

"I believe it means that regardless of our errors and sins, we can be made perfect through Christ," Dudley offered.

"Major?" a sorrowful voice called from Martin's cell. "He's not breathing, Major!"

"Seaman Martin?" Dudley asked, already knowing the answer.

"Yes, sir, Major. He's gone, sir, but there's such a look of peace on his face."

"'Cause he knew he was right with God," explained a cell mate.

Dudley again opened his Bible, this time to the back where each of the men's names and next of kin were listed. He knew he would be writing another sad letter in the morning. As the men worked to move Martin's body through the crowded quarters to the front of the cell, the guard turned the key and retrieved it while Dudley stood to offer a quick, makeshift service:

O death, where is thy sting? O grave, where is thy victory?

The sting of death is sin; and the strength of sin is the law.

But thanks be to God, which giveth us the victory through our Lord Jesus Christ.

The guard returned a few minutes later to a silent cell block. "I'm sorry about your man," he offered sincerely. "Truly sorry. I wish—I wish things didn't have ta be this way."

Looking about him at the human misery that contributed to the lad's demise, Dudley was at a loss to know how to respond. "Thank you for the extra bread," was all he could mutter.

Several prisoners rose at first light to peer through the window as the guards carried Martin's linen-wrapped body across the peninsula to Deadman's Island, the prison's graveyard. Dudley turned to the front of his Bible, to his rudimentary sketch of the graveyard, his effort to map the locations of the men's unmarked graves in case, at some future date, their loved ones would want to come to reverence their sons' and husbands' final resting place.

DeWitt came by and sat near Dudley's cell door. "Major? It's chilly outside and thick with fog, but do you think the men would like a turn outside in the yard?"

Dudley sensed something in DeWitt's voice. "What's behind your offer?"

"Two ships are in the harbor. One's come up from Bermuda, loaded with men."

"And mail?" one man exclaimed hopefully as he wriggled from his hammock.

"Perhaps," DeWitt replied. "But some of those men are ta be dropped off here, and the other ship's headin' back to England loaded with men destined for Dartmoor."

Rumors said Dartmoor was one of the few British prisons worse than Melville. "Do you know who they're sending to Dartmoor?" Dudley asked. "Will the ship be loaded with men from Bermuda, or these men?"

"Can't say. Maybe some of each. I was just thinkin' that either way, things is goin' ta get worse, what with some of these men being stuffed inta the hold of a prison ship for a month, or upwards of two hundred men stuffed inta these cells. It might be your last chance to stretch for a few days. It's not on the schedule, but I could order a scrub in here, and that would get your men out for a bit, leastwise them not called on ta do the scrubbin'."

Two hundred men in each cell? Dudley grimaced inwardly at the ignominy of the situation. "Thank you," he said solemnly.

A half hour later, ten guards marched in, bayonets in hand, to usher the prisoners into the yard. Dudley volunteered to scrub the cell floors, and De Witt assumed guard duty over the detail.

"Change is on the horizon, Major," De Witt whispered. "I don't think this war will last much longer. The scuttlebutt is that the peace negotiations are proceeding."

"Peace?" Dudley said incredulously.

"That's what I hear. Two weeks ago our forces sacked and burned Washington. Everyone seems anxious to finalize a treaty now."

Dudley leaned heavily against his mop and gasped. "Washington is burned?"

"The President's House, your Capitol, the navy yard, and the Arsenal—all gone. Your president even fled the city."

"So Britain will set the terms of peace."

"Any terms will be better than this, don't you agree?"

Dudley continued scrubbing for several seconds, without breaking the rhythm of his work. "I'm a soldier. Regardless of my personal situation, I believe my cause remains as just."

Clearly feeling censured, De Witt withdrew until the scrubbing was completed, then managed to get the three workers out in the yard for a few minutes. They watched as a hundred new arrivals, flanked by twice as many guards, were marched from the direction of the dockyards on the three-mile trek to Melville. The Melville prisoners were separated into two groups, and Dudley watched as one group was marched toward the docks to board the ship for Dartmoor Prison. Mathers was in the mix, and Dudley nodded to the man, knowing he would likely never see him again.

De Witt quickly gathered Dudley's remaining company and ushered them back inside. Knowing how tight the quarters were about to become, they were glad to stake claims on hammocks. Soon, an angry guard unlocked the doors and began shoving bodies through. A few tense moments passed as the new men, exhausted, weak, and frightened, bullied up to claim their spots, but Dudley watched proudly as the old crew made space. When all were settled and all the guards had left, Nathan, the previous week's president, stood up.

"We choose a leader—a president—each week. It's his job to look after the needs of the others, hand out the mail, and make assignments. Our new president's been hauled off, so I'll fill in until we vote again. The major there," he said, pointing to Dudley, "he's the preacher in here. We have a little singing and prayer each night. Anyone take issue with that?"

No one did and with the meeting ended, they fell into their hammocks. An hour later, DeWitt brought in the mail and the men scrambled to the front, eager for any word from home. Nathan took the bundle and began calling names, and the precious letters and packages were passed from hand to hand until they reached their intended recipients. When the last treasure had been distributed, the disappointed sighs that escaped from the unblessed were quickly subdued by the generosity of others. Dudley opened his own precious parcel and plopped a morsel of Beatrice's apple cake into his mouth, reserving a second portion before passing the rest among the others. Leaning into the jute of his hammock, he began to read her letter, fighting the sting in his eyes, which pictured her standing beside him.

CHAPTER 17

Thursday, September 8, 1814
Fort McHenry

Abel knew two things about his military career—that belonging to the Fencibles was more a fragile privilege to be lost than a right he could depend on, and that if he wanted to hold on to that privilege, he had to appear content and avoid confrontation. Sometimes he would almost rather forfeit the rewards than endure another demeaning day with Hildebrand and Skully haranguing him.

Markus's little joke had left them wary of Abel the first day of water duty, and Abel thoroughly enjoyed the way they cut a broad path around him. He chose the duty he wanted, cranking the stubborn well handle, while Hildebrand and Skully took turns leaning over the well to retrieve the filled buckets and then emptying the buckets into casks on the wagon. Once all the containers on the wagon were filled, the three men drove the wagon to the areas where water was needed, and they filled all the storage containers. Since Hildebrand and Skully appeared to be afraid of Abel, he let them know that messing with Caleb was the shortest path to his wrath, and they seemed to leave the boy alone.

The first and second days left Abel bone-ragged by nightfall. His back ached from stacking balls and powder near the guns, and his arms ached from cranking the well. Still, he preferred cranking the well to leaning over it and staring down its deep throat into the black water. He could work hard and he could work long, but he couldn't abide the water. Unfortunately, Hildebrand and Skully were about to figure that out.

It was early in the morning but the three men had already filled and emptied close to two hundred buckets when Captain Nicholson and Sergeant Carpenter called Abel away from water duty.

"I understand you've got experience rigging explosives," Nicholson said.

A new duty assignment? Abel enthusiastically answered, "Yes, sir."

"Excellent. General Samuel Smith, commander of the Baltimore forces, is considering a plan to block the entrance to the Baltimore harbor by sinking old vessels in the Patapsco River to the east of the fort. The plan still needs to be approved by Baltimore's Safety and Vigilance Committee, but if it is endorsed, Captain Rodgers could use a few more men experienced at setting explosives. I'll place you on that detail."

A cold shiver ran through Abel like a hundred snakes slithering across his every nerve. His knees felt like jelly on a hot day, and he felt certain every man in the fort could hear the thunder in his chest. He swallowed hard. "I'll be on the ship?"

"That's right. The powder and lines are in the powder magazine. You might want to check on the supplies to be sure you'll have everything you need." Nicholson pointed to his left just before he and the sergeant turned back toward the office. When Abel didn't move or make a sound, the two men turned back around and found him nearly frozen in place, his eyes wide and his mouth clamped shut. "Is there a problem?" Captain Nicholson asked.

Abel heard the question, but he couldn't make his mouth say the words—not out loud, and certainly not in front of his tormentors.

"Abel?" Nicholson repeated. "Abel?" The name came louder this time, and Hildebrand and Skully began to snicker.

Nicholson was clearly becoming agitated, and now Sergeant Carpenter came striding over to Abel. "Do we have a problem, Private?"

"I—I—I can't get on a ship, sir. I—I—I just can't."

Nicholson stormed over. "What do you mean you can't? Are you afraid?" The question was uttered as if the idea was completely incomprehensible to the captain, and Abel shrank.

"It's the water, sir. That's why I joined the army and not the navy. I can't get on a ship."

"Are you defying a direct order, Abel?"

Abel felt clammy and weak. Other men had treated him poorly—embarrassed and demeaned him—but that was their sin. This day, Abel was afraid, and for the first time, he was ashamed of himself. "I'll do anything else, sir."

Nicholson glanced at Hildebrand and Skully, who were erupting in laughter. "Those men are laughing at you, Abel. Do you realize that?"

Abel's hands curled into fists, but his anger was directed at himself. He had managed to help Jed blow up the docks before the mercenaries came, but he'd been near the land, and friends were nearby. But a boat? In the middle of a river? He wanted to vomit. "That's the last thing I would ever want. You know how badly I want to be here. I would die before I'd dishonor myself or you. But I can't do this." His voice trembled with emotion. "My fear of water goes way back. Isn't there something you just can't do, sir?"

Nicholson's face melted into compassion momentarily, and then a new fire lit his eyes. He reached up, placing his hands on Abel's shoulders to look at him eye to eye. "You're asking the wrong man, I'm afraid. I believe we can do anything we want to do badly enough. If you're determined to surrender to your fears, I'll send another man. But understand that your fear has just given your two associates power they can hold over you."

Abel watched the captain stride away, and he knew disappointment fueled the man's brisk steps. Abel wanted to run after him and promise to conquer his fear, but he just couldn't.

Sergeant Carpenter stood beside Abel with his back to Hildebrand and Skully. "You asked the captain if there was something he just couldn't do, and he said you asked the wrong man. Do you know what he meant by that?"

Abel shook his mighty head, keeping his eyes riveted to a spot of ground.

"In 1801, what Captain Nicholson wanted more than anything else was for Thomas Jefferson to be elected president of these United States, but the voting in the electoral college resulted in a tie between Jefferson and Aaron Burr. Electing the new president then fell to the House of Representatives, where the captain was currently serving the state of Maryland.

"It was February 11th. The captain was just a judge then, and very ill, so ill that his doctor felt he was about to draw his last breath. It was then that a courier arrived detailing the dilemma in Washington. Though it was snowing, the judge would not allow an entire nation's destiny to turn on his concern for his own well-being. So, he had his sickbed loaded onto a wagon and he rode into Washington with his wife by his side, so he could cast his vote.

"He was placed in a committee room to rest between ballots. Thirty-five were cast, all ending in a tie. In between each, the captain's dear wife Rebecca administered medicines to keep him lucid. When the Federalists realized he was determined to cast his vote for Jefferson until his last breath, a few delegates were so moved they stepped away from the vote, handing the advantage to the Democratic-Republicans, who elected their candidate, Thomas Jefferson, the third American president. That's what a man can do when he wants something badly enough, Abel."

Abel trembled at the challenge. "I'll go, but if I panic, I could put others at risk."

"Then stay. And work on that fear, because now others know your weakness, and that's about as deadly a thing as a man can have happen to him."

Nothing more was said as Abel walked past Hildebrand and Skully and returned to pulling water from the well. He saw it in their eyes, the joy they felt over knowing his Achilles' heel, and he dreaded that fact, knowing that somehow, someday, he'd have to conquer that fear or they would exploit that weakness to his detriment.

CHAPTER 18

Thursday, September 8, 1814
An atoll near Bermuda

The storm blew by, leaving warnings of another in its wake. Time was short and Jed now faced the moment of truth. He had never actually smelted ore himself. He had studied the process in one of his classes at the University of Pennsylvania, and he had watched Jack do it several times, but he had never actually done the work. And here, on a beach with limited supplies, he had to improvise. He silently prayed for good recall, to remember everything Jack and his professors had tried to teach him.

As he recalled the appearance of the furnace at home, his mind seemed to be enlightened. He described the items to Ethan, who, along with a friend—a young seaman named Edward Tenneyson—went through the ship, scavenging for suitable items with which to build a furnace.

"I need something that can withstand a great deal of heat, Ethan, like a large ceramic or clay pot. Have you seen anything like that on the ship?"

Ethan clapped his bandaged hand against his good one. "Cook has a big clay pot he stores pickles and kraut in!"

On and on, Jed described what he needed, and Ethan and Edward proved to be most able assistants, exploring every nook and cranny on the *Iphigenia*. When the pair had found everything

Jed felt he needed, they filled the boat and rowed to the atoll. Jed enlisted a crew of eight to dig a large pit in the sand, which they lined with stones to form their furnace. Wood was limited on the atoll, so Jed sent four more men to bring back any piece of wood on the ship that could be spared. Barrels, boards, and empty crates were broken down and added to the pile while Jed formed an enclosed clay "stove" to burn the wood into charcoal, an essential element in smelting iron ore.

They needed a sustained fire, a luxury when the skies portended rain. Ethan and Edward combed the atoll for every piece of driftwood they could find, and the men raced against nature to cut enough wood to keep the fires stoked sufficiently to create the necessary amount of charcoal. After a nearly sleepless night, morning broke and Jed finally announced that they had enough charcoal. The crew celebrated, lifting Ethan on their shoulders, and Jed wondered over the camaraderie exhibited by the pair's former tormenters.

The next step was creating a bloomery—a rudimentary furnace capable of sustaining a fire hot enough to smelt the ore. A tunnel was dug into the sand pit and lined with a few halves of clay pots with their bottoms broken off. When covered with sand, this tunnel formed the conduit to deliver air from the bellows. It was noon when the furnace was finally ready. A hot wood fire was started and burned for one hour to warm up the furnace, and then the pit was filled with charcoal and burned for another half hour.

Jed looked at the pile of charcoal. If they ran out, the ore would be brittle and unmalleable. And if that happened and he failed, he might not get a second chance. Captain Smith could rescind his agreement, and Jed might never get home to Hannah.

As the charcoal burned down, equal-weighted measures of ore and charcoal needed to be added at twenty-minute intervals. The burns Jed had received at the bridge explosion in Washington were scarcely healed, and the heat of the fire penetrated the forger's gloves and apron, causing him pain. And as day wore on to evening, fatigue so numbed him that his concentration began to waver. While resting on his shovel, he nearly fell asleep. If he had done so, he would likely have slipped into the furnace. At that moment, a pair of arms wrapped behind him, gently moving him to safety. It was Roust.

"It'd be a pity to see you die now, when you're very nearly free. Go on board the ship and rest, Lieutenant. I'll spell you out here. We'll just keep doing what you were doing until we run out of charcoal or ore, right?"

"Exactly. The last addition must be charcoal only, about twenty pounds. And save twenty pounds more for working the metal. When those two piles are all the charcoal you've got left, top off the fire with one pile and let the fire burn itself out. Then come for me."

"Lieutenant Ramsey asked for you. Said he thought he only dreamed you up. When I told him you were real enough, he was as happy as I've seen him. I told him you'd be tending him from now on, but he said he'd rather lie there and die. So I told him it would be my honor to carry on. He seemed to accept that all right. I was wrong to treat him so poorly, but I'll make amends."

Jed was speechless.

More kindness followed. One man rowed him to the ship and another man offered his hand to help him aboard. These modest gestures nearly overwhelmed him.

Arthur was awake when Jed slipped into his cabin. "Jed, is that you?"

"Yes, Arthur." He slipped to one knee and lit a lantern so they could see one another face to face. Jed clasped his hands over Arthur's. "How are you? You are an answer to my prayers."

Arthur laughed, bringing on a coughing spasm. Finally, he was able to speak again. "It's hard to believe that I could be the answer to anyone's prayers. I'm but half a man now, Jed. I long for death to release me from this bondage."

"Don't say such things, Arthur. It's a miracle you've made it this far. You're the one who always believed in God's will. Perhaps it is His will that you live."

"It is a miracle that I am still here, but I think I was spared so that I might spare you. I know the Earl of Whittington quite well. When we arrive in England I'll call on him and ask him to repay a great debt he owes me, by pleading for you. He's a powerful man, Jed, and a fair man. I feel certain he will provide the final nudge you need to be set free."

"I'll gladly take your help, Arthur, but don't be so quick to surrender your own life."

"The life left to me is no life, Jed. Military surgeons are among the best in Britain. They believe there is no more to be done. I am a disgusting wretch on earth, but beyond this life I am whole and free. So I will ask God to sustain me during our travels, and then I will pray for Him to take me home."

Jed pressed his face into Arthur's hands, his tears wetting the man's fingers. "What right have I to be so blessed when you suffer so?"

"Do not weep for me, Jed. My heart is calm. I was blessed to find Frannie and briefly experience love, but unlike you, no other life hinges on mine. Let me render what small service I can to help you return home to Hannah and Frannie. Then I can move on without fear or regret."

Jed's head felt like lead, too heavy to move. Still clasping Arthur's hand, his cheek pressed solidly there, he clamped his eyes shut and brought Hannah's face to his mind. He saw her dark hair fall over her shoulder as her green eyes gazed with wonder on the bundle resting in her arms. And then he saw Frannie sitting nearby, her face a mixed study of familial joy and personal sorrow. Jed knew Arthur's death would be the cause.

One long, shuddering breath restored Jed's composure. "Is there anything I can do for you, my friend, to make you more comfortable, or to help pass the time?"

Arthur's eyes brightened. "Just sit and talk to me a while each day. I hear the way the men speak of me. I'm a burden now, but I'd enjoy it if you could read to me from the Bible, or tell me stories from the Willows to help pass the dreary hours. I'd also be so grateful if you'd pen a few letters and final thoughts for me."

"Anything, Arthur, anything at all. May I also have some paper so I can write to Hannah? I know the letters can't be posted until we reach shore, but I'd like her to know that it was thoughts of her and the baby that sustained me."

Arthur squeezed Jed's hand. His eyes remained closed as a smile played on his lips. "The answer as to who sustains each of you is evident, but what woman can be told that too often?"

Jed's cheeks turned red and he laughed joyfully. For the first time in weeks he felt the comforting warmth of his marriage to Hannah, unmarred by his crushing guilt over the toll his impending imprisonment would take on her. And then he remembered his makeshift bloomery and all that hinged on his smelting success. If that failed, he would likely be tossed back into the ship's hold, from which only Arthur could rescue him. Dear Arthur.

"Roust told me you won't allow me to tend you. I would—"

Arthur raised his hand to halt the words. "Please Jed, grant me this one thing—to not be reduced in your eyes the way I am in the other men's."

Jed felt his throat grow tight. "It would never be so, but I'll honor your wishes."

"I wonder how Frannie is. I hope she and Mr. Shepard find their way to one another. It would bring me peace to know she was well loved and happy."

"Don't assume your death will bring them together. Frannie doesn't give her heart easily, nor does she let go easily once it's been given. She will mourn you for a long time, I fear. Let that be one more reason for you not to surrender as long as there is any hope for a good life."

Arthur closed his eyes, obviously unwilling to debate the point any further.

"Shall I read to you for a while?" Jed asked.

"Thank you, but not tonight. Roust told me what you've been doing the past two days. You rest in your bunk awhile. We have days for talking and reading ahead of us. It's a comfort just to have a friend close at hand."

The knock on the door was somewhat panicked. "Lieutenant Pearson! Come quick! I think somethin's gone wrong with the iron."

Jed leapt up and raced from the cabin to the ladder, where three other worried men waited for him. During the row to the atoll he prayed he could salvage the metal. Everything hinged on his success. When they landed he ran to the furnace, anxious yet afraid of what he might find. He looked inside and his arms began to shake.

"Hand me a shovel!" he called out. He took the tool and began to pry the gray, lumpy mass from the sides of the pot.

"Is it ruined?" Roust asked anxiously.

Jed dumped the mass into the sand and fell to his knees. Raising his arms to the sky he began to laugh. "It's a perfect bloom! It's the most beautiful thing I've ever seen!"

"It don't look like any iron I ever saw," said one of the sailors.

"That's because you're used to seeing iron bars. We still need to work this on an anvil."

Jed directed them to build another hot fire. Working one quarter of the bloom at a time, he would heat it red hot and then pound it between his hammer and the anvil until it was flat and hard and consistently colored. Slowly, it transformed before their eyes.

The sky began to darken again, warning of another wave of bad weather. "Show me those items we need to duplicate," Jed said.

Roust brought over the broken pieces and Jed heated the iron again and again, hammering it to shape and strengthen it. One by one the pieces emerged—pins, clamps, bands to secure the mast— as the edge of the storm brought rain that made the fire sizzle. *Just a few more minutes,* Jed thought to himself as he shoved the implement back into his dying fire. A few more pounds with the hammer against a form and the last pin emerged. He plunged the red-hot metal into a pail of water and the sizzle made him smile. "We're done!"

A loud cheer erupted through the group, stifled quickly by the crack of thunder.

"These parts won't do us any good until we get them mounted on the ship," one sailor said. "Unless Captain Bliss says they'll do, we're no better off than we were."

There was one more barrier between Jed and his freedom. They packed up their supplies and rowed back to the ship in the rain to show the parts to the captain.

Captain Smith stood by as the *Iphigenia*'s sailing captain examined the parts Jed had manufactured. "Will they do? Are they strong enough to get us to Bermuda?"

Captain Bliss scowled and frowned as he tapped and banged the parts, nearly driving Captain Smith to distraction. "Captain!" Smith called out. "Will they work or not?"

Captain Bliss eyed Jed curiously. "I don't know how you did it, but you did. You made parts that are strong enough to carry us clear back to England."

"Are you certain?" Smith asked, seeming afraid to accept their good fortune.

"Pearson here made us good strong parts and spares to boot," Bliss exclaimed. "Let's get them mounted, boys! We need to get ahead of this storm!"

Jed worked alongside the men, tightening bolts and mounting the mast supports until the sails were unfurled. He was soaked to the bone but felt utterly exhilarated. Knowledge beyond his own had been given to him this day. He knew that. Never before had he felt so aided, so *known,* and he wondered if this was how Hannah felt when God spoke to her. Jed counted his diverse prayers that had been answered, and the small miracles he had experienced. But he couldn't explain the dreadful cruelty the men had shown to Ethan—the same men who had cheered with him today.

Jed entered Arthur's cabin and lit the lantern, then turned the flame low. Surprisingly, Arthur was wide awake.

"I take it things went well today?" he asked hopefully.

Jed sat in a chair in the corner and leaned back.

"I never doubted you," Arthur said when Jed didn't respond.

"That's just it, Arthur. It wasn't me. I feigned the necessary knowledge to have a chance at freedom, but I had never really smelted iron before. Jack always did the smithing on the farm."

Arthur lifted his head from the pillow to study Jed's face. "Are you saying you think God helped you today, that He worked a miracle in your behalf?"

Jed pondered the question. "Yes, I suppose I do think that."

Arthur dropped his head back down as a smile spread across his lips.

"And the men—it was so curious. A few days ago they wished to torture and kill me." The bitterness returned to Jed's voice momentarily. "They even mutilated the hand of the poor cabin boy because he dared to show me a few kindnesses, and then the past few days, as we've worked together, their hearts softened as if I was a new man to them. And the boy! You should see how they've treated him. It's just so curious."

"Who can estimate the impact of war on men? It can bond men like brothers, and bring out the very worst in otherwise good men. I'm so sorry for what you and the boy have suffered."

Jed shook his head. "I pity poor Ethan. How will these events color his opinion of mankind? But me? I would suffer it all again to understand the nature of man." The power of his next thought brought him to the edge of his seat. "I once believed that man was inherently good. I stopped believing it, but I do again. War—and life itself, I think—can cause us to react with our poorest self, when if we'd but halt and think a moment longer, goodness could prevail."

"Who sounds like a vicar now?"

Jed leaned back again and chuckled. "I never want to lose this feeling, Arthur."

"Oh, you will, sadly. We all do sometimes. But though this may be the first time you've recognized it, this is not the first time the Lord has worked through you, Jed, and neither do I think it will be the last. Where are we headed now? To Bermuda?"

"No, to England. Our course is set straight for England."

Arthur raised his head and looked at Jed. "Straightway to England?" The news clearly pleased him. "Then perhaps I will have the opportunity to make amends with my father before I die."

CHAPTER 19

Friday, September 9, 1814
The Willows

The group sat on the porch, watching the children play in the first pile of autumn leaves, when they heard a wagon rumbling by on the River Road. Jack rose casually and moved to the railing to peer past the brush, obviously attempting to identify the wagon. Soon Timothy was by his side, finally wearing work clothes like Jack did. One by one, the women joined the men—Frannie by Timothy, Bitty by Jack, and Hannah on the end—each of them hoping, praying to see Markus ride in.

"Something's wrong, isn't it?" Hannah asked. "Markus should have been home by now."

The tension in Timothy's eyes belied his response. "He's only two days late. Any number of things could be holding him up. They could have been detained in their departure. Or perhaps he's visiting some of the flotillamen at the Lazaretto Battery."

"No," Frannie said. "He knows we'd worry. If he made land, he would have sent word."

Jack removed his hat and wiped the sweat from his brow. "That's Stringham's rig headed up our lane." He looked to Hannah and Frannie. "Better let Mr. Shepard deal with this."

Frannie boldly stepped down from the porch. "I can handle Frederick Stringham, Jack. Our former engagement is water long passed under the bridge. I no longer have any feelings for Frederick, ill or otherwise. It's his poor wife I worry about."

Stringham sat ramrod straight in the wagon box as he drove the rig up the lane, though everyone knew the poor fellow still suffered terribly from pain in his back and hips.

"Poor Penelope is rounder than ever," Bitty said. "That's a sure sign someone's either very happy or very unhappy."

Hannah's face fell into a sad smile. "How is it then that she seems to also be smaller?"

"It's her shoulders," Jack said. "Rounded over. I've seen that look a hundred times when a slave is so beat down they don't ever straighten up."

Hannah gasped. "Jack, you don't think he beats her, do you?"

Jack looked at Hannah with compassionate eyes. "There's lots of way of bein' beat, aren't there?" She slipped her hand in his and rested her head on his shoulder.

Frederick drove the wagon as near to the porch as he could without running Frannie over. He clearly did not want to look at her, though each time he did his feelings for her were apparent.

"Hello, Frederick. Hello, Penelope. Good to see you both," Frannie said matter-of-factly.

Frederick withdrew his hat and met her eyes, lingering there. "Hello, Francis." Moments passed before he acknowledged the others standing on the porch. "Good day, Mrs. Pearson," he added, completely ignoring Jack and Bitty, and offering but a brief nod to Timothy.

Penelope looked at Frannie with pained eyes, and the Willow's "wild woman" became so fully discomfited that she climbed back onto the porch and stood as far from the wagon as possible.

Hannah stepped forward. "Would you two care to join us on the porch, Mr. Stringham? We have some freshly pressed apple juice."

"Thank you, but no, ma'am. The wife and I have been traveling from Baltimore most of the day and we're anxious to get home.

I have a business proposition to present. Even though I suffered greatly from the mercenaries' attack, I am sympathetic to your current situation. It grieves me that you are without your husband, so I feel you deserve the first opportunity."

Hannah fought her revulsion for the man. "And what would that be?"

"When the fire destroyed White Oak, I was left in considerably more dire straits than you good folks. The majority of my cash reserves are needed to rebuild the house and barn, leaving little for seed or equipment or workers."

"You mean slaves," Hannah said bluntly.

Frederick's mouth tightened before he smiled. "I am not the one who is out of step with the times, but if dealing with a slave owner is too unpalatable for you, I'll take my offer elsewhere."

He began to back up the wagon when Bitty nudged Hannah. "Don't let him get away."

"The man is a beast, Bitty."

Bitty's eyes bore down on Frederick as she nodded. "Remember that surprise I was talking about a few days ago, Hannah? This is it."

Hannah was still confused but turned back to Stringham. "On second thought, I'd like to hear about this opportunity."

Stringham pulled back on the reins. "Are you saying you were a little too hasty?"

Hannah wanted to scrape the man off her property. "Perhaps so. Please continue."

"Very well. I'm selling off a few sections of White Oak land." He patted his breast pocket. "I went to Baltimore to have deeds drawn up to twenty 20-acre tracts. Since the land I'm selling borders your property, I felt I should come to you first."

Hannah looked at Bitty, whose eyes were misting. She, Frannie, and Jack moved in close. Hannah turned to Jack. "What do you think?"

Jack remained unemotional as he replied, "Jed's grandfather believed land was the most important thing a man could own. I think if Jed were here he'd buy every acre he could."

Those were the words Hannah needed to hear. She turned back to Stringham. "And how much do you want for each tract?"

"I'm asking a very reasonable price—fifteen hundred dollars for each."

Frannie was aghast. "That's thirty thousand dollars!"

"Yes, but for prime, waterfront farm land, perfect for growing tobacco and convenient to the river."

"But still . . ." Hannah sighed. "Thirty thousand dollars. We'll need some time to consider your offer. Could we have two weeks to assess things here?"

"Very well. Two weeks. If I haven't heard from you by then I'll post my offer in Calverton. I'm sure there are a host of families who would leap at the chance to buy a twenty-acre plot of farmland. We could have an entire little village of new neighbors in a year or so."

Hannah knew Frederick was baiting her. "Two weeks then."

"Oh, and by the way, I picked up a traveler along the side of the road four days ago, a woman by the name of Jenny. She said she was a houseguest of yours, crowded out by all the bodies living in your house. Pity . . . pretty girl. Odd that she ran off dressed in formal attire. It almost looked as if she was running away from something, or someone."

Frannie stepped forward and said, "Timothy and I went riding after her, but now I understand why her trail went cold. Where did you take her?"

"Baltimore, although that was another oddity. She asked to be dropped off on the outskirts of the city, though we offered to drive her straight in."

"That was very kind of you, Mr. Stringham," Hannah said in an effort to move him along. "We'll contact you within two weeks, then."

"Yes, two weeks, then," he repeated before turning his wagon to head down the lane.

Hannah stood firm as the wagon rolled away. As soon as it was beyond the bend she turned to the group. "Do we even have thirty thousand dollars in cash?"

"I've got some savings and a healthy portfolio I acquired during my days at Le Jardin," Frannie said.

"You have a variety of holdings you could liquidate, but not within two weeks," Timothy explained. "And so many people are defaulting on loans right now that the banks' terms are unreasonable. And with Jed away, well . . . But you wouldn't need to buy all the parcels."

"Yes, we would. We're not a conventional farm. We'd rather have one cantankerous, slavery-loving neighbor than ten bordering Willows land and causing trouble for us."

"I see your point," Timothy said.

"Cantankerous? Stringham is so much worse than that. He makes my skin—" Then Hannah caught herself. "That was thoughtless of me, Frannie. Forgive me."

Frannie's feelings seemed uninjured. "He was a much different man when I cared for him. His father made him what he is today."

"But I do want that land," Hannah went on. "Let's pool all our resources. Jack, can you tell me what we can sell within two weeks? And Frannie, please see what you can pull together. I wish I had something of my own to contribute, but I came here with nothing but my wedding ring."

"Anything we can scrape together from this farm is now partly your contribution, Hannah," Frannie said. "Don't worry. We're going to find a way!"

"Can we put in too?" Bitty asked Hannah softly.

"Of course, Bitty. Do you want to buy some of Stringham's land?"

"What would one acre cost—one hundred fifty dollars, right?"

"That's right," Frannie answered.

Bitty looked at Jack. "I got one hundred dollars comin' from Abel and Caleb. Should be here any day. And another thirty from Jed, plus . . . have you got another twenty, Jack?"

"I believe so."

Bitty squealed and jumped into her older brother's arms.

"What's gotten into you, woman?" Jack asked. Bitty wrapped her arms around Jack's neck and placed a dozen kisses on his cheek. "What on earth has got you all fired up?"

Bitty motioned for Jack to set her down on the porch. Then she looked into his brown eyes. "I don't take the credit for all this, but me and the Lord been workin' for this day, Jack."

"Sister, I have no idea what you're talkin' about. You've been askin' the Lord to get you some of Stringham's land?"

"Just one acre, Jack, one special acre. Do you understand now?"

Soon understanding filled Jack's eyes, and he took her hands in his. "I do now. I surely do now. And you think Abel will be all right with this?"

She nodded. "Before Abel and Caleb left, I heard Stringham might be selling some land. Back then it seemed impossible. I think that's one reason Abel joined the army—to earn that money for me." She wiped away a tear as she turned to Hannah and Frannie. "Next to my freedom, it'll be the best gift I ever got. You know what acre I want to buy, don't you?"

Frannie reached for Bitty's hands. "I think I do, Bitty."

"I don't expect Mr. Stringham will sell directly to Jack and me. Will you buy it for us?"

"It would make us very proud, Bitty."

The steady pounding of a horse's hoofs caught their attention, and again they all moved to the railings. "That's a single rider comin' up from Calverton way," Jack said.

They held their breath as the rider turned up their lane. It was dusk and visibility was difficult. Hannah's eyes were fixed on

Jack, who peered into the darkness as he slowly moved down the porch and to the lawn below, all the while studying the rider's motion and form. "He's about the right build!"

Timothy raced down to stand beside Jack, and soon the women huddled by the men in the growing darkness. As the rider barreled toward the house, Hannah noticed the absence of the Irish seaman's trademark bounce as he rode.

It was the same courier who had delivered Markus's previous orders. He slipped to the ground and bent over to catch his breath. Timothy rushed over, inviting the young man to sit and rest a while, but the courier immediately straightened and pulled a letter from under his shirt.

"President Madison wants your reply tonight," the courier announced, then gladly received the dipper of water Jack offered and the biscuits and jam Bitty ran and brought.

Timothy read the letter while everyone else awaited the news. His expression grew more dour with each second, and finally he slapped the letter angrily against his leg. "The cartel ship left on the fourth as planned, but it never returned to dock. President Madison was wondering if we had any additional information."

"But if they're only two days late, why is President Madison so concerned?"

"Because the British fleet gathered all their ships at Tangier Island, Frannie, and now they're on the move again. It appears . . . it appears they're heading for Baltimore."

CHAPTER 20

Friday, September 9, 1814
Aboard the British fleet

The British fleet left Tangier Island on September 9th, sailing north with Key and Skinner aboard the HMS *Surprise,* while the American tender, the *President,* was escorted along under armed guard. The dinner games continued the next night as Key's and Skinner's attendance was again requested. They were escorted to the *Tonnant,* where maps were spread and where battle details, troop deployment, and casualty estimates were openly discussed. Neither of the Americans could force their food past the ever-growing lumps in their throats. At the end of the evening they were escorted back to the *Surprise,* and Key had made a decision.

"I'm not going back over to that ship. I can't bear to listen to them plan the destruction of Baltimore any longer. It is barbarous to subject any man to such a thing. I'd rather starve."

Skinner rubbed his forehead. "Hunger aside, we're not safe yet, Mr. Key, nor do we have Dr. Beanes. If we are obstinate, we may yet forfeit all our lives."

Key paced to the wall and banged his fist against it. "Never was man more disappointed in his expectations than I have been as to the character of British officers. With some few exceptions, they are illiberal, ignorant, and vulgar, and seem filled with a spirit of malignity toward everything American."

"That is because you are not a warrior by nature. We can still hope their threats of burning Baltimore will be unrealized."

Key sputtered and then grew quiet before he spoke. "I suppose I'm most irate because of the circumstances that brought us to this situation. Days after President Madison signed the declaration of war, Alexander Contee Hanson, the publisher of the *Federal Republican*, published anti-war articles that left Baltimore frenzied. The Democratic-Republicans wanted this abominable war, including Mayor Johnson, who I feel failed them as a leader. Anyone who opposed it met with violence. Now look at what they've brought upon themselves." He bowed his head and folded his hands. "And yet I must place my faith in God, believing that He will hear the prayers of the innocent believers whose piety leavens that lump of wickedness."

"Wickedness didn't make them cry for war, Frank. Their fathers fought for liberty, and after a generation of privilege, they saw it threatened. Their error was their reaction to their divisions. I read accounts of that riot. George Washington's friend Henry Lee was severely wounded there."

"The famed Light Horse Harry," Key mused. "He was severely wounded defending the right to a free press, a principle for which he and Washington had fought in the Revolution."

"And how is General Lee now?"

"The injuries he sustained in Baltimore left him physically debilitated, and poor investments landed him in debtors' prison. His brother signed a bond freeing him, but Lee sailed to Barbados seeking a warmer climate to recuperate, which violated the terms of his bond. I'm told the courts are currently filing against his brother, and he will now be ruined. And Harry's young family will once again be cast from their home and forced to rely upon the mercy of family members for shelter. Harry's youngest is only seven. What will life be like for his little Robert E. Lee? And it all began in Baltimore." Key shook his head. "This city that wanted this war is about to get their comeuppance, and yet my heart is so inclined to the suffering that will fall upon the women and children."

"We should be nearing Baltimore tomorrow evening, and our hosts will call for us again to tell us their plans to destroy that city. As much as we despise their dinner conversations, let's not rile them. Their stories about burning Baltimore could be a ruse. Let's allow them to have their fun at our expense and not give them justification for further anger."

Friday, September 9, 1814
Baltimore

"Hear ye! Hear ye! The honorable Mayor Edward Johnson presiding!" The aged bailiff made the announcement to the clamoring throng of people in the stuffy town hall.

"Mr. Stromberger," whispered the mayor's slightly rumpled legal advisor, Harvey Baumgardner, "these are not official judicial proceedings." The forty-six-year-old Baumgardner's eyes crinkled as he smiled at the older gentleman. "The mayor wants to see firsthand what concerns are impacting the city during this escalation. A simple call to order will suffice."

Stromberger shrugged his shoulders. "I don't know how to conduct whatever it is we're having here today." He straightened his narrow shoulders, stood front and center before the assembly, and made a second attempt. "The assembly will now come to order. Those citizens with business to bring before the mayor can line up behind this podium here." He pointed to the lectern set up in front of the center aisle. "Out-of-towners' business will be heard last. The riffraff being charged with offenses can take a seat here in the front."

Harvey shook his head over the complete discombobulation of the American legal system occurring in Baltimore since the burning of the capital. He knew he shouldn't be surprised. Mayor Edward Johnson had a reputation for employing unorthodox means to accomplish his agendas. Baltimoreans supported his bold, sometimes brash style, including his handling of the riot that erupted over Alexander Contee Hanson's articles condemning President Madison's call for war. Despite the bloodlust that had enveloped the city, residents had returned to the polls weeks later and re-elected the man whose actions had actually heightened the tensions.

At this moment, Mayor Johnson waved to Stromberger from the door, indicating that he was finally ready to enter. The bailiff nodded and ordered, "All rise!"

The scuffle of feet and chairs was brief as the mayor entered, pulling on the lapels of his brown tweed suit with one hand and smoothing the thinning hairs atop his head with the other. Once the mayor was seated, Stromberger handed him a copy of the day's business. Johnson glanced at it and gestured for Harvey Baumgardner to hurry over to him.

"What on earth is this?" the mayor asked as he scanned the sheet. "The Committee of Safety and Vigilance was set up to ensure discipline in our city. I can't attend to all this."

"These items all fall within the jurisdiction of your committee," Harvey said.

Johnson read through the day's docket, scribbled some notes, and then pointed to the five red-uniformed British Army deserters sitting directly in front of him. "You shall be taken to jail, where you shall remain until your fleet leaves our waters. Pray America wins this engagement, for if your own commanders discover you hiding in our fair city, I do not think it will bode well for you."

"Mr. Stromberger, arrange an escort of these men." As the bailiff attended to that duty, Mayor Johnson moved on to the next subject. "I see a number of reports of suspicious strangers within the city limits. Who here has filed a report of observing unpatriotic behavior?"

Several men and two women stood. Mayor Johnson gestured to a tall man dressed in black who was seated in the back of the room. "Mr. Fletcher, would you come forward, please?" The gentleman did so and the mayor continued. "The safety committee has contracted with Mr. Fletcher, a fine detective, to handle all such suspicious characters."

He handed Fletcher a stack containing the individual complaints that had been filed. "I'd like you to begin investigating all these cases right away."

Harvey Baumgardner rushed to Johnson's side. "Mr. Mayor, you cannot set this man off to investigate individuals solely on the suspicion of a neighbor. Many of these reports are so ludicrous they should simply be thrown out."

"Anti-government chatter was overheard in one case, a man was overheard discussing troop movements with a stranger, a group of men were caught discharging weapons for entertainment when our ammunition is reportedly limited, and unknown persons were seen skulking about. We can't have that during wartime, but neither do I have the time to hear each case. Mr. Fletcher will determine which cases warrant further action. Move him and his informants to another room, and hold the accused in the jail until he gets things sorted out."

"We're going to jail them solely on hearsay?"

Johnson pulled his glasses down his nose. "We're not arresting them, Mr. Baumgardner. We're merely detaining them until they can be interviewed. Most will merely be fined five dollars to encourage more politically harmonious behavior."

Two law officers arrived in the company of Stromberger, and soon the deserters and those being held for unpatriotic behavior were herded up. One man made a loud inquiry as to whether the Constitution still mattered in Baltimore.

Harvey's fleshy face went from pink to red. "I'm sorry, Mayor Johnson. I can't allow men and women to be jailed for expressing their constitutionally guaranteed right to free speech."

The mayor seemed shocked at his aide's attitude. "Don't you believe our city must be protected from spies and insurrectionists, Mr. Baumgardner? We saw them raise their ugly heads in Washington—American spies passing reports of our troops' strength and movements to the British. Americans giving aid to the enemy and carrying messages. I'll not have it in this city."

"There are proper ways to handle such things, sir."

"Good heavens! Do you not realize that we are in a war, Harvey? Now let's continue."

When the mayor looked at the next item of business on his sheet, a change came over him. He cleared his throat. "The next item involves families rendered indigent because their head of household is away at war defending our city. How many of you dear ladies have come for this reason?"

Eight beleaguered women stood, each with several small children. Six of the women held tiny babies in their arms.

"And you, dear ladies," the mayor went on, "are without any other means because your husbands are missing work to serve in the militia under Major General Smith?"

Each woman nodded and clutched her children close.

"General Smith and I have enacted a plan to help families struggling under this burden." Johnson studied the faces of the fatherless families and scribbled something on several pieces of paper. "Each of you mothers take one of these vouchers to the city's comptroller. He'll provide you with a modest monthly living allowance throughout the duration of your husband's militia service. If you need further assistance, come and see me again."

One by one, the women came forward, thanked the mayor, took a voucher, and left the room to convert the paper into cash. Harvey knew this was why the people of Baltimore loved Mayor Johnson and would likely re-elect him again. He was decisive and effective. If your causes aligned with his, you were pleased with his take-charge manner, despite the temporary mangling of the Constitution. But if your cause or concern opposed Johnson's, no appeal to the rule of law would sway the man—at least not in the short term.

This was why the mayor and Harvey's brother-in-law, Jed Pearson, had clashed so ferociously during the Baltimore riots. Jed was trying to save Light Horse Harry Lee, who had come to Baltimore to stand with Hanson and the cause of freedom of the presses, and Mayor Johnson had sided with the pro-war crowd.

Harvey winced at the memory. He knew Jed would never admit it, but the two had also clashed because they were too much alike—strong-willed, principled, willing to hurl themselves into the fray. Harvey thought about his wife's sister, Hannah, who had been severely abused as a child. How pleased he was that she and Jed had found their way to one another. Harvey hoped that when Jed was freed from prison, the extended family could all be more sociable, but first he needed to get his own house in order.

Harvey sighed and returned his attention to the affairs of Baltimore's governance. Less than an hour had passed since the session had begun, and the room was nearly cleared. The final cases involved everything from the need for more shovels and pickaxes to build barriers around the city's perimeter, to General Smith's third request for more cartridges and balls with which to arm the muskets.

Another overwhelming problem represented in the room concerned the mass of refugees flooding into the city. Some were family members of the militias pouring in from other states. Some were rural residents who had fled from lands that lay in the path of the anticipated British march, and who now sought shelter in the heavily armed city. With the city so engaged in defense, and with so many of the local merchants now serving under General Smith, services were running low, food was a problem, and so were sanitation and housing. The mayor referred people to various other rooms where committees and subcommittees had been set up to handle the remaining problems.

When the room was cleared he leaned back and rubbed his eyes. "Our city's problems are escalating as the number of people arriving increases. We'll need to convene another meeting of the Committee of Safety and Vigilance to find solutions to these problems. General Smith wants us to pull answers out of thin air, but we simply can't do it."

Rather than listen to the mayor whine, Harvey stroked his ego. "I suppose it's a sign of his confidence in you that he believes you can manage things."

"You're right. He is a brilliant man—from his heroic service as a commander in the Revolution, to his political career here in Maryland and in the U.S. Congress and Senate. Though everyone said there was no money with which to reinforce Baltimore's defenses, Smith found a way. You do know that I personally recommended him to lead our forces here in Baltimore, don't you?"

Harvey smiled. "It was a brilliant choice, sir."

"Yes, yes it was. Look at what he's done to fortify this city and Fort McHenry, Harvey. He's served my constituency well."

Harvey smiled inwardly at the mayor's ability to deliver himself a compliment within every one he offered to others. "Yes, he's a great man whom I'm looking forward to working with directly in these coming days."

"You still plan to abandon this office? General Smith has fifteen thousand men serving him. You serve your city and nation best by helping me hold Baltimore together. And besides, at forty-six years, you are beyond the legal requirement for service."

"You also have an army of advisors at your disposal, Mr. Mayor, and the role of legal advisor is rather unnecessary under the circumstances. I want my service to the military to be more than merely handling acquisitions. I want this leave of absence so I can actually serve with the militia. I volunteered despite my age because someday I'd like my children to know their father fought for the principles he believes in."

"Children? Aren't you and that inhospitable wife of yours separated?"

"I've been rethinking our situation. And I'll ask you kindly not to refer to her in such a manner, sir. After all that's transpired in Washington, I've given our marriage some additional thought. In the total scheme of things, the things of man matter little. Our monuments fall, our cities burn. Only our families, and the imprint each individual makes on the lives of others, really amount to anything. I want to give my marriage another try."

"My apologies, Harvey, but does your wife want any of these same things? She seems as unsociable a woman as any I've met. Now that you've provided her with a home and an income of her own, she might be quite content to live her life alone."

That thought hadn't occurred to Harvey. "She still comes to see me several times a week for things that could easily be settled by letter. No, I feel she is as lonely as I. Her mother is unstable and her father always catered solely to the woman's needs, leaving his daughters without a real parent of any kind. My wife has no experience with the possibilities a good family can offer, and rather than rising to serve as the head of my home, I was a mouse who ran from her outbursts. We failed each other. So, after the war, I'm bound and determined to give it another go."

The mayor nodded. "So you report to General Smith tomorrow?"

"Yes. I'll leave as soon as we're adjourned for the day. I've trained my co-counsel to handle all my duties, so you shall be well served in my absence."

Mayor Johnson extended his hand. "Then I wish you well, Harvey, and I hope the war ends quickly and you are very soon returned to us."

The mayor's kind words warmed Harvey as he walked the five blocks to his town home to pack and attend to the essentials men must attend to, however unlikely their need. He wrote a note with the names and addresses of Myrna, his parents, and his attorney, then feeling the entire process was a bit melodramatic, he wrote a brief, humorous poem:

> *Conscientious Harvey went to war,*
> *Wrote this list and closed the door.*
> *When I get home I'll laugh at my worry.*
> *If I get shot, call my attorney.*

Harvey chuckled at himself, and then in a bold, spontaneous move he added,

Myrna,

It is said that when a man goes to war, he carries his loved ones in his heart. That's where you are, my dear—in my heart—and when I return, shall we not make another try?

Your husband,
Harvey

He patted the note and smiled, knowing that if Myrna came by looking for him and happened upon the note, her heart might soften regarding him.

The next morning he dressed in his custom-tailored militia uniform. He admitted to certain vanities, his wardrobe being one, though he sadly admitted that he had allowed his appearance to deteriorate since moving from the home he and Myrna had so briefly shared.

Once dressed, Harvey left the bustling city and all its complications, heading his dappled horse to Hampstead Hill, also known as Loudenslager Hill, where the camp serving as General Smith's headquarters was set. Harvey had been to the camp on many occasions, serving as the liaison between the mayor and the general, but not for nearly a week, and today provided a spectacle he could only imagine from the works of great artists who captured scenes of war in their paintings. Though stands of oak clustered in several directions, he was still afforded views of Forts McHenry, Covington, and Ferry Point; the Babcock Battery and several other earthen batteries; North Point; and the Chesapeake Bay. And everywhere he looked, there were people—soldiers, and the women who camped with them to cook and tend to their laundry and medical care.

Harvey found Samuel Smith, the venerable old major general, standing under a canvas fly with several advisors. They were all peering through spyglasses toward the Patapsco and conversing animatedly with one another.

Smith looked as if he too had been pulled from a canvas. Tall and strong, with a face carved deeply by life and experience, his very presence instilled confidence and courage. He was over sixty years old, but he showed no sign of frailty. Rather his body was lithe and lean, moving with the grace of a gentleman, while his voice thundered with the authority gleaned from decades as a statesman.

Smith moved to his desk under the fly and began dashing off notes. When the initial flurry of activity settled, Harvey moved closer to report in.

"Lieutenant Baumgardner!" Smith called out in welcome, which thrilled Harvey. "What brings you here today in full military dress?" He turned to his companions and said, "Gentlemen, if you have not met my friend Lieutenant Baumgardner, prepare for a treat. He possesses an inexhaustible collection of anecdotes and stories that will delight you. He's also a fine attorney and the aide to Mayor Johnson."

Harvey bowed and blushed, slapping his arms nervously down to his sides. "You are too kind, General Smith. Today, I am here to report to you full time. I've resigned my services to the mayor in order to serve on the battlefield with you."

Smith didn't respond at first, but Harvey worried as he watched his future commander's face cloud. "Have you any military experience, Lieutenant? You've been a priceless clerical aide, but have you served on the field?"

"Well . . . well . . . no, sir, though I—I fulfilled my militia rotations last year, and I'm a fine fox hunter and an able shot. I won the city's turkey shoot twice in five years." He held up two fingers but quickly folded them into his palm when he noticed the other officers stifling their laughter. General Smith merely smiled. Harvey knew how foolish he sounded, and he regretted his words as soon as they were spoken. Though he often acted overly gregarious to compensate for his innate shyness, he was not a foolish man by nature. He'd been the valedictorian at Harvard the year he graduated, and here he was spouting off like a schoolboy in order to serve with these men.

Smith rose and placed his hand on Harvey's shoulder. "There are many places to serve your country, Mr. Baumgardner. All are noble if they place you where you are needed. You have done for these troops what no one else could do, arranging for supplies when the coffers were empty, serving as the liaison between the mayor and me, freeing me to focus my attentions here, on the field. I wouldn't trade a hundred armed sharpshooters for the service you have rendered."

Harvey picked nervously at his fingers while he absorbed the praise that simultaneously delighted and disturbed him. "Thank you, General, but I would . . . I'd so love to have a taste of the experiences here, something to share with my family someday."

The general's urgency softened to understanding. "The glory is thin behind a desk. I understand that. We're in a difficult moment here, Lieutenant. We received word yesterday that the British left Tangier Island and are now sailing north. We suspect they mean to land their troops to the east and make a run on Baltimore from there while their navy assaults us from the water. I'm afraid the battle is only hours away."

"Could I not stay for a few days, sir? Is there no service I can render to you from this vantage point? I could serve as your secretary, or deliver messages to the troops. And if you need something from the mayor's office, I'd be right here to advise you, and ready to dispatch myself back to town as needed. I could save valuable time by being at your disposal."

Smith studied Harvey's earnest face. "You are too effective at arguing your case, Lieutenant. Yes, I'll agree to your request. I'll be delighted to have you on my staff during this engagement. I hope you won't live to regret what you will see."

CHAPTER 21

Saturday, September 10, 1814
At the mouth of the Patapsco River near North Point, Maryland

John Skinner found Francis Scott Key standing on the deck of the HMS *Surprise,* staring into the watery depths as if avoiding the view of the shoreline where Baltimore's vast reach appeared as a thin line on the northern horizon. It pained Skinner to note the changes that had occurred in Key's posture over the past week—the rounded shoulders, the bent head, the loss of bounce and energy in the generally hopeful man. Key's jacket hung more loosely over his already thin torso. Skinner knew it was true of himself as well. Night after night they had sat at the table with the British officers, listening to their war plans and casualty figures, unable to swallow their food. Skinner and Key said little, hoping not to give the British further excuse to unleash the power of their might on Baltimore, but now it seemed to matter little.

Skinner walked over to Key, a man he had only met a week earlier. He felt a bond with this man, forged from sharing this horrible burden. He laid his hand on Key's back and realized he was in the midst of prayer. Embarrassed by his interruption of the tender moment, Skinner was comforted by Key's hand, which moved to cover his as it rested on the railing, though the man's head remained bowed. In time, Key raised his head a few degrees to study the ribbon of land ahead. "It is going to happen, isn't it?

I know we've heard them discuss every disgusting detail, but I kept hoping that perhaps—just perhaps—it was all for show. But it's not, is it?"

Skinner swallowed the lump that had formed in his throat. "No, it's not. Admiral Cochrane is claiming the *Surprise* as his flagship. He planned to move us again and I asked him to please return us to our own vessel. He has agreed, with the provision that an armed detachment remain with us to prevent us from trying to escape and warn our people."

"As if there was anything at all we could do," Key said cynically. "And Dr. Beanes? We've not even seen him to know if they've kept their word regarding his treatment."

"We'll know soon enough. He'll be moved with us."

Key's expression turned bitter. "Five days we've been held captive, holding their promise to release William into our hands, and yet they've continued to treat him hostilely while denying us the right to see him or assess his condition. I'm tired of their games and intrigue."

"It's nearly past . . . nearly past."

Key's attention shifted to the west, toward the point where Fort McHenry sat, her grand flag but a speck against the late-afternoon sky. "Do you think our forces know the fleet is here?"

"The British spied lookouts at our batteries frantically signaling to one another, but it was just a matter of amusement to our hosts. They know their Congreve rockets will still give them the element of surprise as soon as they are launched. You saw them used in Washington, didn't you?" Key nodded numbly, and Skinner went on. "Those hellish things sail so far that the fleet can anchor beyond reach of any retaliatory strike we might attempt to launch, leaving them untouchable. We may likewise be at risk when Fort McHenry's big guns fire at the fleet."

"Six nights ago we sat with the men of Fort McHenry and heard the story of Major Armistead's bold, defiant flag. I wonder how long it will continue to fly, or if we shall ever see those brave men alive again . . ." Key's voice caught and broke before he continued. "You met my brother-in-law, Captain Nicholson. He is married to my wife's sister. They and their children live right in the city. The devil is coming for them, and I can do nothing to warn them."

Skinner again reached for Key's shoulder, squeezing it gently. "They'll be bringing Dr. Beanes up and then it will be time to transfer. I hope Captain O'Malley and the crew are well. I feel terrible for dragging him into this when his presence served no purpose."

"Perhaps if I make another appeal to the British—for the women and children."

"Our begging is a matter of disgrace to them. No, we'll gather up Beanes, and then make your continued petitions to the only hope that remains—to God Almighty."

Skinner took Key to a door near the stern that led to the hold, where British sailors were attending to their duties. Key was uncommonly rigid and stern-faced, while Skinner remained aloof, knowing he might still need to advocate in their behalf.

The creak of the door opening caught both of their attentions. A haggard, broken man appeared in the opening. His graying hair was slicked to his head from sweat, curling haphazardly at the ends into the tangled sprawl of his gray beard. His filthy hands shook as they rushed to shield his deprived eyes, which squinted into pained slits from the sting of light cast by the lowering sun as it slipped through a cloudy horizon. He grimaced and cowered as he seemed to notice the outline of figures standing directly before him.

"William?" Key said in disbelief. "Oh, William!" He groaned as he swept Dr. Beanes into his embrace. "Dear, dear friend, what have they done to you?"

"Frank? Frank Key? Is that you?" Beanes clutched at his friend like a frightened child. The man began to weep. "Thank you, God! Thank you. Thank you!"

Key lifted him and began scrutinizing his condition, touching his arms and lifting the proud old physician's drooped head. "Dear William, you're still in your nightshirt."

"I asked them to allow me to dress, but before my pants were fully on they dragged me out of the house. I tucked it in as best I could."

Key's expression betrayed his sorrow. "Did they hurt you? Can you walk? And where are your glasses?"

"I grabbed them off the nightstand by my bedside, but I dropped them in the scuffle. I hope my sweet wife was able to find them. But how did you know to come for me?"

"Mr. West and Frannie Pearson sped to Georgetown to report your capture. Timothy Shepard tracked me down and we petitioned Dolley Madison to get the president's support." Key smiled. "Your seizure has caused no small stir in Washington."

Beanes clutched desperately at Key. "But it remains? The presidency? And the Constitution?"

Key's eyes darted to their captors, judging their reaction to the questions. Proudly, boldly, he replied, "Yes, William. They both remain."

A prisoner cortege waited to move them to their cartel ship, which had pulled alongside the *Surprise*. Markus stood on the deck with a smile as wide as his outstretched arms. With great care, the group assisted Beanes, who was weak but determined as he climbed down the rope ladder onto the *President*. There was another warm greeting as Markus drew him into his own arms, and once the good doctor was settled, the British details rotated and a British captain took control of the American vessel's helm, moving her into the center of the British fleet.

CHAPTER 22

Sunday, September 11, 1814
Baltimore, Maryland

It was early morning when a horse thundered through camp to the tent where General Samuel Smith maintained the headquarters for the Baltimore defenses.

"A rider's in, General," reported his aide. "The scouts at the Lazaretto Battery are reporting that the British fleet has reached the Patapsco. They're rallying near North Point!"

General Smith called for Lieutenant Harvey Baumgardner and said, "Send a courier to the mayor. Tell him to sound the alarm!"

As Harvey hurried to attend to that duty, General Smith gathered his officers around the map that stretched across one of the three tables set up under the canopy. General Winder, commander of the forces at Bladensburg, was here now as well, and General Smith looked to him and then leaned over and tapped the spot marked North Point on the eastern bank of the bay at the southern confluence of the Patapsco River. "This is where they intend to land."

A general named John Stricker, commander of the Third Brigade of the Third Division, Maryland Militia, moved battle markers to new positions on the map. "It's fourteen miles from there to the city if it's a yard. My men drill there. We know every rock and tree along that path."

Stricker's highly touted brigade was composed primarily of men from Baltimore City, a proud crew comprised of five regiments, including the elite Fifth Regiment, affectionately dubbed the "Dandy Fifth." He was a solid soldier, but a Baltimorean through and through. Two years earlier, during the infamous Baltimore riot, Stricker gave his word to safely convey the rebels to jail, where they were turned over to the protective custody of Mayor Johnson. The then fifty-three-year-old Stricker was struck by a stone and nearly blinded while protecting his charges, but once the mayor assumed custody of the men, Stricker went home. And when the mobs rushed the jail, Stricker refused to call out his militia, citing an unwillingness to have his men fire upon their neighbors. But now Stricker's men would face a common enemy. Would they stand fast when bayonets and rockets were raised by their foe? It was the great question.

Smith remained optimistically cautious. "The British strategy could play soundly into our defensive plans. Our numbers are large but most of our men have little training. We have three earthwork defenses between North Point and the city, and a large number of hastily constructed redoubts and entrenchments, but the work has been rushed and remains untested. Ultimately, our success will depend on the will of the men. If our forces get overrun we have positions to move back to, but you commanders must assure that your men pull back and return fire, rather than break and run."

The topic was an especially sensitive one to General Winder, whose loss at Bladensburg was primarily due to the lack of resolve in his troops. Stricker nodded to Winder and then declared to Smith, "My men will not flee the field, sir. You can count on each of them to do his duty."

"Excellent. General Winder and his men will provide support." Smith turned to Captain John Rodgers, a sea dog still roiling with fury after the disaster in Washington. "You command the most battle-tested men in our forces, Captain. The remaining flotillamen have faced everything in the British arsenal, and your seamen and marines claim to be hungry for the fight Alexandria denied them by capitulating. Now is their time to rally. I need your men to secure all the batteries. Baltimore will not be another Alexandria. This city will not cower and furl her flag. Tell your men I'm depending on them to batter that fleet before the British guns can destroy our entrenchments."

"The assignments are made, sir. Commodore Barney's men are split between the Lazaretto Battery and Fort Babcock. And my men are as ready and determined as they. These men will not falter, General."

"Good. The Safety and Vigilance Committee meets tomorrow to vote whether or not to proceed with a blockade of the Patapsco. If the measure passes, I'll want you to see to it personally. We cannot allow British ships to get past Fort McHenry. Our city's defenses are too soft to withstand British mortars and rocket fire. McHenry must not fall, and those batteries and the blockade must hold the British fleet at bay." General Smith's expression was dour. Everyone knew how fragile the plan was. If one part failed, Baltimore would be lost.

They spent the next few hours laboring over every detail until they heard cannons firing off the alarm, warning citizens that battle was now imminent.

Stricker looked at his watch. "Noon. Most of the city is still in church. Let us hope a prayer for the troops was offered at every pulpit."

General Smith nodded. "And let us learn from the mistakes at Bladensburg, gentlemen. We'll not sit here and wait for the British to come knocking on our door. I want to take the fight to them so they've no misunderstanding about Baltimore's resolve. Give your men my best, Captain Rodgers. General Stricker, gather your men and prepare to pull out. I want the enemy to walk off their ships and straight into American musket fire."

Stricker and Rodgers bowed, but before the men left the perimeter General Smith began utilizing Harvey. "Lieutenant, we expect the British to land here at North Point, and that should bring them roughly along this path." He drew a relative marching route that meandered toward the city. "Make copies of this and distribute it to all the generals, please."

Harvey nodded and quickly set to work. He read the names of every farm and building along the projected path, and his heart nearly stilled when he realized the Gorsuch Farm lay directly on the trail. "General, am I reading this correctly? Are you now expecting that the British will march close to the Gorsuch Farm and along this route?"

"Yes. Taking into account the terrain and where the more forested places make moving troops too difficult, we can assume they will generally follow this route."

"Sir, my in-laws' Coolfont Farm lies near this road. My wife's mother is ill and her father is an older man with no sons. Except for their slaves, they are all alone there. Perhaps I could—"

"Lieutenant!" Smith raised an eyebrow at Harvey. "Every man on this battlefield has family at risk. For some it is their very own farms and children who lie in harm's way, but if we each lay down our arms, desert the line, and run home, all will be lost. You're a soldier now. It's what you chose. Now it's time to act the part. I need those maps marked and distributed."

"Yes, sir," Harvey replied with a heavy heart.

Sunday, September 11, 1814
Fort McHenry

Three miles south, at Fort McHenry, Abel stood lookout on the ravelin, looking deep down the throat of the Patapsco River. The British fleet was now visible from McHenry's wall.

He was so consumed with worry he didn't hear the footsteps behind him, or the snickers of the other three Baltimore Fencibles on duty with him who saw the trick about to be played. Abel was deep in thought, fretting about Markus, who was five days overdue, and wondering if yet another Willows man had been taken prisoner by the British.

He considered brawny, scrappy Markus, knowing it was unlikely he would be taken without a fight. More likely than not, he figured, Markus was hurt, or worse. Abel's fists clenched at the thought, and he was in this tense posture when the joke was sprung. Five buckets of cold well water were thrown at him simultaneously, stunning him and temporarily disorienting him. As he lurched in reaction to the cold, Hildebrand and Skully came up from behind him and gave him a push, yelling, "Fly, nigger! Fly!"

Abel dug in his mighty legs and feet and pushed back against the forward thrust. Swinging his arms backwards as a counterbalance, he caught Skully in the face with his elbow. He heard a crunch and then a squeal of pain. Hildebrand's attention turned to his friend, and in that moment, Abel twisted and caught the man in a chokehold, while the other assailants ran down the steps. Both Captain Nicholson and Sergeant Carpenter arrived to find Skully's face covered in blood and Hildebrand looking slightly blue from lack of oxygen.

"Let him go, Abel!" the sergeant ordered. Abel's black eyes sent Hildebrand a warning glare before he complied.

Hildebrand coughed and sputtered as he was released, but as soon as he was able, he began pointing at Abel and shouting, "He tried to kill me. I'll see you hang, boy!"

Sergeant Carpenter studied Abel, who stood before the officers, dripping wet but offering no excuse. Carpenter turned to the other three Fencibles and asked, "What happened here?"

The three men shrugged but said nothing.

Captain Nicholson seethed in obvious disgust. "I think the truth is fairly obvious, Sergeant." He walked a few paces away, shaking his head with each step. Suddenly, he spun on his heels and glared at the three men, his face a changing landscape of worry and anger. "Our ground forces have begun their march to North Point, where the British fleet is anchored and preparing to land troops. We think they're also going to make a naval assault on this fort within hours—not days, gentlemen! Hours! An entire city, and perhaps the Union itself, may well rest on our ability to repel this assault, and you'd rather go at one another. You hate each other more than you hate the enemy who wants to burn you out." He glared at Hildebrand and the three mute members of his Fencibles, and gestured toward Skully. "Get your partner to the infirmary, and once he's patched up, all of you wait for me in my office!"

Abel remained at attention well after the group was gone, bearing the scrutiny of his officers.

The captain sighed. "What are we going to do, Abel? I can't have such disputations amongst my troops."

"I didn't—"

"I know who started the trouble, but that's of little concern to me. Those men are excellent artillerists, and your strength makes you an outstanding asset, but together, you are all worthless to me! So what am I to do?" The captain ran his hand through his hair in frustration. "Pack your things, Abel."

Abel's mouth fell open and his heart pounded in his chest.

"I'm sending you and Caleb to join Colonel Foster's militia group for a few days, to let this simmer down a bit."

"But am I—am I still in the army?"

"For the time being, Abel." Nicholson turned and began to walk away.

"Captain, I'd turn myself inside out to stay under your command."

Nicholson stopped but did not face the big man. "It would just about take that, Abel, but I don't really think you would, or even *could* do what it would require for you to fit in." He finally turned, sympathy etched into the lines of his boyish face, and then he resumed his stride to the edge of the ravelin, where he stopped to stare out at the water.

Sergeant Carpenter looked down and shook his head. "Do you understand what he's trying to say to you, Abel?"

"No, sir."

"Have you noticed how well the men tolerate Titus, even befriend him? But they can't abide you, and do you know why? You see, they don't fear Titus. They still feel superior to him, and Titus accepts that. But you see yourself as their equal. You're better educated than many of the enlisted men, and you're smart in other ways as well. Add that to the fact that you're bigger and stronger than most of these men, and you become a threat to what most whites see as the order of things. Most whites simply aren't ready for slaves to become freemen and take their full place in society. And now that the men know about your temper and your fear of water, they'll taunt you until you retaliate, knowing that no white jury or judge will ever tolerate that."

It was the attitude Abel expected from most whites, but he hoped he could expect better from these men. "Are you saying I need to bow and scrape if I want to stay in the army?"

"This isn't about the army, Abel. This is about your life. Those men don't merely want to drum you out of the military. They want to destroy you. You're caught up in a second war, one with stakes just as high as this one with the British."

Abel called across the ravelin to Captain Nicholson. "Do you agree with the sergeant? Will they never accept me unless I dip and beg? Is that your advice to me?"

Nicholson sat on the edge of the ravelin and met Abel's eyes. "All we can do is help you clearly see what you are up against, and then you must answer that for yourself."

"I joined the army so I could determine my own future and my children's futures."

"It's not as simple as that. Even men of good conscience have allowed themselves to dip their fingers into the alcohol of slavery, knowing that once tasted, it is difficult to set aside. You know how I revere President Jefferson. He knew from the day he laid out the Declaration of Independence that slavery was an evil that would divide our country, but it was only figuratively referred to in that document because the nation wasn't ready to let it go. Over the years he has written and spoken on the subject in the strongest of terms, yet he still maintains slaves on his property. Oh, he treats them very well, like family in some instances, but Jed Pearson treated you well while you were still enslaved. That was never enough for you then and I doubt you'll accept anything less than equal treatment here, a thing you are not likely to enjoy so long as there are men here who can't yet accept that mindset."

Abel looked from Sergeant Carpenter to Captain Nicholson. "Can you, sirs?"

Sergeant Carpenter spoke first. "Those men-at-arms should be your brothers. They are fearful and narrow-minded, but they are your reality if you remain, Abel. Unfair though it may be, how you perform together is all that matters to me, and that largely depends on them accepting you. That is, if the captain decides to even keep you."

Abel looked squarely at Nicholson. "Captain, I want to remain. Will you have me, sir?"

"For now, do as I ask and stay with Colonel Fosters' group for the next few nights while I try and talk some sense into that group."

Abel pressed him again. "But you will consider allowing me to stay, won't you, sir?"

"Yes, Abel. No one gets everything he wants, no matter how noble his cause, but some things are worth fighting for. Each man must decide for himself what he's willing to lay his life down for." The captain turned to stare out at the water. "Some fight only for themselves, some do it for the hope of a better world, some sacrifice themselves for another."

"You're thinking about Markus and Mr. Key and the delegation now, aren't you?"

234

The captain placed his hands on the grassy perimeter of the earthwork and leaned on it heavily. "They should have been back days ago. They went to free one man, and it appears they may have forfeited their own freedom instead."

"Leastwise they were free to choose their own course. That's all I'm asking for."

It was a scene not unlike the day the Baltimore militias marched proudly out of the city, naively expecting to rout the British from Washington, with banners waving and the citizenry cheering. And though the outcome of that grueling march had sorely sobered both the new recruits and the more tenured citizen-soldiers alike, the Third Brigade set out again at 3:00 on the afternoon of the eleventh, dressed in their blue coats and white trousers, with their hearts filled with bravado and ballyhoo. They were now swelled to fifteen hundred men with the addition of several companies of Maryland Artillery, the First Maryland Rifle Battalion, and the Fifth Cavalry Regiment, but it was the Dandy Fifth that led the way. They had their packs loaded with one day's rations and thirty-six rounds of ammunition. They were a predominantly volunteer army composed of tailors, shoemakers, carpenters, teachers, grocers, farmers, doctors, and more, all bearing arms and filled with fire and spit, simultaneously bound for North Point and for glory.

Stricker followed General Smith's orders and marched his men seven miles southwest to a narrow section of land called Patapsco Neck, bounded on the west by Bear Creek, and on the right by the Back River. All along the way, his men created obstacles to hedge up the enemy and slow their progress. Upon reaching the Methodist meetinghouse, Stricker called for the column to make camp while he sent scouts out to find the British line and reconnoiter the area. General Smith's military prowess was no surprise to Stricker, and yet he had to applaud the old war dog on choosing an excellent spot for their first entrenchment. Two primary Baltimore roads—Long Log Lane and Trappe Road—crossed at this juncture, and the funnel-shaped Patapsco Neck gave the Americans a strategic advantage, requiring the British to bunch up in order to pass.

Furthering strengthening his defensive position, Stricker positioned Captain Biays and his one hundred forty cavalrymen three miles further south at the Gorsuch Farm. These mounted soldiers would be the first to come upon the British column, with the ability to speed away to the second line, positioned one mile further north of the Gorsuch Farm and two miles from Stricker's main line. Captain Dyer's trained sharpshooters were positioned here near a blacksmith shop on Long Log Lane, trained to hit and run on the enemy as they approached.

By 10:00 PM, the American stage was set, filled with men anxious to engage the British, who, unbeknownst to them, were still shipboard and asleep in the Patapsco River.

Fourteen miles south, the British fleet was making final preparations. Ross stood at the ship's railing, staring off at the American shore where British boots would land early the next morning, on the 12th of September. He heard a voice from behind.

"Are you also unable to sleep?" Admiral Cochrane came and stood beside him, his hands grasping the rails and working them as he too now stared landward. "George Cockburn has been sleeping like a baby since 7:00." The two men huffed sarcastically at their comrade-in-arms.

"Lamps are still lit on the American cartel ship. Apparently, they aren't sleeping either."

"How could they, knowing the new world they've built is changing moment by moment? The *Iphigenia* will soon arrive in Liverpool, and Captain Smith will inform Parliament and the Prince Regent of our victory at Washington, and everything will change in Ghent. The peace negotiations will stall, or our delegates will press John Quincy Adams and his American delegation to surrender vital concessions to us or face more of the same. And then, two weeks later, another ship will arrive with news of our victory here. And then we'll capture New Orleans and control the Mississippi, and the Americans will have no recourse but to sign over whatever we require to obtain peace."

"Do you feel that certain about tomorrow?"

"Robert, what were you hoping to find by staring at that shoreline?"

Ross couldn't face his friend. "Assurance, I suppose."

Cochrane laid a hand on Ross's shoulder. "There is no such thing in war, Robert. We both have lived long enough to know that, but we've gone over the plan until we've exhausted every concern. The plan is solid, and reports from spies tell us that the quality of Baltimore's defenses has been greatly overestimated. McHenry remains a formidable obstacle, but once the city falls, the fort will quickly follow. And we will have substantially reduced her strength by that time with our bombardment. Once you and your men are entrenched, we'll begin the assault of Fort McHenry as a diversionary tactic. Our big guns will pound the fort, and I daresay those American militia forces will respond as they always have when our Congreve rockets are fired. Their lines will break, either in fear or because they are racing to support McHenry. In either case, we will reduce their army's numbers, opening the city to your superior ground forces while enabling us to protect your flank with our firepower."

"Yes," Ross replied. "The plan is solid."

"Where is that pre-battle vigor? Are you questioning our decision to go?"

Ross smiled. "No. Second guessing is deadly in battle. I know that, and yet I cannot shake this feeling of dread. To how many grieving wives and mothers will I find myself writing letters in the coming days?"

"George Cockburn would ask you how many schools and jobs and hospitals the Crown will be able to build if we are successful at breaking America's back at the negotiating table because we were victorious here."

"Of course. And he'd be right, as much as I hate to equate men's lives with such things."

"We often fight to maintain commerce, which drives government so government can care for its people." Cochrane sighed. "Now get some sleep, Son. It's nearly 8:00 and you launch at 3:00."

CHAPTER 23

Monday, September 12, 1814
Baltimore, off the North Point shore

It had been a restless evening for Major General Ross and a busy one for the cooks, who prepared three days' rations for each man to place in his pack. As the mission would be conducted as a coup-de-main, or surprise attack, the men were required to carry everything they would need for the entire engagement. Twenty rounds of ammunition were added to the sixty each soldier normally carried. Additionally, for such a rapid expedition, each man packed only a blanket, a spare shirt, and pair of shoes. Personal items like brushes and razors were divided between pairs of comrades who would carry and share the items.

The men slept in their clothes to be ready to disembark at a moment's notice. Most were packed and asleep quite early, but Ross found Lieutenant Gleig awake in his berth after 8:00 PM, writing a letter as the general prepared to lay his own head down.

"Lieutenant? You should be resting."

"Yes, sir. I'm finishing up a letter to my family, just in case, sir."

Ross sat on a stool by Gleig's bed.

"Arthur Ramsey was my best friend, sir. Losing him as we did, well, it makes a man realize how fragile life is."

"He was still alive when he was carried aboard the *Iphigenia*. Perhaps the surgeons were able to save him."

"I heard about his wounds. I believe I'd rather die straight off than live maimed that way."

"Are you frightened about tomorrow, Lieutenant?"

"That's just it. I feel invigorated, in a nervous sort of way. It's hard to explain, but I wrote it in a letter to my parents so they would know I wasn't afraid, just in case."

He handed the letter to General Ross, pointing to two specific paragraphs.

> *But no man, of the smallest reflection, can look forward to the chance of a sudden and violent death, without experiencing sensations very different from those which he experiences under any other circumstances. When the battle has fairly begun, I may say with truth that the feelings of those engaged are delightful, because they are, in fact, so many gamblers playing for the highest stake that can be offered. But the stir and noise of equipping, and then the calmness and stillness of expectation, these are the things which force a man to think.*

> *On the other hand, the warlike appearance of everything about you, the careless faces and rude jokes of the private soldiers, and something within yourself, which I can compare to nothing more nearly than the mirth which criminals are said sometimes to experience and to express previous to their execution—all these combine to give you a degree of false hilarity (I had almost said painful, from its very excess). It is an agitation of the nerves, such as we may suppose*

*madmen feel, which you are inclined to wish
removed, though you are unwilling to admit that
it is disagreeable.*

Ross handed the letter back to Gleig.

"In the event the worse does happen, and I were to die, General Ross, do you think reading this will give my parents a measure of peace to know that I wasn't fearful?"

"I think it's beautiful—and quite accurate—and that it will make them very proud."

The lieutenant's letter energized and comforted Ross. Yes, they were gamblers playing for the highest stakes, and he was now anxious to play his hand. When he arrived at his cabin, he slipped into a brief sleep. He rose after 2:00 and stood confidently in the dim moonlight at the starboard rail of the *Surprise,* dressed in full regalia. It was a perfect night. The heat of the previous day was past, and a full moon shone brightly against a cloudless canvas, illuminating the shoreline and everything on it. The tide broke gently around the anchored fleet in a soft hush, disturbed only by the whispered voices of men as they rose and assembled.

In time, Admiral Cockburn joined him, watching his blue-jacketed marine detachments preparing to disembark. Ross's breast swelled with pride at the sea of red-jacketed warriors who stood shoulder to shoulder on the decks of the British fleet. The living machine began to move with precision, and within four hours nearly five thousand men and dozens of horses would be moved aboard barges and small boats, and would land on the shore from whence they would commence their march northward.

Bugle calls sounded and the soldiers moved into formation, directed by Ross and Cockburn, who were anxious to pull out and begin their march. The heat was already smoldering as three companies of light infantry led the way, with Cockburn's six hundred armed seamen nested in the middle between more infantry and marines. Ross issued orders to Colonel Arthur Brooke, his second-in-command, to remain at the landing site until the last of the forces were on shore, while he and Admiral Cockburn began their march. Brooke and the remaining men would follow in due time.

Less than an hour passed before three American horseback sentries, or vedettes, were captured. Cockburn pulled out his timepiece. "Forty-eight minutes and we have three prisoners. I'd say things are going very well."

Ross was elated. "We'll find a suitable spot for breakfast and interrogate them then."

"There's a family farm a mile ahead with ample room for all our troops. The family's name is Gorsuch. We've reconnoitered the area and it would make a safe place to break."

"Fine. Then ask the Gorsuch family if they would be so kind as to host a few British officers with a good, hearty breakfast."

The Gorsuch family obediently obliged. While eggs cooked and bacon fried, Ross and Cockburn turned their attentions to the captured American scouts, who exaggerated the number of Smith's militia troops while failing to mention Stricker's men, who were decidedly closer.

"Twenty thousand militia troops?" Cockburn said mockingly. "Do you take us for fools?"

Ross smiled at the scout. "I wouldn't care if the number is correct. All we'll be seeing are their backs as they retreat. Shall we have our breakfast?"

At the conclusion of breakfast, Ross thanked Mr. Gorsuch for the fine meal.

"Should I have the wife prepare supper for you and your company on your return this evening?" Mr. Gorsuch asked.

"My return? No," Ross answered. "I shall sup this night in Baltimore, or in hell."

By 7:00 AM the companions of the captured American spies were racing into camp with reports of the British landing. Stricker quickly moved his men into strategic positions, making the best use of his firepower. All was set as they awaited the enemy. A tense hour passed when word arrived that Ross, Cockburn, and their troops were breakfasting at the Gorsuch Farm. The arrogance of the situation made Stricker livid.

"Take an artillery company and a four-pounder to that farm and shake the British from that place!" Stricker said with a growl.

He had no sooner given the order when a false report of British positions sent his rifle corps scattering off the line, leaving Stricker struggling to quickly fortify the abandoned position.

Reconnaissance information grew thin for a time. The British were reportedly on the move again at 10:00, having progressed some five miles, but the American line was so fluid that Stricker scrambled to simply keep his own troops in place. By 1:00 PM, he had sent a small detachment of volunteers forward under the command of Major Heath. Following the sound of rifle fire, they soon drew near the advancing British line, but what no one realized was that another detail was also on the field—sharpshooters from Jed Pearson's squad at Bladensburg, Captain Edward Aisquith's company—some of whom had embedded themselves into trees, awaiting an opportunity to fire on the advancing British line.

"September 12th and it's as hot here as midsummer," Admiral Cockburn complained as he pulled his handkerchief out to mop at his brow. "My horse is lathered from the heat."

"At least it's cooler here in the woods," Ross answered.

"Yes, where we're picking through the trees like a flock of chickens."

"The Americans built and abandoned an impressive entrenchment a short distance behind us. They may still be near, expecting us to travel along one of the good roads. With any luck, our advance party will locate them first and then we can bring up reinforcements before they detect us—"

Deadly gunfire pierced the forest air, exploding bits of bark like shrapnel in such a random path that it was impossible to detect the location of the shooters. The British advance line returned fire, dropping a few of Heath's embedded American riflemen and setting some off in a rapid retreat, while others dug in amid the trees, determined to fight on.

"Can you determine the shooters' positions?" Cockburn asked as he pulled back on the reins to back his horse deeper into the brush.

Ross scanned the tree line for gun smoke. "It seems to be coming from multiple directions, even falling from the sky, though the number of guns is few. I'm going back. I'll return with the light infantry companies."

He and his aide-de-camp turned their horses and moved a few dozen yards away, oblivious to the fact that two eighteen-year-old American volunteers had set their sights on Ross's scarlet coat.

Daniel Wells and Henry McComas had chosen their perch well, some twenty feet above the ground in the thick boughs of an old tree. Captain Aisquith had hand-picked these men for their shooting skills. They had served with Jed Pearson on the line at Bladensburg, and now these two youngsters saw the best prize on the battlefield turning their way. They tracked Ross in their sights for a few seconds, and then in succession, they each fired.

Ross felt the sting in his right arm and the jerk of his torso before he registered the sound of the shot. He had experienced that feeling before—the queer about-face with death that Gleig had so eloquently described the night before. The prophetic timing of the man's thoughts did not escape him. But this was even more surreal than Gleig's description. More than pain, more than shock, Ross actually felt the life ebbing from him as he slumped forward. He seemed powerless to stop his fall. He didn't hear the sound of his aide-de-camp screaming, but he felt him at his side in an instant, catching him before his shoulder hit the ground.

He now began to vaguely register the frantic rush of boots and hoofs, narrated by the shouts of his aide-de-camp crying for a surgeon and summoning Admiral Cockburn. Events around Ross mattered less and less as his last conscious thoughts turned to the love of his life—his loyal wife. It pained him to think of her receiving the news. She had spent so many nights alone, loyally waiting for his return from wars, and far too many nights suffering a soldier's deprivations to come to the battlefield to nurse his broken body.

But not this time. He knew he would never see her again.

Cockburn came and knelt beside him, the admiral's expression of concern instantly shifting to disbelief and then to true sorrow. He took his comrade's hand. "But—but how is this possible? I was just with you, Robert."

Ross reached a frail hand to his neck and motioned to Cockburn. "The locket. Please see that my wife gets it. I commend her and my children to the care of my king and my country."

A swarm of stunned British soldiers raced to the scene, refusing to believe the news of their beloved commander until they saw it for themselves. Lieutenant Gleig was among those grieving soldiers watching as the general's aide swept past, crying that the general had been shot and begging for a surgeon. But the truth of the loss didn't sink in until they saw the general's horse plunging onwards, without its rider, the saddle and housings stained with blood.

The disbelief was the same for the rest of the men as Ross was loaded onto a cart for the harrowing five-mile journey over rough terrain back to the ship.

"Don't let them see me," Ross mumbled. "It will damage their morale before battle."

Despite his last request, the news of his death spread like fire. Admiral Cochrane had already moved half the fleet up the

Patapsco, positioning his ships for their attack on Fort McHenry. Ross's body was rowed to the *Royal Oak,* the very ship he had languished upon in the Patuxent as he debated whether or not to rescind his decision not to go to Baltimore. The question had now been definitively settled, and the hero of Bladensburg was stored in a barrel of rum to preserve his body until his interment.

Grief swept through the British troops as they learned of the devastating loss of the leader they loved and trusted. Their one consolation was that the shooters, Daniel Wells and Henry McComas, had been spotted in the trees and were now as dead as their general.

Ross's underling, Colonel Brooke, had overseen the last of the troops disembarking and was within a half mile of the shore when the news of Ross's death reached him. Dozens of issues faced Brooke as he raced to the front of the line and assumed command. He knew these men were devoted to Ross, but he also knew they were the finest soldiers in the world, and his faith in them proved well founded. Burying their sorrow, the soldiers picked up their guns, reformed their columns, and marched ahead two more miles to the Bouldin Farm. There they found Stricker's American forces embedded behind a fence and among the trees. Between the two armies lay a large, open field that would soon churn with artillery fire.

CHAPTER 24

Monday, September 12, 1814
North Point, Maryland

The British launch at North Point had proceeded so quietly that it was nearly over before Markus even knew it had commenced. He awoke to an endless relay of barges and small boats moving men and horses, and he knew the work of death and conquering would shortly begin. As he stood at the railing of the *President,* his paramount emotion was despair as he considered the helpless situation of his crew and his countrymen.

He and his crew watched the division of the fleet as seventeen ships—including Cochrane's temporary flagship, the *Surprise,* plus frigates, bombers, and a rocket-launching ship—broke from the rest of the fleet, moving north toward Fort McHenry. Markus and his men turned from time to time, hungry for glimpses of the fort's brazen banner, which still issued a challenge as she fluttered above the star-shaped garrison. They could now see the battle plan unfolding, and they would be forced to sit off North Point like guests at the Roman Coliseum, watching the destruction unfold.

The Britons and the Americans on the *President* stayed to themselves for the most part, each needing some separation during the tense hours. Several times over the course of the day the men could hear the unmistakable sounds of gunfire and cannon explosions. The Americans' mood was somber and filled with angst, surprisingly like that of their British guards, who also watched and worried.

In the early afternoon a new excitement began along the shore, which had finally become quiet after the final transport of soldiers. "Something's happened," whispered Skinner to the other Americans, whose rapt attentions turned to the shoreline.

Dr. Beanes squinted but was unable to see anything without his glasses. "What is it Frank? What's happening?"

"It looks as though several cavalrymen have raced to the waterfront followed by a detail of soldiers, but they're in no formation and they seem to be in distress."

The British guards moved to the railing and began conversing in hushed tones.

"A blanket-covered cart's bein' rolled up, Dr. Beanes," Markus said quietly. "I think the British've lost a man—a leader, by the look of things."

The British guards aboard the *President* peered anxiously through the spyglass, watching the body being lifted and moved to a boat. And then they saw the unmistakable marker, Ross's honorary sword, dangling by the side of the body. There was a haggard intake of breath as the shock settled over them, and then stunned silence as they tearfully watched the boat row to the *Royal Oak,* where the litter was lowered to bring the body on board.

"We'll allow your men their privacy," Skinner said to the British guards. When the Americans had slipped below deck, he looked at the group. "The fallen leader was General Ross. Their ground operation could now be in peril. What do you think, Captain O'Malley?"

Markus shook his head in worry. "Admiral Cochrane won't take this loss lightly. It's Washington all over again, boys, and just like when the sharpshooter fired on the peace delegation, the ante's now been upped. If anything, he'll use Ross's death to spur his men on. They'll fight like dragons now, and pity the city if they break through our lines."

★ ★ ★ ★ ★

Heath and his company raced back to Stricker's line after the skirmish, with an incredible supposition to share. "I think General Ross is dead!"

"What?"

"I can't be sure, but men were firing from the trees, and then the guns went silent and we heard men shouting for a surgeon. The entire line was disrupted!"

"It must have been Aisquith's men. The line would only have been disrupted if the casualties were high or if a leader was struck. How heavy were our losses?"

"About a dozen down. More were wounded. They're being tended to now."

"Recheck the battle lines. If Ross has fallen, his men will be roaring for a fight."

Stricker's theory soon proved true as the small British advance team met the Americans across Bouldin's field, fully containing them while their artillery and reinforcements hurried up the line. The British unleashed several of their legendary Congreve rockets, but during this engagement their inaccuracies made them more a spectacle than a threat, until one landed far off target, igniting a fire to the east.

"Check the map," Stricker ordered. "What property is ablaze over there?"

One of Stricker's captains pulled a map from his pack. "I believe it's Coolfont Farm, sir, owned by the Stansbury family."

"Relatives of General Stansbury? Send a detachment to save the family members."

The firefight increased in ferocity, lasting nearly an hour, though the results of the battle were difficult to assess as mud, dirt, tree litter, and bomb fragments sprayed the air. Casualties mounted on both sides, but Stricker began to see the weakness in his line. The Dandy Fifth fought valiantly, holding their ground and pummeling the elite British line, but few of the other American infantry or artillery companies were equally committed to defending their positions. Stricker dashed off a brief report of the situation to General Smith and handed it to an aide. "Deliver this immediately, and bring me word back."

The cavalryman took the note and raced for Baltimore and General Smith, who was monitoring the field through his spyglass from Hampstead Hill. He received the missive and read:

> *Owing to the disgraceful example set by men who pledged their honor to hold the line fast but who instead seem prone to abandon our flanks with inexcusable cowardice, I may be required to withdraw my troops to our previously determined secondary position. British rockets have set fire to the Stansburys' farm. As I believe they are relations of the general, I have sent a detachment to rescue survivors.*

General Smith studied Harvey Baumgardner, who had been riveted to the plume of smoke rising near his in-law's farm. "Lieutenant," Smith said, "was your wife a Stansbury?"

Harvey's eyes closed halfway as he braced for the worst. "Yes, sir."

"It's believed it is their farm the British set ablaze. Is your wife there, Harvey?"

"No, sir. Myrna's at our farm, to the north of the city."

"I'm glad for that. However, General Stricker is sending a detachment to attend to the survivors at Coolfont. Would you like to go along on that errand?"

Harvey shivered. "I would, sir."

"Very well. Return to General Stricker's position with this officer. Report back here after you've attended to your duties."

Harvey saluted and grabbed his hat, rifle, and haversack. An hour later he was on the field, regretfully having the military experience he had longed for. He chastised himself for his naiveté as he rode past wounded men pleading for relief. He reported in to General Stricker, volunteering to be part of the rescue detail.

Stricker stormed back and forth between unit commanders, exposing weaknesses in their lines. "The detail has already left, Lieutenant," Stricker informed him. Harvey's eyes widened and he froze in his place as the general went on. "Hurry now or stay, but do not delay, Mr. Baumgardner! If things worsen, as I fear they will, it will be too dangerous to send you later."

Harvey was visibly shaking as he mounted once more. He gave his horse a firm kick, and they bolted away from the Bouldin Farm toward Coolfont.

General Stricker turned back to his commanders and barked, "The flanks are beginning to fail! Look! Make better use of those cannons! Did you give the order to fall back?" A captain assured the general he had not, but the news was of no worth to Stricker, who realized that holding their tactical position was becoming increasingly unlikely, making any type of offensive strike unthinkable. The British had evidently come to the same deadly conclusion.

"Look, look!" Stricker yelled to the commanders of the Fifty-first and Thirty-ninth.

Stricker watched the perfect British line begin to push forward across the barren field toward his men. Yard by yard, the British line progressed, the soldiers reserving their cartridges until the Americans were in clear range. The American line fired a successful volley, dropping some of the enemy, but the red line moved on, undaunted. When the order was finally given for the British troops to fire, muskets and cannons filled the air with a deafening staccato. The cries of the American dying and wounded echoed across the field while their comrades ran in every direction, leaving their fallen behind. By 4:00 PM, disgusted and disgraced, Stricker gave the official order to pull back and regroup, leaving the British in control of the Methodist meetinghouse, where their own injured men were being sheltered.

The first retreat brought the American line a mile closer to the city. They assessed their casualties and braced for another British attack. Losses were lighter than expected—24 killed, 139 wounded, and 50 known men taken prisoner. Stricker was unsure of the ratio of British dead to wounded, but he knew more red coats lay on the field than blue. And even though they had been beaten back, at least his fleeing men had regrouped and not raced home as they had done in Bladensburg. Pride filled Stricker's heart as he considered who it was his little volunteers were slowing down—Ross's elite European guard, many of whom had served with the Duke of Wellington himself!

Stricker's spies returned, reporting that the British were standing down and resting. The general knew they had to be exhausted from their pre-dawn launch and march, but he also knew he was facing an enemy like no other, an enemy trained to push beyond fatigue.

When another battle engagement didn't immediately materialize, Stricker moved his line still closer to both the city and General Smith's entrenchment, to a place called Worthington Mills, six miles from the heart of Baltimore. General Winder and his men followed suit. An increasing number of incoming volunteers multiplied their numbers, adding a measure of much-needed hope to the group. Other volunteers poured in from Virginia and Pennsylvania as military riders pounded north and south with news of the British advance. Still, the evening was unsettling. A solid rain had begun to fall, adding to the misery of the day's humiliation on the field. Poised for a night assault, the Americans dug in and waited.

★ ★ ★ ★ ★

Every nerve in Harvey Baumgardner's terror-filled body was raw. He cringed over his incalculable ignorance—equating his precision at a turkey shoot to his readiness for war—marveling at how any man could have the courage required to face what he had seen today.

The rain fell, adding weight to his uniform and making every movement more difficult and unwieldy. He saw the patrol ahead and whipped his horse to catch up. The sound of pounding hoofs caused the Americans to spin their horses around and meet Harvey with raised muskets.

"No, no, no, no, no!" Harvey cried. "I've come to join you on General Smith's recommendation. The Stansburys are the parents of my wife."

"We're risking our necks to save a crazy old loon," one soldier remarked.

"Stop!" Harvey said. "Yes, she's troubled, but her death would cause great sorrow to her good husband and her daughters. Please, when we arrive, allow me to approach her first."

Another member of the group pointed to the sky. "The fire is spreading. Even with the rain falling, see how wide the plume is growing?"

Chills gripped Harvey as he considered the horror befalling the Stansburys, and the impact the loss of Myrna's parents would have on her. He kicked his mount and rushed ahead of the group, anxious to reach the farm. Behind him, the battlefield was eerily quiet.

It had been a year since he'd last visited Coolfont. Dread washed over him as he recalled the events of that day. Myrna had harangued him to visit the farm, to convince her father to assign her his power of attorney. After arriving at Coolfont, Myrna went upstairs to visit with her mother, leaving the men alone. Harvey raised the issue, and Bernard quickly agreed to limited terms, but what Myrna didn't know was that Bernard had sought Harvey's assistance in making modifications to his will, changes that would not please her.

As he rode on, he considered the odd relationships that existed within the Stansbury family. Beatrice, the oldest daughter, had fled her family to achieve a measure of happiness, and Hannah, the youngest, was for all intents and purposes disowned and dead to them in this life for marrying Jed Pearson. This left Myrna in the peculiar position of doting only-child and martyr, two roles she embraced fully. As traumatized as she would be over their deaths, that loss would force the need to read the will, and that would create another abyss between Harvey and Myrna at a time when he had hoped to mend things. He cursed the war and the fire.

A filthy blanket of smoke hovered over the farm's untilled fields, while a tree line obscured the view of the home and barn, where flames still leapt above the highest boughs. The scene beyond the trees was Armageddon—blistering heat, steam, and destruction. Now nearly consumed, the barn had evidently taken the rocket strike, and judging from the sickening smell of burned flesh and hair, Harvey assumed most of the horses had perished in the flames.

The fire was devouring the carriage house that stood between the barn and the farm's once-stately home, providing the flames access to the home, which was now fully engulfed.

The old stable hand, Mobey, sat in the rain with his hands covering his head. Harvey dismounted and ran over to him. "Mobey, where are Mr. and Mrs. Stansbury?"

Tears streaked his brown face. "Da slaves all run off 'cause they thought da British was settin' them free. Massuh Stansbury tried to get da missus out of da house, but she's crazy over da cannons and da fire. She just shot him with his own rifle. They's both inside in da fire!"

Harvey glanced at the raging inferno and decided to make an attempt to search for survivors. He had barely reached the porch when Susannah Stansbury burst through the front door onto the covered porch, still dressed in her nightclothes, and brandishing a pistol. Still lovely at fifty-three, her countenance was nonetheless menacing. Her green eyes were wild and wide, and her graying auburn hair was piled upon her head in complete disarray. Harvey noticed the bloodstain on the sleeve of her flannel gown.

"Stay away from me, you redcoat!" she screamed as she struggled to cock the pistol.

Harvey raised his hands defensively. "Please, Mrs. Stansbury, it's me, Bernard. I'm Myrna's husband. I've come to help you."

Susannah ignored him, as her complete attention was now focused on steadying her hand so she could ready the pistol for firing. Noting her shakiness and her mental state, Harvey supposed he had time to reach her before she could successfully fire a round.

Taking an anxious breath, he rushed toward her, hoping to overwhelm her before she could shoot, but as he reached the bottom step he heard the click as the gun cocked. There was neither time nor place to seek cover. He faced her with a plea for mercy and a prayer that recognition would hit her before her finger pulled the trigger.

She raised the gun directly at his chest and studied his face until her face softened into a welcoming grin. In a greeting as sweet as honey she said, "Mr. Baumgardner, how nice of you to come," while seemingly forgetting the gun she held aimed at his chest.

"The gun, Mrs. Stansbury. Please . . . point it away."

She looked at it and back to him, and her face clouded again, darkening into fear and then rage, and in an instant she pulled the trigger.

Harvey fell backwards in a heap in the mud, in full view of the remainder of his arriving group. Susannah Stansbury watched the uniformed horsemen riding in and heard their shouts as they kicked their horses and increased their pace. Shrieking wildly, she tossed the gun at them in defiance before running into the house and bolting the door behind her.

The soldiers pulled Harvey's body away from the house and checked his pulse, but there was none. The man had been murdered by the very woman for whom he had advocated minutes earlier. They saw her crazed face in the front window, hiding behind a lace curtain as she screamed and smacked the glass, ordering them to go. They next saw a pained man, with a crimson patch across his right shoulder and chest, clutching at her skirt, dragging himself to a stand beside her. He tried to pull her toward the door but she resisted, pushing him away. The soldiers saw him look toward the ceiling in terror as he slumped to the floor.

The soldiers looked up as well, just in time to see a cloud of sparks erupt over the roofline. There was a loud *whoosh* as the roof collapsed, turning the entire building into a merciless fireball, settling the fate of Bernard and Susannah Stansbury forever.

CHAPTER 25

Monday, September 12, 1814
Two miles south of Fort McHenry

It was 7:30 AM when the ship carrying the news of General Robert Ross's death reached Admiral Cochrane on the *Surprise,* which was anchored with his attack squadron two miles south of Fort McHenry. His personal sadness was as deep as his respect for this honorable young veteran, and his anger was multiplied that Britain's hero had been cut down by an amateurish enemy. He wanted retribution and he wanted the consequences to be severe, and Colonel Brooke would be his avenger. The decision to destroy the city or place it under contribution was solely up to Brooke.

Cochrane counted down the hours before the next phase of the battle would occur. Each unit had to play its part perfectly for the strategy to succeed. Brooke's troops would advance on the city, while Cochrane and the fleet began the bombardment of Fort McHenry, creating two active battlefronts that would divide the Americans' attentions and faculties. Partway into the assault on the fort, Captain Napier would command a third group in an attack up the Ferry Branch tributary, which lay along the lightly defended, marshy perimeter to the west of McHenry, guarded only by the Babcock Battery and a small fort named Covington. Cochrane believed each of these positions could be easily reduced with a few strategic blows, forcing the Americans to pull men from their line at Hampstead Hill, weakening their line to the east sufficiently to allow Brooke's men to punch through to Baltimore.

It was a good plan, but doubts still plagued Cochrane. He had agreed to this campaign in part because of Ross's skill and courage. Could he count on Brooke to perform as boldly? Doubts crept in again. Had Ross been careless? Were these American forces so very different from those at Bladensburg? Had Ross been right in predicting that the defeat in Washington could steel these people in ways he had not calculated?

The captain of the fleet, Admiral Codrington, encouraged Cochrane to cancel the attack. So many new variables had been introduced. The shallow waters of the Patapsco hampered his fleet, requiring him to rely only on his lower-draft vessels—frigates, a few bomb ships, and one vessel capable of launching the terrifying Congreve rockets. But Cochrane pressed on.

He awoke the next morning to a sky still heavy and hazy, which served as a solemn backdrop for the British vessels aligned in an arc facing Fort McHenry. There sat the bomb ships *Terror, Meteor, Aetna, Devastation,* and *Volcano,* with the rocket ship *Erebus.* Cochrane knew Brooke's men would begin their march toward the city at 6:00 AM, timed with the *Erebus*'s first rocket launch. It would have to be enough.

Tuesday, September 13, 1814
Fort McHenry

The restless defenders were alerted to the battle's onset by the hissing of the initial volley of three fiery rockets delivered from the *Erebus.* The rockets soared high over McHenry, bursting through the murky haze. Though they fell far from the target, they provided the expected signal to Brooke's land forces and also served as the Americans' first tutorial on what lay ahead.

Fort McHenry's military complement was normally one hundred soldiers, but with the influx of volunteers racing to her perimeter, over one thousand men were now committed to the fort's defense. They knew if Fort McHenry and the surrounding artillery batteries failed to hold back the British fleet, the British would sail toward the port of Baltimore, where those deadly guns would level the city and pound Hampstead Hill. At that point, Britain's ground forces would have free rein to lower the Stars and Stripes, raise the Union Jack over the city, and place Baltimore under tribute, or worse.

The five gun bastions, or points of the star-fort, were manned by regulars under Captain Evans, as well as by volunteers under Captain Nicholson, with whom Abel had initially served. Two companies of Sea Fencibles or naval militia, which included a detachment of Commodore Barney's flotillamen, were positioned to fight from the lower ranks of the fort, and six hundred of General Winder's infantrymen and Captain Foster's men were placed in the outer ditch or moat in case the enemy attempted a landing there. Abel was now stationed here.

The British rocket blast was followed by frigate shots that fell in the water, short of the fort. The ships sailed in closer, providing Armistead and his American soldiers with a rare opportunity to actively defend themselves.

"Stoke up the furnace and bring up the balls!" Armistead shouted to the men tasked with heating metal cannonballs until they were red hot and therefore able to ignite their targeted ships. He shouted to the Sea Fencibles, "Ready the twenty-four-pounders!" Then he ordered Nicholson and Evans to fire the forty-two-pounders. Soon every cannon in the fort was spitting out hot and cold cannonballs at a rate of up to three balls per minute per gun, pounding the frigates in the river.

McHenry's defenders could see wood splinter and hear the delayed echo of each hit, and they responded with cheers and joyous songs. Their celebration was short lived. The captains of the frigates quickly pulled up anchor and adjusted their sails, limping beyond the reach of McHenry's guns. Now the British bomb ships and the *Erebus*'s rockets ruled the day.

It was a cat-and-mouse game for a time as the bomb ships fired their first few rounds into the water, inching forward until they had obtained the desired firing range. McHenry's artillerymen remained vigilant, but their cannons' barrels were too short to match those of the bomb ships, and fewer balls hit their marks. By 2:00 PM, the British ships had calculated the perfect distance from which to pummel Fort McHenry from beyond the reach of her guns. Unable to mount an active defense, the powerless Americans stood by their guns in the pouring rain and watched helplessly as the British bombs sailed directly at them.

The two-hundred-pound spheres were fitted with a trailing, lit fuse that burned to the hollow, powder-filled center. When the bombs exploded high in the air, the jolting concussion was followed by hundreds of pieces of jagged shrapnel that ripped and tore whatever they touched as they fell. When the bombs exploded closer to the ground, those same pieces were propelled in a wide scatter pattern at speeds that penetrated walls and severed limbs.

On and on, the British fired without answer from the Americans, who stood by their guns in the downpour, praying a ship would advance forward so they could return effective fire. It was the ultimate ignominy for Abel, who suffered as he watched Titus standing by his gun on bastion two while another man stood in Abel's place on bastion one, filling the great guns with the forty-two-pound balls he had been trained to load and fire, while Abel stood in the rain with a useless musket watching the enemy bear down upon them.

A bomb flew directly at the line of infantrymen standing in the moat, and the men of Foster's company braced for the worst, scrambling to press themselves into the packed earthwork. Abel tucked Caleb beneath him, forming a shield over the boy just before the bomb exploded in midair a dozen yards before it reached them. Jagged chunks of shrapnel bit into their backpacks and the backs of their legs.

Reports of the damage and injuries from inside the fort kept coming. Captain Evans had a bomb land at his feet. Fortunately it never detonated, but another bomb killed one of the women as she raced within the fort's perimeter bringing refreshment to the soldiers. And there was nothing they could do to stop the barrage.

Abel saw the small fleet of twenty-four derelict vessels being towed to the mouth of the Patapsco near Fort McHenry in an effort to block the river's entrance and further hedge up the British naval advance on the city. The sailors dodged falling shrapnel as they rigged explosives and anchored the ships in place, scurrying from one vessel to another in a race to scuttle the hulls before the British guns could splinter them into ineffectiveness. Some men began hacking away at the hulls with axes, and Abel saw an opportunity to redeem himself.

Several small rowboats were pulled up on shore. Abel saw them and turned to Captain Foster. "I'm going."

"Are you sure?"

Abel nodded. "I'd rather face my worse fear than stand here like a target." He squeezed Caleb's shoulder and the frightened boy melted against him. "Stay right here beside Captain Foster, Caleb."

Caleb nodded tearfully, and Abel pulled away as Captain Nicholson's words ran through his mind, spurring him on and quieting his fears. *I believe we can do anything we want to do badly enough. . . . I believe we can do anything we want to do badly enough. . . .*

Abel pushed the nearest boat into the water and closed his eyes as he jumped inside. For a few seconds he just sat there, still as stone, grappling with his fear. He thought of his father besieged by the mill wheel and struggling to keep his head above the water.

I believe we can do anything we want to do badly enough. . . .
Abel looked at the men scuttling the ships. Then he picked up the
oars and began to row.

Robert Stockton, the scrappy young man assigned the
responsibility of creating the blockade, stopped momentarily to
assess whether the arriving man was a friend or foe.

Abel managed to offer a shaky hail. "Private Abel from
McHenry! I've come to help!"

Within moments of Abel reaching the fleet, a man standing
on a dilapidated schooner waved him over and pointed to a rope
ladder. Abel made a shaky transfer onto the schooner, whereupon
the man handed him an axe and led him down below deck. "The
name's Beverly, Abel. We're running out of time to rig them all
for detonation, so we have to sink a few the old-fashioned way.
Start hitting her below the waterline. Once you see water rushing
in, hightail it above deck."

Abel swung the axe with trepidation, fearing a full swing would
flood the ship too quickly, trapping him inside. The first cut produced
barely a trickle, but the second swing splintered a board and the third
opened a hole the size of his foot. The appearance of rushing water
made him dizzy and he trembled, his legs becoming too weak to bear
his weight. He wanted to sit down or vomit or both, but he knew if he
didn't keep moving the ship would be his grave.

The man named Beverly peered down below and said cheerily,
"Good job, Abel! A few more whacks should send her down."

The confidence in his voice buoyed Abel up, settling his
fears. He was now aware that even a gaping hole would require
several minutes to admit enough water to overwhelm the vessel.
With that reasoning, he swung the axe two more times, releasing
a gush of water that again made him weak-kneed. And then a
bomb burst nearby. The thunder of the explosion echoed in the
empty hull, which also reverberated from the watery spray and
splintered wood. Abel slogged through to reach the ladder as the
depth reached his ankles and then his shins. One arm held the axe

and the other reached for the next rung as he climbed up, but the water kept rising. When he reached the deck he could barely pull himself through the hatch. He had lain there for a moment when Beverly returned to him.

"Can you rig explosives?"

Abel sat up, gasped, and nodded.

Beverly handed Abel a keg and some fuses, then pointed to a brig. "Row to her and plant small charges in the stern and one in the belly whilst I give this old girl a few more beauty marks, eh? Remember, just make a hole big enough to sink her. We need the hull to remain intact." He patted Abel's arm as another close blast shook the air, raining hot, iron debris on the deck. One piece caught Abel in the shoulder, but his hand shot to it, raking it off. For three-quarters of an hour he worked to ready the old brig. Then he signaled to Beverly, who in turn signaled to Robert Stockton, who gave the okay to light the fuses.

Abel lit his long fuse, raced back to his boat, and began to row furiously. With each pull on the oars he had to swallow bile, and when he reached the shore another bomb burst fell in time with the rhythm of the detonations. Small rumbles and churning water was all the show they produced. Abel let his knees have their way at last, and he collapsed onto the marshy shore and sat there as the ships slowly went under.

Caleb ran up and wrapped his arms around his father. "You did that?"

"I just helped."

"Now those old British won't be able to get to Baltimore."

Abel set Caleb down beside him and ruffled his hair as another bomb fell on the beachhead. The pair shot to their feet and ran toward the moat as the troops began pulling out.

"We've been ordered back behind the fort. We'll be safer there," Captain Foster said, handing Abel his musket. "Good job, Abel. Now keep your musket near in case we need to defend the shore."

Abel nodded and took the gun in one hand, securing Caleb to his side with the other. As they moved to the far side of the fort, another bomb hurtled toward bastion two, where a team of Captain Nicholson's artillerymen stood by their twenty-four-pound guns. Screams of pain and shouts for the medics echoed within the walls of the fort and down to the empty moat.

That blast was followed by another forward push by the British, who appeared ready to test the success of their eight hours of assault. Frigates moved forward and broadside to unleash their cannons on the fort's brick and earthen wall, while the *Erebus* increased her rocket fire. The silent American guns began to roar again, once more settling the matter of their resolve. Again the British ships effected a retreat, but not before the *Erebus* was severely handicapped, along with several of the frigates.

As if incensed by the Americans' tenacity, the British bombardment intensified with a new ferocity. From the back wall Abel watched messengers move constantly between Baltimore and the fort, handling the communications between Major Armistead and General Smith. The news from the field at Hampstead Hill was encouraging. Though the British troops had advanced to within a mile of the American entrenchments, every other advance on their part had been countered by American forces and had eventually proven futile.

It became increasingly apparent that the British ground advance was dependent on the fall of Fort McHenry, enabling the British fleet to sail unimpeded into the Baltimore harbor and pound General Smith's defenses. But the blockade was now in place. Would they storm it? No one knew. All the Americans seemed certain of was that everything hinged on the fort's ability to withstand the bombardment and repel the fleet's advances. To this point, General Smith's two-year effort to fortify her had proven brilliant. Though scarred and battered, every wall stood firm. The question was how long the assault would continue, and whether McHenry and her men—and the citizens of Baltimore, for that matter—were equal to the test.

The blasts were deafening at the fort, but their psychological effect left the citizens of Baltimore unnerved. Up to five bombs could be seen in the air at a time. One bomb would fall, rattling walls, toppling knick-knacks, and shaking windows, and then quiet would settle again for just a moment. Too quickly, another blast would come, followed by a rocket sailing in a red streak, its deadly hiss igniting the sky with a glowing trail before it burst, raining fire on the land and people below. The pattern repeated with sixty to one hundred explosions per hour for the first eighteen hours. Then the pace slowed, but a total of twenty-five terrorizing hours had passed with few reprieves.

Dr. Samuel Renfro saw the hospital fill with patients. Some were casualties from the battlefield in need of surgery; a few were foolish spectators who had placed themselves in harm's way as they stood in the open, watching the spectacle unfold. But most of the patients had come for issues related to their nerves or their heart. Adults and children came crying and moaning, unable to manage their normal tasks. They couldn't think, or sleep, or comfort their children, and no place provided the safety or peace for which they so desperately hungered. The unyielding pattern of shock and awe was simply so psychologically devastating that some of the city's inhabitants were literally being frightened almost to death.

Jenny Potter Tyler was one of these. Six miles north, in a backstreet Baltimore café, she abandoned her waitressing duties and crawled under a table, biting her fist as she cowered from the relentless, thundering blasts. Her employer tried cajoling her out but she locked her arms around a table leg and huddled there. It was simply too much for the overwrought woman, a repeat of the same foul terror that had met her in Washington, where she sought refuge after escaping another dreadful situation. She began to wonder if any place was safe anymore.

Myrna Stansbury heard the blasts clearly on her farm north of Baltimore. The relentless thunder unnerved her enough to make riding into Baltimore seem a more palatable choice than quaking in her home. She ordered a carriage readied and had one of the stablemen drive her eleven miles into town—through sixty-six bomb blasts, each of which left her shrieking almost until the next one began. The horses fought the reins, snorting and stomping the ground with fear, requiring the driver to endure a wrestling match to keep them on the road. She had the driver take her straight through to City Hall, where she exited as another concussion began. Myrna let out a shriek that brought Mayor Johnson to the front door to see the cause of the new alarm. She ran straight to him, nearly tackling him. "I need to see Mr. Baumgardner right away!"

The mayor paled. "He left my staff to join General Smith on the battlefield."

Myrna huffed and smacked her handbag against her. "So, he did it? He told me he would. And he did it? Where is he? You must help me find him! I'm having palpitations, and I'm worried about my parents. I need him, Mayor Johnson!"

The mayor set his hands on her shoulders gingerly, attempting to steer her into the building, but Myrna would have none of it.

"I was . . ." the Mayor began. "Just this minute I was preparing a letter . . . to inform you . . . My secretary and I were coming to see you."

A queer understanding was communicated between the two of them in that moment, and Myrna crumpled beneath Johnson's sympathetic touch. "No!" she cried mournfully. "No!" The word carried for seconds, sliding up and down in pitch like the cry of a wounded cat, while Myrna beat her handbag against her body all the more.

The tears beginning, she stomped her foot, suddenly oblivious to the bombs as an even greater shock now washed over her. The mayor led her inside to his office and sat her down, preparing her for the other news he had to share—the news about her parents. Myrna's response was unexpected as she simply shut down, seemingly unable to accept the enormity of her loss.

Her driver was summoned and the mayor escorted her to the hospital. Samuel Renfro attended to her, hearing the full report of the losses she had suffered. His thoughts turned also to Hannah as he wondered how she would take the news. She had to be informed, but looking at the patient load awaiting him, he knew it would be hours, perhaps even days, before he could pick up and travel to the Willows, and that would be too long. With great consternation, he dashed off a note and sent a courier racing to deliver it to Hannah.

CHAPTER 26

Tuesday, September 13, 1814
The areas surrounding Baltimore, Maryland

As evening dusk settled in, the bombardment did not lessen, though Admiral Cochrane's confidence of victory dimmed. Shots periodically fired from the fort's cannons assured Cochrane that McHenry still stood, forcing the admiral to admit he had underestimated the strength of the fort's construction and the tenacity of her defenders. The blockade of the river was also not anticipated, and it rendered him unable to provide naval support to Brooke's significantly outnumbered troops. Without that support, the troop casualties would be egregious. It was too great a risk to the overall plan for the next phase of the American campaign, when the battle would shift south to a new and more critical theater where the troops would be essential.

It was late in the evening when he sent a letter to Colonel Brooke, outlining the situation and admitting that he was pulling the fleet back. If Brooke continued, he and his men would be left on their own, but he advised against this course. Near midnight, Cochrane stilled his fleet's guns, aware that while he waited for Brooke's reply, a third planned front that had failed to receive word of the retreat, began to move.

A twenty-vessel fleet and twelve hundred men under the command of British Captain Napier began moving through the darkness toward the tributary to the west of Fort McHenry. They rowed forward in stealthy silence along the coast, lit only by the rockets' light. And then the bombardment ceased, forcing them to navigate their vessel through the darkness, past McHenry, until they approached the Babcock Battery and Fort Covington without detection. Somewhere along the way, eleven ships carrying the bulk of the troops fell off course heading east. Captain Napier's group remained on target, but it was now reduced to a rocket boat, five launches or barges, three gigs, and only a fraction of the men.

Sailing Master John Webster was the first to hear the approach of Captain Napier's portion of the attack group. He fully recognized the threat these ships posed to Fort McHenry and Baltimore. Rockets fired at such close range threatened the integrity of the fort and the safety of the American ground forces. Coupled with the danger incurred by the successful landing of British troops behind American lines, these ships could ostensibly change the balance of the battle. With the defense of the city now squarely on his shoulders, Webster ordered the men of the Babcock Battery to open fire, assailing the British with their full military complement. Fort Covington soon joined the defense with her guns, and the British cannons and rockets replied.

After a period of blessed silence, Admiral Cochrane heard the exchange of fire and was compelled to resume the bombardment of McHenry to protect his men who were scattered in the darkness all across the Patapsco. Once again, rockets and bombs began racing across the sky.

The battlefield became fluid and confusing. General Smith's American scouts could see their enemies' camp less than a mile away. They didn't appear to be readying for combat, but the American troops on Hampstead Hill, like their brothers along the coast, remained vigilant, not knowing if the relaxed posture was part of a feint, or if in reality, the British were preparing to stand down.

★ ★ ★ ★ ★

The American detainees on the *President* had received no news regarding the progress of the land campaign, though communication vessels moved constantly between Cochrane's *Surprise* and mounted couriers waiting on shore. The only conversations were those shared with the visually impaired Dr. Beanes, who asked repeatedly what flag currently flew over McHenry.

The echo of another round shook the timbers of the ship's cabin. "What time is it now?" Beanes wondered.

"Nearly midnight," Key replied. "You should try and rest, William."

"Rest? They've been firing those wretched guns for eighteen hours. When will it stop?"

The air stilled momentarily except for the gentle rhythm of the rain, which sounded so peaceful between the gun blasts. Markus's thoughts were of Abel and Caleb as he answered, "Dr. Beanes, so long as the British are assailing the fort, we at least know McHenry still stands."

Key grabbed a great coat and went above deck to check the scene. A blustery wind blew across the water. He stared off in the direction of the fort, but the darkness offered no clue about the flag or the state of the fort. Key heard the echo of the last blast and felt comforted to see darkness in the direction of the city—no fires or other reminders of the horror that had beset Washington a few weeks earlier. He studied the panorama east from North Point to the west where Fort Covington lay, and all was dark and still. When another bomb blast suddenly lit McHenry, he saw it—the defiant flag—still waving over the fort.

"How much can they endure?" Key asked aloud. He stood there a moment more, savoring the scene. When he returned below deck, he anticipated Beanes's question. "Our banner still waves," to which Beanes nodded in relief and laid his head back against the hull.

Markus tipped his head to the side, attuning his ears to something. "Do you hear that? No bombs have fired in the last few minutes."

Every ear strained now as the men counted the silent seconds. They scrambled up to the deck and looked out over the horizon. Blackness surrounded them, and no burst of light or beacon allowed them to survey the fort. Rain pelted them as the wind increased.

Their British guards likewise studied the silence. Still, no one spoke. Instead, they sat in the rain for half an hour, the Americans almost wishing to hear another bomb blast.

"Do you think the fort has fallen?" Key whispered.

Markus's face was tense as he pulled out a spyglass and peered into the darkness. He saw a vague outline of the fort, but he could not find a trace of the mighty striped flag.

"May I?" Skinner asked as he reached for Captain Ferguson's glass and peered at the fort. "Neither do I see it, but what did Major Armistead say? When it rains or when the wind exceeds a certain strength they replace the garrison flag with a storm flag, remember?"

Holding to that hope, the men sat and waited for the truth to be revealed.

An hour passed, and the sounds of cannon fire sounded from the east.

"That's the Lazaretto Battery," Captain Ferguson said. "Flotillamen are stationed there."

The cannons went unanswered and the air became still. Half an hour passed before the light of a rocket and the pop and flicker of distant gunfire echoed west of Fort McHenry. Concern filled the men's eyes as the ferocity of the assault increased to a deadly fusillade.

"That's the Babcock Battery and Fort Covington, manned with flotillamen," Markus explained. "The British are hittin' the perimeters now. They must be attemptin' ta land along the shore."

He pressed the spyglass to his eye again, straining to identify the cause of the battle. "Our boys are answering with everything they've got. They're good lads, everyone."

The unmistakable brilliance of a Congreve rocket shot from the location of Cochrane's *Surprise,* igniting the sky over Fort McHenry again. The men examined each inch of the fort's outline for a trace of the flag.

Dr. Beanes squinted, trying desperately to make his weak eyes work. "Please tell me that you see the beautiful Stars and Stripes flying above the fort."

Painful moments passed and then Skinner pointed with a shout. "Look! The rocket's glare illuminated the smaller storm flag for a second, a few yards above the rampart. It's small, but it's there! McHenry still flies the American flag!"

"Thank you," Key prayed as concussion blasts filled the night sky.

"Say a prayer for my brave boys there on the batteries," Markus said. "They've a perilous fight ahead of them tonight."

"I will, Markus. I'll pray that God keeps His watchful eye on all of them tonight."

The *Surprise* began a slower fusillade, belching out two-hundred-pound bombs every few minutes, but little light was given off, leaving the men on the *President* unable to determine the fort's fate. After two hours the cannon fire slowed, but the bombs continued to sail from the *Surprise* all night. The rain also continued, settling into a gentle drizzle as dawn neared. When it stopped, a light fog rested on the water, limiting visibility and turning the river an eerie gray.

It was another night in which the Americans barely slept. The steady bombings persisted, leaving them distraught over the outcome of the night battle. Francis Scott Key rose to discover a pre-dawn sky blanketed by fog. He raised the spyglass to study the horizon. Behind him came Skinner, Beanes, and Markus.

"Can you see it, Frank?" Dr. Beanes asked timidly. "Oh, please say you see it."

Key gave Dr. Beanes a sad smile. "It's still too dark and foggy to say, my friend."

One by one, the Americans rose and silently stared off toward Fort McHenry. At nearly 7:00 AM, the guns stopped their barrage and the air became still. Francis Scott Key was the first to notice. "Listen," he whispered. "It's been several minutes since the last blast."

"You're right. Either McHenry's finally fallen or the British have abandoned the assault."

"Look again, Frank," Dr. Beanes pled. "The first light of dawn is now breaking."

Frank Key raised his spyglass to his eye but still could not see through the mist.

Markus noticed a solemn stillness on all the British ships anchored near North Point. There were no haughty celebrations, no earnest activity, and he wondered what that meant. "Look at the British ships. Do they seem oddly quiet?"

Skinner's hopes rose for a moment and then leveled once more. "They're probably simply fatigued. They've been manning a twenty-five-hour assault."

Markus shook his head. "But it seems more than fatigue. A victory energizes a soldier. This is a dread silence. It reminds me of us after Bladensburg."

Beanes hung his head. "Perhaps they too are worried at what the dawn will reveal."

"We must maintain our trust in God, William. We have been a foolish people at times, and we suffered our comeuppance in Washington, but our cause is still just. God has reached His hand down from heaven and rescued this land in the past. Let's pray He'll do so once more."

Skinner leaned heavily against the rail. "My heart swelled last evening as I glimpsed that flag against the last gleam of twilight. Never before has a banner been so personal to me."

"Other nations have their kings and crowns, their castles and their parliaments that they point to as the symbols of their nation," Key replied, a sense of reverence in his voice. "Our presidency passes from man to man, as do the seats in our congress. In truth, our people are the symbols of our republic. The British have destroyed even the few icons we had. Now our president has no home and Congress no house. They destroyed it all—everything but our beautiful, defiant flag. If she survives, I will never look at her with indifference again."

He reached into his pocket and found a letter and pencil there. Pulling up a barrel for a seat, he began jotting on the back of the paper.

"What's that you're writing?" Beanes asked.

"These very thoughts. I never want to forget what we feel at this moment."

Soon, he placed the paper and pencil back in his breast pocket and returned to studying the ribbon of sky over Fort McHenry.

"Dawn's first light is breaking. We'll shortly know the city's fate." Apprehension tainted Skinner's voice. "I can make out the rampart, but I still don't see the flag."

"We may have to wait for the mist to lift."

More minutes passed and then movement in the air above the fort caught Key's attention. "John, Markus, look! High above the fort! I think I see the garrison flag!"

They thought they saw it also, but was it merely hope or want that filled their eyes? Then a bright beam of morning light burst through the clouds like a heavenly beacon, clearly illuminating the fort's star-spangled banner. A cheer erupted from the group as all the crew joined in the joyous moment of release. America had prevailed! This was more than a success for Baltimore, or a Maryland triumph. This was a national victory. Key saw it so clearly.

William Beanes's face became wet with tears of gratitude. Francis Scott Key again removed the paper and pencil from his pocket and began to write the overwhelming feelings he was unable to express vocally.

In time, Skinner and Markus began a dialogue with their guards, who explained the night's events. The ferocious firefight of the previous evening between British Captain Napier's small band of conquerors and the Americans at the Babcock Battery and Fort Covington had lasted for two hours. British casualties ran high, and around 2:00 AM Captain Napier acknowledged the futility of the effort and began a careful retreat. The fleet laid down cover fire and began a slow and steady firing rhythm. As they pounded away at Fort McHenry, their diversion protected not only Napier's men but also Colonel Brooke's ground forces, which had begun their own retreat at 3:00 AM.

Skinner was given details regarding the protocol leading to the release of the Americans on the *President*. Colonel Brooke would make a guarded retreat, expecting to have his troops back at North Point in two days, during which time the American detainees would remain under guard on the *President.* Then the guards would leave, and the Americans would be free to sail to Baltimore and home.

A sense of gratitude swept over Francis Scott Key. He had kept his promise and helped to free his friend, and soon he would be home with his own family. More than that, a new sense of national pride swelled within him in a way he had never before felt. Over the next two days, while Skinner spent hours in conference with Cochrane and Cockburn, attending to the political details of their diplomatic mission, Key stole away to add to his notes, expanding upon the tender feelings of his heart as he had searched the horizon for a banner of red, white, and blue.

The siege at McHenry took a hefty toll on Major Armistead. The hero had spent days without sleep, standing vigilantly in the rain beside his men, and as his body surrendered to the fatigue, he fell deathly ill. Before he retired to bed, he commended his men, heralding each of them for performing at or above his every expectation. Four men had lost their lives and twenty-four more had been wounded. And while the major understood the triumphant mood sweeping through the fort, there were important matters of honor to be attended to regarding the fallen.

Abel was ordered to report to Captain Nicholson on the morning of the fourteenth. As he re-entered the fort he was anxious to ascertain his standing with the military. On his way to Captain Nicholson's quarters, he passed the four flag-draped bodies lying in the back of two wagon beds. He removed his hat as he passed and then knocked on the captain's door.

"Good morning, Abel," Nicholson said as he moved to invite him in. "I was told you voluntarily joined the blockade team." The captain smiled. "That's the act of a true soldier, and because of it, I'm asking you to stay. I've spoken with Hildebrand and Skully, but I can't promise you things will be any better with those two."

Abel nearly leapt off the floor. "Will Titus be staying on also?"

Captain Nicholson's eyes widened and his mouth drew tight. "Abel, haven't you heard? Titus was killed on bastion two. A piece of shrapnel hit him and severed an artery. He died very quickly."

Tears sprang to Abel's eyes. "He had a wife and children. They live in Philadelphia."

"I know. I want to be sure his family receives the compensation due him. We'll bury him here in Baltimore, but I'd like you to travel to Philadelphia and personally return his belongings to his family. Captain Foster has already agreed to accompany you."

Abel swallowed hard and nodded. "Yes, sir. He was pleased just being a member of the Pennsylvania militia. I talked him into enlisting here."

"You're not responsible for what happened, Abel, but you can help us see that his hopes for his family are realized. McHenry will remain on high alert until the British are completely off Maryland soil and out of the Chesapeake. Admiral Cochrane assures us the troops will embark on their ships in two days. Soon after that the fleet should move down the bay, but how long they'll lurk about in our waters is anyone's guess. Once they're gone, you can leave."

"Yes, sir. Has there been any word about Markus and Mr. Key?"

"Admiral Cochrane assures us they are fine and that they'll be released once the last soldier is aboard the fleet." The news momentarily brightened Abel's face, and Nicholson went on. "The men who helped build the blockade are receiving commendations. You'll be receiving one too."

"But I barely sank one ship."

"Your willingness to volunteer is being applauded. However, I fear it will be one more thing Hildebrand and Skully will hold against you. They were injured in the blast that killed Titus. They'll recover, and they'll receive commendations as well, but they'll be none too pleased at your success."

CHAPTER 27

Wednesday, September 14, 1814
The Willows

The thunder of the Fort McHenry bombardment could be heard along the Patuxent and as far north as Philadelphia on the thirteenth and into the morning of the fourteenth. Hannah and Frannie tried their best to reassure Bitty of Abel and Caleb's safety, but everyone's nerves were on edge. The wretched bombing had the cows so upset they couldn't give milk, and the horses were frenzied, racing wildly until Jack secured them in their stalls so they wouldn't break a leg.

After a restless night, the noise suddenly stopped, and new fears gripped the Willows' residents as they paced and fretted and prayed. The children refused to leave the house, afraid the soldiers would now come and set their new church and cabins on fire. The women were bottling apple slices to keep themselves busy when Jack burst into the kitchen.

"A rider came in from Baltimore," he practically shouted. "He says the battle's over and we won! The British couldn't take down Fort McHenry, and now all their troops and ships are leaving Baltimore!"

After a few moments of stunned silence, the women cheered and jumped and hugged one another until the children ran into the kitchen.

"What's wrong, Bitty Mama?" little Helen cried as she crawled under the table.

Bitty fished her out. "Nothin's wrong, child. Everything's just fine! Those British are leaving the city. Your pa and Caleb done beat them soundly!"

"What brought the rider in, Jack?" Hannah asked.

"I practically forgot. He brought a letter . . . for you."

"More good news?" Frannie asked as she wiped an errant hair from her face.

Hannah broke the seal and began reading, and the letter's sobering effect was soon clear.

"What is it, sweetness?" Bitty asked as she set Helen aside and approached Hannah.

Hannah sat quietly and refolded the single page. "It's from Samuel. He's treating Myrna at the hospital. Her husband Harvey is dead."

Frannie sat beside Hannah and took her hand. "I'm so sorry. He was such a kind man."

"It gets worse." The words' hollow tone caused everyone's eyes to grow large with worry. "My mother is the person who shot him, after she shot my father."

"Jack, fetch us a pitcher of fresh water," Bitty said as she tended to Hannah.

Hannah dropped the page and numbly wrapped her arms across her abdomen as if caressing her baby. "A British rocket set my parents' house on fire. Harvey volunteered to try and rescue them, and mother shot him and then ran into the burning house. All three of them are dead."

Frannie moved to Hannah, who remained stiff and unwilling to be consoled. Jack returned with the pitcher and Bitty sent him out again. "Jack, quick, fetch the reverend."

"I need to get to Baltimore." Hannah stood abruptly, strode to the door, and stopped. "I suppose I should write to Beatrice and tell her." She headed back to the kitchen drawer where she kept her writing paper. The drawer stuck and when she jerked it open, she bent over with a groan. Bitty and Frannie rushed to her and gingerly moved her to a chair.

"You've got to calm yourself, darlin'," Bitty said gently.

"Is it the baby, Hannah? Good heavens. What if it's the baby?"

"It's not the baby, Frannie," Hannah snapped. "I just wrenched my back a bit."

Bitty cupped Hannah's young face in her small hands and stared into the expectant mother's green eyes. "You took your hurt out on the drawer. Admit it, child. You're hurtin' and sad, and probably frightened too. There's no shame in feeling those things. Your parents done you wrong, but it doesn't make you stop lovin' them, or hopin' things will get better."

"As long as they were alive I always held out hope that perhaps someday—"

"Of course, and with a baby comin' you had added reason to want things to be good."

Hannah began to cry and Bitty drew her head to her breast. "There, there. We both understand. Here we are, three women and not a mama between us. I wish I could say the day will come when you won't ache over the loss of your folks, but that's just not so. Family has the most powerful tug on a heart. But it's goin' ta be all right, and you'll never be alone."

Hannah wiped her eyes. "Thank you, Bitty. I know that. I cling to that."

"Someone needs to travel along with you," Frannie said. "I'd be happy to go, but perhaps Bitty would like to be your companion so she can see Abel and Caleb."

Bitty's eyes lit up. "Only if my going would give you comfort."

Hannah fumbled with her apron. "I could use you both. Myrna is ill and there are three funerals to plan and legalities to be attended to. Jack and the reverend can manage things here."

"Couldn't we also settle on those White Oak parcels while we're there?" Bitty asked.

The land purchases had slipped Hannah's mind since the bombardment had begun. "I suppose we could if we can sell the tobacco for a good price. It will still require every cent we have in the bank plus half the horses—Markus's pride and joy. I wish he were here. He's the expert on selling the horses and the tobacco." Her voice began to break. "I hope he's all right. It's not like him to give his word and then be a week late."

Frannie wrapped her arm around Hannah again. "Don't fret. Timothy suspects he joined the flotillamen fighting at the batteries."

"I'm overwhelmed with everything. We need to tell Frederick we'll take the land before he sells it to someone else. His attorney is in Baltimore, so we should be able to settle on the deeds as soon as we sell our goods and collect the monies." It all seemed too daunting to Hannah. "Where is Timothy? His help would be valuable right now."

Frannie's face grew sheepish.

"Frannie, why did Timothy ride off to Washington yesterday?" Hannah stared at her. "He promised he would remain here until Markus returned."

"He asked me to marry him again and I declined. He left in a terrible snit. I suppose I finally convinced him to pursue Miss Bainbridge. I'm not sure I'll ever see him again."

Jack walked in, and behind him came the reverend, dressed in his black pants, white shirt, and collar. He was sweat soaked and his sleeves were rolled up to his elbows as if he'd been working. He removed his signature black hat with its broad, round brim and bowed humbly.

Frannie took Hannah's hand. "Tell me what you'd like to take on the trip, and I'll begin packing bags for both of us."

"And I'll put a nice basket of food together for us," Bitty said. "When do we want to leave?"

"In the morning, I suppose," Hannah answered. "Samuel lives in a rooming house in the city. He said there are plenty of rooms available, since most of the residents moved out when the British arrived."

Frannie left to attend to packing, and Bitty pulled on Jack's arm. "I've got some favors to ask of you," she said as she dragged him through the back door.

"May I sit?" the reverend asked Hannah as he removed his hat.

"Where are my manners? Forgive me, Reverend. I'm so sorry. I'm just out of sorts.

The reverend stilled her hands. "I'm so sorry about your loss. Truly, I am."

Hannah's lips quivered as she fought the rising emotion. "Thank you." She stood, retrieved her hand, and began wiping down a jar of canned apples.

The reverend clasped his hands together, holding his hat. "Jack asked me to offer you some words of counsel . . . some comfort, but it seems you'd prefer not to speak."

"It's not you. I'm trying to be strong. I promised Jed."

"I understand, but one good cry hardly qualifies as a breakdown, just as one unique spiritual opinion does not qualify one as a heretic."

Hannah laughed sadly as she sat down. "Madness runs in the women in my family. I began to think I was delusional or crazed like my mother, but perhaps she too had this gift. Perhaps her parents only treated her as if she was mad because they didn't understand."

"And now you'll never know the truth," the reverend said, taking a seat in the chair next to Hannah. "Is that what grieves you?"

"Partly. I think I simply longed to have a mother's love." Hannah wiped her eyes with a corner of her apron. "But I've discovered that God can fill emptiness with a warm peace. I now have the assurance that He knows me and is aware of my concerns.

"And what saved you from believing you were crazed? Your friend, Reverend Schultz?"

"Yes. My sister Beatrice and I stayed with him for a time. I had lost faith in the gift, believing it to be more a curse than a blessing. The reverend helped me see how it was from God, and how it was I who had abandoned Him."

"And the gift returned?"

"Not constantly, but Emmett taught me that when I want to speak to God, I must pray. And when I want to hear His word, I must read what He has already written, and then listen, and He will show me how it applies to my life. It has worked for me."

The reverend seemed stunned by her comment. "If you hold fast to those truths, Mrs. Pearson, I believe the answers to all your questions will eventually be revealed to you."

Hannah and Frannie dressed in their best suits. Frannie's was green, and Hannah found that only her blue dress suit would fit her growing belly. Neither young woman—particularly a very motherly looking Hannah—felt prepared to negotiate with Frederick Stringham.

"Why are we so nervous, Hannah? This would be a small purchase to Jed were he here."

"Then you be the spokesperson. We're committing thirty thousand dollars, Frannie! Have you ever done such a brash thing? The largest single purchase I've ever made on my own was a new copper bathtub for Jed's birthday, and that was less than seventy dollars!"

"Oh, no, Hannah. I'll come along, but you must do the speaking. Frederick unnerves me and he knows it."

Frannie drove the wagon up the lane to White Oak. The small home Frederick shared with Penelope sat to the right of the lane.

It was still intact, and there were signs of rebuilding the manor house, which once sat to the left, but the overall appearance of the property, from the barns to the sheds to the fences, bore the charred reminders of the fire.

Suddenly Hannah felt ill and went to the side of the wagon to retch. Soon, she sat up, chilled and shivering. "The sight and smell of fire makes me think about my parents' final moments." She turned to her sister-in-law. "I can't do this, Frannie. Not here, not today."

"I'll do it," Frannie said, her former grit returning in answer to Hannah's need. She slapped the reins down on the backs of the team and proceeded up the lane.

Penelope Stringham sat on her front porch peeling apples. Dressed in a drab blue gingham dress that was neither stylish nor fit her well, she looked twice her thirty years. She set the bowl aside, adjusted her dark topknot of hair, and hurried across the grass to meet the Willows' ladies.

"It's so lovely to have company! I've missed you both so. Come in, come in!"

Frannie glanced at Hannah, who said, "We've come to speak to your husband about purchasing the land." Penelope's smile turned to disappointment and Hannah added, "But if you don't mind, I could use a glass of water. Frannie can discuss the particulars with Frederick."

The smile returned as Penelope offered a chubby hand to help Hannah down. "Frederick's taking measurements at the manor house, Frannie. I'll see to Hannah."

Hannah sent her sister-in-law a sympathetic glance, and the two parted.

Frannie took a deep breath and strode to where a new brick corner was being constructed. She saw Frederick Stringham overseeing the work of three slaves, all good masons, who were attending to the work. She paused to assess the man who had once captured her heart. It had been more a love based on friendship than passion, but she had loved him until Frederick had allowed his father to destroy their once-beautiful bond. Frederick was a shadow of the gentle man she had once cared for. His body was shriveled from an injury inflicted upon him by Dupree, but it was her former fiance's angry manner that most unnerved her. He barked and stomped like his father had, looking much like him as he ordered workers about, seemingly enjoying the way the slaves cowered at his authority. Frannie wanted to walk up to him and slap him for becoming so like the man he had once despised, but she buried her anger, determined to attend to the duty at hand.

"Frederick?" she called out.

He turned and was transformed at the first sound of her voice, the hard lines of his face melting and his manner softening. "Frannie? What a delight! What brings you here?"

"The land purchase, Frederick. I'd like to discuss that with you, if I may."

Like Penelope's, his happiness dimmed when he learned that business was at the root of the meeting. Nevertheless, he took Frannie by the arm and gently led her to two chairs set up near a table under the tree, where the grand floor plans were spread.

"It's going to be lovely, Frederick."

His gaze fell reverently on the plans. "Thank you. I want to honor my father's memory."

Frannie wanted to offer her opinion of what measly tribute she felt the man's memory warranted, but instead she moved ahead to the matter at hand. "We'll take the entire parcel, Frederick, all four hundred acres, but I want to be sure exactly what land is included in the deed."

Frederick's face brightened. "Would you like to take a ride along the boundaries?"

Frannie looked at her outfit and paused. "All right, but do you have a sidesaddle?"

"A sidesaddle?" he teased. "I never thought I'd hear those words fall from your lips, but I suppose we've both changed quite a bit these past few years."

Frannie didn't linger on the mention of their past. She smoothed her auburn hair back as they entered the newly built barn. It was twice as large as the Willows' barn, though only four horses were stalled there. Frederick found a sidesaddle and readied a bay gelding for Frannie, then saddled a chestnut mare for himself.

As they set off, Frederick proved he was still among the most skilled horsemen Frannie had ever known, but now, in his slightly crippled state, the difference was more pronounced. He was graceful and fluid and his eyes were filled with the confidence and joy she remembered. They rode to the border where the two properties met. The parcel stretched two acres across the riverfront, running two hundred acres deep along the Willows border. It was beautiful, prime land surrounding the old Wye oak, the spot where the pair had courted, but the parcel didn't encompass the one piece of land Bitty so desperately wanted.

"I'm glad you'll be keeping the tree," Frederick said. "One of us should always keep it."

Frannie ignored the comment. "I need one other piece of land from you, Frederick. It's so near the parcel we assumed it was included."

"What land is that?" He leaned toward her. "Whatever you want is yours, Frannie."

She cringed at the intimation underscoring the words. "We want the plot where Jack and Bitty's sister and her family are buried."

In an instant Frederick's face darkened. "So you can slander my father's memory?"

"No! So Jack and Bitty can finally have some peace."

Frederick pulled up hard on his mount's reins, yanking on the bit and causing the poor animal to cry out. "It's not part of the offer."

"Please, Frederick. You were the one who notified us about their murders and saw that they were properly buried. You know this is the right thing to do. Please, grant us this request."

"You want this very badly, don't you? How badly, Francis?"

Two gourmet cookies remained on a china plate beside a pitcher of exquisite punch. Penelope touched Hannah's hand encouragingly. "Eat up, Hannah. You're eating for two now."

"I couldn't eat another bite, Penny, but I'll gladly take them with me if you don't mind. We so enjoyed all your wonderful delicacies when you stayed with us last summer."

Penelope beamed with delight as she popped from her chair to fetch a napkin in which to wrap the cookies. "I do love to bake, but Mr. Stringham is not one for treats, and, as you can see—" she blushed crimson "—and as he points out from time to time, I've eaten more than I should."

"Most men would feel blessed to have a wife who can cook as you do."

"My parents sent me to France to study cuisine there, hoping it would improve my opportunities. I'm afraid I became an embarrassment to them as well—nearly thirty, with no prospects." As she wrapped the cookies Hannah noticed the beautiful embroidery on the napkin.

"Don't speak of yourself so. You're marvelously talented. Did you do this napkin as well?"

Penelope blushed again. "It's gets lonely here. Mr. Stringham retires to his bed around eight, and I am left alone for several hours, so I sew or read until I turn in upstairs. I used to love to play the piano at night, but since his room is off this one, I fear to wake him."

Hannah was shocked by the life Penelope described, and Penelope must have seen it on her guest's face.

"I've offended you by sharing details of too personal a nature. I'm so sorry."

Hannah reached across and took the woman's hand. "No, Penny. I'm not offended, merely sad for you. You are such an accomplished woman, educated in the arts and a skilled cook. Your company is delightful. Why do you remain with a man who treats you so coldly?"

"Because I have seen the man he could be—the man Frannie once loved—and I dream that in time, perhaps when White Oak is restored and we are free of this obligation he feels to his father's memory, he will become that good man again, and a good husband."

"And what if he never becomes that man, Penny? I hope you know you can always come to the Willows and find safety and friendship there."

Penny bowed her head and blushed brightly once more. "Thank you. From the bottom of my heart, I thank you, but Frederick can give me something you and the Willows cannot."

Hannah caught the insinuation. "You want a child."

"When the time is right. You see, during his recuperation I was his nurse and his support. He asked me then why I stayed, and I told him it was because I had nowhere else to go and neither did he. I also asked him for one great favor, redeemable at the time of his choosing, and he granted me any desire of my heart if I would stand by him. This is what I will ask for when the time is right."

"And that is the extent of your marital warmth?"

"If he changes and finds me suitable, I will welcome him. And if he doesn't and this matter is resolved merely contractually, I will still count myself well served to have a child."

Frannie arrived, offering the women a smile Hannah knew was intended to mask her anger. "I hate to rush off, Penny, but Hannah and I must be going."

Hannah quickly embraced Penelope and then made a hasty exit, hurrying to keep pace with Frannie's angry stride. "I assume things did not go well with Frederick."

"The parcel does not include the burial plots, though I all but begged him to include that small piece. He fears we'll use it to ruin his blessed father's good name."

"Tell him we'll promise not to disclose his father's complicity in their deaths. We just want the land so Bitty and Jack can pay their respects whenever they want."

"Oh, he wants that and far more," Frannie went on. "He wants a document from us attesting to his father's good character so the matter can never be raised. And he wants more than our assurances."

"What could he possibly want? More money?"

"Much more—ten thousand dollars more."

Hannah gasped. "For a quarter-acre plot?"

"We can't say a man is good when we know he's been the devil!" Bitty cried.

"Then he'll refuse to sell the other parcels to us, Bitty. He'll find private buyers." Frannie looked away. "We could have twenty new neighbors along our border."

"We can't have that," Hannah said. "He knows we've got to agree to his terms. But where will we get another ten thousand dollars?"

"I'll divest myself of all my holdings," Frannie answered. "I'm not sure it will be enough to meet his price, but it will be a start."

Bitty leaned over the table and pressed her forehead to the surface. "This is all my doin'. I'm sorry. I just wanted to honor my sister and her family."

Hannah placed a hand on Bitty's back. "I understand, Bitty. Sometimes we love them all the more once we don't have them any longer."

Frannie peered out the window. "Jack's packing the wagon. If we're going to leave at first light we should get some rest."

CHAPTER 28

Thursday, September 15, 1814
Baltimore, Maryland

The closer the wagon drew to Baltimore, the more the women could feel the ebullient spirit enveloping the region. People were in their yards and fields again, shoppers were on the streets, and children were visible instead of sheltered away.

"Except for the soldiers standing guard along the coastline, it almost feels normal," Frannie said as the wagon passed a family picnicking under a tree. "Maybe everything will be all right again." Suddenly, she pulled the reins hard, stopped the wagon, leapt to the ground, and raced over to a tree where a poster was nailed. "Oh, dear!"

"What is it, Frannie?" Hannah asked.

Frannie held up the poster of a woman in a lavish blue gown. The name Genevieve was printed across the top, with show dates listed below, except the face had been gouged out and the word "traitor" had been scrawled across the page. "Jenny is Genevieve, Hannah. It's her stage name, just as mine is Francesca. From the looks of this, she could be in trouble."

Frannie crawled back up into the wagon box and they hurried on across town. It was 2:00 in the afternoon when they reached the city center, and Frannie began organizing their busy day.

"Hannah, I'll drop you off at the hospital so you can visit Myrna and hopefully get some advice from Samuel. Bitty and I will get us settled at the rooming house. I'll try to slip over to the bank to check on the amount in my investment account before they close. And Bitty, I assume you just want to get to the fort and check on Abel and Caleb."

The three divvied up the tasks and set about their work. At the hospital, Hannah was told Myrna was on the second floor, but before she reached the stairs she heard Samuel's voice as he spoke to the staff. She waited until he concluded his instructions, but when he saw her, his eyes filled with compassion and he moved to her, drawing her to him in a warm embrace.

"I'm so sorry, Hannah. Come sit a moment. Did you just arrive?"

Before she could answer, he led her to a bench and sat beside her, drawing her head to his shoulder. For the first time since the news arrived, Hannah allowed the tears to flow freely as Samuel quietly held her. Next to Jed's embrace, Samuel's was the one she most needed at that moment.

"You, Jed, and I have been through a lot together in the past three years—dodging the mobbers as we fled Baltimore after the riot, doctoring you when you fell sick on the way back from York. I love you like a sister, Hannah, so I hope you won't mind that I wanted to spare you some of the grisly business of attending to your parents. The slaves and looters dug through the rubble to see what they could take. Once I heard that, I asked the sheriff to pull their bodies out and bring them back. You wouldn't have wanted to see them that way. I arranged for them to be buried at St. Paul's. Myrna seemed relieved to have that duty attended to. If you want to hold a memorial service, I'll help you. Anything I can do, anything at all, you need only ask."

Hannah sighed with relief. "Thank you, Samuel. Thank you so much. How is Myrna?"

He frowned and shrugged. "She's fine physically, but she's emotionally unstable, crying one minute and then shouting the next. She's frightened half the staff away."

"She's afraid. She has no one but Beatrice and me now."

"I know. She's been asking for you. She's in the room at the end of the hall. There's more. Most of your parents' slaves escaped, but there was one older man who was still there. He looked as if he hadn't eaten in days."

The news brought Hannah's head up sharply. "That's probably Mobey! Where is he?"

"He's in a room down the hall. And we've one more patient you'll be interested in seeing. Jenny Tyler's here."

"Did someone harm her? We saw a poster with her name scratched out and the word 'traitor' written across it."

"She suffered a breakdown. Lots of people did during the bombardment, but this goes deep, Hannah. Something bad has happened to her, and she won't talk about it with any of us."

"I suppose we'll be taking them all back to the Willows."

"Just focus on your sister right now. Everyone else is resting."

"One more thing, Samuel. Have you heard anything from Markus? He never returned to the Willows from his trip with Mr. Key."

Samuel's brow furrowed and he frowned, though it seemed to Hannah that he tried not to.

"Oh, no," she muttered. "It's bad news, isn't it?"

"We just don't know, Hannah. Their ship never returned to dock. We assume they're in the hands of the British."

It was almost too much to consider, and clearly Samuel felt as distraught and powerless as she. She turned and walked to Myrna's room and found her sister in her own misery, lying on her side, curled into a ball. She held a letter in one hand and a handkerchief in the other. As soon as she saw Hannah she reached for her.

"The soldiers went to Harvey's town home to get a suit to take to the undertakers, and they found this lying on the table. He loved me, Hannah, he really did, and he wanted to give our marriage a new start. He loved me, and I pushed him away. What a wretched fool I was."

Hannah had no words of comfort. She could only hold her sister and pray Beatrice answered her letter and came quickly.

"Where will I go? What will I do?"

Hannah stroked her sister's hair. "You're welcome to come to the Willows and stay."

"Thank you." In the next moment she asked, "Do slaves still live in your house?"

The snide comment rankled Hannah, but she reminded herself that she was, after all, dealing with Myrna. "Most of the residents have moved back into their own cabins now, but they move freely around the house and property. It is still their home too."

She could see the panic rising again in Myrna. She was tempted to allow her sister to stew a bit, but she was too exhausted and rung out to play games. "I'm sure Harvey has made provisions for you, and though our parents' house is gone, their land is still very valuable."

"That's true," Myrna answered, seeming stronger now that the first crisis was averted. "I hear the slaves have run away. I'll file runaway papers on them as soon as I'm well."

"Don't, Myrna." Hannah's voice was firm and resolute. "Let them go. We know they worked harder while Mother and Father owned them than most people could in five lifetimes. Just make peace with things. Mobey remained behind, but he's too old to make his way in the world. Emancipate him and let me take him to the Willows. I know there's nothing in Father's will for me, so grant me this one tiny thing."

Myrna's expression softened. "I'm sorry Mother and Father disowned you and cut you from their will. Regardless of the pain you caused them, you still were their flesh and blood. I have the power to decide their estate now, and I think it's wrong for you to get nothing, so—"

Hannah held her breath. Myrna could reinstate Hannah's inheritance, and that would solve their problems with Frederick Stringham.

"—Mobey is yours. I'll draw up the papers."

Myrna's lack of generosity no longer disappointed Hannah, though she felt a brief sting. "Thank you. I'll be going now, Myrna. I want to tell Mobey the good news."

"You'll come and take me to Harvey's service tomorrow, won't you? And then to the reading of our parents' will at 1:00? Everything will be so final. I'll need your support."

Hannah didn't turn to offer her reply. "Very well. I'll be here."

✶ ✶ ✶ ✶ ✶

Even though the British had sailed back to North Point, Abel and the other men of Fort McHenry were still on alert, since the British fleet had a reputation for reappearing and rearing its ugly head again and again. Bitty was excited to at least get Caleb back for a few hours. She brought him to the rooming house for the evening to share supper and tour the city together.

Hannah told Frannie about Jenny, and the pair decided it was time to confront the woman. On the ride to the hospital Frannie shared her bad news. "My stock portfolio is still worth less than three thousand dollars, Hannah. Not enough to solve our problems."

"Myrna is now a wealthy woman. Perhaps she'll extend a loan to me if I beg her."

"I'm sorry you'll have to give her that satisfaction."

"After everything that's happened in the last month, groveling to Myrna seems far less unpalatable than it would have otherwise."

They reached the hospital and entered Jenny's room. She was wide awake but staring at the blank wall. She smiled as they entered, then lowered her eyes. "Dr. Renfro told you I was here, didn't he? You needn't have come. I'll be out of here soon, and then I'll be on my way."

Frannie sat on the edge of her bed, forcing Jenny to look her in the eye or turn her head to avoid her altogether. "We saw the posters, Jenny. A sheriff even came by the house asking questions about you. We want to help you, but you need to trust us and tell us the truth."

Jenny turned her head away. "I know you would help me if you could, Frannie, but there's nothing you can do. The only option I've got is to keep on moving. And that's exactly what I plan to do in the morning."

"At least tell us the truth and let us see if we can help."

Jenny turned glassy eyes back to Frannie. "Please don't think poorly of me once you hear." Jenny blinked rapidly as she appeared to gather her thoughts. "Remember all that money I was saving to buy a little grocery? Well, my pa talked me into starting an outpost in the Kentucky Territory. He figured we could trade with the trappers and the settlers. He went on ahead with half my savings and built us a little trading post. I got three letters from him pretty quick, then nothing more. I was worried, so I packed my bags, took the rest of my savings, and headed off."

She laughed sarcastically as tears began to form. "What was I thinking—a lone woman traveling in the wild? I hadn't even made it out of Pennsylvania before bad things began happening, terrible things. You try to be invisible, but it's hard to hide when there are so few women, so you have to fight someone off every time you buy a meal or rent a place to sleep. I barely made it to Kentucky alive, though what I was when I got there was closer to dead."

Frannie reached a hand to comfort her friend. "I'm so sorry, Jenny."

"I found the trading post. Jeremiah Tyler was running it. He said my father made him his partner until an Indian supposedly killed him. I think Jeremiah actually killed my father.

"I started running the post with Jeremiah, but the same kind of troubles started all over. Jeremiah asked me to marry him. I didn't even care about love or such things—I just wanted to be safe, and I figured being married would save me. But Jeremiah had a mean streak. An older man lived in a trapping camp nearby. Everyone called him Doc, though he did a bit of lawyering too. He was real nice to me—set my shoulder and arm twice and stitched me up a few dozen times.

"He taught me some nursing. I suppose you can't be a patient that many times without picking up a few things. I told him about Jeremiah beating me, and you know what he told me? He said a man in those parts was more likely to be censured for beating his horse than for beating his wife. Imagine that." Jenny laughed sarcastically. "I told him I was once a singer in Philadelphia with nearly five hundred dollars saved, and that the last I heard, my troupe was in Washington. I told him I'd pay him one hundred dollars if he could get me there.

"Instead, Doc wrote up divorce papers and told Jeremiah he'd pay him one hundred dollars if he'd sign them so he could marry me legal. And Jeremiah did it." Jenny's laughter began again but soon turned to tears. "My husband sold me for one hundred dollars."

Now Frannie and Hannah began to cry.

"Jeremiah must have decided that having a maid and a cook was worth more than a hundred dollars to him, because he came to Doc's tent and tried to drag me home. I grabbed the first thing I could reach—an iron skillet—and hit Jeremiah. Then I took my money and a gun, stole his horse, and rode out of there, only resting when the horse was about to collapse.

"I finally reached Washington, and our soldiers were everywhere. I went to the Columbia Hotel to ask the proprietor if he knew if the Le Jardin singers were in the city. When he found out I was one of the 'Flowers of Le Jardin,' he begged me to hire on with them and sing for the soldiers. He bought me dresses and printed advertisements, scheduling me to perform for three weeks in Washington and then on to Baltimore. And then the British arrived.

"All day long I heard muskets firing and cannon blasts and rockets hissing, and that night the fires were blazing right outside the window. The British commandeered the house where I was staying, and they asked me to entertain them. What was I to do? The American men had treated me so poorly that I was terrified of what an enemy might do. So I sang, and they gave me presents, telling me they were from Dolley Madison's jewelry box. How was I to know it was true?

"The butler offered to help me get away in return for one of the rings. The only place I could think to go was the Willows. He placed me behind him on a horse and we rode away, and the next memory I have is of waking up in the wagon bed with Dr. Renfro and Mr. O'Malley. They were so kind that for a time I dared hope I could stay, but once I saw that poster in your drawer I knew the sheriff was looking for me, and that I'd have to keep moving on."

"Maybe not. Do you still have the divorce papers?" Hannah asked.

"Yes, but they were never filed, and they won't spare me from the assault charges my husband raised. They say I'm a horse thief. They hang people for that!"

"Those papers may at least prevent him from carrying you back to Kentucky."

A spark of hope appeared in Jenny's eyes.

"I have to meet with an attorney tomorrow," Hannah said. "Let's see what he thinks."

CHAPTER 29

Friday, September 16, 1814
Baltimore, Maryland

Hannah was waiting when Myrna was released from the hospital, and the two headed to St. Paul's church to spend a few moments at their parents' graves. It was a painful exercise for Hannah. Torn between her sorrow at their deaths and her anger at having been dismissed from their lives, she remained stoic, while Myrna melted into a spectacular display of grief.

It served the widow well as they moved into the packed chapel for Harvey's funeral. His people studied her with scornful glares throughout the mass and the glowing tribute from the mayor, but Myrna was undeterred as she allowed her grief full expression.

From there, the sisters walked to the law offices of Sanford and Hutchison for the reading of their parents' wills. The ancient Mr. Sanford wore a puzzled expression when he entered the room where the secretary had situated the women.

"Forgive me for keeping you waiting, ladies. Some legal details required verification, but we're ready to begin. Mrs. Baumgardner, you are the sole beneficiary of your late husband's sizeable estate, including his farm, his town home, and all his financial assets. You are a very fortunate woman. Your husband was a wise investor, and with a little care, you should be quite comfortable for the remainder of your life."

Myrna's tears were real, but with her handkerchief dramatically at the ready, she dabbed at her eyes, punctuating her loss.

"You will also enjoy the additional security provided by your share of your parents' estate, but there appear to be some discrepancies. When I visited you yesterday, you told me you were the executor of the estate and that of the two beneficiaries, you'd be the only one present."

"Hannah is not a beneficiary," Myrna blurted. Clearly noting Mr. Sanford's appalled reaction to her statement, she added, "My sister is here to offer me moral support during this painful time."

Sanford's bushy eyes arched. "Hannah? Hannah Stansbury Pearson?"

"Yes," Hannah said cautiously.

"Very curious indeed. Well, Mrs. Baumgardner, I for one am certainly glad your sister is so benevolent and obliging. It will save me considerable travel and the trouble of tracking her down, because she is also a beneficiary of your parents' estate."

Myrna bolted forward so forcefully the table shook. "What? That can't be! Let me see that. I read that will the day it was written!" Then, obviously recognizing the impropriety of her outburst, she turned to her sister and smiled. "Of course I'd be thrilled if Father had a change of heart and included you, dear, but we must make certain this will is authentic and that the bequests reflect his wishes."

"Oh, I assure you the will is authentic. It bears your signature, and the codicil is likewise authentic. I checked the signature against our records."

Myrna's voice had risen three pitches and now possessed a pinched quality. "And may I ask who witnessed the codicil?"

"Why, your husband, Harvey Baumgardner, on the 13th of July 1813, the same day your father turned over the power of attorney to you." He set the document on the table and turned it so she could see where he pointed. Myrna's coloring paled and then flushed purple. "Strange he relinquished control of his estate to you but he didn't have you witness the codicil."

"Yes, well, it was intended to be a surprise, a wonderful surprise. Hannah, I'm so delighted Father took my advice and left you something too. It was only right."

"You three daughters are named equal heirs, Mrs. Baumgardner, except for a few individual bequests of items that were destroyed in the fire."

Hannah fell back against her chair, stunned.

"You three will need to come to some agreement as to how you wish to handle the real estate holdings and the physical property, including your father's furniture manufacturing company. I will be sending you each checks for your shares of the monies held by the bank, less any outstanding debts. But since there are no mortgages or liens, everything else appears very straightforward, and the probate should be brief. You may enjoy knowing that the specific bequests are as follows . . ."

Hannah barely heard the rest of the details. There were deserved acknowledgements of Myrna's devotion and loyalty, and in token of her loving service to her parents she was to have been given all her mother's personal effects, including her beautiful jewelry collection—save one piece. Their mother's wedding ring, the pianoforte built by Johann Andreas Stein in Germany, and their father's violin were to have gone to the eldest daughter, Beatrice, the most proficient musician of the family. And Hannah, the daughter who always questioned everything, was to have received her father's entire library. The happy news nearly broke the woman.

When the meeting concluded, Hannah asked to speak to Mr. Sanford alone, hoping to receive some insight into her parents' change of heart. "Was there a letter or note explaining the cause of the change in the will?"

"No, I'm sorry, but perhaps you'll find your answers

as you consider the meaning of the gift they bequeathed to you."

The advice was sound. "How long will it be before the money is available? My husband is a prisoner of war, and those assets would be very helpful right now."

"A few weeks, but I could provide a letter of credit you could draw upon immediately."

"Thank you. That would be perfect. And could I trouble you for one more thing, sir? Could you look this document over?" Hannah handed him Jenny's divorce petition. "Is it filled out correctly and written to be binding?"

Sanford read the document through, commenting as he went. "Hmm, yes, yes. Everything is in order. It merely needs to be filed."

"Could you please handle that for Mrs. Tyler?"

CHAPTER 30

Friday, September 16, 1814
Baltimore, Maryland

The *President* pulled into the Baltimore harbor late in the evening of the sixteenth, twelve days after it set sail to rendezvous with the British fleet. Baltimore was still in a state of high alert, its leaders fearing the British would regroup and return. Soldiers and sailors were everywhere, making it appear as if the mighty host of Egypt had arrived in the city since they had departed, so great was the number of troops still arriving from Maryland, Pennsylvania, and Virginia.

Though the harbor seemed to be in a state of excitement, the men were sober when they landed. The city and its people had spent days adjusting to the battle's toll—the deaths and the destruction—but the battle's effects were still fresh and raw for the isolated men of the *President*. All were exhausted from their ordeal, but the duty that had brought them together was now completed, and as they bid one another good night, they knew they had shared a singular experience from which they would never be able to truly walk away.

Francis Scott Key saw the toll of Dr. Beanes's harrowing, twenty-day captivity, the majority of which had been spent in deplorable, torturous conditions. The sixty-five-year-old doctor was dehydrated, weak, exhausted, and pained in every joint.

Beanes desperately needed rest, so Key took his friend to the Indian Queen Hotel and got him settled, then settled himself in his own room and pulled out the poem he had begun during the bombardment.

The framework of the poem pleased him. Taken from his thoughts and the conversations shared on the ship, the words accurately expressed his emotions that night. He had spent eleven days with his liberty stripped from him, experiencing a helplessness the privileged attorney had never before known. Britain's exercise of her might had dredged up raw, unflattering passions in him, both unfamiliar and uncomfortable—anger, resentment, defiance. These were emotions gentlemen eschewed, but they stoked the fire in the belly of Key the soldier and Key the poet.

Gripped by apprehension and anxiety, he had awaited the breaking of dawn to discover the battle's outcome. These feelings composed the first stanza. In the second he sought to adequately convey the joy he felt at the first glimpse of the star-spangled banner. His defiance of the foe filled the third stanza, which expressed his disgust that where Americans were fighting for their homeland and liberties, many of those in British uniforms were hired soldiers who fought for lucre instead of loyalty. The fourth stanza was intended to illustrate the gratitude he felt as he considered the unique blessings America afforded her people. Underscoring everything was Key's acknowledgement of God's hand in the establishment and defense of the infant nation.

Key had heard the agonizing stories of men's sacrifice during the Revolution, but he had also heard their testimonials of inspiration, of deliverance, and of miracles. Similar miraculous events had been witnessed in this war, and Key had seen many with his own eyes. Some men would call them coincidences, but he knew the help was divine, despite the frequent ignorance and arrogance of America's people. Key looked back at his poem, made a few small changes here and there, copied it into neat form on fresh paper, and set his pen aside.

✯ ✯ ✯ ✯ ✯

On the morning of the seventeenth, Skinner was anxious to race off to Fort McHenry. His talks with Admirals Cockburn and Cochrane, particularly on the fourteenth and fifteenth, had been enlightening, and Skinner prepared for hours of debriefing and pages of reports he would need to write.

Markus was also anxious to head to Fort McHenry to check on Abel and Caleb, and to see the bombardment's effects firsthand. He also wanted to check on the flotillamen stationed at the Babcock Battery and Fort Covington, knowing they had sustained some of the heaviest fire.

Key's concern for Captain Nicholson weighed on his mind, and he knew the reverse was also true. He joined Skinner and Markus as they headed to Fort McHenry. Key carried along a copy of the poem to share it with his brother-in-law.

Pride, joy, ballyhoo, and bravado were in abundance at the fort, but strain and stress were also apparent, and no man discounted the fragility of the freedom they cherished. Major Armistead was still bedridden. As second-in-command, Captain Joseph Nicholson was now in control of the fort until the temporary commander arrived.

Key presented his poem to Nicholson. "The most exquisite feelings overtook me as I witnessed the bombardment from the ship. I drafted a poem expressing them. I've wondered if your feelings were similar."

As Nicholson read the poem, his reaction was powerful and immediate. "You exactly captured the emotions of that night."

"Thank you, Joseph. I'm so pleased you like it."

"Its feel is familiar."

"Most likely because I set its meter to a tune I've used previously—'Anacreon in Heaven.' It was running through my mind as I wrote the piece."

"So it's actually a song!"

The remark caused Key to blush. "Allow me to explain. Through the clouds of the war, the stars of that banner still shone in my view, and I saw the assailants driven back to their ships. In that hour of deliverance and joyful triumph, my heart said, 'Does not such a country and such defenders of their country deserve a song?' Let the praise, then, if any be due, be given, not to me, not to the writer, but to the inspirers of the song."

"Frank, this must be printed. After the defeat in Washington, and with the British still skulking in the bay, the people need some inspiration. They need this."

"May I?" John Skinner asked. As he read the poem, his head began to nod in agreement. "I agree with the captain, Frank. We must get this to a printer this very morning."

Key balked at the praise, but Skinner insisted. "If you'll allow me, I'll see to it."

"Mr. Skinner, the newspaper offices have suspended operation because the men are on the battle lines," Nicholson said.

"All but the *Baltimore American*" replied Skinner. "Their offices are still operating. The apprentice is Samuel Sands, a lad too young to go to war. He is still printing a reduced paper."

"Excellent," Nicholson replied. "But indulge me, Frank, and allow me to first write an introduction so your modesty doesn't dilute the importance of the piece."

Nicholson composed his thoughts and handed the paper back to John Skinner, who read his explanatory comments:

> *The annexed song was composed under the following circumstances—A gentleman had left Baltimore in a flag of truce (for the purpose of getting released from the British fleet, a friend of his who had been captured at Marlborough). He went as far as the mouth of the Patuxent and was not permitted to return, lest the intended attack on Baltimore should be disclosed. He was*

therefore brought up the Bay to the mouth of the Patapsco, where the flag vessel was kept under the guns of a frigate, and was compelled to witness the bombardment of Fort McHenry, which the Admiral had boasted that he would carry in a few hours, and that the city must fall. He watched the flag at the Fort through the whole day with an anxiety that can be better felt than described, until the night prevented him from seeing it. In the night he watched the bomb shells, and at early dawn his eyes were again greeted by the proudly waving flag of his country.

"Marvelous! I'll have broadsides printed with this addition and the tune title, and then I'll return with the copies."

Within an hour, copies of "Defence of Fort McHenry" could be seen all over the city, and soon after that a copy was handed to every soldier in Fort McHenry. The broadsheets spread like a prairie fire, and while newspapers hungered to resume business and get their hands on a copy from which to set their type, vocalists began preparing to perform the song.

Sunday, September 18, 1814
Near Hampstead Hill, in Baltimore

Some Pennsylvania militias arrived in Baltimore too late to meet the British on the field of battle. They now provided needful but less glorious service to their country by relieving the exhausted and starving troops who had met the enemy and who were sorely in need of rotation. A Lancaster militia had among their troop two brothers, Charles and Ferdinand Durang, troubadours and actors who sought glory on the battlefield. With the glory thin, the brothers were relieved they had also brought along their flutes to pass the time. A member of their company approached them with one of Key's broadsheets and asked, "Have you seen Key's poem?"

Ferdinand reached out a hand. "Let's have a look at it. To the tune of 'Anacreon in Heaven,' eh?" He began to hum the tune as he counted out the words. On the next try he began to quietly sing the words to the tune. "It needs a bit of tweaking to fit. Charles, pull out your flute and play a few bars of 'Anacreon in Heaven,' will you?"

Charles obliged, and with a few tries the awkward phrasing became less so, and the tune became more engaging. More and more of the men gathered near the group to learn how the poem could be sung, until the camp filled with Key's tribute to the star-spangled banner.

It had been a busy trip for the Willows women. After settling Myrna's affairs and arranging a team of men to move her from the farm to the town home, Hannah had the exquisite privilege of handing Mobey his freedom papers. The old stableman cried and pressed the document to his chest, but when offered the chance to move to the Willows, he declined, preferring instead to join Myrna's employ, enabling him to remain in the city. Hannah was dubious about the idea, but Myrna seemed oddly pleased by the request, and once the parties agreed to a modest salary and living arrangement, the deal was struck.

Hannah and Frannie finally secured Jenny's promise not to run again, though the women had purposely spent the majority of their free time in the neighborhood near the rooming house to avoid any confrontations that might occur if people recognized Jenny.

After church on Sunday, Hannah and Bitty left for a few hours to help Myrna settle into the town home, leaving Frannie and

Jenny alone. The two women decided to take an afternoon stroll, but the evening air grew chilly and Jenny ran back inside to grab a wrap. It was at that moment that Markus arrived to visit Samuel.

Frannie saw her friend heading up the street and called out to him. Unable to wait for him to see her, she lifted her skirt hem and began to run.

He heard her before he saw her, but once he did he too began a dead run. Soon, he scooped her up in his arms. "You're the best thing I've seen in weeks," he said as he twirled her and set her down. "For a time I wondered if I'd ever see the likes of home and all of you."

"How are you?" she asked. "We've been worried sick about you. Hannah and I considered storming the fleet!"

Markus squeezed Frannie once again as they began walking back toward the rooming house. "You should never've doubted that I'd keep my word. I promised I come back, didn't I? Abel told me you were here in the city somewhere, else I would've headed right back ta the Willows. So what's keepin' you here? I assume the funerals are over. How's poor Hannah bearin' up?"

"Samuel's worried about her. She's not getting enough rest and she cries a lot. She thinks no one notices, but we're all aware that she's at the end of her rope."

They had chatted all the way back to the rooming house. Markus turned to Frannie. "Let's get you girls home then, and get things back to some kind of normal for her."

"We plan to leave soon. Hannah still has a few more details to attend to with the land deeds and the bank."

Markus saw Jenny Tyler a block further down the street. "What's she doin' here?"

Frannie followed his gaze. "Jenny? She was in the hospital. Samuel's been tending her."

"I thought she left the Willows two weeks ago."

"How could you know that?" Frannie saw coldness fill his eyes. "Is something wrong, Markus? You look irritated."

"She's no good, Frannie. She's a traitor. I'm glad she's left the farm."

Frannie stopped in front of him and placed her hand on his chest. "You don't know the entire story, Markus. It's not like you to judge someone. Let her explain."

"No explanation can justify aiding an enemy that's done what they've done to us."

Jenny approached the pair, speaking to Frannie while her gaze was set on Markus. "I couldn't find you, Frannie. Well, hello, Mr. O'Malley, it's very nice to see you again."

Markus returned Jenny's warmth with a cold, silent stare that unnerved Frannie so completely she turned to Jenny and asked, "Could you excuse us for a moment?"

Jenny's gaze shifted between the two. "This is about me, isn't it?"

"This is about a certain traitor named Genevieve." Markus's eyes narrowed in contempt.

The recoil in Jenny's body was physical, and Frannie noticed people's attentions shifting their way. "That's enough, Markus! Let's go inside and discuss this before you cause her more trouble."

"Her kinda trouble needs to be handled by the soldiers at the fort."

Something must have snapped in Jenny Tyler. She stormed up to Markus and glared straight into his eyes. "I thought better of you, but you think you know me all about me? You want answers from me? Then do it! Take me to the fort!"

Her words clearly caught Markus off guard. He looked to Frannie, but she had only fury in her eyes.

Frannie pulled Jenny aside. "Are you sure, Jenny? I don't think this is wise."

"I'd rather face my accusers head-on than worry every time I walk down a street that some thug or brute is going to try to punish me for something they don't understand."

Without waiting for Markus, Jenny began storming toward the fort with Frannie by her side. Fully chagrined, he called out, "Let me at least get a wagon so you don't have to walk!"

But the women kept marching on. Markus cursed them both, cursed the British, and then cursed himself as he headed to the livery and hitched up Samuel's team. By the time he reached the women they had covered nearly a mile. "Get in," he said, but they kept walking. "Darned fool women, get in the wagon!"

Frannie cast Markus a scorching look and marched on with Jenny in the lead. He softened his voice to a more reasonable tone. "Please, get in."

Frannie's jaw was set so hard it looked like it would crack. She convinced Jenny to climb in, but neither woman would give Markus a look or a word. When they reached the fort, Markus spoke to the guard, who brought Sergeant Carpenter to the gate. After Markus briefly explained Jenny's business at the fort, the sergeant escorted her through the sally port and to the junior officers' quarters.

It was the longest hour of his life, next to the last one with Lyra. Frannie sat on the wagon with her eyes fixed on the water, unwilling to venture into any conversation with the man. Finally Markus could take it no longer, and he asked her angrily, "How can you sympathize with a woman who entertained the same men who're makin' your brother suffer?"

"What you really mean is how could I sympathize with a woman who entertained the men who murdered your wife. Isn't that it? Have you ever stopped to think that maybe their situations were similar? Except when Lyra was afraid, she ran, and when Jenny was afraid, she had nowhere to run, so she did what they asked her to do—she entertained them."

"How can you compare the two?"

"Because I know how it feels to be that afraid for your life. Remember when I was kidnapped, Markus? I fought back, but Lyra ran, and Jenny sang. It's that simple."

"And you're so sure she did it out of fear?"

"Yes, I am, and you would be too if you took half a minute to listen to her. You saw the condition she was in when you found her. Why are you so unwilling to believe her?"

Markus knew the shameful reason. He marched to one of the fort's guards, who escorted him to the junior officers' barracks. He rapped on the door, and soon Sergeant Carpenter answered.

"Come in, Captain O'Malley. We're about through here."

"Yeah. About that, I may have made a mistake in bringing Mrs. Tyler in. I'd like to take her home now."

"Under the circumstances, we think you did exactly the right thing."

"Well, ya see, there are some extenuatin' circumstances that need ta be considered."

"Really?" Sergeant Carpenter turned and addressed Jenny, who was making her way to the exit. "Mrs. Tyler, is there anything more you'd like to tell us?"

Jenny appeared in the doorway, regarding Markus with a cold glance. "No, sir, Sergeant. I've said all I had to say."

"I'm sorry for everything you've been through. Women suffer in wartimes in ways men can't fathom. We'll pass the word on to the men. You shouldn't be subjected to anymore harassment or threats. We appreciate the information you've passed along. This could be very useful to General Jackson. And thank you, Captain O'Malley, for seeing her safely here."

Jenny walked past Markus, paying him no regard. The three returned to the wagon, and before Markus helped Jenny up he said, "You've no cause to answer me, but would you tell me what the sergeant was thankin' you for back there?"

"For information, Mr. O'Malley. You see, while those British officers were drinking and vying for my attention back in Washington, they were also bragging about their plans for the next campaign—New Orleans. They're going to attempt to take control of the Mississippi, and I was able to provide a few details about dates and troop strength."

"So you were a spy."

"No. I was a captive. Just like you. Except I know how to listen."

Markus was appropriately censured. He drove back to the city in a shamed silence, hoping for a chance to apologize to Jenny, but when they reached the city limits the sound of singing in the streets caught the women's attention. Markus pulled back on the reins, preparing to face the wronged woman, when he heard her ask Frannie, "Isn't that Ferdinand Durang?"

"It is, with Charles on the flute!" Jenny and Frannie climbed to the ground and hurried to where the crowd was gathered, leaving Markus chewing on his planned apology.

The women chattered excitedly as they hurried toward the throng, arm in arm, leaving Markus sitting idly in the rig. He knew he had disappointed them both deeply. What hurt more was that he knew what was really at the root of it. For that he was ashamed.

"Charles! Ferdinand!" Frannie shouted above the crowd's chatter.

Ferdinand Durang spied Frannie in the crowd and nudged his brother. Soon the music stopped and the two men parted the group and moved to the women. "Francis! Jenny! It's so wonderful to see you." Ferdinand turned to the crowd and exclaimed, "Ladies and gentlemen, may we present two of the finest singers you'll ever have the pleasure of hearing? Two of the Flowers of Le Jardin de Chanteuses in Philadelphia—Miss Francesca and Miss Genevieve!"

As the crowd offered a round of applause, Ferdinand leaned close to Frannie. "How long has it been since we've performed together? A year?"

"More like two. Not since President Madison's inaugural party."

"Then that's two years too long. Would you ladies like to join us? We could use some harmony."

The women looked excitedly at one another and nodded. "Where are you performing?"

"Just for the public on the street corners right now. Who knows but that a venue will open for us if the locals like our performance!"

Frannie bit her lip, hungry to say yes. "We'll only be here for a few more days, but it would be wonderful to perform again. I haven't sung in public since the war broke out. What do you think, Jenny?"

"Nothing would make me happier."

"All right!" Frannie was nearly giddy. "Our accommodations are at the rooming house on Eutaw Street—apartments 4 and 5. Come at 7:00 and we'll rehearse."

CHAPTER 31

Sunday, September 18, 1814
The Atlantic Ocean, on board the Iphegenia

Jed finally understood the extent of Arthur's injuries. He had lost control of his bladder and bowels, requiring that he be diapered and changed several times a day. Additionally, his incisions failed to heal properly because the sanitation was so poor, resulting in infections that caused him to suffer extreme pain and an almost constant fever, though Arthur never complained. The truth was plain enough to see by the gray of his complexion and the tautness of his mouth and brow.

Jed did what he could to distract and entertain his friend, and true to his word, Roust now addressed Arthur's needs with the greatest compassion and care. Improvement was evident, but the surgeons were unwilling to offer any further hope for the young chaplain. To them it was a miracle he was still alive. Still, Arthur fought on, knowing Jed's hope lay in a pardon from Lord Whittington, a pardon Arthur felt he could secure.

While Arthur slept, Jed had spent the afternoon on the forward deck, mesmerized by the blue and gray patches of the sea that mirrored the movement of the clouds. His hair was neatly trimmed as was his beard, but other than these gentlemanly improvements, he rather felt like a sailor, dressed in a cast-off set of work clothes— white cotton pants and a blue, tunic-like cotton shirt. The ensemble was unsurpassed for comfort and ease of movement, two essential elements when men were climbing rigging, as he was learning to do. Jed had never sailed the ocean before, but he now understood its pull and romance. Weather patterns changed frequently, requiring sails to be shifted and furled or unfurled, and imaginations were expanded to invent creative solutions to a myriad of problems. But no adventure could satisfy his hunger for Hannah and home.

He was beginning to count on freedom again, not just at the end of a prison sentence, but in lieu of one—so convinced was he of Arthur's connection to Lord Whittington. He again awoke happy after a sweet night's rest, clean and shaven, in a bed with sheets, his dreaming filled with visions of Hannah and a child he would now meet while it was still an infant. The dreams were both comforting and disturbing, filling him with such a physical hunger to hold his wife again that he cried out to her in his sleep. Several nights he had awakened to find his fingers scraping the sheet in a fevered attempt to reach her, to become tangled in her raven hair as they swam in the river by the mill. He longed to ride with Frannie and go fishing with Markus, Jack, and Abel.

Jed wanted to feel fatigued from building a future, instead of rotting day by day. It mattered not to him if they planted tobacco or corn, whether they raised thoroughbreds or Arabians. The minutia was meaningless. He simply wanted to get home. And now he believed he would.

Young Edward Tenneyson approached him. "Thanks for saving our skins back there, sir. I s'pose you're dreaming of home now. This is where I come when I miss my home."

"So the navy hasn't completely captured your heart yet, Edward?"

"You know, sir, sometimes I'm not sure I'm a good fit for the navy."

Captain Smith approached and the boy quickly departed. "Lieutenant, we could use a fourth tonight. We're playing that card game the men picked up on shore—poker."

Jed knew how they "picked up" the game on shore—from American spies who bivouacked with the British troops. "Who is playing?"

"Myself, Captain Gottfredson, and Ensign Pickering."

Jed had discovered that Pickering was the beast who had mutilated Ethan's hand. "No thank you, sir. I believe I'll read to Lieutenant Ramsey tonight."

"Well, come to my cabin if you change your mind. It would be helpful to have someone who knows the game present to be certain we're playing correctly."

Jed walked back to Arthur's cabin and found him still sleeping. His wounds had improved enough that he was now able to be partially dressed, and on this day he wore a white shirt loosely bloused at the waist and hanging over blue military trousers slung low and unbuttoned beneath. His hair was clean and had been cropped short, circling his head in a soft, brown mass of waves that framed a cleanly shaven face much leaner than it had been just a few months before. Though slightly older than Jed, Arthur appeared boyish and innocent, and far too gentle a soul to be a casualty of war.

Jed scooted the wooden chair under the small porthole and tried to capture enough light to pen a letter to Hannah without lighting the lamp. He had filled nearly every spare piece of paper secured from Captain Smith, who was allowed to believe the sheets were for Arthur. A few pages were indeed filled with letters to Arthur's parents, and a few more held the British lieutenant's observations on the war, meant for Lord Whittington's eyes. But the rest of the pages had been handed to Jed, who filled them for Hannah and their coming child.

The creak of Jed's chair awakened Arthur, who stretched his arms and grimaced from the pull on his abdomen.

"How long have I been asleep?" he asked.

"About four hours, I'd say. How are you feeling?"

Arthur appeared to assess his condition. "Somewhat better, I think."

"You always say that." Jed was dubious and laid a hand on his friend's head to check for fever. "But I must admit, you do feel cool to the touch."

Arthur smiled. "And I'm hungry. When's the last time you heard me say that?"

"That's wonderful! I'll get you a bowl of whatever I can find in the galley."

Jed returned shortly and helped prop up Arthur so he could feed himself. "You do seem much better, but then your care has vastly improved. You couldn't sit at all the other day."

After Arthur ate, Roust arrived to prepare him for bed. Jed strolled the deck again and then returned to present Arthur with the evening's options. "What shall I read from the Bible tonight? Psalms? Revelations? And then perhaps a few poems from Thomas Gray?"

"Oh, yes, Psalms. And then the poetry would be lovely."

Jed read for nearly an hour until his voice became raspy.

"Thank you, Jed. That's enough for tonight. I'll say my prayers now and go to sleep. Go and join the card game. Captain Smith stopped by earlier seeking your company."

Jed's eyes narrowed as he shook the idea off. "I've no interest in cards this evening."

Arthur frowned. "You love cards. It's because of Pickering, isn't it?"

"I can't abide the beast! If I got the chance, I'd strangle him with my bare hands."

"Deserved or not, we can't risk that. And yet you can't sit in here, day after day, reading to me until you're hoarse."

Jed folded his arms and leaned back into his chair. "You're feeling better. Why don't you entertain me for a while?"

Arthur gazed at him incredulously. "Shall I juggle, or dance a jig?"

"Either will do," Jed replied with a smirk, delighted to see some fire return to his friend.

"Actually, Jed, I'm grateful you've asked. There are some things I'd like to discuss with you before we reach land."

Jed tensed, assuming he knew what some of those things were.

"I hope you'll try to have an open mind and not allow recent events to taint your opinion of Britain and her citizens. War does queer things to both. England is a lovely land filled with good, earnest people, and you hail from two of her noblest families."

"Which means absolutely nothing to me."

"Can you truly say it doesn't thrill you at all to know your family line can be traced back to the days of Christ? Or that the same blood that flows in your veins once flowed in some of the most noble men in history?"

"You have told me we are actually cousins. That is as noble as I care to be, especially since I've been struggling to remain one step ahead of all the supposed family members trying to kill me. I haven't seen much reason to appreciate the connection."

Arthur sighed. "Yes, my father tried to have you killed. I can barely say it, and I make no effort to excuse him. I'm overwhelmingly grateful his plot failed, but knowing your family heritage is still your right." Arthur settled deep into his pillow as if anticipating a lengthy telling. "Your grandfather, the first Jonathan Pearson, was born out of wedlock to a young couple who represented two of the finest families in England. His mother was my great Aunt Fiona Ensor—the daughter of a member of the House of Lords—and his father was a man named Mitchell, the heir to a member of the House of Commons."

"I know the story well enough, Arthur, but it has no bearing on my life. Frannie told me our grandfather was sent to America as an indentured schoolteacher when it was feared the truth of his birth was about to be revealed. Britain and her nobles banished him. My family's life began in America. The rest of my bloodline is merely history."

"I wish my father would have had such a casual concern about such things," Arthur said. "Father grew up hearing only half the story—how his mother had once been loved by the wealthy American rebel named Jonathan Pearson, though she had somehow ended up married to a fisherman who indentured my father on a ship at age eight.

"My father's childhood was difficult, Jed, and he cursed your grandfather and his successes. This is why he aligned himself with the British Navy and Dupree, so he could destroy the Pearsons, whom he blamed for his poor fortune and the betrayal of England, his mother, and himself."

Jed felt his anger rise over the mention of Arthur's father, the man who had sent Dupree to destroy Jed's family and the Willows. He stood, needing to break the tension he felt. He leaned against the hull, laying his arm alongside the small porthole as he stared blankly out. "I cannot forget that if not for your intervention your father would have had his way. Frannie, Hannah, and I would all be dead now, along with everyone else at the Willows."

"I thank God I was given an opportunity to warn you and your family." Arthur's voice trembled and then strengthened again. "But let me also say that my father appears to be a very changed man now. I'm not sure what happened, but somehow knowing the truth has finally brought him peace." The worry lines reappeared on Arthur's brow. "His life is very tarnished, but I believe his heart is now new. If only it had happened sooner."

"And what of my benefactor, Lord Whittington?"

Arthur dropped his head back to his pillow. "Ah . . . Lord Whittington. What do you want to know?"

Jed returned to the chair, anxious to explore this subject. "How do you know the earl, and why does he owe you a great favor?"

Arthur laid his arm across his eyes and sighed in disappointment. "It's another tale of my father's sordid past. Three years ago, we all attended church together. I was finishing up at divinity school, and the earl and his son Daniel would speak to me after mass. I didn't realize at the time that he was investigating my father for bribing an MP—a member of Parliament. One day I overheard Lord Whittington arguing with Father, who as much as admitted to everything. But since there was no witness willing to testify, Father knew he would go unpunished. I was angry and disillusioned, and I turned my back on my father and turned to the earl instead."

"After all he's done, you still feel the need to reconcile with your father?"

Arthur's arm flew away from his eyes. "He's changed, Jed. I know it! Please understand my part in all that's happened. Because I turned away from him, things became much worse. The bitterness between the two men increased until my father hired men to watch the earl's castle. Lord Whittington believed his intent was to kidnap Daniel. My father claims he did it simply to have a report of my activities. In any case, one of the men Father hired to spy on me broke into Daniel's room and murdered the boy's governess before his eyes."

Jed hung his head to avoid Arthur's gaze. No matter how much Stephen Ramsey loved and admired his son, Jed had tried Stephen in his heart and found him guilty on all counts.

"I see it in your eyes. You think he's as guilty as the murderer. So did the earl." Arthur's voice grew heavy and his body seemed to slump further into the pillows. "I continued to champion my father, and that led to a break between the earl and me. Still, he trusted me and my mother, and fearing for Daniel's life, he asked me to perform one final favor—to safely carry the boy into my mother's care. I told him he was choosing the wrong course in tearing his son away after such a devastating trauma, but he insisted. My unheeded advice has proven painfully correct. According to Daniel's letters, he and his father barely speak now."

"If you and the earl are also estranged, how can you be sure he'll help me?"

"Because, though he erred with his son, Lord Whittington is a good man, an honest man, and he'll rule on your case with that honesty. But secondly, he knows I am perhaps the only person who can turn Daniel's heart back to his father. I'll play that card if I must."

"Thank you, Arthur. I wish I had an equal gift for you."

"But there is one thing you can do for me that would bring me immense pleasure. Tell me all about Frannie—how she became the 'wild woman of the Willows.' Since I won't know what her future holds, I'd enjoy hearing how she came to be the woman who captured my heart."

The all-too-familiar lump returned to Jed's throat. He tried to begin with a laugh as he described the strong-willed, redheaded baby sister who defied convention from birth, but the topic was too tender, and from the first word, he settled back and allowed the memories to flow sweet and strong. After an hour's storytelling, he looked at Arthur's face and saw resigned sorrow beneath his smile.

"She loves you, Arthur. She's had many a suitor, but never once has she given her heart to another as she has to you. Not even with Frederick. They were more friends, really. But not you. If you have any will left, promise me that you'll try to get well and return to her."

CHAPTER 32

Tuesday, September 20, 1814
Baltimore, Maryland

Timothy Shepard was in a full sweat, though the temperatures were mild that Tuesday afternoon. Dusty, dirty, and not knowing where to begin looking, he headed to the fort, seeking any news of the women. Caleb grabbed his infantry cap and neckerchief, his two proudest possessions, and volunteered to guide Timothy to the rooming house, but there was no answer at either of the women's apartments. They tried Samuel's door, but his apartment was also empty. In frustration Timothy said, "Come on, Caleb. Would you share a meal with me?"

Caleb's eyes lit up and the two headed uptown to the busiest part of the city. Vendors once again sold their wares on the streets, while newsboys hawked newspapers fresh from the press as printers began to be dismissed from the battle lines to serve the war effort in a new capacity—publishing the victorious news of the repelling of the British from Baltimore. And the most popular paper of the day was the *Baltimore Patriot,* who scooped its competitors by featuring the first newspaper publication of Francis Scott Key's poem, "The Defence of Fort McHenry."

Timothy purchased a copy and took it with him to the restaurant the pair chose. After ordering, he opened the paper and began to read. "Mr. Key wrote a poem about the bombardment!" he uttered softly to himself. As he settled in to read the poem he was so moved by the words that he began again, reading aloud, so he could share it with Caleb.

Caleb stood during the reading and fished something from his pocket. "I've got my own copy, one of the first ones, straight from Mr. Key's original."

"May I see that?" Timothy asked.

"Sure. Everybody at the fort got one." Caleb handed the sheet of paper to him.

Timothy looked it over, then smiled and handed it back. "Have you read it all the way through, Caleb?"

"Read it? I memorized it already!"

Impressed, Timothy leaned back and smiled at the precocious youngster. "All right, recite some for me."

Caleb stood, dressed in his soldier's cap and neckerchief, and began in a voice soft and serious, reflecting the meaning the poem held for one who had survived the events depicted.

> *O! say can you see by the dawn's early light,*
> *What so proudly we hailed at the twilight's last*
>   *gleaming,*
> *Whose broad stripes and bright stars through the*
>   *perilous fight*
> *O'er the ramparts we watch'd, were so gallantly*
>   *streaming?*
> *And the Rockets' red glare, the Bombs bursting in*
>   *air,*
> *Gave proof through the night that our flag was still*
>   *there;*
> *O! say does that star-spangled banner yet wave,*
> *O'er the Land of the free, and the home of the*
>   *brave?*

L.C. LEWIS

*On the shore dimly seen through the mists of the
deep,*
*Where the foe's haughty host in dread silence
reposes.*
*What is that which the breeze, o'er the towering
steep,*
As it fitfully blows, half conceals, half discloses?
*Now it catches the gleam of the morning's first
beam,*
In full glory reflected now shines in the stream,
'Tis the star-spangled banner, O! long may it wave,
O'er the land of the free and the home of the brave.

And where is that band who so vauntingly swore
That the havoc of war and the battle's confusion,
A home and a country shall leave us no more,
*Their blood has washed out their foul footsteps
pollution.*
No refuge could save the hireling and slave,
From the terror of flight or the gloom of the grave,
*And the star-spangled banner in triumph doth
wave,*
*O'er the land of the Free, and the Home of the
Brave.*

O! Thus be it ever when freemen shall stand,
*Between their lov'd home, and the war's
desolation,*
*Blest with vict'ry and peace, may the Heav'n rescued
land,*
*Praise the Power that hath made and preserv'd us
a nation!*
Then conquer we must, when our cause it is just,
And this be our motto—"In God is our Trust,"

And the star-spangled banner in triumph doth wave,
O'er the land of the Free, and the Home of the Brave.

When Caleb finished, he stood silent and still, staring into Timothy's eyes, which were now moist. Timothy reached a hand across to the lad. "Well done, Caleb. Well done."

Unbeknown to either of them, the other patrons in the establishment had also tuned to the lad's recitation, and now the men rose and displayed their own copies of the *Baltimore Patriot,* while the women joined them in offering Caleb their own grateful applause.

"It's for you, Caleb. They're applauding your recitation."

Caleb turned slowly, his eyes bright with wonder, and smiled. Gently removing his cap, he dipped it and bowed, then replaced it and sat. A reporter from the *Patriot* came over and asked Caleb's name for the story he was writing about the city's reception of Key's poem.

"I'm going to be in the paper?" Caleb asked the reporter.

"You sure are," the man replied. "And where did you get your cap? Is your pa a militiaman?"

"It's my cap. Me and my pa are soldiers at Fort McHenry. Well, I'm sort of a soldier, but my pa is one of Captain Nicholson's Fencibles!"

"Is that right? Why, that'd make a swell angle for my story. A colored soldier at Fort McHenry. Yeah! I like the sound of that. Think your pa would talk to me?"

"He's not much on talking, but maybe he will if I tell him I'm already going to be in your paper. I'll take you to him."

Caleb's food was packed in a sack so he could take it along. He smiled at Timothy before he left. "Thank you for all this, Mr. Shepard. This has been one of the best days of my entire life! I never thought it could be this way anywhere but the Willows—

not having to hide my smarts, and having people like me and not be all worried about me being Negro or white."

"I'm glad you had a good day, Caleb. I did as well. And thank you for the recitation. I'll remember it always."

As Caleb headed off on an altogether new adventure, Timothy became contemplative. He couldn't help the smile that kept creeping onto his own face. Like Caleb, he hadn't known life could be so sweet and good, and it wasn't just the turn in the war that had set his heart on fire. It was something more, and he had Frannie to thank for that.

After paying for the meals, Timothy headed back outside, allowing himself to be swept along with the crowd that was swarming toward strains of beautiful music. He pushed through to the middle of the crowd to see the source of the sound, and there he found Frannie and Jenny singing in a quartet with two men, while another man accompanied them on the flute. The accompanist and one of the male vocalists were unfamiliar to Timothy, but the other was none other than Samuel Renfro.

Anxious to catch his friends' attention, Timothy waved and called Frannie's and Samuel's names one by one. When he felt a tap on his shoulder, Timothy turned and saw Markus O'Malley. The naval officer was neatly dressed in a blue Sea Fencibles' uniform, his smile beaming and his hand extended.

"I take it ya didn't know Samuel could sing either, eh?" Markus asked.

Timothy bypassed the handshake and drew Markus in for an embrace. "First things first! How are you? I've read the account in the paper. What an ordeal you've been through."

"Aye," Markus said with a chuckle. "'Twas a bit dicey at times, but I think it'll prove ta be one o' the great honors of my life."

"I have no doubt. I'm proud of you, Markus."

Markus stepped back. "I did nothin' to earn any praise. It was just an honor to be an American and see our boys give them brutes a good fight. Now Samuel's the one I'm proud of!"

Timothy laughed and returned his gaze to the singers. "I had no idea he even sang."

"Aye, those other two are the Durang brothers, friends of Frannie and Jenny from their singing days. They bumped into them yesterday and they needed another fella singer, so Samuel obliged them."

Timothy listened to the beautiful harmony. "They're marvelous."

"Aye, they are."

Timothy noted the thoughtful tone in Markus's reply and the melancholy written on his face. "You look exhausted, but I suppose that's to be expected after your ordeal."

"Aye, I suppose that's what it is."

Puzzled by Markus's answer, Timothy eyed him curiously. "Let's move forward so they know we're here. I need to speak to Frannie anyway."

"No thanks, but you go on along. I'd just as soon listen from here, incognito, as they say."

Now Timothy knew something was wrong with Markus, but this was neither the time nor the place to pursue the matter. He picked his way through the throng until he reached the front. Again the song ended, and again the musical group began moving forward to a new corner with a large portion of the crowd following along.

"Frannie!" Timothy called out.

When she saw him, Frannie smiled happily and waved her hand over her head at him. Timothy moved in closer and wrapped an arm around her and nearly shouted to be heard above the din of voices. "I've forgotten how beautifully you sing. You're marvelous!"

"Thank you. I feel sublime. Ferdinand and Charles have been signed to a six-week contract to perform at Captain McCauley's tavern beginning in October. And imagine what their finale number will be? Mr. Key's poem set to 'Anacreon in Heaven!' Isn't that splendid?"

"Only you could be so happy over someone else's good fortune. But I should still scold you! I nearly died of fright when I returned to the Willows on Thursday evening to find you women gone. Jack told me you had come here. I waited three days for your return, debating whether to race here and find you or to continue vigilantly at the farm. Where are Hannah and Bitty?"

"Attending to business in town."

"Alone? Without me? Twice I rode into Calverton and asked around if anyone had seen three disobedient women on the loose. I should throttle you all, you know."

Frannie raised a playful eyebrow. "You should never have left us in the first place!"

The comment drew a sobered acknowledgement from Timothy. "I know, I apologize, but I didn't know how to face you after you turned down my proposal yet again. But you were right to do so, and I followed your advice."

Frannie looked at him in confusion. "What advice of mine did you follow?"

"I called on Lucinda Bainbridge to settle the matter concerning her feelings for me. I wanted to put the notion to rest once and for all, and you had so filled me with frustration and humiliation that I felt I had nothing more to fear. So I went to her home, told her I was fond of her, and asked if she felt anything at all similar for me. And she does, Frannie! She said she felt altogether the same. Isn't that wonderful?"

Frannie frowned. "Astonishing."

The sparkle in Timothy's eyes dimmed. "You don't seem pleased. Is this not the very thing you wanted from me? To end my hovering and have me move along so you aren't encumbered like a master with an annoying pet at her feet?"

"Of course it is. I'm very happy for you." Frannie signaled to Ferdinand that she needed a moment, then grabbed her skirts and fled to a lone corner, with Timothy following her. When he reached her he was more frustrated than before, and angry as well.

He took off his hat and raked his fingers through his brown hair. "What do you want from me? You say you love me but not as a husband, and then you try to make a match for me, and when it works—when someone I could care for does actually love me in return—you yank me back like a dog! Is that what you want? A dog on a leash?" His breathing was rapid and his eyes narrowed angrily. "You don't really want to be happy, nor do you want that for me. You love drama, Frannie. That's what this is all about. To you, life is a grand stage, and you prance about playing a part, but you have no idea about how to actually live a real life, or love anyone!"

In a reflex, her hand moved to slap him, to stop the hurtful words. He caught it and held it fast as he studied her. His face relaxed, and as compassion filled his eyes he brought their hands to his heart and held them gently. "You're so easy to love, but you're so afraid to love back. We're different, you and I. I can't be happy playing endless games of run and chase. I need attachments and stability. I want a wife and a home and children, while you commit yourself only to phantom lovers who can't commit in return. I hope it works for you, Frannie, but I am done."

She covered her eyes with her hands to hide her tears. "If Arthur lives, I'll find him, and I'll find my happiness. And if he doesn't, then I at least know what my heart requires. In either case, I do want you to be happy. I'm not sad because you found love. I'm only sad because it will change our friendship."

"I promised to always be here for you, Frannie, and I shall, but from here on, *we* shall be here for you. We've spoken of you already. Lucinda knows of our friendship. She will always welcome you into our home."

"It will never be the same, but I wish you every happiness. You two will have a wonderful life together. You are well suited to one another."

Timothy's face relaxed once again. "Yes, we are. America is going to survive this war, but she'll need strong leaders who'll help the coming generation remember how close we came to failing. I want to be one of those men, and Lucinda will help me." He moved to Frannie's side and slipped her arm within the crook of his own. "And what will you do next?"

"I haven't thought beyond Jed's return home. All my plans hinge on that."

"You need something more—for yourself. Promise me you'll think about that."

Frannie nodded and the two walked down the street to join the group, who had been carrying on in two-part harmony on the store's stoop in her absence. Timothy and Frannie had barely arrived when a mustached man in a seaman's uniform started yelling from the back of the crowd. He was a head taller than most of the men in the crowd and half again as wide, and as he approached the singers, he waved a colorful handbill in the air.

"Jenny's in trouble!" Frannie said, letting go of Timothy's arm. She tried to find a path to reach Jenny, who was just beginning to understand the nature of the confusion. Before Frannie could reach her friend, bodies began parting like a wake in the sea as another man barreled through the crowd. Jenny seemed equally frightened by his arrival as Markus O'Malley stood before her, facing the crowd, his broad, squat frame positioned to take on any comers.

Immediately, the seaman recognized the officer's bars on Markus's uniform. Pointing his handbill at Jenny like a sword, the seaman attempted to win Markus's support. "She's a traitor, sir," he shouted. "A filthy British-loving traitor who cozied up to the enemy after they burned Washington!"

Markus shouted a rebuttal, but the collective gasp of the crowd drowned out his words. A general shift in the mood of the assembly preceded more finger-pointing as murmurs escalated to the shouting of angry epithets. Jenny shrank in horror and began to cry as Markus moved directly in front of her, commending her to Samuel's care. That action caused him to also become the subject of derisive comments. A balled page of newsprint was thrown at him, then another, and then a stone, but Markus remained in his place.

Frannie stepped up beside him, directly into the fray, and the sight of her bravely standing there appeared to stun the crowd. "Do you have a plan?" she whispered to Markus.

"Not a good one," he replied before stepping forward and addressing the throng. "I was just like you this very mornin', condemnin' this woman without a trial on the hearsay of someone who isn't even here to face 'er. You all have your papers and you've read Key's poem, but have the words 'The land of the free and the home of the brave' not meant anythin' to ya? This little lady climbed up here and sang those beautiful words for us, knowin' these hateful posters were plastered all over the city. Seems to me a person can't get braver than that. And what about that line 'When our cause it is just'? Does this feel like American justice to you, friends? It sure don't to me."

"Was she with the British or not?" bellowed the sailor.

"Yes, yes, she was, as a prisoner, just like me and Mr. Key and the rest of our company were during the bombardment. Yes, friends, I was there in that ship with Mr. Key, and I can tell you there's nothin' more frightenin' than havin' an enemy strip away your liberty. That's what they did to 'er that night, so, yes, she was there. Did she sing for them? I can't say, but I can tell you that this very mornin' this fine lady went to see the captains at Fort McHenry and delivered important information about the British and their next military campaign. Now that's real patriotism to me, and I applaud 'er courage."

He started clapping his hands together slowly and deliberately. Frannie joined in next, followed by Timothy, then Samuel and the Durang brothers. They maintained the rhythm until a few people in the crowd joined in, and soon everyone began to either clap or leave. When the clapping finally halted, the crowd slowly slipped away. Jenny looked as wrung out as a rag.

"Thank you, Mr. O'Malley," she said.

Markus bowed slightly, never meeting her eyes. "It was the least I could do, Mrs. Tyler. I'm sorry for any hurt I caused ya earlier." He laid a gentle hand on Frannie's arm. "You're about the bravest person I know." As he turned to leave he noticed Timothy studying her, his eyes filled with admiration. "Ain't she, Timothy?"

Mr. Shepard glanced away and said, "She's a wonder."

Samuel moved forward to shake Markus's hand. "Well said, friend." He shifted his attention to Timothy. "So the prodigal son returns. And where have you been?"

"Washington. There's much activity there with the government, and I'm needed there. Markus, are you ready to resume the watch at the Willows?"

Markus's eyes closed as if he were savoring a delicious treat. "Aye. I'm hungry for green fields, solid ground, and hard work."

"Then I'll return to the Federal City," Timothy said. "I'm needed there in Washington. President Madison was set to reconvene the Congress yesterday."

"Where are they meeting now that the Capitol Building is in ruins?" Samuel wondered.

"At the patent office. After much cajoling the British were convinced it was a public entity and not government property, so it was spared from destruction, but there is considerable discussion about moving the capital to a new city. I suppose that will be the first item of debate."

"So many problems," Markus mused. "I'll stick to farmin' and mendin' fences."

"The problems are great and many," Timothy went on. "The first order of business will be to assess and strengthen the military. Then a full inquiry on the events that led to the failure at Washington will commence. I hope to begin rebuilding the Congressional Library, but our biggest worry may stem from all the rumors of secession being whispered in three New England states."

Markus was incredulous. "Some of our own want to divide us after all we've already been through?"

"The whole of New England feels they've suffered heavily as a result of the war, but Massachusetts, Connecticut, and Rhode Island are the most vocal on the matter."

"Well, tell them to see what we've suffered here. That ought ta settle their whinin'."

Timothy huffed in agreement, then stood and offered his hand to his friends. "Well, then, I suppose I should be on my way."

"When will we see you next?" Samuel asked.

Timothy's eyes stole briefly to Frannie, whose attention was fixed on him. "I think I'll be heavily engaged in the capital and unable to get away for the foreseeable future, but my door is always open. Aside from Jed, you are my dearest friends. God be with you all." He tipped his hat to the women and began to walk away.

"I'll walk a ways with ya." Markus likewise tipped his cap to Frannie and Jenny before departing.

Samuel quickly joined the pair as well, leaving the Durang brothers and the women standing on the stoop.

✮ ✮ ✮ ✮ ✮

Jenny slipped her arm through Frannie's and leaned close to whisper, "Thank you for standing up for me back there. And Mr. O'Malley was unexpectedly kind as well, wasn't he?"

The words fell on deaf ears as Frannie's attention remained wholly on the departing frame of Timothy Shepard.

"Are you all right, Frannie? You look as though you've lost your best friend."

"Not my best. He's on his way to a British prison, but I've lost my second-best friend."

Jenny laid her head on Frannie's shoulder. "I guess it's just up to us to make good on all those dreams we dreamed at Le Jardin."

Frannie watched as the three men disappeared around a corner. Then she offered her friend a half smile, clamping her hand more confidently over Jenny's. She sighed long and low, then wiped the last tears from her eyes, straightened, and set her shoulders. "And we will, Jenny. We will."

CHAPTER 33

Monday, September 26, 1814
Melville Island Prison

Since the news of the fall of Washington, Major Dudley Snowden felt his own hope ebbing. He no longer felt the spiritual assurance that he would make it off Melville Island alive. Only two things kept him from surrendering to the deadly malaise that had freed so many others from Melville through death—Beatrice's daily letters, and God's word.

The letters arrived in passels of ten to twenty at a time. Dudley would sort them out by date and read them quickly, one after another, and then he would read them again and again until the next batch arrived. Some of the men were so hungry for any mention of America and the minutia of normalcy that he would pass around the less personal pages so others could enjoy the delicate penmanship of a woman and remember the cause that had sent them to war. Dudley felt guilty for his thoughts of dire melancholy, for what man could be more loved? But still, despite his good fight, the depression set in.

He opened his Bible less frequently now, as fewer and fewer of the men called for those sacred passages of hope and deliverance. When he did read from the holy text, it was primarily for his own comfort. Dudley wondered if the soldiers who fled the line at Bladensburg had any idea at all what they had thrown away. It was unfathomable to him, particularly now, that any free man could open the way for a despot to seize his homeland. Dudley knew any one of the men in his cell block would stand his ragged body on the line right now, merely for the privilege of facing the enemy again and declaring with unwavering surety in the principles of America, that their cause was just.

For days the men had endured the most painful taunting as their British captors flaunted the destruction of the Americans' capital in their faces. Then the prisoners' agonizing questions abounded: "Is Madison still our president? Do we still have a government? Do you think they rallied somewhere else, sir?"

The next batch of Beatrice's letters had been long delayed after the announcement of Washington's fall, and when they finally arrived the news on these matters was thin. And then Dudley felt the change—the unmistakable tension, the underlying anger, the deterioration in the quantity and quality of their already-meager rations. He had experienced it all at the prison camp at Lachine, near Quebec, and though the effects were grievous to the Americans, he knew some American victory was the cause, and that gave him and his men hope.

Dudley tried to engage DeWitt in a conversation in order to confirm his assumption, but not even this gregarious guard would speak with the Americans. As the week wore on to two, Dudley worried about the other prisoners, some too sick and weak to endure further privations. Then one day, the arrival of a ship drew nearly every guard to the docks or at least to the yard. Then, and only then, would DeWitt whisper an exchange to Dudley.

"You'd do well to have your men stay real quiet for the next few days, Major. The British men have heavy hearts, and it wouldn't take much for them to light into any American."

Dudley's thin, frail hands gripped the bars as he drew his sagging face near to whisper in reply. "But why? You've taken our capital. What could cause your men this much distress? We've felt it for weeks now."

DeWitt glanced about nervously, though he was the only British soldier in the area. "We've had a few bad turns, we have. Two weeks after our sterling victory at Washington, another of our fleets was setting in Lake Champlain, preparing to land ten thousand of Britain's best on New England's shores. Your ragged American fleet sent them into a full retreat. Some say a British victory there would have been enough to make you Yanks surrender this war. Instead, you disrupted our supply lines and lengthened it, but that's not the worst of the news. You see that ship in the harbor? The *Royal Oak?* Major General Robert Ross, a beloved commander, was shot dead in Baltimore during the attempt to take that city. The men are grievously feeling his loss."

Dudley groaned at the report and asked urgently, "Did they succeed, Sergeant? Did Baltimore fall?"

Dewitt's eyes shifted again as he checked every corner and entrance to assure the privacy of their conversation. "I'd hold this news a few more days, Major. Considering the mood our troops are in, if your men speak of these things, it would prove most unpleasant for everyone."

"Yes, yes, you have my word. I won't speak of any of this until after we receive news in a letter from our families. But Baltimore is my home. Please tell me her fate."

DeWitt scuffed his boot on the floor for a moment or two, checking the entrance for any sign of arriving soldiers. Then he pressed his cheek as near the bars as he could while pretending to be leaning there, checking the sole of his shoe. "She's fine, Major," he whispered. "Baltimore still stands. We lost the battle and our beloved General Ross, but Baltimore and Fort McHenry still stand."

CHAPTER 34

Friday, October 7, 1814
Liverpool, England

From the first sighting of land, Jed and Arthur stood on the deck watching the shores of England draw near. Admittedly, Jed was as excited about reaching shore as Arthur, knowing that despite their different reasons, both men's deliverance and peace waited there.

Jed was dressed in donated attire, the very best pieces of clothing owned by the few crew members as tall and broad as he— black dress slacks, a white shirt with ruffles at the throat and cuffs, a blue cravat, and a gray coat. He was awed by their kindness, and despite the slightly odd look, he felt like an aristocrat.

He was drawn to the very depths of humility as he stood next to Arthur, his selfless benefactor, who was in far greater need than he. For the first time since the explosion, the gentle Brit was dressed in a clean uniform, sitting somewhat upright in a chair, propped up by pillows and rolled blankets. Jed studied his friend's countenance and noted peace there despite the obvious toll of the explosion six weeks before. Arthur's once-boyish jaw was now slack and lean, appearing like that of an old man, not a youth of twenty-six years. Jed feared each time he shaved him that a nick would go straight to the bone. The gold epaulets of Arthur's red jacket hung limply over his narrow shoulders, but his vitals' region was thick with bandages, leaving the sweet young man shaped like a two-legged red pear.

As shocking as his appearance might be to those who knew him, there was one detail that undeniably identified Arthur despite his pain and infirmity. His eyes sparkled with gratitude for the one gift he had asked God to grant him—the blessing to return to England's green shores. Jed wiped his moist eyes as he considered the man. He would have counted himself blessed to have Frannie and Arthur marry. As convinced as Arthur was that he was on heaven-borrowed time, Jed still prayed that God would heal his friend and spare his life. He wondered if it was a selfish request.

Half an hour passed. Jed's nose crinkled as they drew deeper up the Mersey River to the port at Liverpool.

Arthur smiled and nudged Jed. "What do you smell?"

Jed chuckled. "Rotted fish."

"No, that's pure British perfume, my friend." Arthur closed his eyes and drew in the aroma. "This is where my father began—in Liverpool—and these are the smells he wanted to rise above. To me, they simply mean I am home."

Jed wanted to avoid discussing Stephen Ramsey. "Is London far from Liverpool?"

"It's a two-day trip by carriage with a good team and a healthy companion. I suppose it may be easier for me if we travel by boat, though it may take us longer. My father's new residence is an estate on the fringe of the London suburbs, but he still owns the London town home where I was born. That's where we'll be staying until your hearing."

"Perhaps we should pause here for a few days so you can rest in a bed on solid ground."

"First, I want to eat something that hasn't been salted or dried. I'd like to awaken to fresh scones and honey, and fork into a steaming shepherd's pie."

"I have no idea what either item is, but I'm salivating for a taste of both."

"What delight will I have showing you my world!" Arthur grabbed Jed's arm and laughed, but his hand remained there seconds after. "I want you to love Britain, Jed. Her people are good and her ways are strong. I hope you will try to bring friendship between our nations. And remember, these are also your people."

Jed didn't answer. The hurts and aggressions doled out in recent months were still too raw, but this land had produced Arthur, and that alone opened Jed's heart to the exercise.

He studied every inch of the shoreline and the activities there as they sailed into the bustling harbor. The docks seemed to be just another sea, as fluid as the ocean and equally mesmerizing to the eye. As Jed stared at the people and products waiting to be loaded onto or pouring forth from ships, he deduced that these people could easily be standing on a dock at Calverton.

The ship anchored and three sailors, including young Edward Tenneyson, helped Jed carry Arthur to a dinghy and set him inside before a wooden arm swung the small craft, suspending it over the water. Slowly, it began to be lowered into the river. Jed, Captain Smith, Smith's secretary, a ship pilot, and the sailors climbed down the rope ladder and joined Arthur inside. The vessel shifted and swayed something terrible until it settled on the murky waters dotted with dead fish. The strain of the movement was written in the gray of Arthur's face.

As they rowed to shore, Jed saw other faces studying their boat. Some were simply curious children fascinated by the arrival of the warship *Iphigenia,* but most were men who stopped their work, waiting for whatever news the ship and its crew would bring.

Arthur craned his neck to get a better look at the crowd.

"Do you recognize someone on the dock?"

Arthur relaxed. "I thought I saw the Spaniard. No matter . . . I'm sure I was mistaken."

"The man indebted to your father?" The thought of meeting Arthur's father, or his associate, unnerved Jed.

"Don't worry. As I said, I was mistaken."

340

Jed's worry faded as the boat tied up at the pier, where he and the three sailors carefully lifted the litter to the dock. As they moved through a crowd, a young boy in tattered clothes and a cotton cap ran alongside, tugging at Captain Smith's sleeve, jabbering in a British accent more exaggerated than Arthur's.

"Sir! Sir! Are you come from America, sir?"

The child clearly annoyed Captain Smith, who was struggling to part the crowd to facilitate Arthur's transport. Pushing the lad aside he replied, "Yes, boy, now hurry along."

The child ran up again, tugging the captain's sleeve even harder. "From Mary-land, sir?"

One of the other sailors brusquely kicked at the lad, sending him scurrying ahead. "We've got a wounded man here, boy. Out of the way."

"No harm meant, sir. Just please tell me if you've come from Mary-land! I've been hired to watch for Lieutenant Arthur Ramsey's ship."

Arthur grabbed Jed's hand. "What did he say? Stop! Let me speak to him."

Captain Smith now had a hand on the lad's shoulder. "Lieutenant, this boy seems to want to speak to you."

Arthur raised his head and reached out a hand to the lad. "You say you've been hired to watch for Arthur Ramsey's ship? Who hired you, Son?"

"A Spanish man, sir. I get a shilling for every military ship's arrival I report, and a five-pound note when I locate the ship carrying Arthur Ramsey."

"Then tell the Spaniard he owes you five pounds. I am Arthur Ramsey."

The boy raced away but returned momentarily. "Where shall he find you, sir?"

"Tell him . . . tell him I'll be awaiting him in the Boar's Head Inn and Tavern." Arthur looked up at Jed, who stood scanning the dockyard, studying every face.

"I don't think my father is here, Jed, but I need to get a message to him. I'm not asking you to meet him. I won't put you through that."

Jed offered no reply.

As the boy raced off again, one of the sailors asked Captain Smith, "Shall we head there now, sir?"

Captain Smith nodded. "Yes, but give me a moment." Smith placed one hand on Jed's shoulder as he addressed Arthur. "Lieutenant Ramsey, I now entrust Lieutenant Pearson to your watch on your honor as an officer in His Majesty's Royal Navy. He is still a prisoner, and you both must remember that. Here is a duplicate copy of his file I had made for you. The contents will be necessary for your meeting with the earl. I must run along now to make my report to my superiors, but I'll schedule Pearson's hearing in one week, on the fourteenth, at the offices of the Admiralty, at 1:00. Mr. Pearson's future peace and freedom will require that you both make it there at the appointed hour. If, for some reason, well . . ." He turned his attention to Jed. "If Mr. Ramsey is unable to attend, you, Mr. Pearson, must get yourself there or risk being a wanted man whose guilt will be assured by your failure to appear. Have I made myself clear?"

"Quite clear," Arthur answered with a wry smile. "We will both be there, Captain."

"Good. I'm putting my own career in jeopardy by allowing you to serve as his guard, Mr. Ramsey, particularly in your fragile condition. I'm trusting you both to act honorably here. The Admiralty may send guards to your London home to check on Pearson." Smith offered Jed his hand. "Thank you, Lieutenant. It has been a privilege. I'll do my very best for you, sir, as I promised."

Jed clasped both his hands over the captain's, knowing this would likely be the last time they would see one another before the trial. "Thank you for restoring my hope, Captain Smith. My very life now lies in your hands, sir."

Smith shook Jed's hand. "I fully understand the import of this hearing, Lieutenant." Smith took Arthur's hands next. "You'll be in my prayers, Mr. Ramsey. God speed to you both."

Smith and his secretary strode away and quickly melted into the throng, leaving the pair in the care of the sailors, who now carried the litter toward the Boar's Head Inn. Once there, Arthur raised his hand and asked Jed, "Would you help me stand? I'd like to walk in on my own."

Jed noticed the boyish playfulness in Arthur's eyes. He helped Arthur to sit up and then to swing his legs around until they touched the ground. Then, carefully supporting his friend's weight, Jed helped him to rise. "Are you sure this is wise, Arthur?"

Arthur offered a sly smile. "Roust and I have been practicing." To the sailors he added, "Thank you for your help. You are now dismissed."

Jed turned to young Edward, whose friends were cajoling him to head to a pub. "We never got to have that talk, Edward. Follow your heart, and watch out for Ethan, will you?"

The pair shook hands. "I will, sir, on both counts. I—I wish you the best, sir. I truly do."

Jed watched the lad leave, then hovered close to Arthur, who clearly basked in the sights and smells of England's working class—the clamor of voices, the heady aroma of stout mixed with the lingering odor of fish and the sea. Pointing to a table in a forward corner, Arthur began hobbling forward when a frantic voice at the doorway stopped him cold.

"I'm looking for my son—Arthur Ramsey! He's a soldier just arrived from America and he's injured. I was told he was here."

Arthur turned to the man, who now proceeded to grab arms and collars, demanding answers from every person in his path. The father's and son's eyes finally met, but recognition and acceptance appeared to come slowly to Stephen Ramsey. The man's initial reaction was agonizing shock as he scanned the fragile, distorted being before him. Jed watched Ramsey's color drain as the reality hit him—that this broken man was his beautiful, angelic son.

The mixture of sorrow and joy consuming Arthur's face was equally wrenching. He had described his father as a handsome man looking younger than his fifty-three years, but the man standing before Arthur was nearly completely gray and dressed in a blue cotton suit whose expensive cut was marred by the tight fit, stretching the buttonholes of his vest across an expansive midsection. He appeared more like a contented family man than a powerful broker of business.

"My son!" Ramsey said with a groan. His body shrank inwardly, but then he straightened himself and flew to Arthur, gathering him up in his arms. "What have they done to my boy?" He took Arthur into his arms gingerly, hesitantly, and wept, while Jed remained transfixed, almost numb, absorbing the fact that this grieving father was the man who had tried to murder his family.

Behind the pair was an exquisitely clothed younger man with jet black hair tied at the nape of his neck. His stood like a matador, serenely erect and elegant, a warmth emanating from his coal black eyes that seemed familiar and genuine. He made his way to Jed with his hand outstretched. "This is a good thing you have done today in bringing this man's son home, señor. Allow me to introduce myself. My name is Juan Arroya Corvas," he said in a heavy Spanish accent.

Jed stared at the man. "The messenger. Another of Stephen Ramsey's victims."

"That is past. Mr. Ramsey has released me from our arrangement. I am here today in service to Arthur Ramsey."

Jed's eyes narrowed suspiciously.

"I know that expression," Corvas said. "Those are the eyes of someone Ramsey has crossed. Are you also indebted to him?"

"Indebted to him?" Jed spat back. "That man owes *me*, only he couldn't repay his debt to my family if he had a hundred lifetimes."

The Spaniard shrank back, and then Jed saw shame reflected in his face. "You are the American, from a place called Maryland," he stated sadly. "Yes . . . hello, Mr. Pearson."

Fire flashing in his eyes, Jed bolted toward Corvas. "How do you know me? Did Ramsey also enlist you to harm my family?"

Corvas paled and dropped to his knees, clasping his hands together and bowing his head as if in prayer. "I did not plot against your family, sir, but I confess that my hands are not clean. Though I did not know his intentions, I am the weak man who delivered the assassin Dupree to Mr. Ramsey. I have spent these past years trying to undo the harm I've caused your family."

"Do not speak to me of my family! How did you know our ship was arriving today?"

"I didn't. For days I've been paying that young boy to watch the harbor and report every incoming military ship to me."

"And how long did you plan to do this? You had no idea when or if we were arriving."

Corvas finally raised his eyes to meet Jed's. "Until the end of the war if need be."

Jed cast a distrustful glance at the man. It was then that Arthur and Stephen Ramsey approached him. Arthur's father stood ramrod straight with his hands by his sides. "Mr. Pearson, I am Stephen Ramsey, the man who sent Dupree to your door."

Jed had not counted on facing his nemesis, but now the devil that had tortured his family's peace for two long years stood before him, extending a hand. Jed stood stone still.

Ramsey sent his own gaze downward. "There are no words to express my regret for what I have wrought upon your household, Mr. Pearson. Were I as agile a man as Juan, I too would be on my knees, but I stand here, nonetheless, begging your forgiveness."

Jed flatly ignored the plea. He had spent too many sleepless nights plotting to kill this man with his bare hands, hoping to make Ramsey realize the same terror he had unleashed at the Willows. But now Arthur watched anxiously, and his goodness and loyalty cooled Jed's fury. Jed directed his response to Juan Corvas, but his cold stare aimed at Ramsey made it clear his intentions were meant for both men. "Get off your knees, Corvas. Your piety comes far too late."

As Corvas rose to his feet, Ramsey met Jed's stare. "I suppose you'd like to kill me."

The men's eyes locked and Jed fought the urge to use his hands, which had curled into fists of their own accord. He wished Ramsey were stronger or less accommodating. Jed didn't want his enemy to be repentant—he wanted to feel justified in his hatred. But he could see Arthur's sweet eyes, praying for him to make peace.

Jed felt his shoulders sag. "I know what you'd like from me, Arthur, but I cannot do it. I cannot forgive this monster. Not now. He stole our peace during what could prove to be the only months I had with Hannah. How can he ever give us that back?"

Arthur looked away as Jed pointed his finger in Stephen Ramsey's face. "A man I loved was murdered by Dupree. I cannot absolve you of that good man's blood, nor do I wish to. Were it not for Arthur . . ." Jed growled. "He believes you are changed. I only pray he is right."

"He is, Mr. Pearson. I swear he is. And I will do my best to prove that to him and to you."

Arthur slumped against a chair and all attention returned to him. As Stephen Ramsey moved to his son, he cried out, "Hurry, Juan! Bring my carriage here!"

As Corvas hurried away to attend to the task, Jed helped settle Arthur into a chair, then moved to a corner of the room, away from the sight of Stephen Ramsey.

"Let me take you to a hospital, Son—"

"No, Father! We have more urgent matters to attend to. Speak with me about these."

Stephen sat back, his worry obviously unabated. "Very well. I'll do whatever you say if you'll promise to let me take you to a doctor and have you seen."

"Once we are finished." Arthur took hold of Stephen's hand. "I hope you know that I love you. So much ill will has passed between us, but I do not want to be your judge. I leave that to God. I want there to be no disputations between us, only amity and love."

A sudden peace filled Stephen's countenance, but Arthur drew a deep breath and went on. "Still, I was there when Dupree attacked the Willows. I saw the horror—and it was horror, Father—meted out to women and children alike. It was only through the grace of God that more weren't killed. You can never repay this family for what they have suffered, but you do have one opportunity to try."

Stephen Ramsey, normally the epitome of cold control, seemed incapable of mounting any defense. He bowed his head to his hand. "I'll do anything, Son, anything."

Arthur could now barely bear up his head. "Jed Pearson has been falsely accused of a war crime. The documentation should be sufficient to prove that, but I—I plan to petition Lord Whittington to review his case and plead for him. If something should happen to me—make me unable to see this through—I want your word that you will call upon the members of the Admiralty in whose favor you are, and advocate for Jed Pearson."

"Why would you not be able to ful—No, Arthur! You're not saying that your time is so short?" Ramsey stood and searched through the window. "Where is Corvas with that carriage?"

"Give me your word, Father."

"I'll hail a cabbie, Arthur. We'll head straight to the hospital—"

"Your word, Father!"

"You have my word, Arthur. Of course I'll do all I can for Mr. Pearson, but right now you are my concern."

Juan Corvas appeared, driving Ramsey's custom rig. As soon as he saw it pull up, Ramsey lifted his frail son and began heading to the carriage.

Arthur stalled his father a moment longer. "I want you to know that I wish you to be happy, Father. If that happiness lies in a union with Mrs. McGowan, then do it and be happy. It pleases me to think that you will have a chance to be a father again. It truly does."

"Are you so quick to forfeit your own life, Arthur?" Ramsey asked urgently. "I am not so willing to replace one son with two others. I expect to be the father of three."

Arthur smiled, noticing a gang of young hooligans gathered in front of the tavern. One of the lads had seemed especially interested in their arrival as they rowed to shore, and he kept peering through the glass at them. As they exited the pub, one boy received a series of hearty pats as the group scurried away.

Jed entered the carriage first to pull Arthur's shoulders, while Stephen Ramsey remained on the ground, guiding his son's legs into the conveyance. The group of boys ran full tilt down the street. Several of them skirted so close to Ramsey that one boy actually bumped him. After a groan and a gasp, Ramsey began to fall.

"Father!" Arthur shouted.

Corvas jumped down from the driver's box and laid Ramsey back against his own chest. The man's breathing was labored and he was unable to speak. A crimson patch spreading against Corvas's chest revealed that Stephen Ramsey had been stabbed in the back.

CHAPTER 35

Monday, October 10, 1814
London, England

The bells of London pealed loudly on the morning Stephen Ramsey was to be buried, as they had for the past two days, not in response to Ramsey's death, but in reaction to Captain Smith's report about the sacking of Washington. Jed stood at the window of the guest room at the Ramseys' London home, his heart breaking with every celebratory ring.

There was a gentle knock at the door. "Come in," Jed called out flatly as he continued to stare out at the citizenry's primarily joyful reaction to the news that caused him such pain.

The Spaniard opened the door. "Forgive me. The physician—he is satisfactory?"

Jed was slow to trust the Juan Corvas, although he couldn't deny the man had proven himself to be invaluable. After handling the legalities associated with Ramsey's murder and funeral, Corvas had traveled ahead to London to arrange medical treatment for Arthur, but not before securing a physician to attend to him during the grueling trip. Additionally, Corvas had contracted the service of two nurses trained specifically in the care of military wounded. Jed marveled at how Corvas had attended to each of Arthur's wishes with the utmost respect and detail, causing Jed to believe the Spaniard's efforts were simply *too* perfect. "Very satisfactory."

"And for you, Señor Pearson? Is there some service I can render to you?"

"No, thank you." Jed turned, making no attempt to hide his skepticism. "I want nothing from you."

Corvas's face flushed and then he bowed. "You can trust me, señor. I am not your enemy."

Folding his arms across his chest, Jed leaned back against the wall and eyed the man. "Then let us speak candidly, shall we?"

Corvas nodded and gestured for Jed to continue.

"You were supposedly oppressed by Stephen Ramsey and forced into delivering Dupree into his hands, whom he in turn loosed on my family and farm. Then you and your alleged oppressor both show up at the dock like two chums, awaiting a ship you couldn't know was even coming. Moments later, Ramsey is murdered, leaving his frail son, Arthur, the heir to a vast fortune, and now you want to serve him as well? I hope you can see how this would make me suspicious of you, Mr. Corvas."

"A man who has walked a filthy trail will still leave dirty footprints, even when he moves to higher ground, Señor Pearson. And I am trying to move to higher ground. Yes, I forgave Stephen Ramsey for making me his errand boy and soiling my hands with his deeds. Forgiving him was easier than I expected when I saw how tortured he too had become. As for my interest in helping his son, I spied on young Arthur for three years. I carried his father's letters to him, reported on his movements. In the same way I participated in your terror, I helped his father torment him because I was too weak and afraid to stand up to Stephen Ramsey. But he does not bear all the guilt. I had no wife or children he could torment—only me—and I had a choice. All he could do to me was take my life, but I feared him more than God. That is why I attempt to undo the bad I have done, señor. I want nothing from you, but I desperately want God's forgiveness."

It was as honest a confession as Jed had ever heard.

"I will leave Arthur Ramsey's household if that is what he desires, but first I must confess one more critical thing to him, as soon as he will see me."

Jed offered no challenge. "Come with me."

He opened Arthur's door carefully, surprised to find the man nearly dressed and tying his cravat. The toll of the journey to London was evident, returning Arthur's face to the wan color he had worn weeks earlier, but his back was straight and his spirit seemed unusually determined.

"You're dressed! Are you certain you're up to this?"

Arthur nodded. "I took the opportunity to tell him I loved him when I had the chance, Jed, but it would pain me to miss Father's service." He peered past Jed to where Corvas stood. "Thank you for securing the services of such skilled nurses. It is only because they have tended me so well that I feel able to do this. I am in your debt."

The comment brought a smile to Corvas's lips. "Mrs. McGowan fell faint when news of the tragedy reached her. My cousin Amado went for a doctor to attend her. He doubts she will come."

"I can only imagine her sorrow. Her life was about to transform, and now this."

Corvas bowed once more and remained in that position of obeisance, leaving Jed to explain, "He needs to speak to you, Arthur. He says the matter is critical."

"I have a few minutes before I must leave for Father's service." Arthur secured the knot in his cravat and then pointed to two chairs. "Please sit."

Jed complied but Corvas remained standing. "I will remain in your service as long as you desire, Mr. Ramsey, or I will leave as soon as my warning is delivered."

"Warning?" Jed leapt to his feet again.

Corvas glanced quickly at Jed before returning his attention to Arthur. "Yes. There was no time to speak of this before I raced for

London, and you arrived so exhausted last evening that I dared not raise the point then, but I may know who murdered your father."

Arthur's response was barely more than a flinch. "Was he one of my father's debtors?"

"He was one of Dupree's mercenaries. I know him by one name only—Jervis—and the man he actually seeks to harm is you."

"Jervis . . ." Arthur repeated with resignation.

Jed spun on Corvas. "How do you know this man?"

"My father is the man who originated the debt with Stephen Ramsey. The deeds father performed for him were so heinous that he could only secure the service of liars, outlaws, and thieves for his crew. Jervis was one of them.

"He found me several weeks ago at the Boar's Head Inn. He had barely returned from America and was looking for work. I still carried the copy of your portrait with me—the one your father first gave me when he sent me to track you and the earl's son. Jervis saw it and referred to you as Arthur Benson. I ignorantly corrected his mistake, not knowing he had a grievance with you, and he left, swearing to find you at your father's home and settle the score."

Jed felt his heart pounding in his chest as he looked at Arthur. "Because you betrayed Dupree's men to save us!"

Arthur sat heavily on the bed and stared at the floor. "That seems like a lifetime ago."

"It is very fresh to Jervis, señor. I went to your father's home to warn him, but Mrs. McGowan told me he had been called away suddenly to Liverpool on business. The timing left me suspicious, so I left Amado there to watch for Jervis so he could warn me if he arrived. In the meantime, I hurried here to warn your father. I found him two days ago, and as I suspected, there was no urgent business matter that required his attention. It was then that I decided to hire the boy to watch for your arrival while I guarded him. But, alas, I failed."

"We can't be certain the stabbing of Stephen was planned by Jervis," Jed said.

"You are kind, sir, but any other explanation would require a very big coincidence."

Arthur stood and placed a hand on the Spaniard's shoulder. "So, what would you suggest I do?"

"Post guards here and leave only when absolutely necessary until he is caught . . . or killed. I will check with Amado to see if Jervis has shown up at your father's house."

"Will you stay on for a while longer, Juan?" Arthur asked. "It appears I need your diverse talents as well."

Corvas bowed to Arthur. "I will attend to these details now." Then he quickly left.

Arthur slumped back onto the bed. "Some fine advocate I am. I'm sorry, Jed. I've placed you in more danger. If Captain Smith hears about this he may move you or at least post guards of his own to assure your arrival at the Admiralty next week. If that happens, I'm afraid your liberties will be severely curtailed to model those of other prisoners."

Jed had begun to feel simply like a man again, but here was a reminder that he was still a prisoner whose freedom was fragile. He had one crucial need to fill while his freedom remained, and as if an angel whispered Jed's concern in his ear, Arthur raised the topic.

"Your letters to Hannah, Jed. We must see to posting them today, in case my situation becomes . . . more complicated."

Awe swept over Jed, knowing the magnitude of the complications Arthur was juggling. It was as if the dear man was on a slope watching everything he loved slip away from him, one by one—Frannie, his own health and vigor, his father, his homeland, and possibly his very life—and yet over and over he placed others' needs ahead of his own. He had traveled to the Willows to warn Jed and Frannie about Dupree, and then he had broken ranks to protect Americans at Hampton. When American

Commodore Joshua Barney had been wounded at Bladensburg, Arthur had been among the British officers who extended him safety and protection, and over land and sea, he had succored Jed. Like Markus, Jed too believed Arthur was more angel than man. The examination of Arthur's life left Jed humbled.

"We'll tend to your father's burial service first, Arthur. It's the least I can do. But we should hurry. It's nearly 9:00."

"There's time enough to attend to both, and there may not be another. We'll need some sturdy paper in which to wrap the bundle. Let me think. Oh, yes. Look in the bottom drawer of the highboy. There should be a stack of books I mailed home from college. See if they're bound in something we can use."

Jed found the books wrapped in plain brown paper and bound by pieces of string. He unwrapped the books and held up the paper. "This will do."

Arthur pulled on his day coat. "Ready your parcel. I'll post it on my way to the church."

"Thank you, Arthur," Jed said as he hurried off. His letters were already stacked in chronological order. Pulling a last piece of stationery from his pile, he jotted a few final thoughts, wrapped that page around the whole stack, and tied it tightly.

He examined the brown paper with amusement. One side was clean and ready for a mailing address, but the center of the other contained the corrected address of the London town home. Jed imagined Arthur's frustration at the error as evidenced by the many times the errant characters had been retraced to repair the mistake, turning the spot into a sloppy, nearly unreadable splotch. Still smiling, Jed turned the written side inward, set the letters in the middle, and wrapped the stack into a tidy parcel. After addressing it, he changed into his borrowed ensemble and carried the package to Arthur.

Noting Jed's change of clothing, Arthur said, "You needn't go out. I'll post it for you."

"I'm coming along with you, to your father's service."

Arthur's lips parted but no sound escaped for a time. "Are you certain? After everything he—"

"I do it for you, my friend. A son should not mourn his father alone." Jed held his arm at a right angle, offering it to Arthur for support. Nothing more was said as Arthur picked up his hat and placed it atop his head, signaling that he was ready to head off into the streets of London.

Posting the parcel took a mere moment, but the relief Jed felt was indescribable. He had been able to give Hannah little of himself during their marriage, but everything he was and hoped to be was written there for her to hold forever. She would know without question how desperately he loved her, how fiercely he longed for their child, how hard he was fighting to get home, and now how he was ready to fight the entire Admiralty if need be to assure that outcome.

CHAPTER 36

Monday, October 10, 1814
London, England

Lord Whittington looked out the window of his London town home across to Hyde Park, where people were gathering, newspapers in hand, to discuss the various reports of the drubbing of Washington. Publicly, both houses of Parliament applauded the victory for strengthening Britain's bargaining position at the peace negotiations. They believed John Quincy Adams and his American diplomatic team would certainly capitulate now, but the earl was less certain, knowing as he did the fickleness of wars and victories.

He reread the editorials about Washington's defeat. The *Niles Weekly Register* posted, "The capture of Washington was received in London with great exultation and joy. The park and tower guns will be fired for three days at the twelve noon hour."

The *London Times* declared, "We soon expect to hear of the end of the American Republic. That ill-organized association is on the eve of dissolution, and the world is speedily to be delivered of the mischievous example of a government founded on democratic rebellion."

Some voices called the attack "barbarism," wondering if such an assault would not rally the Americans as they had before. Spencer's mind went to where it was prone to go—to worries over the toll the war was taking on Britain—but he was unwilling to linger there long, fearing he would again descend into the emotional hell of the previous year.

Noting the lateness of the hour, the earl set the papers down and went to the mirror to check the set of his cravat. He cringed at the changes the past year had wrought upon him. His brown hair was rapidly graying at his temples, and the lines etched in his face made him look a decade older than his forty-five years. No sparkle remained in his eyes, for there was no one in his life to revive it. He had no woman to love, other than mother England and her millions of fretful children. Beset by years of war and the subsequent economic problems, she had become a demanding lover, so demanding that the earl's attentions to her had formed a rift between him and his only child, nearly thirteen-year-old Daniel.

Another letter had arrived from the lad. It was a petition, actually, in which Daniel again begged his father to resign his seat in Parliament and join him in Ireland, where he attended school. The earl gingerly fingered the letter, pained by the contents. Raising Daniel had been the widowed earl's only joy. Daniel had been a loving, happy child, proud of his father's work in Parliament, and dazzled by his stories of parties at the Prince Regent's castle. But everything had changed after Daniel witnessed the murder of his nanny, a woman the earl had also come to love. The earl shook his head. He too still ached over the beautiful woman's death. The tragedy had steeled him to work harder in Parliament to strengthen Britain, but Daniel now wanted no part of carrying on his family's seat in the House of Lords. Somehow, that must change.

Lord Whittington missed the aromas of a family—the essence of lilac his wife, Severina, had worn; the freshly scrubbed-and-powdered scent of Daniel when he was a baby; and the delicate wafting of Clarissa's rose water. The earl even longed for his son's musky scent after a football match, noting that the solitary clean air was yet another reminder of how barren his life had become.

The earl picked up the *London Times* and turned to the obituaries to check the time of Stephen Ramsey's funeral service. He had dreamed heinous dreams of revenge against Ramsey for his part in Clarissa's death. It now seemed odd that his nemesis' demise brought him little of the pleasure he had expected, but then again, so much that had happened in his world had been unexpected—Clarissa's murder, Daniel's anger, Arthur's departure for the war in America, Britain's mounting costs and casualties, and now Stephen's death.

Lord Whittington knew it was likely a combination of all of these things that had contributed to his breakdown. He cringed as he considered the spectacle he had made of himself at Parliament. It was why he could ill afford to leave London anytime soon. Every waking moment was spent restoring his peers' and his constituents' faith in him so Daniel could hold his head high when he assumed his father's parliamentary seat. And he would. Lord Whittington would see to that.

The earl picked up his coat from the back of the chair and put it on as he headed out the door. With a nod to his butler, the loyal Mr. Ridley, he left the house to mend another tarnished relationship.

The funeral cortege was moving to the cemetery when Lord Whittington arrived. It was a painfully small assembly with no evidence of Ramsey's intended, Mrs. McGowan, the widow of the beast who murdered Clarissa. Neither had any of the Admiralty showed up to pay their respects to Ramsey, though they had recommended him for knighthood mere months earlier for having provided the services of the infamous spy Sebastian Dupree. Was it because news of Washington's destruction was now consuming their time? Or was it because Ramsey's planned marriage to a murderer's widow had proven the man to be as unfit as the earl had always said?

Lord Whittington steeled himself for his first glimpse of Arthur. Captain Smith's description of the wounded soldier's injuries had sounded too grim to be believed, and the earl studied the funeral assembly, unable to accept that any one of those gathered could possibly be the gentle, gregarious Arthur. Concealing himself behind the cemetery fence, the earl noticed a tall, broad-shouldered young man he presumed to be the American prisoner about whom Smith had spoken. Two older men appeared to be members of Ramsey's household staff, and the other person, shuffling along, stooped and padded . . . *Could that be . . .?* Spencer groaned, praying it was not.

As the reverend uttered a few words over the grave, the rounded, fragile man stepped forward to drop a handful of soil on the casket, relying heavily on the arm of his taller companion. Every nerve in the earl's body confirmed that this broken being whose pained step weakened the earl's knees was, in very deed, Arthur. And despite the pain it caused him, his attention remained riveted on the young man he had loved as a son.

The robed clergyman offered a prayer, the casket was lowered, and the gravediggers commenced shoveling. With a nod to the grieving son, the reverend bowed and left. The members of the staff spoke briefly with Arthur, their expressions reflecting worry over their positions more than grief. Soon Arthur was alone but for the tall man offering him brotherly care.

The earl removed his hat, gripping it tightly before him. "Arthur?" he called out softly.

Arthur lifted his head and peered at him. "Lord Whittington?"

The earl was unsure how to proceed until Arthur released the larger man's arm and approached with three unsteady steps. The earl closed the gap.

"Hello, Arthur. I—I came . . . for you . . ."

Arthur acknowledged the statement with a bowed head. "Thank you. I know there was no love lost between you two, and little good remaining between us either, I fear."

"I'd like to remedy that. May we sit a moment?" Lord Whittington helped Arthur to a stone bench near a wrought-iron fence, carefully lowering him to the seat and then sitting beside him. The earl's awkward hands found no rest in his lap as they worked the brim of his hat. "I heard Captain Smith's report of your injuries. I'm so sorry. I—I feel responsible."

Arthur's eyes slid nearly closed from fatigue. "Lay your fears to rest, my lord. You did only what I asked you to do in securing a post for me with General Ross. It's in God's hands now. I've made my peace with things."

"Has your father's murderer been caught? Do they know why he was stabbed?"

A sad laugh punctuated Arthur's reply. "It's poetic justice, I suppose. My father engaged Sebastian Dupree's services, and I helped stop him, drawing the ire of those denied their plunder. Now Father is dead and I'm supposedly the next target on their list."

"My dear Arthur, is he British? Give me the name of the dog and I will have him found!"

"I know him only as Jervis, but do not trouble yourself. There is some comfort in being in my condition. I have no fear of what any man can do to me now. I only wish for time enough to right what I can before I go, beginning with you."

The earl shrank back. "Me? No, the error was and is mine, all mine. I was out of my mind with grief after Clarissa's death, and I lashed out at you because despite all the charges I attempted to bring down upon your father, you still loved him. I wanted you to hate him as I did. Only now do I understand what your father said to me the night we clashed—that business is business, but the relationship between a father and his son is sacred territory that no man should cross. I unleashed your father's wrath on my household by causing the rift between the two of you. In the end, my actions caused Clarissa's death and my separation from Daniel."

"But you still believe my father was behind the attack on your home, don't you?"

The earl's eyes took on a cold, faraway look as if peering beyond the veil to face Stephen Ramsey in the underworld. "More than ever, only I accept my part as well."

Arthur's tired face looked peaceful as it recaptured the earl's glance. "I cannot prove his innocence or guilt, but let me say he died a repentant man, a man trying to right his wrongs."

"Then your father and I are alike in that, Arthur. It is why I fight so hard for Britain. But I can't make Daniel see that. Perhaps we both will be damned for our failures as fathers. You were right about Daniel on all counts. My son loved you when he was angry with me. Your prediction was nearly prophetic, you know. You told me if I sent him away, even though it was to protect him, he would see it as yet another abandonment. It has been so." The earl stood, shoved his hands deep into his pockets, and leaned against the fence like a tired boy. "He hates me now, Arthur. He says he will deny our seat in Parliament when it passes to him. I cannot let that happen, just as I cannot abandon my post to run to him and tear him from your mother's skirts in Dublin!"

Immediately embarrassed by his outburst, Lord Whittington quickly returned to sit beside Arthur. "Forgive my pettiness. Your mother has been a godsend and she has loved him well, but I fear his loyalty now lies with her and her Catholic Church, and with that blasted Irish tutor of his."

Arthur's eyes darted over to his father's gravesite, where the tall man stood, waiting anxiously.

"Is that the American who seeks my help?" the earl asked.

"Yes. He is Jonathan Edward Pearson, the man upon whom my father unleashed Dupree with the assistance of the British Navy."

"Captain Smith has shared the weak evidence against him. And you believe in this man's character and story?"

"Without question. Please, meet him for yourself."

The earl raised a hand to withhold the meeting a moment longer. "First, let us mend our rift. Please allow me some opportunity to redeem myself, Arthur. I know you believe all that can be done to help you has been done, but will you tolerate me making a few inquiries amongst some medical schools? Innovations frequently occur there."

"Of course. I would be grateful, my lord."

The formal term irritated the earl's sensibilities. "Please, Arthur. Though I know I deserve it, don't treat me so formally. I loved you as a son once. You became a member of my household for a time. You are fully a man now. Can you not be at least my friend? Please, call me Whit."

Ever so slowly, a delighted smile flashed from Arthur's bowed head. "That would please me very much. Whit, may I introduce my friend?" With a nod from the earl, Arthur raised a hand to Jed, who moved to them with a graceful urgency, bowing as he arrived. "Lord Whittington, please meet Mr. Jonathan Edward Pearson of Maryland, from the United States of America. Jed, this is my friend, Lord Whittington. As I promised he would, he wants to help you."

The earl rose and extended his hand, studying the face of the man he had wondered and worried over for so long. "Mr. Pearson, Arthur's past letters have described some of the horror your family has experienced. I feel I already know much about you."

"And you'll help me win my freedom, sir? I am completely innocent of the charge. My only desire is to return home to my farm. I have a wife, and a baby arriving soon."

"First things, first. Come back to my home. Let's sit and talk a while."

The earl's adamance that he would not risk appearing a fool before his peers required Jed to endure hours of questions, as Lord Whittington grilled him from every angle in an attempt to trip him up and expose any flaw in his story. Backwards and forwards the two went, with Arthur as audience as Jed paced across his friend's sickroom, sparring over minutia until he was certain he'd do better facing the court alone than relying on an advocate who doubted his every word.

What did you wear that day? A green sharpshooter's uniform? Where was the alleged explosion that left you wounded and in the home of the shooter? Who placed you there? What was your condition at that time? How deaf were you after the explosion? How disabled were your limbs? Which hand was burned—your trigger hand? How angry were you at the British? What color did you say your trousers were?

Finally, Jed spun around on the earl, releasing all the fury that had been roiling in his gut. "Enough!" He raked his hands angrily through his dark curls as he strove to control himself. "I would rather defend *myself* before your board of inquiry! I know the truth, and, God willing, your admiralty will listen to the integrity of my voice as deftly as they scrutinize my every word!"

Arthur gasped. "Forgive him, my lord! Jed, you cannot speak so to a noble!"

"With all due respect, Arthur, I know and care nothing of nobles and titles. I am an American. That is the nobility I recognize. My justice rests not on genuflection, but on the fulcrum of law and truth, and I would rather hang trusting in those principles than spend a lifetime subject to the whims of my people's oppressors."

His arm slashed through the air like a sword, and the room fell silent except for the sound of Jed's heaving breaths. He glanced at Arthur and saw his sorrow over an opportunity squandered. Jed's pride would not allow him to recant his words. He realized he had likely lost the support of the earl—that in very deed, he might meet the fate he so brazenly described. Not knowing what else to do, he turned and left the room, heading off on his own to think.

His legs shook so fiercely he could hardly cross the threshold before he fell weakly into a chair, gripping its arms until his knuckles ached. What had he done? What had his temper done?

He saw Hannah holding their newborn child as she stood on the porch, day after long day, staring down the empty lane for some sign of his return, a return he had likely forfeited because he was angry and tired and proud. He released his right hand from the chair's arm and used the hand to still the trembling of his lips. He was innocent and yet he was a prisoner, but his staunch American pride would not allow him to yield an inch to his oppressors. *Kiss the bloody nobles' feet if that is what is required!* he told himself, but he could not even rise from the chair.

He heard the even steps of the earl beside Arthur's pitiable shuffle as both men moved down the hall toward his room. Jed closed his eyes and hunched forward, clamping his teeth over his knuckle, the stinging pain counterbalancing the ache in his heart.

The door opened and he felt a tense hand fall tenuously on his knotted shoulder. Time passed as he waited for Arthur's voice to find the strength to utter what he already knew—that the earl had refused to advocate for him. The hand squeezed once, and then the voice began slowly, but it was not Arthur's.

"You must control that temper when we meet before the Admiralty."

Jed twisted and saw Lord Whittington's eyes bearing down on him.

"I must suppose that pride and anger bear some negative sway, even among noble *American* judges," the older man added.

Jed rose slowly, twisting out of the chair to grasp the hand of the earl that reached to him in his torment. His eyes quickly dropped. "I'm so sorry for my outburst. Forgive me, sir. Please forgive me."

Lord Whittington's bearing was warm but even. "An innocent man should be allowed one angry outburst before trial, but only one."

"Are you—are you saying you believe me?"

"I do, Mr. Pearson, and so will the members of the Admiralty if you do not allow your temper to paint you an angry, Britonhating rebel. We are as opposite as we can be on our politics, but we both revere the law. If you can do as you say you do—place your trust in those principles—and otherwise remain levelheaded, we should see you absolved."

"Thank you. Thank you!" Jed's fear erupted in a joyful gasp as he nearly shook the earl's arm off. Arthur beamed at Lord Whittington as if he were his own father, and Jed knew his second chance was due as much to the earl's love of this man as it was to the truth or the law.

CHAPTER 37

Friday, October 14, 1814
London, England

Morning dawned with rain on the day of the hearing. Arthur seemed even weaker than usual, but he insisted on attending. Jed dressed in the humble gray suit the earl had purchased for him after schooling him in the proper etiquette of addressing the court. Early in the morning, a boot black ran a final coat of polish over Jed's already gleaming new boots, while Whit's barber personally shaved him and trimmed his dark, wavy hair to accentuate the two fresh scars he received from the explosion. One ran an inch above and parallel to his right eyebrow; the other increased the dip in the dimple of his chin. The earl hoped the scars would confirm the ferocity of the explosion Jed had survived, therefore validating his claim of having been too injured to have been the shooter the day of the attack on the British party.

"I'm afraid it's time, Jed," Arthur said. "The carriage is waiting."

The finality of the moment caused a wave of nausea to sweep over Jed. "Promise me that if I am found guilty this day, you will send word to Hannah and Frannie."

The slump of Arthur's shoulders matched his voice. "I swear it, Jed. I will send my letter anonymously to spare Frannie, but I will make certain the women know everything. But don't despair.

366

I've prayed nearly through the night for you, and I feel all will turn to your favor."

"Thank you, Arthur. I need a moment alone, if you please."

Arthur closed the door quietly behind him. These were possibly Jed's final hours of freedom—or his final hours of life if the reports of Dartmoor were correct. He rubbed his healed wrists. If things went poorly, he would immediately be chained again and taken away to prison. He took comfort in knowing he had done all he could for his loved ones with the time and resources allowed him. There was but one thing left. Slipping to his knees, he offered an awkward albeit tender petition to heaven. It was not the first, and he knew it would not be the last, as he and God had become quite well acquainted of late.

The ride to the offices of the Admiralty seemed interminable. If their intention was to imprison him, then the sooner begun the sooner ended, Jed reasoned. For himself, for Hannah, for their child, and for everyone else he loved at the Willows, he would plead his case as powerfully as he could. But no matter what, he would not buckle and he would not beg.

The gray stone building that housed the military court was imposing and cold. Captain Smith met their party inside and escorted Jed away, while Arthur found a solitary corner to offer a final prayer. He heard two voices close by. One was Lord Whittington's, and the other belonged to Lord Marshall Northrup, the earl's redheaded cousin whom Arthur had met while residing with the earl and Daniel. Though Arthur tried not to listen, the topic of Spencer and Northrup's discourse grabbed at his heart.

"Marshall?" The earl's voice reflected his surprise. "What brings you here today?"

"It's whispered in Parliament's halls that you're advocating for the American accused of firing on Cockburn and Ross's party.

Is it true? As your cousin and dearest friend, Whit, I've come to ask you to consider what you are about to do. This is suicide! After all you have done to restore the Parliament's confidence in you, you would dare risk everything with this move?"

Whit's voice did not falter but rather became emboldened. "On the contrary, I see this as savvy strategy. President Madison is now attempting to rally international support against us for the Burning of Washington. In turn, we will point the finger of accusation at the Americans, saying that it was the bloodthirsty attack of one of their own upon our peace delegation that forced our hand. Now, if we temper that with a civilized and fair hearing for the suspect, whereby officers of our military like Lieutenant Ramsey and Captain Smith stand as character witnesses for the accused, we bespeak compassion and honor. And if a noble advocates for him—"

"We appear to be pious and merciful," Northrup exclaimed. "This could actually be a boon to your career!"

"Come what may on the matter, I'll advocate powerfully for the man, but regardless of how the Admiralty votes, I will have championed Britain powerfully as well."

"It's cunning. We need to take the high ground on this Washington business. But if you get this man freed, some will note that we tortured an innocent man. I hear his treatment on the *Iphigenia* was heinous, and then he saved the crew. We could come off looking brutish after all. Perhaps it would be better for Britain if you were a little less strident as you advocate for him. I've read Captain Smith's papers. Say good things about what you have observed in Pearson—commend his efforts to save the *Iphigenia*'s crew—but I hear he's an American hothead with a volatile temper. Are we absolutely certain he was not the shooter? He certainly fits the profile."

"I believe he's innocent," Lord Whittington said.

"But you do not know for sure. Allow the board to decide the truth, but consider pulling back your defense somewhat.

You are an impassioned man, and you may set a murderer free."

It was all Arthur could do not to shout, "Foul!" at the top of his lungs. After the earl bid goodbye to his cousin, Arthur stepped into the hall and made his presence known. Forcing his bent body to straighten, he said to Lord Whittington, "So this was all a political move? An act of ambition?"

The earl regrouped and scowled. "Not for me. For Britain! And what does the reason matter if I help acquit Pearson?"

"Will you? Or will you simply defend him powerfully enough to secure him a cozier cell in a better section of Dartmoor?"

"There is much at stake here, Arthur. Do you know any better than I that he is innocent?"

"Oh, yes, I do! And there was a time when you would have known as well. You say you love Britain but you have no confidence in her. Rather than reveal her error and allow her to repent, you would propagate a lie? You lied to Jed about revering the law. I mourn for the days when truth reigned supreme, and when honor was not merely a façade. What happened to you?"

"Mind who you're speaking to, Arthur. This does not have to mar our relationship, but if you choose to allow it to do so, you will close this door."

"Then let it close!" Arthur remained firm, glaring at the man until the earl could no longer bear his stare. With a final shake of his head, Lord Whittington stormed past, leaving Arthur wondering what was about to befall Jed. Legs shaking, heart pounding, Arthur stumbled into the hearing room.

Jed nearly shot from the defender's seat to attend to his friend, but Captain Smith held Jed's arm and forced him back down as the gavel pounded soundly, calling the hearing to order.

Jed stood in his defendant's perch, attempting to adhere to the advice to remain collected and composed throughout the hearing. Lord Whittington was steady, but Captain Smith was as nervous as a cat, increasing Jed's own anxiety.

He scanned the five wigged officers who, with their tight-lipped scowls, reminded him of the old gentry biddies who organized the Baltimore cotillions. The pounding of the gavel by the High Lord Admiral sounded like hammers, bringing Jed sweet memories of building projects at the Willows. Soon the faces of his loved ones came to mind, settling his nerves and diluting his fear.

"In lieu of counsel, the defendant, Jonathan Edward Pearson, has agreed to have Captain Harry Smith and Lord Whittington advocate for him."

As he second-guessed his wisdom in this choice, Jed could almost hear his father's reassuring words, "I trust you, Son," echoing in his head. Jed kept his eyes focused on the floor while the prosecutor spent half an hour describing him as a trained sharpshooter, strategically placed to cut down Ross and Cockburn as they entered Washington, calling him a rabid patriot who forced Briton's hand, setting in motion the events that caused the destruction of the American capital. Jed's head jerked up at the charge, but Smith shot him a glance, silently ordering him to relax.

While the prosecutor sat and Captain Smith rose, the charge reverberated in Jed's head, that if he were found guilty, history would level the responsibility for the devastation of Washington upon *his* shoulders. On the ship, Smith had mentioned the cause and effect of that sniper's shot, but in his extremity Jed had missed his point. He could suffer and survive prison, but the ignominy of having caused the destruction of Washington? He would rather die.

His attentions were riveted on Smith's presentation, even though he already knew every point the British captain would raise—his incapacitation after the explosion, the weak evidence that led to his arrest, the claims that a barber had been the shooter, Jed's service on the *Iphigenia*. Smith called on Arthur, who characterized Jed as an angel of mercy. This was probably sufficient to win him some leniency, but Jed knew the Britons had raised the stakes, making his arrangements with Smith insufficient. A guilty verdict with a lenient sentence would not clear his name. He needed to be found innocent.

The prosecution deftly wore away at Smith's points, claiming Jed's injuries could just as easily have come after the shooting when the British retaliatory strike leveled the home from which the shot was fired. Smith had no witness to the contrary, and everything rested on the earl.

Lord Whittington looked tense as he stood and bowed to the board. "I have only known this man for a few days, but I have been impressed that—that he is not unlike us."

Jed noted the strain in the earl's voice, the tentative way he phrased his words. This was not the same man who had assured him the evening before that he would be found innocent.

"He loves his family, his country, his home. I've found him to be an honorable man who believes in the truth, and the truth that he has declared to me is that he was not the shooter."

The earl's voice grew stronger, but gone was its fire, even as he moved his argument into the questioning phase, where he pointed out Jed's scars and quizzed him on the details of the day of the shooting. Jed noted how the earl's eyes slipped to meet those of the ruddy-faced man in the gallery before his closing argument, which was vague and devoid of personal conviction.

"We may have the wrong man. We must ask ourselves whether Britain is not better served by a show of mercy on this matter, as evidenced by the release of Jonathan Edward Pearson."

Jed's body began to shake as the earl sat down. *Release? Not exoneration?* Where was the promised call for his innocence? Why had the earl led him to believe it was assured?

The members of the Admiralty board whispered among themselves for several minutes before the High Lord Admiral pounded the gavel again. "Mr. Pearson, we see no need to retire for deliberation, as we concur on the decision. The admirable Britons who have spoken in your behalf today are to be commended for their goodness and mercy, but despite the generous defense they have raised in your behalf, we see no evidence of your innocence.

"The good deeds you are reported to have demonstrated to Lieutenant Ramsey and the crew of the *Iphigenia* are inconsequential because they likewise benefited you as well, as is evidenced by Captain Smith's willingness to testify for you. Of course you would latch onto Lieutenant Ramsey. He was a man you attest showed mercy to friends of yours in Hampton, Virginia. No doubt you hoped his goodness would serve you well, as it clearly has in securing the support of his good friend Lord Whittington. Nevertheless, out of respect for these good men's requests for leniency, and our lack of an eyewitness, we are willing to commute the sentence of death normally associated with such a crime, to prison time."

Arthur's gasp could be heard across the room.

"Before we pronounce sentence, Mr. Pearson, is there anything you would like to say in your own behalf?"

Jed's heart hammered so loudly in his chest that he failed to notice Arthur struggling to his feet. He heard him cry out, "I beg forgiveness, my lord, but I have pertinent information!"

Lord Whittington jumped to his feet, searching the gallery for the red-haired man, who was wide-eyed and ashen faced. "He is an ill man, my Lord!" the earl cried out as he moved toward Arthur. "Allow me to attend to my friend."

Arthur strained to make his way forward. "I need only to be heard, my lord. May I have the floor? I must speak more to you of Jed Pearson."

Jed knew Arthur was prepared to throw his own life away in a last attempt to protect him. A single mention that Arthur had warned Jed's family about Dupree, or a word of his relationship with Frannie, would brand Arthur a traitor and likely earn *him* a death sentence.

More chaos ensued as the door opened and two men entered the disorder. The High Lord Admiral pounded the gavel, ordering guards to surround the earl and Arthur. "Secure those doors as well, and take Mr. Pearson away. I will pronounce sentence in my quarters!"

"Please, my lord," Arthur begged. "Let justice be served by hearing the whole truth! I am not a recent acquaintance of Jed Pearson. I know him and his family well because—"

Jed gathered his wits and called out, "Because we are kin! We are cousins, though distant, as many of you also have cousins separated from you by the Great War. Arthur wanted me to know the goodness of Britain and her people, and I have seen it, but not here in this room. Not today. Arthur tells me the strength of Britain is in her people, and I believe that, for it is also true of America. But there the people's voices reign supreme. There, a man must be proven guilty beyond a shadow of doubt or else he is innocent. You say I am guilty, though no witness stands here today to accuse me. Had I been tried in America I could produce the man who saved me after the explosion, but there is no one here to attest to more than my character.

"I am innocent of this crime, yet it is not prison or death I fear but your slander upon my good name! I would rather be shot or hung this hour with the promise that this crime will not be laid to me, than to live a thousand years labeled the coward who caused Washington's ruin. Since you have no sure proof, consign my body to your sentence, but please leave my child an honorable name."

A man leapt up in the back of the court. "Here stands a witness, my Lord—a man who was there the day of the attack. One of Admiral Cockburn's men!"

In the midst of a new uproar, the High Lord Admiral called for a guard to arrest the brazen intruder—Juan Arroya Corvas—and the young sailor standing with him.

Once more, the room quieted enough for the admiral to be heard. "Bring him forward for questioning!" Before Corvas and the boy reached the front of the room, the admiral bellowed, "Who are you, and how did you happen upon this so-called witness?"

"My name is Juan Arroyo Corvas, my lord," Juan said as he bowed with a flourish, causing the hand holding his feathered hat to scrape the floor. "I am the captain of a ship docked in Liverpool. I have many friends along the harbor—friends who overheard this sailor and his colleagues discussing the attack at Washington."

"Is that so? And who might you be, Son?"

Dressed in seamen's blues and clearly terrified, Jed's former shipmate looked barely more than seventeen. His brown hair was slicked to his scalp with sweat and rain, and his hands were twisting his cap into a knot. "Seaman Edward Tennyson, sir, of the *Iphigenia*."

"And you claim to have information pertinent to Mr. Pearson's case, Seaman Tennyson?"

"I don't know about that, sir, but I saw the explosion at the bridge that hurt Mr. Pearson."

The board of admirals chuckled at the lad's humble response.

"Carry on, Son," the High Lord Admiral urged.

"My patrol was sent to scout the bridge but I got separated from them. I saw Mr. Pearson preparing to rig it to blow when I heard the explosion. It wasn't until I saw him cleaned up on the *Iphigenia* that I realized he was the man I saw at the bridge."

"Why didn't you say something then, Son?"

"I—I—I was afraid to cross the other sailors, sir. They cut a finger off the cabin boy just for sneaking Pearson an extra crust of bread."

The High Lord Admiral winced at the report, then pointed to Jed and asked Edward, "And you're certain this is the man wounded at the bridge?"

"I am, sir. I'm sure of it. He was grabbing at his head and hollering. He could neither stand nor walk, and his arms were badly burned. He looked like the walking dead. Scared me nigh to death. Another man came to his aid, but he could barely even get him on a horse to take him away."

"This is very important, Seamen Tennyson, so let me ask you once again. Do you believe Mr. Pearson could have fired upon our peace delegation?"

The boy paused before answering. "No, sir. I doubt he even knew they was there."

A thrill coursed through Jed as he watched the admirals gather to discuss the new evidence. Optimism radiated on Arthur's face, giving Jed greater cause to hope. The men returned to their seats and faced Jed as he held his breath.

"You are an arrogant man, Mr. Pearson, and not a very bright one, considering how willing you were to vaunt your pride in your court system in such a disrespectful display in ours. But we are a nation of laws as much as courtesy, and in view of this new evidence we have decided to drop all criminal charges against you . . . "

Arthur's cheer was stifled by another angry fall of the gavel. Jed shook as relief surged through him, requiring him to grip the rail to remain upright.

"As I was saying, you are still a military prisoner, and you will remain so until such time as you are exchanged or a treaty is struck."

Lord Whittington rose, ingratiating himself before the court. "My lord, in view of the unnecessary distress caused by the allegations, might the court consider releasing Mr. Pearson?"

The response was curt. "The petition is denied, Lord Whittington."

Arthur signaled next and was also recognized. "My lord, in consideration of our kinship and my injuries from the war, might the court consider remanding Mr. Pearson back into my custody to serve as my valet during my recuperation?"

The admirals conferred briefly and the gavel slammed down once more. "We will agree to your petition, Lieutenant Ramsey, with the understanding that you act as an agent of this court and the military. Mr. Pearson is your prisoner, not merely your cousin. Understood?"

Arthur bit his lip, and Jed knew he meant to obscure his joy. "Very clearly, sir."

The gavel fell once more to dismiss the court. Captain Smith rushed in on Jed, extending his hand in congratulations. With his legs still so unsteady, Jed had barely moved a few paces before the earl was also upon him.

"Congratulations, Mr. Pearson. You did not heed my warning about your temper."

"Please forgive me, but what value would you place on your life if your name and honor were to remain forever sullied? But I thank you sincerely for all you did for me, sir."

Arthur arrived, and the earl's discomfiture was apparent. "I see you two have much to discuss. Best wishes to you, Mr. Pearson."

"And to you, sir." Jed took the earl's proffered hand and bid him adieu, then turned his attention to Arthur, whose face erupted into pure happiness as Juan Corvas and Seaman Tenneyson approached. Jed caught the three up in a playful embrace. "God bless each of you!" he cried out, his expression turning serious as he laid his head back as if also thanking God.

Tenneyson hung his head. "I'm sorry for not coming forward sooner. I—I—I was afraid."

"It doesn't matter now, friend. You each came through in my hour of greatest need, clearing me and my name. You have returned my life to me! I'll make you proud of what I do with it!"

CHAPTER 38

Monday, October 17, 1814
London, England

Jed took the tray from the butler and carried Arthur's breakfast up to his room. When he arrived, he was surprised to find Arthur fully dressed from hat to boots. "So you've decided."

"Yes. My attorney is meeting me shortly, and father's attorney is meeting us here. I must attend to these matters with the McGowans."

"Your nurse and I are both ready. And this came for you from Lord . . . from Whit."

Arthur rolled his eyes sarcastically at Jed. "I know the concept of nobility and nobles grates against your sensitivities. However, exercising the proper etiquette is essential if you wish to make connections with people who can help your anti-slavery cause."

"Whit promised to introduce me to William Wilberforce and the other members of Parliament who steered Britain's anti-slavery legislation. I'm honored to meet them."

"I would enjoy meeting Mr. Wilberforce as well," Arthur said. "When did Whit extend this invitation?"

"This morning, for tomorrow. He sent a letter to me, along with this one for you."

Arthur sat on the bed and read the letter. The emotions in his face fluctuated as he read, but the overwhelming one was sadness.

"Is the news bad?" Jed asked.

Arthur refolded the note and placed it on his nightstand. "He has arranged for me to see two surgeons in Oslo. Evidently an entirely new theory of surgical education is emerging there, and a member of the House of Lords who is related to one of the surgeons has offered me a letter of introduction." At Jed's surprised look, Arthur added, "You'll soon see that noble blood supersedes borders, Jed. All these blue-blooded families are interrelated."

"That's wonderful news, isn't it? Why the long face?"

Arthur huffed uncharacteristically. "I've sadly discovered that I wrongly placed the earl on a pedestal, Jed. He is but a man, and as subject as any to vice. Mind that when he bends your ear."

"He is a man to me and nothing more. I'll be wary. But you will see these doctors, won't you? Don't let your disappointment in him make you too prideful to accept his help."

Arthur sighed aloud. "I suppose. We should leave soon, though. The season is already late for travel across the North Sea."

"Then let's book passage to leave this week. Will Juan be coming with us?"

"No. Juan has been a good ally, but I need another favor from him. He and his cousin have been watching my father's house this week. They sent a note telling me a tenant farmer of my father's, a man named Richard Porter, has been residing on the property, supposedly running the household as a favor to me until I can make other arrangements for the McGowans and the house. I need to get this messy business settled quickly, and then we'll leave for Oslo."

The trip that would have taken an hour for two able riders on horseback proved to be an arduous five-hour ordeal in a jostling carriage to accommodate Arthur. He was finally able to ride upright, but he required an additional hour's stop at an inn near his father's estate so his nurse could freshen his dressings. Dusk was settling in when the party arrived at the property's gates. As Arthur studied the plaque with the ornate "R," a look of melancholy crossed his face.

"Does this place hold fond memories for you?" Jed asked.

"The estate was a fairly recent purchase of Father's. I only came here twice."

The driver continued on until a voice called out to them. "Señor Ramsey! It is I!"

The carriage slowed as two magnificent white Andalusian stallions hurdled a hedge and cantered to the window. "Hello, señors. I trust your journey was pleasant, Señor Ramsey?"

"Just fine, Juan, thank you. And thank you for watching over the estate."

"My pleasure. I have hired three other guards to patrol the property. The butler, the gardener, the maid, and the cook are inside. An attorney named Reynolds arrived moments ago."

"Yes, I sent for him. And this Mr. Porter—the tenant farmer—is he not around?"

"He carted a wagonload of sheep to the market yesterday. Mrs. McGowan and her sons left with him, to visit the neighbors."

Arthur was impressed by the man's efficiency. "Juan, I have business to attend to here, and then I'll be leaving for Norway for a few months for medical treatment. Would you and your cousin consider remaining here for that time? Mrs. McGowan and her sons may be moving to a cottage on the property, and I'd prefer not to leave the manor house unoccupied."

Amado shook his head, but Juan overruled him. "Yes, we will stay until you return."

"Very good. Thank you. I'll see to the arrangements for the McGowans then. Move your things into the main house when you're ready. We'll plan on seeing you at supper."

Arthur urged the driver on to the brick manor house, which loomed ahead like a small palace. Arthur counted three stories in the center section, with wings descending on either side, each of two stories' height. A large, curved veranda swept across the front of the house, with a similarly shaped balcony extending from the second floor. Beautifully trimmed evergreens framed a stone walk that extended from the house to the circular drive where the carriage was now headed.

"I had no idea, Arthur," Jed said. "It's larger than the President's House!"

"And equally burdensome, I'd wager."

Soon the butler rushed out to meet the travelers. He offered a gratuitous smile as he opened the carriage door and stood at attention. "Mr. Arthur Ramsey, I presume? Mr. Corvas told us you would be coming, so we've done our best to ready the house for your arrival."

"Thank you." Arthur extended his hand. "And you, sir? You are . . .?"

"Willum Smythe, sir, the butler. I was recently hired by your father, God rest his soul. My condolences, sir, and may I say how pleased we'd all be to remain in your service."

"Thank you. Please tell the cook the six of us will need to eat. And inform the staff that I'll meet with all of you tomorrow morning."

"Very well, sir. I took the liberty of settling Mr. Reynolds in your fa—in your office."

Arthur winced, registering the reference to his father's passing. He and Jed quickly joined Mr. Reynolds in the office, and the three men began studying the farm's accounts. Jed's farming experience and education proved invaluable, and owing to Stephen Ramsey's fastidious bookkeeping, Arthur quickly knew the farm's financial status.

Reynolds frowned. "I don't see any lease or rent record for a tenant farmer named Richard Porter."

"He seems very conscientious. Perhaps Father gave him free rent in return for managing things. My father was certainly no farmer."

"Perhaps," the attorney answered. "As for Mrs. McGowan and the children, your father has already named them partial heirs to the tune of twenty percent."

"He wanted to improve their lives. Are the terms of distribution spelled out?"

"They are not, but I know your father desired that they receive an education if they are capable, or at least that they be taught a worthy trade."

"I've seen how a great influx of money can corrupt. There is a good-sized cottage situated near the main gate. I'd like to deed that house and twenty acres to Mrs. McGowan so she and her boys will always have a decent home. Twenty acres will require them to labor for what they desire, establishing a pattern of industry in her sons—something that, if their father'd had, may have prevented him from becoming a thief and a murderer. Let's establish a trust whereby the family may only draw two hundred pounds a year, an ample sum, until the boys' twenty-fifth year. By then they will be mature enough to handle the money and responsible enough to care for their aging mother. Let's also channel twenty pounds a year into an educational trust fund for the boys. Though they are only three and five years old, choose a good academy and begin making inquiries into where Mrs. McGowan would like to see them go. Does that cover the necessities?"

"Except for the estate's affairs, sir," Reynolds said. "I would be happy to see that the status quo is maintained while you decide what you wish to do long term."

Knowing how unsettled his life was, Arthur nodded. "Please do. Draw up a will for me as well, naming Mrs. McGowan heir to half my estate in the event of my death. If she proves worthy of the trust my father placed in her, I'll sign the document at a later time."

"And the other fifty percent, sir. To whom shall it be willed?"

"To Francis Pearson, an American woman of the Willows Plantation in Maryland."

Clatter in the yard brought Arthur's head up. "Someone's arrived."

Corvas entered and bowed slightly. "Señor Ramsey, may I present Mrs. Mary McGowan?"

A stout woman of about thirty years entered nervously, dressed simply in a black dress and bonnet. She barely met Arthur's eyes, though she dropped into a curtsy, crying softly as she rose. Arthur moved to her, offering her his hand. "My dear Mrs. McGowan. We finally meet."

Her chin fell to her chest. "I still can't believe it. Who would do such a thing?" She pressed her handkerchief to her lips. "He treated me like a queen, he did. Made me feel like a real lady. And he was so good with my boys." Her crying intensified.

"I wish we were meeting under other circumstances, madam. I hope it comforts you to know how pleased I was by how happy you and your sons made him during these final months." Arthur took her by the arm. "You've met Father's attorney, Mr. Reynolds, haven't you?" She nodded without looking up. "He's here to explain the terms of Father's will to you."

An hour passed as the terms of the will were explained. At the end, Arthur asked her if she understood everything and she said that she did, gratefully acknowledging the ease with which he fulfilled his father's intentions. "We'll move into the new house right away," she said.

Arthur noticed the way her hands were shaking. "Are you all right, Mrs. McGowan?"

"I just miss him," the woman said. "I truly do. I know he was wrong to hire my first husband to kidnap that boy, but he changed after that. He was a good man as long as I knew him, and I miss him so."

The admission caught Arthur off guard. "My father hired Mr. McGowan to kidnap what boy? Lord Whittington's son? Are you certain? Are you speaking of the night Lord Whittington's nanny was murdered?"

"Yes," she said with a sniff. "Stephen sent my Trevor there to kidnap the boy to teach the earl a lesson, but things went terribly awry and Trevor killed the nanny and slit his own throat."

Arthur felt sick, realizing that every condemnation the earl had thrown at his father was deserved. He had been responsible for the murder of the woman the earl and Daniel both loved—Clarissa. "And what did my father offer your husband to kidnap Daniel Spencer?"

She finally met his eyes. "Th–th–this inheritance. Didn't you know?"

"Blood money!" snapped Arthur as he shoved the will away.

"At first, but he came to love us! He wanted to make amends to the children."

The door burst open as Jed and Corvas rushed in, hauling a man by his collar.

Arthur shot to his feet and pointed at the man standing before him. "Jervis!"

When Arthur's head spun to glare at Mrs. McGowan, she whimpered, "Richard, who is Jervis?"

"Richard?" Arthur said. "Are you the man posing as Richard Porter?"

"Richard Porter's my real name. My mates call me Jervis. I see you've met the wife."

Arthur's eyes shot back and forth between the couple. "You mean to say you two are—"

"Married!" Jervis said with a snicker. "Yesterday, in town. Had a lovely little wedding night, too, to make it all legal. I'm now her boys' legal guardian, and that goes for that sweet inheritance, too."

"Murderer!" Arthur said angrily.

"You got no proof!"

"I'll give the estate to the dogs before I allow you touch a penny of it. Renounce this marriage this instant, Mrs. McGowan, or I'll use your testimony about my father's reasons for drawing it up to break it and leave you penniless!"

"I renounce it! I renounce it! I only agreed to marry him because he said he was Stephen's friend and that marrying him was what Stephen would want me to do!"

"Mr. Reynolds, file the paperwork immediately to annul this union, and do not release a cent of the inheritance until it is done. And you, Mr. Porter, I will give orders to have you shot on sight if I ever see or hear about you coming near this property again!"

"I'll kill you, Ramsey! I swear I'll hound you every day until I see you dead!"

CHAPTER 39

Saturday, November 12, 1814
The Willows

Bitty rushed about the house, the ends of her black hair bobbing wildly from underneath her cap as she snapped orders to everyone. "Jack, when's that cradle gonna finally be ready? And Markus, you promised me a larder filled with birds by now and there's not but three hanging in the smokehouse! Francis Pearson, we got rugs that need beatin'. You and Jenny don't need me to remind you that Hannah's sister Beatrice is comin', followed shortly by a baby!"

Jack pulled on his red suspenders and scowled at his tiny sister. "Slow yourself down, Bitty, lest you spin yourself into the ground like a corkscrew. Markus and I have been haulin' Willows' tobacco to Calverton so we can make the final payment on Stringham's land."

Bitty flopped into a chair like a puff of blue gingham. "I know, I know. There's just been so much goin' on lately and I want everything to be perfect for Beatrice and for the baby."

"Beatrice has spent a month living with Myrna, Bitty," Frannie said as she knelt beside Bitty. "She'll be so grateful to finally arrive here that she would hardly notice a cow in the kitchen."

Bitty chuckled. "I still want things done right." Then she landed the one point that sobered the household. "It's what Jed would want done if he were here."

Jenny entered the kitchen, her blond hair tumbling from under a bonnet. Her eyes locked momentarily with Markus's before he cleared his throat and turned for the door, saying, "We'd best get this last load of tobacco ta Calverton, Jack. Then we'll set off ta hunt, Bitty." As he exited he cut a wide path around Jenny, his eyes remaining fixed on the bottom of the door.

"I'll put some mint in your cabin, Mr. O'Malley," Jenny said matter-of-factly.

"That'd be nice, Mrs. Tyler," Markus answered, then exited the room with Jack close behind.

Jenny bit her lip and looked at Bitty. "I'm the one who has a right to be vexed, but no matter how cold he is to me, I plan to be nice to him until he's cordial. I'll get to those rugs now."

As Jenny left the kitchen, Hannah entered, her hands placed low on her back as she stretched her bulging belly forward. "I don't think Markus is vexed as much as smitten," she commented, looking at the open doorway through which Jenny had just passed.

"I agree," Frannie said. "He's fallen for a woman he believes is still married. He keeps trying to push her away. That's why he's been so hard on her."

"Poor thing. Love's been none too good to him."

Frannie laid her arm across Bitty's narrow shoulders. "No, it hasn't, Bitty. Hannah, shouldn't she have received the final decree by now?"

"I would have thought so, but even once that's settled there are still a host of things complicating Jenny's life. Captain Nicholson exonerated her of treason, but there are still the charges of assault and horse theft. Guilty or innocent, we're harboring a fugitive."

Frannie cocked her head as if ready for a fight. "I'd like to see that beast of a husband try and testify that she abused him, with all the scars and knotted breaks he gave her!"

"Does Markus know about all of that?" Hannah asked.

"He does not," Jenny answered as she walked in holding the rug beater. "Though he doesn't appear to care a lick for me, he might try to avenge me and get himself killed in the process. Besides, I don't want a man's pity. I've been the subject of every kind of attention but the genuine loving kind, and I'll have none else the rest of my days."

"We promise not to meddle," Frannie said.

"And I'm not saying that I even care for the man. I just don't want to be beholding to any man ever again. I hope you'll respect what I've said."

Chastened, the women fell silent as Jenny left the room again. Bitty provided a needed change of subject. "You should be resting, Hannah. You look a mite puffy today. Let me see your legs."

Hannah raised her hem, revealing swollen ankles. "I must have overdone it yesterday. My head aches a bit as well." The wild barking of dogs sounded in the back yard. "That must be my sister."

Jack reentered the kitchen with a curious smile on his face. "Company's here."

"Beatrice?" Hannah said.

"Her too." The raise of his eyebrow signaled something unpleasant.

"She's there too? What? No!" Hannah huffed. "Jack, this is not amusing."

Frannie caught the secret. "Oh, no! Not Myrna!"

Jack chuckled. "Let's just say I'll be moving back into the cabin during this visit."

"I suppose it's too late to escape into the root cellar," Hannah said with a groan.

Bitty was clearly displeased as well. "Just keep Miss Hissy Fit out of my kitchen!"

Hannah gave her white blouse a quick tuck, then quickly brushed off the dark blue pinafore that now protruded forward past her toes. After returning a stray dark hair to her chignon, she sighed and left to greet her guests. A plastered smile was added just before she reached the door, but as soon as she saw her sister Beatrice, her joy was full and real.

Beatrice bolted from the carriage as soon as it stopped, her green cape trailing behind her reed-thin frame. She halted a few yards from her baby sister and surveyed her womanly form before quickly closing the gap. She clasped Hannah's hands in her own as she studied her tired face. "I know that look. I'm so sorry about Jed."

"I'm so glad you're here. Only you can truly understand my situation right now."

"It's as if we're living parallel lives, two years apart—expectant wives whose husbands are imprisoned. But we'll get through it. We Stansbury women are strong, aren't we?"

The sisters caught one another up in a tight embrace that was cut short by a squeal from the carriage. "Where is the butler?" Myrna whined to Mobey, her driver. "Surely there is at least a houseboy." Then she called out, "Hannah, fetch someone to get our bags at once!"

Hannah rolled her eyes. "Myrna, you know very well we have no houseboy or butler. I'm sure any one of the men will help you if you will only behave kindly."

Myrna harrumphed as Jack and Markus moseyed over, tipping their hats in meager efforts at decorum. "Well, I never!" she declared in obvious frustration.

"It's going to be a long winter," Beatrice whispered to Hannah and Frannie.

"Winter?" Frannie's mouth fell open.

Hannah mouthed her concern. "You don't mean to say that she . . ."

Beatrice stole a glance at Myrna and shrugged. "It was a last-minute decision."

Myrna stormed up to the women, her portly frame shifting left and right with every stomp.

"Beatrice, you remember Frannie, don't you?" Hannah said. "She's become a sister to me in every way."

Myrna jutted her lips near Beatrice's ear, though her volume negated any effort at discretion or hiding her disdain. "She's the en-ter-tain-er."

Beatrice rolled her eyes apologetically at Frannie. "So wonderful to see you again, Frannie. What better company to have over a long winter than a talented musician?"

Frannie turned the tables on Myrna, taking her arm as she flashed her a million-dollar smile. "Just imagine it, Myrna. You and me, sharing every day together for weeks and weeks. Perhaps we could host a party together, invite some of your Baltimore gentry friends."

"My goodness!" Myrna said with a groan, her face turning pale.

"I'd give them a fine show! You'd be the talk of Baltimore."

Frannie relished the rise her game was getting from Myrna, who broke free of her grasp and skittered up to latch onto Hannah's arm like a child being pursued by the boogeyman.

Once inside, the women retired to the parlor, where Myrna began their visit with a long discourse about her sufferings. Bitty strode in and Hannah stood to introduce her. "Beatrice, this is Bitty, the woman I've written to you about. She's cared for Jed and Frannie since birth. She's become a mother to me as well." Hannah gave Bitty a squeeze, and the little woman shyly lowered her head.

"Tea's almost ready. Just waiting on the apple cake to come out of the oven." Bitty checked the time, then relaxed and took a seat. "Don't mind me. Just carry on with your story."

The blood drained from Myrna's face. "You're . . . joining us . . . here . . . in the parlor?"

"The baby is with her grandma in her cabin in the meadows, and the cake needs a few more minutes, so I've got time. I'd enjoy sitting a spell."

Hannah quickly intervened. "Beatrice, what have you heard from Dudley?"

A soft sadness shadowed Beatrice's effort at a smile. "He mentioned the men's devastation over the news of Washington's defeat, but I haven't received a reply to my letter about the victory at Baltimore. And I sent him a copy of Mr. Key's poem. I hope it will rally the men's spirits."

"I'm sure it will. It's a wonderful poem and now a song, but they've changed the name to 'The Star-Spangled Banner.' Frannie has performed it. Tell them, Frannie."

"It's incredibly popular in Baltimore already," Frannie explained. "Sheet music is being printed for it under the new title, and the poem is appearing in papers all over the coast."

"It's an adequate effort," Myrna said grumpily, "but it's not as if Key was Shakespeare."

Hannah returned her attentions to Beatrice. "Does Dudley know you're here now?"

"I wrote my schedule in a letter. I've asked the postman to forward my mail from Tunbridge to here. I'm sure there will be a delay as the first few letters catch up."

"In Baltimore we can receive two deliveries a day if something important arrives. As I tried to tell you, we should have stayed in the city, Sister."

"I'm sure Dudley is delighted to know I'm here with Hannah."

"Well, yes, you must comfort one another. How blessed you both are that your husbands are merely in prison. It was given to me to bear the greater burden of widowhood—alone."

Hannah ignored Myrna. "What are the conditions at Melville?"

Beatrice's gaze fell to her hands. "I know so little of Melville. Dudley's letters are filled with questions of home with very few references about prison life, causing me to assume it is too unpleasant to share with me. Perhaps Dartmoor is a better facility. Let us at least pray it is."

"It's all right, Beatrice. I know Jed is fine. I just know it."

Beatrice smiled. "Your spiritual gift is still a wonder to me. I'm glad the feelings it brings you are peaceful."

"It's the devil's work, I say," Myrna argued. "Visions and apparitions—eek!"

Hannah pressed a hand against her pounding head and rose from her seat. "I'll go check on the apple cake."

Bitty already stood in her way, as tense as a strung bow. "No, missy. For the sake of your sister, you'd best let me leave and check on the cake."

Hannah returned to her seat under duress just as Myrna said, "You're too removed from God's word out here. Where is the nearest church? Where shall we worship?"

"We have a chapel right here on the grounds," Frannie answered, "and a minister."

"That's lovely," Beatrice said with a smile. "I adore the intimacy of small, quaint chapels."

"Small and quaint is that and no more," Myrna put in. "Now, I always say, if you want to find God, seek a church with a good choir, plenty of candles, and stained glass. God will be there."

Beatrice gasped and bolted to her feet. "Hannah, I believe I would benefit from a walk."

"A walk? Yes, I'd adore a walk." She struggled to her feet, wincing at the effort. As an afterthought she added, "Frannie, Myrna, would you care to join us?"

"You go on ahead." Frannie chuckled. "I think I'll check on Jenny."

Myrna appeared to have a sudden attack of some ailment. "I really should go rest."

"By all means then. You rest, dear." Beatrice's voice was as sweet as honey.

Bitty already had two shawls in her hands, and she wrapped one around Hannah's shoulders. "I believe I'll come along and give that cake time to cool."

The three women walked across the yard and through the barren tree line that separated the main yard from the meadows, where the chapel and the residents' cabins sat.

Hannah watched Beatrice rub her hands over her arms. "Are you cold, Beatrice?"

"No. I just didn't notice the charred trees before." She faced Hannah with a shudder. "You were nearly burned out! I know you wrote that, but I couldn't comprehend it until now."

"We lost Bitty's father-in-law that day. So many families along the river were burned out by the British. We count ourselves among the fortunate ones, except for losing sweet Jerome."

"My sister and her family were murdered for trying to get us word about the coming attack," Bitty explained. "But the land they're buried on is ours now. Now we got some peace on the matter."

Beatrice sighed. "I'm sorry for your losses, Bitty. I hear your husband and son are soldiers now."

"My, oh my, yes! My Abel's a real Baltimore Fencible. He got a commendation for his service during the battle at Fort McHenry. I expect him home soon for a few days' leave. He's carrying a dead soldier's belongings to his widow, but he and Caleb will be here directly."

"I've taken this war for granted living where I do, in Vermont. We receive news of battles along the Great Lakes, but I am quite removed from the effects of war in my little home."

Hannah remembered the verdant beauty of Vermont and the friends who cared for her and Beatrice when the pair fell ill from typhoid. "How are Em and Dr. Butler?"

"Em is as well as ever, though he asks about you often. You should come home with me in the spring and visit. He would love it so."

"And Dr. Butler?"

"Dr. Nathan Smith, the surgeon who saved Joseph Smith's leg, moved on to serve as the first dean of Yale University's medical school, causing a rearrangement of positions at Dartmouth. Dr. Butler is now a professor at the college."

"That's wonderful news," Hannah said. "And the Smiths? How are they?"

"The medical expenses left them destitute, requiring them to move from Lebanon to Norwich, Vermont, so I don't see them anymore, but Temperance Mack updates me on her in-law's situation. They've rented a small farm and hope to have success in that field. Little Joseph is still quite lame, relying on a crutch to get about when his brothers aren't carrying him."

"The poor child. Dr. Butler told me it could take years for his leg to heal, but he at least still has it and, along with it, the hope of walking once again."

They reached the rudimentary chapel with its log walls, framed steeple, and hand-carved cross. Smoke wafted from the brick chimney. "School's in session," Hannah said proudly.

They slipped in through the only door, taking a seat on a bench in the back while the reverend assisted his seven brown-faced students, who were hard at work on their "ciphers."

"Bitty is doing some needlework pieces to adorn the walls. They're beautiful. Why don't you get your pieces to show Beatrice, Bitty?"

Bitty wrinkled her nose. "They're not all that, but I'll get them for you to see."

She left and returned a few minutes later, displaying two rectangles of fabric hung from wooden dowels. As Bitty handed the pieces to Beatrice, the dogs began to bark wildly. The reverend looked out the two windows that faced the road but shrugged, obviously seeing no one. Bitty moved to the windows that faced the field. "I see two horses but no riders. Maybe it's Abel."

She rushed for the door and pushed. It began to open and then slammed shut. Bitty tried to force it open again with no success. Muffled voices were heard and wood scraped on wood as a wedge was placed to bar the door.

"They're locking us in!" she cried as she pounded on the door. "They're locking us in!"

A surge of pain shot through Hannah's head as the reverend pounded on the immovable door, but Hannah soon fell in beside him, screaming. "Let us out! There are children in here!"

Clamor erupted as the children began to cry, racing to the women and clutching their skirts in terror. Bitty's ten-year-old stepson, Eli, pointed to the fireplace, where a more urgent threat appeared. Smoke from the fireplace began pouring into the room. The reverend moaned a guttural prayer of desperation. "God help us! They've blocked the chimney!" he cried, then removed his coat and started to beat the fire out. More smoke filled the room as flaming logs rolled onto the rag rug, creating a new threat before the fire was doused with water from the drinking bucket.

"Break the windows! Help the children climb through!" Hannah shouted.

Eli raced to a window and broke the glass, but as he began to lift his little sister, a musket ball sailed through the window and into the room. "Whoever did this aims to choke us out and pick us off!"

Hannah looked at the terrified children coughing all around her. She pressed one hand against her throbbing temple and the other over her belly as she instructed the children, "Stay low and near the window where the air is fresh. Reverend, we need to pray Frannie hears their shots!"

Eli broke the remaining windows and the enemy answered with gunfire. The smoke began curling out the openings, making the air more breathable.

Hannah forced a smile for the children. "See? We'll be all right. Frannie will rescue us." Then one of their assailants moved past the window, holding a flaming torch in his hands.

"They mean to burn us out!" Bitty's eyes were wild with fear as she grabbed her children and cowered in a corner. Hannah felt Beatrice's hands digging into her shoulders. The room began to spin as she remembered the choking smoke that nearly suffocated all the women and children during Dupree's attack on the Willows. *How many times does a person have to fight for her life?* Hannah thought in desperation. Her baby was days from drawing its first breath of life—a life it now might never know. And this time, Hannah knew Jed could not save her.

She felt a spasm of pain wrap around her belly like a vice, doubling her over against Beatrice. "Bitty," she cried out, groaning as the pain intensified. "Bitty!"

Bitty's eyes went wide. "This can't be your time!"

"Help me, Bitty," Hannah cried out as another pain wrenched her body.

Bitty ran to the window and pled with the assailant. "We've got a mother about to deliver a baby! This church is full of children! For the love of God, you gotta let us go!"

The torchbearer's face jutted through the window. Bitty saw his hat and gasped. "I know you! You're . . . you're a soldier from Fort McHenry. One of them Fencibles."

"That's right. You just better hope your man Abel arrives in time."

✯ ✯ ✯ ✯ ✯

Abel reached his blue-uniformed arm across and ruffled Caleb's hair as he sat atop his horse. "The captain said you were a great asset at the fort while I was away. I'm proud of you."

"So am I," Captain Foster said. "You'll make a fine soldier someday, Caleb."

Abel noticed his son had been unusually solemn since he and Captain Foster had returned to the fort the previous night. Caleb had clung to him like a shadow ever since. "We'll be home before long. You don't seem too excited. Are you sad to be leaving the fort?" Caleb's reply was an aloof shake of his head, causing Abel to glance curiously at Foster.

"I hope you brought a copy of that article home for your mama," Foster said. "Not too many boys get to see their name in the newspaper."

Tears welled in Caleb's eyes as he kicked his horse and moved ahead of the men. Abel did likewise, closing the distance and grabbing the bridle of Caleb's mount until he brought the horse to a stop. Before Abel could reach his son's hand, Caleb slid from his saddle and raced away, with his father and Captain Foster close behind. Abel caught him in a few strides, but as his hand clamped over Caleb's shoulder, the boy cried out in pain, crumpling to the ground.

Abel recoiled, but not before his fingers identified the lumpy feel of his boy's flesh. He had felt flesh marred in that way—swollen and striped—in another place, in another time. Abel shuddered, his breath becoming shallow. Tenderly, he knelt beside his son and tipped his chin until Caleb's eyes met his. Love, sorrow, and understanding passed silently between them as Abel unbuttoned his son's shirt enough to pull it down across his shoulder. Wide, swollen welts crisscrossed the lad's back and shoulder. Some were scabbed where the drawn blood had dried.

"Oh, Caleb!" Captain Foster caught a haggard breath. "Who did this to you?"

"I know," Abel said with a groan. "Hildebrand and Skully."

Caleb buried his face in his father's shoulder and cried so hard he couldn't speak.

Abel's hands balled into fists as he recalled being summoned into Captain Nicholson's office at the request of Hildebrand and Skully, who claimed they were sorry and wanted to make amends. They had lied so convincingly that he had let his guard down. Now, he wanted to kill them. "I'm sorry, Caleb. This is my fault."

"They were kind to me while you were away. They said you were a good soldier who deserved your commendation as much as they did, and they were happy about me being in the newspaper.

But they lied. They just said those things so I'd trust them—so they could hurt us."

"Hurt us?" A chill ran down Abel's spine. "Tell me exactly what happened."

"As soon as the sentry announced that you two were riding in, Skully began suffering one of the attacks he's been having since he was wounded. Hildebrand asked the sergeant if he could have a two-day leave to take him to the city to the hospital, only Skully wasn't really hurt." The boy's lower lip began to tremble. "Th–th–they woke me up before daybreak and hauled me out beyond the gate." Now tears began once more. "They said they didn't want to be part of a military that gave commendations to niggers, and they told me no one wanted to read about coloreds in the paper. They tied me to a post and stuffed Skully's bandana in my mouth so no one could hear me cry. Then Hildebrand took off his military belt and beat me."

Abel began to shake with fury. He felt he would explode if he didn't release his anger, but he saw how Caleb was watching him. He did his best to relax his clenched arms enough to comfort his battered boy before asking, "Why didn't you tell me sooner?"

Caleb sniffed loudly. "They threatened me . . . said they'd shoot us dead if I told you before we crossed the Calvert County line."

"But they wanted you to tell your pa *after* you crossed the line?" Captain Foster asked.

"They're planning on teaching you a lesson, Pa. They're waiting for you at the Willows."

In one motion, Abel stood with Caleb cradled in his arms. Handing the lad off to Foster he said, "I'll kill them." Then Abel headed for his horse.

Foster struggled under Caleb's weight. "Wait, Abel. Think! What you're planning is suicide. If they don't kill you, they'll get you hung. Don't do this!"

But Abel was deaf to Foster's counsel. The blood surged so loudly in his head that he could hear nothing but the words,

"They're waiting for you at the Willows."

Abel's horse jumped in response to the hard kick he delivered as he urged it down the River Road toward home. He laid low, hugging his mount as he planned his strategy. Where would they be waiting? At the manor house? In the meadow? Over and over, scenarios played in his head, but all Abel could see were the stripes on his son's body, and Bitty's fearful eyes.

He heard Foster and Caleb following at a fast pace, but he could not afford to slow and wait for them. The scent of wood smoke was everywhere, and then he saw a haze hover over the distant tree line where the Willows lay. A dry knot caught in the back of his throat like a ball of yarn, turning his breaths into panicked heaves. That same panic set his heart on an even wilder rhythm, but again he pushed the terror down and focused on the perils ahead.

As he neared the edge of the Willows property, the location of the smoke was evident—the meadows. Bitty, his mother, the children! Racing by the first entrance of the horseshoe lane that arced past the manor house, he continued down past the mill and raced across the fields, from which screams and pleas for help could now be heard. He pulled his horse up in a stand of evergreens and saw Emerson Hildebrand wielding a flaming torch before a window as if taunting someone. Abel's heart slammed against his chest. *He's got them trapped in there!*

He thought about shooting him where he stood, but Hildebrand had planned his assault well. If he fell, so would the torch, igniting a pile of straw that would engulf the church. Where was Skully? Abel scanned the area and found Skully holding Abel's mother and baby daughter at gunpoint under a fir tree. Abel knew he could possibly stop one threat, but not both.

In his head, he replayed Caleb's warning: *"They're planning on teaching you a lesson."* Abel urged his horse forward and shouted, "I'm the one you're after. Let everyone else go!"

Both assailants spun in the direction of Abel's voice, brandishing their guns and torch.

"Abel!" Bitty screamed. "All the children are in here, and Hannah's gone into labor!"

The terror in his brave wife's voice pierced him to the soul. Never had he felt more powerless than he did at this moment.

"So that little whelp of yours told you I taught him some manners, did he?"

"You filthy cowards! Instead of facing me, you beat a boy."

"Well, let's just see how brave you are when you're hanging from a rope!"

Abel followed Hildebrand's glance to a nearby tree, from which two ropes tied into nooses now hung. Abel's breaths came out rapid and shallow. Where were Markus and Jack? He at least needed time for Captain Foster to arrive. Trying to stall, Abel said, "Put out that torch, and let's all drop our weapons. Let everyone else go free and I'll surrender to you."

Hildebrand sneered. "You don't tell me what to do! You do what I say! Drop your gun and walk this way so I can see the fear in your eyes."

"First, I need to know everyone's all right."

"My arm's getting tired, Abel. Where's your little nit? I want him, too. Call him out from wherever he's hiding or I'll drop this torch and burn the rest of your family!" Hildebrand taunted Abel as he lowered his torch toward the straw. A few wisps caught, and the fire sent glowing embers floating upward.

"All right! All right!" Abel tossed his gun, raising his hands high. "Let them all go!"

"Skully, we'll get the boy later. Have you got Abel in your sights?"

Skully stepped away from Abel's mother and child to target Abel. "Sure do."

"Tie his hands and get him on his horse, then lead him over and string him up."

Abel stared Skully down, slowing his progress to a tentative walk, though Skully continued to point his gun at Abel's chest.

"Big, brave Abel," Hildebrand said menacingly. "If you're not afraid of losing your own life, then maybe you'll care about theirs." Hildebrand dropped the torch into the straw, igniting a ball of fire that swarmed the wall. As a new barrage of screams erupted from within the chapel, Abel slapped his horse, confusing Skully, then leapt toward the man, grabbed his gun, and fired, dropping Skully with a lifeless thud. Hildebrand squeezed off a shot, clipping Abel in the shoulder as Caleb and Captain Foster rode into the clearing. Foster's gun was raised.

"Let them out!" Abel shouted. "The women and children are in the chapel!"

Foster flew to the chapel and kicked away the brace. The women and children poured from the building, coughing and crying, the children clinging to Bitty's skirts. The reverend carried Hannah to a clearing and laid her down while Beatrice attended to her. "Eli," he shouted, "hitch the water cart and bring it here quickly for Mrs. Pearson."

Bitty raced to her husband, passing Emerson Hildebrand, who ran to his friend, collapsing beside him and crying out, "You killed him? You killed him?"

His grief seemed so sincere that Abel looked to Captain Foster.

"You killed a white man!" Hildebrand shouted.

"I was protecting my family."

"It was all a joke! You killed a white man over a joke, and now you're going to hang."

Abel felt panic rise in his throat. Looking from Captain Foster to Hildebrand he explained, "He beat my son and nearly incinerated a dozen women and children!"

"It was a game," Hildebrand insisted. "We'd get a slap on the wrist for laying a few stripes on your boy. And the green timbers on that chapel would have taken half an hour to catch fire. We would have had everyone out before then. But you murdered a white man, and you'll hang for that!"

Bitty pressed herself against her husband. "Abel, what are we going to do?"

The cart rolled by, Hannah coughing between spasms of labor. Beatrice walked beside the cart, her eyes so full of rage that Hildebrand cowered from her.

Abel looked desperately to Captain Foster as he pushed his wife away. "Bitty, go on to the house and tend to the children and Miss Hannah."

As Bitty left, Hildebrand's wide eyes fixed on the wagon. "There were white women in there? We didn't know! We thought it was just freed slaves and their slave-loving teacher."

"The courts might not care that you scared the freedmen nearly to death, but your trick put Mrs. Pearson at risk, and she and her sister could press attempted murder charges against you. Looks like you might swing next to Abel," Foster said. "But there is a way out." Both men seemed to understand that their lives hung on his plan. Foster continued, "Abel, the courts may not uphold your defense in a murder trial, but no one will raise an eyebrow if I say I killed a known scoundrel like Seaman Skully, who was endangering the women. I'm not doing this for you, Hildebrand, but I'll lie and risk imprisonment or worse to save Abel." No one spoke.

"Hildebrand, you return to Baltimore and explain how you and your friend became separated. That's your burden. And pledge to tell no one about Abel, or we will all hang."

Hildebrand slumped into a pitiful lump. "You're consigning us to live a terrible lie."

Foster spun on him and spat, "It is not I, but you who has wrought this sin upon us! There is no other justice for Abel, so I leave it to you. Your sport has already cost your friend his life. Do we end the game with a score of one man dead, or four?"

Jack and Markus returned home laden with good news about the tobacco sale and with their horses loaded with game, when the children rushed in on them, scrambling to be the first to share the grisly details of their imprisonment in the church by angry soldiers gunning for Abel.

Markus bolted from the wagon to fire questions at Abel, forcing him to square the children's story against Captain Foster's suggested explanation—how the good doctor had fired a "miracle shot" from the tree line that had brought Skully down. Harder yet was redirecting the children's memories away from Hildebrand's complicity in the events.

"You're sure everyone's safe?" Markus asked Abel.

Abel couldn't meet his eyes. "I'm sorry, Markus. It's my fault. I'm the one they came for. Thanks to God, everyone's safe, but Hannah went into labor in the middle of it all."

Abel ached as he watched the Irishman castigate himself. "I should never have left!" Markus pressed his fists to his temples, ranting all the way to the front porch. "I promised Jed!" He turned again to Abel. "You're sure this Skully is the only one? I need to know if someone else is goin' ta show up here with a gun or a torch because he has a vendetta against you, Abel."

Abel cringed, knowing Hildebrand was still out there. No matter how Abel answered, someone could suffer—those he loved or Dr. Foster. "Another soldier came around, but Dr. Foster checked him out and sent him away. He's all right." Abel knew that was a lie.

Markus stared him down. "I bloody hope you're right, Abel, because you'll be leavin' soon, and there's few of us here ta protect these women and children."

Frannie met Markus on the steps and placed her hands on his chest to calm him. "It's as much my fault as anyone's, Markus. Jenny and I went riding. I heard the shots but I assumed they were because you and Jack were hunting."

Markus drew her close and kissed her head as Jenny quietly watched the scene play out from the porch. Then Markus spun back around on Abel. "Where were Royal and Sookie?"

"They were bringing the stock in from the back pastures," Frannie answered quickly. "Abel wouldn't have known. He had just arrived when he was ambushed."

The news quieted Markus. "I'm sorry, Abel. I haven't even told you how good it is to have you home." He turned back to Frannie. "How's Hannah?"

"Her sisters and Bitty are with her. Jenny and I are heading up there now to help."

Fortunately for Abel, Hannah's distress and preparing for the baby's birth supplanted everything else for the women. Abel pitched in to help Jack and Markus prepare the meat for the smokehouse, while the children ferried regular updates about Hannah's progress and asked Abel to retell the story of their rescue again and again.

A pall of fear settled over Abel as the breadth of the lie soon became clear to him. His salvaged life seemed as fragile as a house of cards. In his heart he felt his actions were justified, but supporting them with a lie was so onerous a burden he considered confessing to free himself. However, with Captain Foster's life also hanging in the balance, he vowed to remain silent.

CHAPTER 40

Monday, November 14, 1814
The Willows

The strain of labor took a sorry toll on Hannah. Midnight came and went, taking with it Bitty's confidence in her ability to help the expectant mother. Late in the night, Bitty sent Jack racing to Calverton for the local doctor, and Markus raced away to Baltimore to fetch Samuel back.

With each push Hannah felt her head would burst, until between the headache and the fatigue she knew her reserves were failing. The women maintained a faithful vigil by her side, but just before dawn Hannah requested that Beatrice bring her stationery box to her bedside, and asked her to read the first few lines of each until she found the one she sought.

"Will you pen a letter for me?" she asked her sister. "I want to include some of Jed's sentiments from this letter." The tender message of the final composition was painfully, agonizingly clear.

November 13, 1814

My dearest Jed,

Of all the nights I've missed you, tonight I miss you most sorely. Today our child was to be born, but instead I go to him. God calls me home, my darling Jed.

Two years ago, you penned a letter to me that gives me courage and peace this night. My hope hangs on these words—for us, and for the angel child that we will not meet in this life. Do not weep for us long, my darling, for if God is as just and kind as we believe, you will find the way across time, beyond death thinly veiled, and back to us.

Do you recall these words? They are now mine.

"Short indeed was the time apportioned to us to love on this earth. And if it so be that we are separated by death, be comforted that I leave this earth with glad expectations . . . hoping that God has a plan for His children, and pray that surely, such a Being as you call Father, being greater than mortals, would offer mercy beyond that which mortal man or woman could hunger. And if love can indeed transcend death, than I shall spend my eternal days waiting and watching for you to cross over and into my embrace, to warm my cold soul once more."

Let love warm your heart in life, my love. I will wait for you.

Yours always,
Hannah

Jack never found the doctor in Calverton, but Samuel and Markus arrived near dawn, drunk from lack of sleep. Despite his size, Samuel raced up the stairs two at a time.

Bitty wailed as soon as she saw him. "I can't get the baby out! I can see its head but after every push it slides away. And Hannah's fully spent. She isn't even responding anymore."

Samuel cleared the room, washed his hands and arms, and performed his own exam. When he met the others in the hall his face was pale and grim. "The cord is wrapped several times around the baby's neck. Hannah has other problems. How long has she been swelling?"

"Today was the first I noticed it, I swear!" Bitty wrung her hands. "She said her head hurt, and then we got scared out of our minds, and she breathed all that smoke!"

Samuel laid a comforting hand on her shoulder. "You've taken very good care of her, Bitty. Markus told me what you've been through today. I can't even imagine it, but this long, hard labor is endangering Hannah's life. If she doesn't deliver this baby soon, she could suffer a stroke, or worse. I'll try again to clear the cord, but it's a painful procedure. I'll give her a few moments to rest before making another attempt."

Half an hour passed. Hannah's agonized moans filtered through the door to the women on the other side. When Samuel emerged, sorrow was etched on his face. He slumped against the wall, his chin falling to his chest. "I was unsuccessful. I couldn't clear the cord." A collective gasp sent the women into one another's arms. "You all know how dear Hannah is to me, so it grieves me to say that if the baby is not soon delivered, our Hannah will die."

"And you don't believe she will be able to deliver her child, do you?" Beatrice asked.

Samuel shook his head before he uttered, "I do not."

"It's not fair!" Frannie cried. "Surely there's something you can do. Jed can't lose them both, not after everything they've been through! Please, can't you save one of them?"

"There are only two options. One requires that we sacrifice the child with no guarantee of Hannah's survival. Or I could attempt to remove the baby surgically. There is a procedure called a cesarean section."

"I've never heard of such a thing," Beatrice said.

"It's a matter of absolute last resort. I'd make an incision across Hannah's abdomen just before she passes. It may save the child."

Beatrice shuddered. "And if you perform this procedure sooner?"

Samuel's head came up abruptly. "I've never . . . It's painful, and the risk to the mother is grave. Only fifteen percent pull through, but the child's chance for survival increases."

The weight of the news seemed to crush the two sisters. Beatrice wrapped an arm around Myrna before asking the doctor, "How severe would her suffering be?"

"I could dull her senses with opiates, but there would still be considerable pain."

Beatrice tightened her arm as Myrna began crying. "We are her nearest blood kin, Dr. Renfro. I give you permission to operate now."

Myrna pushed away from her sister and wailed. "No, Beatrice! You cannot do this! She is also my sister, and I will not have her splayed open like an animal!"

Beatrice's own eyes were shining, though she remained unflinching. "Think of Hannah, Myrna. Some chance is better than none. Hannah has the strongest will and spirit of us all. This is the choice she would make if she could. You know that, don't you?"

Myrna lifted her head, clearly not convinced at all, but moment by moment her face softened until she nodded. "Then we are agreed, and may God forgive us if she dies."

"Very well then." Samuel wiped his tired eyes. "I'll need supplies—alcohol, lime water, hot water, several towels—and someone to assist."

Jenny looked up from her quiet corner. "I'll assist if you'd like."

Samuel nodded. "Very good. Then let us prepare."

A pall hung over the house as everyone else retired to pray, or pace, or both. Markus was on the porch when the postman arrived with two packages—one large, one small—and some letters. "Does a Mrs. Jenny Tyler live here?" he asked from his saddle.

"Aye."

"I need her to sign for this package," the postman said, displaying the smaller of the two.

"She can't be disturbed. Can I just sign for it instead?"

The man shrugged, indicating the signature line. After Markus obliged, the postman tucked his notebook into his saddlebag and raced away. Markus checked the mail and set it down as Frannie came out to the porch, her eyes red-rimmed and her lips trembling. He opened his arms and she fell against him, burying her face into his shoulder.

"I can't believe what's happening! She's probably dying up there. I've never sat and waited for someone to die before."

"Hush now! Don't go givin' up on Hannah just yet! She's a fighter."

"I know you're right. Was the postman just here?"

Markus pointed to the stack of mail. "Yes. There's a letter to you from Timothy, something official for Jenny there, and a package for Hannah."

Frannie picked up the letter, read the return address, and tucked it into her pocket. The small package was sent from the Office of Sanford and Hutchison, Atty, and addressed to Mrs. Jeremiah Tyler. "Any other day this would have been exciting news."

"What is it?"

Frannie paused. "It's probably Jenny's divorce decree."

Markus's brow furrowed conspicuously but he didn't inquire further.

Frannie picked up the larger package, read the sender's name, and fell back into a chair. "It's for Hannah, and it says the addressee is Jed. Oh, Markus, what if these are his personal effects. What if he's—"

"Don't go assumin' the worst, Francis," he snapped. "Let me see. Is it his handwritin'?'"

"Yes!" Frannie's eyes brightened and then dimmed again. "He's all right, and she's . . ."

A slap sounded from the master bedroom window, followed by a weak cry. Markus and Frannie closed their eyes and froze. "Come on, baby! Cry! Cry!" she cheered. Seconds later, a strong wail could be heard, and Frannie's shoulders shook. "Thank you, thank you!" she repeated as she met Markus's gaze. "I'm going up to be with Hannah. I'm going to open her package for her. She has a right to know he's all right, and that he sent something to her."

The two friends climbed the stairs to find Bitty grim-faced, bearing an armful of bloodstained towels. "It's a boy. Looks just like his father did the day he was born." She wiped her nose with a corner of her apron.

"How's Hannah?" Markus asked.

Bitty blinked, clearly trying to stave off her tears. "She's a brave one, that girl. I never saw such a thing as what she's been through to give this baby life. She's lost so much blood."

Frannie gripped Markus's arm tightly. "Can we sit with her?"

"Not until she's sewn up," Bitty said. "Markus, you'd best wash and change from those hunting clothes before you go in. Samuel says half the mothers who survive this far die from childbed fever. We've got to keep things real clean. But Jenny did real good. What a blessing she was in there."

An hour later, Frannie and Markus they were admitted into the room. Hannah lay shrouded in white sheets, as still and white as death. Her dark-rimmed eyes and sweat-soaked hair evidenced the strain of the ordeal. Samuel looked nearly as worn, with sweat marks under his arms and down his back. Jenny silently gathered the blood-soaked linens and towels while Bitty fussed over the baby. Beatrice and Myrna sat on either side of their sister, holding her hands and praying.

"Does anyone know what name Hannah intended for her child?" Samuel asked. "I must record his birth."

Bitty knew. "He's to have his father's name, except he'll be the fourth, and we're to call him Johnny. Should I send to Calverton for a wet nurse?"

Samuel laid a finger across his lips. "No. Prop the baby beside his mother and let her suckle him as long as she's able."

Finality began to set in. Frannie unwrapped Hannah's package, revealing the stack of letters. She looked to Samuel for approval. "Jed made it to England. He sent her these letters. May I—may I read these to her? She should hear Jed's words, in case . . ."

Samuel nodded slightly. "Somehow, I think she'll hear every word."

He and Jenny gathered up his instruments and left the room as Frannie pulled a chair close to Hannah's side. Taking the entire bundle, she began to read, beginning with the most recent note, the one used to wrap the others.

October 13, 1814

Sweetness,

I arrived safely in Liverpool three days ago. A most hopeful turn came my way. A British captain named Smith believes in my innocence and has agreed to serve as my advocate at the hearing. Another benefactor has come to my aid, and I am resting comfortably as I prepare for trial. Whatever befalls me, know this, that my every thought, my every action, all of it was aimed at bringing me back to you.

Your time must be drawing close. I pray daily for you and for the son or daughter you carry, placing my complete trust in Frannie, Bitty, Markus, and Jack to provide all you need until I return. Write down every moment so I will not miss a minute of this child's life.

I will write more very soon, for as long as I am able. I pray you'll find some comfort in my musings. I tried to press a lifetime of love into these few pages. I pray they sustain you until we are united. These are the memories that will nourish my heart until then. Invest the love you feel for me in our child, and tell our child that Papa loves them dearly. Until we are together again, you are ever, ever, ever on my mind.

All my love,
Jed

Unable to offer the women any words of consolation, Markus muttered a prayer in Hannah's behalf, made the sign of the cross, and left the room. He found Samuel on the front porch, leaning heavily against a column and staring blankly out at the barren November landscape. Markus moved to the rail and stood silently beside him for a time.

"That couldn't've been easy for you, lovin' Hannah as you do," Markus finally said. "It was very brave."

A twitching around Samuel's mouth was his only response.

Markus let out a sigh. "It's a good sign that she's made it so far, isn't it? Don't we have cause to hope?"

Samuel pushed away from the column and turned, placing his back there now. "If she does make it, we have Jenny to thank for it. I doubt an instrument ever touched Hannah twice without being sterilized with alcohol in between, and ready before I asked. It cut our surgical time down considerably. And she administered the drug in the smallest amounts necessary while keeping Hannah still enough to allow me to make clean incisions and to suture her inside and out. I've never worked with a finer nurse."

The groan of the door preceded the arrival of Jenny and Bitty, who each had items in their hands. Bitty placed two bowls of venison stew on the railing.

"You two eat up, you hear?" she ordered with a wag of her finger.

Jenny handed Samuel his medical bag. "I've cleaned and repacked all your instruments. I think I'll enjoy a breath of fresh air before I check back in on Hannah."

"Thank you for assisting. Your skills have given Hannah the edge she needs to survive."

Jenny bowed her head shyly. "I don't know if that's true or not, but I thank you for the honor. Helping use what I learned eases the suffering it took to learn it."

She glanced briefly at Markus as she passed him. Samuel picked up his bowl and took a spoonful of stew, and the two men watched as Jenny walked across the lawn and disappeared behind a large oak tree.

Samuel pointed his spoon in her direction. "The day we found her was a double blessing. We needed her as much as she needed us."

"What do you think she meant by that, about her sufferin'?"

Pointing his spoon again, Samuel said, "Go ask her."

412

Markus pushed his red hair behind his ears and straightened the collar on his plaid shirt as he made his way across the lawn. He heard Jenny's soft cries before he saw her sitting on the grass behind the tree, curled up with her feet under her like a small child. He coughed to announce his arrival and watched her quickly wipe her eyes and assume a stoic, upright position. He shoved his hands deep into the pockets of his brown trousers and hunched his shoulders around his neck.

"I wanted to thank you for all you did to help Hannah today," Markus began. "Samuel said he's never worked with a finer nurse—not even at the hospital."

"I was glad to have a chance to repay her kindness to me."

"I know I've been an ornery cuss, and I don't deserve the time of day from ya, but I was wonderin' what you meant back there about the sufferin' it took to learn what you know."

"It doesn't matter. What's done is done."

Markus scrunched his shoulders again. "If it bothers you, it matters."

Jenny studied him for a moment, and he watched her stubbornness fade into resignation. "My husband used to beat me senseless, Mr. O'Malley. He'd send me to the doc to patch me up enough to warm his bed and cook his food. Things would go all right for a while, but then I'd make the coffee too strong, or a sock would work a hole in the toe, and he'd break my arm or bust my head open again. Sometimes the doc would keep me for a few days, and I'd help him mend other people, too. So you see, I learned what I know about medicine firsthand, the hard way."

Markus just stood there, unable to offer a response.

"I haven't known much kindness from men since my pa died. I pretend to be able to handle myself, but the truth is, I'm really not very brave." Two tears trickled down her cheeks. "I know I should have fought off those British soldiers, but I was just too afraid."

Markus crouched beside her, slipping her small hand into his. "I'm sorry."

"I know. I know what kind of man you are. You're stubborn and pigheaded, and you ought to listen more, but I also know you're kind and gentle and good. Frannie told me about the man who hurt her—how you and her brother were so caring to her. You didn't expect anything in return. You just were her friend. I wondered what it would be like to feel that safe and loved."

He rubbed his thumb into the palm of her hand. "Don't you worry. No one's ever goin' to hurt you again."

For three hours Frannie read Jed's letters to a sleeping Hannah. Those watching over her heard the words, not as voyeurs, but as guardians empowered by them, elevating their thoughts from grief to hope, until they began willing her to be made well through their faith and prayers. The love expressed so tenderly by Jed made anything less unthinkable.

Line by line, the couple's unique bond was revealed—how the tender connection that had begun when they were children had sustained Hannah through her mother's madness, and had served as the impetus for Jed to become the man he needed to be. It was all there—the agonies of their trials and separations, the exquisiteness of their momentary peace, forgiveness for those complicit in their heartaches, and wondrous dreams for the future.

Jenny entered the room with a handful of supplies. She touched Hannah's forehead and announced happily, "She's warming up a bit!" A quick glance at the bandages also produced a smile. "I'll need you all to leave while I change her dressings."

Bitty carried the baby out of the room, and the rest of the women followed. Beatrice and Myrna decided to go to their rooms to rest, while Frannie headed to the kitchen with the stack of letters. She organized them back into a neat bundle, and when she reached into her pocket for the string, she found Timothy's letter. After tying up the bundle, she sat down, broke the seal, and read the latest Washington news, including the item dearest to Timothy's heart—the re-establishment of the Congressional Library, a project in which he was invited to assist.

President Jefferson had offered to sell the government his personal library of over nine thousand books for twenty-four thousand dollars, to replace the volumes lost during the burning of the Capitol. Timothy noted that the collection contained works on every conceivable topic, each selected from around the world by Mr. Jefferson's own hand. Timothy's one concern revolved around the attitudes of those who needed to approve the purchase. While the Senate seemed inclined to approve the measure, the House members were balking, claiming Mr. Jefferson's choice in books reflected an "infidel philosophy," a matter Timothy wished to debate with them.

The next paragraph held the news Frannie was expecting and was finally prepared for.

> *Miss Bainbridge and I have decided to forego a long engagement and are planning a winter wedding. I hope you will be pleased for us. Know that I share this news with you before anyone else other than our families, so you will see in what high regard we both hold you. We hope you will come and toast our marriage, Frannie, and in due course, if things should proceed between you and Mr. Ramsey, we will be most pleased to toast your own.*

Timothy used his whole name to close the note, and Frannie saw that as the final break of their old relationship and the beginning of a strange new one, with Lucinda Bainbridge as his wife. Frannie was too spent to care, though his mention of Arthur Ramsey tore at her heart.

Jenny returned from Hannah's room and sat at the table across from Frannie.

"You're smiling," Frannie said. "Is it because you think Hannah is doing well?"

"Oh, I can't say. I don't know anything about this surgery, but as surgeries go, she's doing fine. She got real cold and clammy after losing all that blood, but she's warming up some. Now we need to watch for fever. But her wounds are clean, and her bleeding is stopped. She moaned when I changed her dressing, but I'd rather see her respond to the pain than not. Bitty's putting the baby back to nurse again, and Dr. Renfro is keeping an eye on them."

Frannie unfolded the brown paper to rewrap the letters. "So, there's another cause for your smile. And what might that be? A certain Irishman?"

Jenny blushed crimson. "Did you put him up to talking to me?"

"Of course not, but I think I know what did." She left for a minute and returned with the parcel from the attorneys. "This arrived today. Markus signed for it."

Jenny fingered the parcel nervously before opening the seal and removing the documents. "I'm too nervous. Will you read it?"

Frannie scanned the document, understanding little of what was written, but the last page was unmistakable—an official certificate of divorce. "Look, Jenny. You're free from that tyrant! He even signed it. It's over." She handed the document back across the table.

Jenny touched Jeremiah's signature with her finger. "I wonder how they got him to sign it. I guess it doesn't matter. So you think this is why Markus finally spoke to me?"

"I think this mattered very much to a man like Markus."

Jenny's smile returned and faded again. "It's strange. As terrible as Jeremiah was to me, I still feel sad somehow. There

416

was always a part of me that dreamed he would change and that things would get better. I suppose it's hard to let go of a dream."

She gathered her papers and left the room, leaving Frannie alone again to finish her task. When she flipped the brown wrapping paper over to smooth out the last wrinkles, the smudge caught her eye. The handwriting looked oddly familiar. *Jed must have been in a hurry,* she thought. But then she realized the handwriting wasn't Jed's. As she examined the smudge more closely, a shock jolted through her. She noted the corner where the return address was situated. The name was Arthur Ramsey!

Frannie's hands shook so badly she could scarcely untie the bundle. She peeled the first letter from the stack and searched for a single line: "Another benefactor has come to my aid, and I am resting comfortably as I prepare for trial." She read it three times, her every sense telling her she was right. Arthur was still alive, and Jed was with him!

She bolted from her seat and paced the floor. Why had Jed not disclosed the news to her? Arthur must have asked him not to. What had he said at their parting? "You can no longer hide behind that armored façade, Frannie. You were made to love . . . and you need to be loved by someone. You must promise me that you will not surrender and lock your heart up again."

Arthur might think he was too broken or sick to love her as he felt she deserved, but she wouldn't let him push her away without a fight! Frannie copied the address onto a piece of stationery and tucked it into her pocket, knowing that when the time was right, she would sail to England, find Arthur, and wait there until he listened to reason.

She wanted to run upstairs and share the exciting news with Hannah that their men were together and everything would be all right. For a second, life seemed perfect again, with hope abounding, and then she remembered that life wasn't perfect at all. A thread of life seemed to be all that was holding Hannah on earth.

A scream split the silence, followed by a crash as something hit the floor. Frannie's blood chilled as she thought of what the cause might be. She ran to the base of the steps and waited, listening for the confirmation of her worst fears. When she heard nothing, she steeled her nerves and raced up the stairs to find Hannah's bedroom door wide open with Myrna standing in the doorway. The washbasin was overturned, with its stand lying on its side in a river of water that pooled around Myrna's feet. Frannie inched forward, needing to have her answer yet afraid to have it. Peering past Myrna, she looked at Hannah's sickbed and gasped. Hannah was propped upright with several pillows. Bitty and Jenny stood beside her, their hands busily attending to some duty. Frannie saw the subject of their concern—Little Johnny was meeting his mama for the very first time as Samuel teared up over the wondrous scene.

Hannah turned, the serenity in her face belying the stress evident in her bedraggled hair and gown. "Isn't he perfect?"

Hannah's progress was slow but steady. When Markus had told Samuel of Hannah's distress, he had left the hospital with a cursory and exaggerated explanation that a family member needed him. Now he desperately needed to return to the hospital. Two days after Hannah's emergence from the edge of death, he confidently turned her care over to Jenny and Bitty and left for Baltimore.

Days passed with Hannah remaining too weak to leave her bed. Frannie spelled the women off so Bitty could spend a little time with Abel before he returned to the fort, and so Jenny could catch some rest. On the fourth day of the child's life, Frannie was rocking little Johnny when his fussing woke his mother.

"There are some things only mamas can do," she teased as she nestled Johnny near Hannah's breast. "You can't know how frightened we all were over you, Hannah." Frannie handed Hannah the letter she had written to Jed. "It pleases me to give this morbid thing back to you."

"It pleases me even more not to have to send it," Hannah replied. "Will you help me post a glorious birth announcement to this little boy's papa?"

"Of course." The baby gave a loud, impatient wail. "Just a moment more, Johnny."

"You're the picture of contentment, Frannie," Hannah said as she scooted to sit up.

Frannie reached out to take her sister-in-law's hand. "I think I'd be very good at this."

"I'm sure you'll be wonderful. Are you rethinking Timothy's proposal?"

"Timothy and Lucinda have announced their wedding date—a Christmas ceremony."

Hannah's face sobered in concern. "You're taking it well."

"Because I have wonderful news of my own," Frannie whispered. After moving her chair close, she clamped her hand over Hannah's. "Jed mailed his letters from Arthur's house! The return address said Ramsey, Hannah. Arthur is Jed's benefactor! I have a complete address, too."

Hannah's eyes lit up. "Arthur survived the voyage? And he's helping Jed?"

"It has to be him! How else would Jed have come across a sheet of wrapping paper with Arthur's name on it? Imagine! Arthur not only survived, but he's well enough to help Jed."

Hannah pressed her lips to her baby's head. "Did you hear that, Johnny? Daddy will be home sooner than you know." Worry lines appeared on her brow. "Frannie, what did you mean when you said you have a complete address? Do you mean to go searching for Arthur?"

"Would that sadden you because you can't come along?"

"Not at all. Johnny's safety must come first now. I'm content to wait for Jed's return." She began to chuckle. "Besides, he'd skin me alive for considering such an escapade. But neither do I think you should go, Frannie. A woman crossing the sea alone in the dead of winter to travel to an enemy nation . . ."

"Jenny has agreed to accompany me. And along with sending my regrets about missing the wedding, I've asked Timothy for a favor. We have American prisoner exchange officers stationed in London. I've asked our savvy Washingtonian to arrange letters of introduction for Jenny and me. If Timothy can secure those, we should be quite safe. And considering that he is very sensitive to my feelings at this time, I doubt he will refuse me anything."

"Francis Pearson, I doubt your brother would approve."

"We'll know soon enough, won't we? We plan to depart as soon as you're well."

Abel's long, truthful explanation about the agreement struck between himself, Hildebrand, and Captain Foster did nothing to ease Bitty's concerns. If anything, the pacing and hand-wringing only intensified.

"You got to tell Markus the truth, Abel! He'll keep your secret."

"I have another plan, Bitty. If I'm not here, Hildebrand won't bother the Willows. We could move on, start fresh somewhere else. We're free. I've got skills to get good work."

Her face twisted in obvious disappointment. "This is our home, Abel! These people are our family! And you'd be a deserter. You'd have the whole military looking for you. How long do you think a big man like you could go without being identified?"

He crouched low to see eye to eye with his wife. "We could go west and homestead, Bitty, to Tennessee or Ohio."

"Please, Abel. First, go tell Markus the truth."

420

Abel's mighty heart was heavy as he walked away. He knew he'd almost prefer to pull up stakes and run than tell his friend he had lied to him. No matter what others had done to him, he had always had his honor.

He found Markus and Jack in the barn. Markus held a horse's foot between his knees as he worked the hoof with a file. Both men looked up as Abel entered.

"Need some help?" he asked Markus.

"I got it."

Jack chuckled. "Markus is vexed because Frannie talked Jenny into sailing to England."

Markus shot Jack a scathing look that only increased Jack's laughter. "Well, I've got milking to do. Markus is sorry company, Abel. You'd do best to occupy yourself elsewhere."

"I'd appreciate it if you'd stay a minute, Jack. There's something I need to tell you both." Abel couldn't meet their eyes. "I lied about what happened the other day. There may be more trouble coming." The rhythm of Markus's strokes halted momentarily and then resumed without a word. "Did you hear me, Markus? I didn't tell you the whole truth about the attack."

Markus dropped the horse's foot and tossed the file in a box. "I know."

"I didn't lie just to save my own hide. I'm saving Dr. Foster's, too." Abel slumped hard against a stall. "It's a terrible mess now and I don't know what to do." He told the story from start to finish, lingering on Hildebrand's claim that it was all a "joke," and the hellish pledge made by the three men to pin the entire attack on Skully in return for Hildebrand's silence about Abel's mortal shot.

"Dr. Foster bartered his good name to save my life." Abel rose to his full six feet eight inches, a giant with the face of an angel, and declared softly, "I'd give myself up right now to keep everyone here safe, but Dr. Foster might be jailed for lying, or get something worse for doing it to cover a freed slave's murder of a white man."

Jack cast a worried glance at Markus. "And if Abel comes clean about Hildebrand now, they might say he's lying to cover his tracks."

Markus nodded. "In which case Hildebrand might still remain free to threaten us."

"What should we do then?" Abel asked.

"It's not right that any man can be charged with a crime for protectin' his family." Markus sighed. "But the law may take years to change. In the meantime, you need to return to Fort McHenry and keep an eye on Hildebrand, and we'll double the watch here."

CHAPTER 41

Saturday, December 24, 1814
London, England

Snow fell softly on Christmas Eve, the day Jed and Arthur returned from Oslo. It was a stronger, more confident Arthur who emerged from the carriage that day, but Jed knew the prognosis had somehow fallen short of his hopes. Though his outward health appeared normal and nothing specific was said, the fire that once danced in Arthur's eyes was still absent.

Jed bolted through the door as soon as it was opened, running straight for Arthur's desk, where he knew the butler laid the mail. Relief shot through him as he caressed the ink on the first of Hannah's many letters, and then the ache resumed.

"Hannah received my package. Look at all this mail." He closed his eyes and kissed a letter, uttering, "Thank you, Lord," as he fingered the pile. "Come help me, Arthur. Somewhere in here is news of my baby's birth! Help me sort these by date."

The inequity of the piles became painfully apparent. Jed had dozens of letters from Hannah, who appeared to have written daily. There were also notes from Bitty and Jack, and pictures and cards from the children. Arthur's stack was pitiably small—bills, a letter from Corvas reporting on the farm, a Christmas note from Arthur's mother thanking him for stopping by her home in Ireland with his American friend on their way home from Oslo, and a single holiday invitation. But Jed couldn't dwell on that at this moment. He was anxious to know one thing, and he settled into an overstuffed chair to discover the answer.

"I have a son!" he soon announced joyfully. "Hannah named him after me." His eyes glistened, making reading difficult. Then, blinking rapidly, he repeated the news in a whisper. "I have a son named Johnny. Arthur, I have a son."

Arthur strode across the floor to his friend. "That's wonderful news, Jed. Congratulations. I'll break out a good bottle of wine and we'll toast to his safe arrival."

Then Jed's face sobered, his hand covering his open mouth. "Not such a safe arrival. I very nearly lost Hannah." Silent seconds passed as he continued reading the letter. "Markus sent for Samuel, and he removed the baby surgically. Surgically?" He folded over and dropped his head into his hand. "I nearly lost her, Arthur. Hannah nearly died. I need to get home. My family needs me and I need them. When will this blasted treaty be signed?"

"Soon, I hear. Let's pray it's very soon."

"I've failed her so many times when she's needed me. We've been separated by our families, by my pride, and by the war. When I get home I'll never leave her again."

"And yet by the amount of correspondence shared between you and William Wilberforce, I assumed you had decided to proceed with your anti-slavery efforts."

"I have, but Hannah will be right there by my side. She was the catalyst behind me freeing my slaves. She's been behind every good thing I've ever done."

Arthur eyed him skeptically. "Has William told you what his work cost him? Slavery incites powerful passions in men, Jed. They see their livelihoods being threatened, and they will not be easily persuaded to change. It nearly cost William his fortune, his reputation, and his life."

"Hannah and Johnny will always come first, but I will find a way to effect some change. Understanding even what little I do of how a captive man feels, I know it must change."

"And how is Frannie? Are any of those letters from her?"

"Two." Jed chuckled. "I suppose my sister was content to simply know I'm alive. Either she's too busy to write, or too sad. You should tell her you're alive. At least give her that peace."

Arthur held up his hand to end the discussion. "Please let this go. It's better this way."

"I don't agree. I'd rather you tell her you never want to see her again than leave her grieving for you. Isn't that precisely what you wanted to spare her from?"

"Have you ever been so coldly rejected by someone you loved? It is worse than mourning them. I won't break her heart further. Give me time. I'll find a better way. For now, I'll go pull a good wine from the cellar so we can toast your son's birth."

Jed read on. When Arthur returned, Jed looked up at him. "Markus sent along details about the American victory at Baltimore. A new anthem has emerged titled 'The Star-Spangled Banner,' written by one of Timothy Shepard's friends, Francis Scott Key. He sent along a copy of the text." He handed the page to Arthur. "It's quite stirring. Markus said the nation is rallying around the flag as never before. And there's more, Arthur. General Ross was killed at Baltimore."

Arthur lowered the page and stared at Jed in disbelief. "General Ross is dead?"

"I'm afraid so. I know how deeply you cared for him."

"The doctors shielded me from the news. No wonder the rumors say the treaty will come soon. The war has turned since Washington. America has found her inspiration and now brave General Ross is dead . . ." Arthur poured two glasses of wine. "Whit has invited me to a party to celebrate the New Year. He mentioned his regrets at not being able to invite you as well, but he feared it might cause the Admiralty to revoke the leniency of your terms."

"I understand. I'm grateful to simply not be at Dartmoor. In fact, I feel guilty about my comfort here, considering that many of my countrymen are suffering. Could permission be obtained to do something to ease their situation, at least for the holiday? Additional rations of food and clothes, and perhaps some medicine?"

"I'll ask Whit tonight. Daniel is visiting, and things are not going well between father and son. Whit has asked me to speak with the boy in his behalf."

"Will you tell him what you've learned about your father?" Jed asked as he took a glass.

"I dread it, but I must. The ripples from that night's events have altered so many lives."

"There's no use in looking back, Arthur. You did your best with what you knew."

"Such as it was." He raised his glass. "To Jonathan Edward Pearson IV."

"Thank you. And to the future. May it be bright and filled with peace."

CHAPTER 42

Saturday, December 31, 1814
London, England

The stream of carriages headed for the earl's party flowed through Hyde Park, guided through the night by the glow emanating from the brightly lit home. Arthur paused on the landing, enjoying the cheer of the holiday decorations, exquisite tapestries, hundreds of candles, and evergreen boughs bound in trailing ribbons.

Lord Whittington stood beside Daniel, who was barely inches shorter than his father. The sober lad beamed as soon as he saw Arthur, breaking from his father's side and barreling over while calling out, "Arthur! I've missed you!"

Arthur's face erupted into a smile. "This cannot be you, Daniel! You're nearly a man. Let me look at you."

"Father said you had been wounded and that you went to Oslo for treatment. Are you well now? You appear well enough to challenge me in rugby, though I must warn you, I've improved my game. I've learned a few tricks living in Ireland."

Arthur placed a loving hand on the young man's shoulder. "Give me a few more weeks to heal and we'll test that claim, all right?"

Clearly flustered, the earl took his son's arm and softly scolded him. "Decorum, Daniel. You are not a Labrador pup." He smiled at Arthur. "I'm so delighted you came."

"Tell me about America, Arthur," Daniel said. "What's it really like? I dream of going there someday."

"Daniel," his father interjected as he gave the boy's formal coat a firm tug. "This is not the time for boyish daydreaming. We have guests, and you have responsibilities to attend to."

The boy appeared to deflate as his eyes met Arthur's. Lord Whittington must have caught the change in his son's mood, because he smiled sheepishly at his guest and said, "No one is dancing. Daniel, ask the conductor to liven the music, will you?"

While the boy left to attend to the errand, the earl moved Arthur to a quiet corner, his eyes conspicuously avoiding the young man's as he said, "I wasn't sure you'd come after our last exchange. Please, let me explain about that, Arthur. I haven't been well, though I know that sounds ridiculous considering all you've been through. You know I've sternly fought to keep Britain's actions honorable in this war, but I suffered a breakdown on the floor of Parliament, and my reputation has been sorely effected. That day at the hearing, my cousin saw a chance for me to redeem some credibility amongst my most strident opponents. I know how that exchange must have sounded to you, but I meant Jed no harm. I simply hoped to do myself some good."

Arthur remained unmoved. "I've said nothing to Jed about our conversation. My thanks are to Juan Corvas for finding Jed's witness. I doubt Jed would be free otherwise."

"I have thanked God many times for that bit of Providence."

"My error was in setting men up as more than men—making heroes of them and then either refusing to see their weakness or discarding them when they falter, myself included."

"You're speaking of me?"

"No more than my father. I recently discovered that he did send McGowan to your home to kidnap Daniel that night. I'm so sorry, Whit. And I'm sorry I didn't believe you."

The earl's shoulders rounded. "At least I now know I was right, for whatever good it does me. The life I loved ended that night. You've seen the contempt Daniel shows for me and his title. Will you talk to him for me? I need my son, back, Arthur. He's all I have."

"Of course I will. Let's find him."

The men found Daniel standing near the refreshment tables, overwhelmed by an older couple's attentions. Arthur bowed to the couple and said apologetically, "Please excuse us. The earl sent me for his son." He swept Daniel to freedom, whispering, "Shall we begin our season of competition with a game of chess?"

"Thank you, Arthur. I may let you win out of appreciation!"

Arthur noted the joyful change in Daniel as he led the way to the lad's room, where a chessboard waited on a table. The pair sat across from one another and sparred equitably for a time, but Daniel beat him in a challenging first game.

"I can hardly fathom that you'll be thirteen soon," Arthur said. "You were barely ten when we met."

"Father treats me as if I were still a boy." Daniel leaned forward. "Did you know a boy becomes responsible for his own actions—like a man—at age thirteen in the Jewish culture?"

"I have heard that, but you are not Jewish, my friend."

Daniel eyed him cautiously. "What would you say if I told you I may convert."

Arthur nearly dropped his rook. "What? That's no joking matter, Daniel."

"I met a Jewish girl in Greece last summer. Her name is Ruth. Her family owned the inn where my tutor, Mr. Healy, and I stayed, and we've been writing to one another ever since. I'm quite taken with her culture and teachings."

"How old is this girl? What have you been asking her?"

"She's my only friend my own age, but at twelve she is already treated like an adult. I was in Greece on Clarissa's birthday, and missing her badly. Ruth explained her beliefs—how our dead loved ones are nearer than we think, and how life continues beyond the grave. I felt peaceful, Arthur. That night was the first time I slept soundly since Clarissa was murdered."

"Daniel, you have been taught these principles from birth with the understanding that this peace comes from the sacrifice of our Lord Jesus Christ. Perhaps you need to strengthen your own faith, not look for another. Converting away from Christianity is no small matter." Arthur heard the sound of singing. "Your father's entertainment has begun. He'll soon come for us, so please listen to me, Daniel. Perhaps you liked Ruth so well that anything she might have told you would have turned your head."

Daniel appeared to consider the notion. "I've never met anyone like her. She works hard but she is the happiest person I know, and I was my happiest with her." He pulled a satchel containing dozens of letters from under his bed. "Read this." He handed Arthur a single letter with a recent date. "Her parents plan to promise her in marriage to someone this year. She won't actually marry for years, but once she is promised she won't be able to write to me anymore."

Arthur read the note and struggled to know where to go with the conversation. "Daniel, these are very . . . adult concerns. You shouldn't be worrying about such things now."

Daniel's face clouded and he stormed away to the window to sulk. "Father says I am too much a boy. You say I worry over adult concerns. Which is it?"

"Ruth's world is not yours, but your expectations and obligations are similar. She will be promised to a Jewish young man and she'll meet the obligations of her culture. You will rise to meet yours—to serve the people of your shire as their earl. And you will fall in love and choose to marry someday. Be patient, and if you do, I promise you, you will be happy, Daniel."

"Are you happy, Arthur? Have British politics and war made your dreams come true?"

Arthur removed his gaze from the boy's probing stare. "Life is about more than fulfilling our own dreams. We are each obligated to serve others as well as ourselves, Daniel. And we place our hope in Christ that our good efforts and faith will someday be rewarded."

Daniel abruptly stood and walked to the window. "But mustn't men also be free to choose their own way? Am I just to be herded along like an animal? I'm willing to serve my fellow man, just not the way Father wants. I want to be a doctor, Arthur. Mr. Healy says I have a gift for medicine, and Ruth's father knows so much about healing herbs. He said he would teach me so I could combine Western medicine with the ancient. And I want to go to America and be free to choose the life I want. Is that so terrible?"

The door thrust open and Lord Whittington entered, his face stormy and dark. "These doors are too thin to hide your deceit, Daniel. So this is the cause of your reluctance to fulfill your duties!"

Arthur rose to stand between father and son. He placed his hands on the earl's arms to restrain him. "Please, Whit. Calm yourself. Little good comes from confrontations made over half-heard conversations. We were both involved in such an impasse a few years ago with my father, and we know what a debacle that became."

"I've heard enough and I've been patient enough," the earl declared. "Too patient and too lenient, perhaps. Please leave, Arthur. I need to speak to my son alone."

Daniel stood defiantly. "It's all right, Arthur. I want to talk to him as well."

Arthur made another appeal to Lord Whittington, but one look at his steeled expression assured him that no one could delay what was about to unfold. With a final mournful glance back at Daniel, Arthur left and closed the door.

✯ ✯ ✯ ✯ ✯

Unbelievable as it was, Jed reached a new level of loneliness this night. These were the first waking hours he had been truly alone since his agonizing days chained to the hold of the *Iphigenia.* But it was more than the lack of company. It was the letters, the reminders of home.

It was the gentle way Hannah looped the "J" when she penned his name, the tender endearments of "darling" and "my love" that kissed every few lines. It was the description of their baby's first moments—moments Jed had missed forever—and of Hannah's near death, when others had hovered over her in his stead.

It was 128, the number of days since he had last seen Hannah, and 134, the number of days since he had last held her in his arms as a free man. During the long weeks in Oslo, Jed had hungered for those letters, assuming they would ease his loneliness, but he had been wrong. The first glimpse of Hannah's penmanship harrowed up a terrible, physical longing that made him moan with sorrow.

He lay on his bed staring at the ceiling when he heard the knocker pound against the front door. It was an unfamiliar sound at this house where so few people called. *The butler will get it,* he told himself as he plunged again into his well of despair. A few moments passed before the butler's heavy footfalls sounded on the stairs, soon followed by a knock at Jed's door. "Yes," he called out in a voice he knew reflected his desire to be left alone.

"Mr. Pearson, there is a gentleman here to see you, sir—a Major Stebbings."

A major? An icy chill settled into Jed's heart. Had the Admiralty decided to revoke his privileges? He quickly tidied his appearance and slid into his coat and boots, then headed into the hallway. At the foot of the dimly lit stairs stood a round, fortyish man with but a fringe of dark hair. He was dressed in formal attire with a bright red cummerbund that only accentuated his girth.

Before Jed reached the landing the man asked, "Are you Jonathan Edward Pearson from Maryland?"

"I am, but I don't understand . . ."

"It will all be very clear to you in just a second. Please, wait here."

Stebbings stepped back out into the snow and returned, guiding a woman through the doorway. She was wrapped from head to foot in a scarlet-dyed woolen coat, scarf, and hat. Before he identified her she rushed toward him crying out, "Jed!"

"Frannie? Frannie?" he repeated as she fell into his arms. "Oh, Frannie! Is it really you or a heavenly apparition?" he muttered as he clutched her to him.

"It's me," she cried. "Oh, Jed, we've been so worried about you. We've all missed you so. It's taken me six frigid weeks to get here, but I'm really here, Jed."

He pulled back and questioned her. "But what made you dare to come? You thought I'd be in prison now." Panic set in. "Is Hannah well? And Johnny? Is he also well?"

"They're both very well, Jed," she said. "The reverse side of the paper you used to wrap your letters had a return address on it that said Ramsey. I knew Arthur had to be your 'kind benefactor,' and I was so desperate to see him that I asked Timothy to help me. A diplomatic envoy was traveling to Belgium, and Timothy arranged for me and my friend to sail with him."

Mr. Stebbings returned through the open doorway, leading a young blond woman by the arm. He cleared his throat. "Excuse me, Miss Pearson. I hate to intrude on this happy reunion, but I wanted to get Mrs. Tyler settled before I depart."

"Forgive me, Jenny! Jed, this is my friend, Jenny Tyler. And this is Major Josiah Stebbings, who headed the security detail at the peace conference in Ghent. We met him there and he offered to escort us back to London. He has been most obliging in helping me find you."

"Miss Tyler, the pleasure is mine," Jed said, bowing to Jenny. As he rose, he offered the officer his hand. "And Major Stebbings, I am forever in your debt, sir."

"They are a brave pair. I daresay I'd go into battle with either of them." Mr. Stebbings offered them a bow. "Ladies, it has been an absolute delight, but I'll now take my leave. I believe I'll arrive at the earl's party just in time to be fashionably late."

After the major departed, Jed hung the women's coats in the foyer closet and settled Jenny into a room where she could rest. Then he and Frannie moved to the parlor to catch up.

"Tell me everything about home," he began excitedly. "Is Hannah fully well? Oh, Frannie, I barely received her letters. I almost lost her. How could that be?"

The memory clearly sobered Frannie. "It was terrible, Jed. Samuel saved them both, with Jenny's help. She served as his nurse and assisted during the surgery. Hannah's well now. And your son is beautiful. Bitty says he looks exactly as you did when you were born."

"I'll never be able to make all this up to Hannah. I've put her through so much."

"You didn't cause this, Jed. And she's not angry. She loves you more than ever before."

Jed's lips formed a tight, quivering smile. "We have lived our lives in a crucible. She allows the bad to burn away like dross while she becomes more perfect with every trial."

"I hope Arthur and I will fare as well. How is he?"

Jed took her hand. "He's been through countless surgeries, Frannie. He wanted to die on the ship. Helping me was his reason for surviving. We've just returned from two months in Oslo, where surgeons again operated on him. Physically he is much improved, but he's different now. His spirit has dimmed, and I don't think he will receive you."

"He loves me, Jed. And he needs me."

"That's the problem, Frannie. I don't think he wants to need you. He doesn't want to need anyone. I only wish I knew what was still troubling him."

"Where is he? Please, take me to him."

"I can't. I'm still a prisoner and not at liberty to move about, but I don't think I would take you to him if I could. Now is not the time—"

The door opened and Arthur filled the reflection in the foyer mirror as the butler hurried to take his hat and coat and hang them in the closet. Jed stood to ease the announcement as Arthur pulled Frannie's scarf out of the closet and brought it to his nose, lingering over the fragrance as sorrow washed over his face.

"Where is she?" he asked.

Jed could almost feel the pain radiating from the man. Frannie was beside Arthur before Jed could answer, her hand reaching tentatively toward Arthur as she called his name.

"You shouldn't have come, Frannie." Arthur refused to look at her but Frannie persisted. The couple blocked the doorway and Jed's exit, forcing him to remain for the torturous exchange.

"Arthur, I love you. I needed to see you."

"I didn't want you to see me like this . . . a broken fragment of a man. I want you to forget me. I have nothing to give you."

Frannie rushed to him, framing his face within her hands, forcing him to look at her. "I could never forget you. I have given you my heart, and I cannot be whole without your love."

Arthur's mouth hovered near hers for seconds, the ache, the hunger painfully evident. His eyes were moist and shining as Frannie brought her mouth up in a kiss, brushing her lips as gently as butterfly wings against his. He moaned in response, then his eyes flashed open and he pushed away. "Go home, Frannie."

She stood her ground and fired back, "I know you love me." Again she returned to him, pressing her hands to his chest as her eyes searched his face. "Look at me and tell me you don't love me in return, and I'll go."

He was slow to answer her challenge, taking moments before he brought his eyes to meet hers. The hard line of his lean face softened with each tick of the clock. "It's because I do love you—because you deserve what I cannot give you. Listen to me. I'm no

435

longer a complete man, Frannie. I'm an aberration, unable to be a proper husband and unable to father a child!"

Frannie was dumbstruck for a few moments, but she soon rallied. "I don't care! I will not enjoy those joys if you turn me away, because I'll remain alone. I'd rather have your heart than any other man's physical comfort."

Hope flickered in his eye for a moment before going dim again. "You say that now."

The comment stunned Frannie. "Do you doubt my fidelity?"

Arthur took her hands and pressed them to his lips. "No! Not yours. Never yours. The fault would be mine." His voice began to tremble. "Even now, standing here, I have a man's want, a man's desire. I could not bear this torture daily—to be allowed only this and nothing more. But worse would be the ache I would suffer each time I saw passion flush your cheeks, knowing I would be the reason it could not be answered. And children, Frannie. I cannot deny you that joy. You were meant to love and to be loved. That's why you must go. Please!"

Frannie tightened her hold on his hands. "We are more than our passions, Arthur. Don't reduce us to that alone. You, as you now are, are more man to me than other men, because of your heart. Let me stay a while and show you what life still could offer us. Please."

The door thundered with the rapid pounding of several fists. "Open up! Police here!"

Arthur pulled away and opened the door. Three officers rushed in, followed by Lord Whittington, who immediately confronted Arthur. "Is he here? Have you seen him?"

"Who are you talking about?" Arthur asked anxiously.

The earl pounced on him, his finger pointing in accusation. "Daniel is missing! He would have come to you." To the officers, he barked, "Search the house!"

Arthur spun around, protectively tucking Frannie behind him as officers began tearing through his home. "What are you doing? Do you think I would lie to you?"

"You challenged my authority in front of him tonight, giving support to his wild ideas!"

"Look at you, Whit! He's not a criminal! What happened after I left?"

For a second the earl's defenses came down, leaving only a heartbroken father. "We argued bitterly. He denied his title, saying he wanted to choose his own life and attend medical school in America. I saw a letter on his bed. I assumed it was more of his tutor's efforts to 'expand his view of the world.' I picked it up and read a bit, but it was from a Jewish girl in Greece, begging him to return there and telling him what he would need to do to convert! I forbade him to ever write to her again and he railed against me, assailing everything my life stands for." Lord Whittington looked at his open hand. "I hit him, Arthur. It was the first time I've ever struck my son. Then I left his room. When I went back later to check on him, he and his bag were gone, along with one hundred pounds he stole from my safe."

The police returned to the foyer. "He's not here, Lord Whittington. Are you willing to file a formal charge against the boy?"

Arthur laid an anxious hand on the earl's shoulder. "You can't! Consider what you're about to do! You're hurt. I understand that, but is your pride worth more to you than Daniel's love?"

Frannie gasped softly at Arthur's words, and the hypocrisy of his counsel clearly stunned him equally. Making no effort to conceal his distress, he leaned toward her, reaching for her, but the moment was lost on the earl, who shot back fiercely.

"How dare you equate duty with pride! You are as naive and foolish as Daniel." Lord Whittington addressed the captain. "I'll file whatever paperwork is necessary to have him dragged back."

"You're a fool if you file charges, Whit! Daniel is not a criminal. He's your son."

Lord Whittington glared at Arthur. "A friend would not challenge me. I see no friend in you, and unless Daniel returns of his own volition, neither have I a son." The earl turned quickly, leading the officers away.

The encounter must have exhausted the last of Arthur's reserves. Obviously aghast at the evening's events and devoid of further fight, he pulled Frannie to him and tightly pressed his lips to her brow. "Too many doors have closed for me. I cannot bear to close another tonight. Forgive me, Frannie. Don't leave me. Please tell me you'll still stay."

Her tears fell alongside her smile. "Of course I will, Arthur. Of course I will!"

CHAPTER 43

Sunday, January 1, 1815
London, England

The paperboys stood on the street corners early as if knowing the day's sales would be grand. "The treaty is signed! We have ourselves a treaty!" they shouted to the rooftops. Soon shutters flew open as people shouted down to confirm the announcement. Pennies fell to the ground below, and the vendors plucked them up in exchange for copies left on the doorsteps.

Jed raced down the steps in his pajamas, barely taking the time to tie his wrapper as he flew out the door, nearly accosting a busy lad who was scrambling to gather his coins and distribute his papers. "I'll take four!" Jed exclaimed, dropping coins into the boy's hands from the money Frannie had brought him. He moved but one step away before the need to confirm the reports for himself overwhelmed him. Racing past the glorious headline, which simply said, "Treaty Reached in Ghent," he devoured every hopeful, precious word that confirmed Frannie's earlier report.

By the time he re-entered the house, Frannie was on the staircase, smiling hopefully. "It's good news—I can tell by your expression!" She hurried down the stairs and he swept her into his arms, crumpling the papers against her back.

"You were right! The treaty is signed!"

Jenny was now on the landing, and Arthur's weary face emerged from his bedroom door. Jed set Frannie down and raised the headline high like a trophy while Frannie stood beside him, reading the remainder of the article.

"We have a treaty, Arthur! The war is ended! Isn't it marvelous?"

Jed climbed the stairs. His mood sobered as he turned his attention to Jenny. He met her with his hand extended, taking hers and placing a kiss there. "I understand I have you to thank in great deed for helping Samuel save my wife and son. I'm overwhelmed with gratitude. Thank you, thank you."

He squeezed her hand and offered her a paper. Then his exultant mood returned and he rushed to Arthur, pressing a paper to his chest. "Peace, Arthur. Imagine it! After two hard years of turmoil we finally have peace. I'll soon be going home!"

"It's not quite that simple," Frannie cautioned. "According to the paper and Major Stebbings, both governments must approve the treaty first. Our delegates need to sail home and have the terms ratified by the Congress and signed by the president, and then they must sail back to London with the signed document before the war is actually ended. That will take months. And the soldiers on the front must be notified. They will fight until they receive some official word."

Jed looked expectantly at Arthur.

"I'm afraid she's right, Jed. But your John Quincy Adams has held our delegates' feet to the fire throughout the negotiations. I'm sure what they did there will pass both government's approval. You should be home in a few months."

Jed's enthusiasm curbed only slightly. "A few months," he repeated, embracing his friend. When he pulled back, the look on Arthur's face was somber and pensive. Jed followed his gaze to its end, to Frannie's strained smile. With a final pat, he withdrew from Arthur and crooked his elbow at Jenny. After escorting her back to her room, he returned to his own, leaving Arthur and

Frannie alone to sort out the future. A trace of guilt stung Jed each time he considered the limited joy peace offered some victims of the war. A political treaty would stop the warring, but it would not end the inner turmoil the war would continue to inflict.

When Jed rejoined Arthur and Frannie, a stiff ease had settled in between the pair, who sat across the table from one another, their daily papers spread before them, sharing bits of news like an old married couple. It pained him to see his fiery sister reduced to such an anemic life, but he knew he would suffer the same deprivations to share whatever marital joy remained if Hannah were ill. But when he placed himself in Arthur's shoes, the question was more difficult to answer. He had experience enough with his own wrestlings to know how onerous a burden a man's pride could be, and he didn't know if he would be able to handle it any better than Arthur.

Later, the foursome gathered around the piano, singing and laughing as Jed's awkward bass joined the three gifted singers, but he noticed how quickly Arthur stiffened when Frannie touched him, and he saw the pain in Arthur's eyes when his gaze inadvertently lingered on her face.

Over the course of the next few weeks, there was reason for hope. Frannie's contact with Major Stebbings opened the door for Jed to arrange some relief for the Americans suffering in Dartmoor's hell. Jed, Frannie, Arthur, and Jenny sent warm socks, blankets, and baskets of foodstuffs to the prisoners. It was precious little, Jed knew, but it confirmed the changing British mood, which in turn confirmed the coming peace, and it provided Arthur and Frannie with a mission they could share.

The couple's bond grew as they worked together. Jed could imagine Arthur returning to the ministry with Frannie by his side, serving others and replacing his and Frannie's lost physical passion with a spiritual and emotional one. But in the quiet moments the anguish always reappeared as Arthur flitted about Frannie like a moth to a flame, clearly hungering to savor the warmth and passion she embodied, but recognizing the threat his limitations posed to his fragile manhood.

The strain of their situation took its toll on the entire household, prompting Jed to dim his joy over every letter from Hannah, and casting a pall over Jenny's excitement when letters began arriving for her from Markus. Though the budding romance was a great source of delight to both Jenny and Frannie, they must have known it would be an irritant to Arthur, for they stole away to Jenny's room each time a letter arrived.

The first of Markus's letters posed dozens of questions about Jed's and Arthur's well-being, though both women knew Hannah could supply every detail on those subjects. Together, Jenny and Frannie composed an equally sterile recounting of everyone's health and diet, concluding with a single personal note asking about Markus's well-being, and a wish that he was fully mended from the wounds he had bravely received while precipitating Jenny's rescue.

Markus's next letter began with a droll account of the weather, the chess-game scores between Jack and him, and plans for the spring planting, with a carefully couched request for Jenny's return by spring so he could show her the beauty along the Patuxent. In the third letter, sent before Jenny's first could have arrived, Markus took a bold leap, recounting details of his life with Lyra and his sorrow over her death. Then he wrote:

> *When I think of the abuse you suffered at a man's hand, a man who should have protected and cherished you, I feel to beg you never to give your heart again to a man who cannot make you feel truly safe and loved.*

Loving is hard the second time around. For you, trusting will be the challenge. For me, it is letting go. I made a vow, the forever kind, that still claims a bit of me, but you are free to love again. But if those British blokes win your fancy, just promise me you'll choose wisely.

Frannie spilled backwards on the bed and cheered. "He's in love with you, Jenny!"

"He said no such thing," Jenny replied. "In fact, he said he's made a 'forever vow' that still 'claims a bit of him,' to his first wife. How is that good news?"

"I know Markus too well. He's hot or cold, but never lukewarm. And he's private. He would never share these details about Lyra unless he's wrestling with himself over you!"

A rap on the door was answered by Frannie, who found a smiling Arthur standing there. "Just what are you two ladies up to in here? I heard you squealing like schoolgirls."

Frannie glanced back over her shoulder at Jenny. "We think Markus is falling head over heels in love with Jenny. Isn't that the most wonderful news?"

The corners of Arthur's mouth twitched as if he were struggling to maintain his smile, but the narrowing of his eyes was not lost on Frannie. She touched his hand and gazed into his eyes. "Aren't you happy for them? Now Jenny and Markus can be as happy as we are."

Arthur laid his hand tenderly against Frannie's cheek and she snuggled into his palm. He looked at Jenny and said, "I'm very happy for you both." Then he returned his attention to Frannie. "Everyone deserves to be so happy."

CHAPTER 44

Sunday, February 19, 1815
The Willows

Barely two months of age, little Johnny was already as fat as a spring piglet. Hannah tied him to her and carried him about the house like a papoose, never daring to have him beyond arm's reach. It had been several weeks since Frannie had left for England, and though Hannah desperately missed her sister-in-law's energizing spirit, she gladly gave her up in return for the positive developments occurring between Arthur and Frannie.

Hannah quietly affirmed that either wisdom or providence had prevailed in separating Frannie from Myrna during the long, frigid winter. It was a season like none Hannah could remember, with temperatures so low Markus feared the livestock would die in the night. Ice and hail left the trees looking as if they had been dipped in liquid glass. It was beautiful but treacherous, and since everyone hunkered down indoors and barely ventured out, Hannah and Beatrice were forced to endure Myrna's incessant expressions of misery.

The men hitched an ox team to a sled to ferry supplies between the main house and the meadows, and when that proved too daunting all nineteen Willows residents took shelter in the two main houses. Myrna kept to her bedroom with some dire malady, while the rest of the women quilted every piece of fabric in the house. There had been no communication in or out for days as Hannah, Beatrice, and Markus watched their outgoing letters stack up and awaited an opportunity to have them posted. Weeks earlier, the *National Intelligencer* had confirmed Timothy's report that a peace treaty was expected, and Hannah ached to know if the delegates had finally struck their agreement.

The temperatures warmed for two days but returned to freezing at night, causing a thick crust of ice to harden over the deep, packed snow. The men tried shoeing the horses with studded shoes to make it to Calverton, but within a few dozen yards one horse went down, nearly breaking a leg. Frustration inspired another plan as they filled a bucket with hot coals, tied on snowshoes, and walked to the end of the lane to build a fire and catch any news passing along River Road.

Hours later, Jack and Markus stomped back into the house. Markus met Hannah with a twinkle in his eye.

She took a deep breath. "Do we have a treaty?"

"We do!" He produced a broadsheet that made Hannah squeal with joy. "We caught a neighbor who'd come fresh from Calverton. He said a reporter rode up from Washington with the news. The treaty was signed in Belgium on Christmas Eve. It arrived here the other day, the Congress passed it unanimously, and the president signed it on the seventeenth!"

Hannah nearly leapt into his arms but remembered Johnny bundled near her chest, so she settled for a hug instead. She clutched her hands over her baby, then tipped her head back and shouted for Beatrice, bringing her sister to her in a run.

"What on earth is the cause of this celebration?" Beatrice asked.

Hannah caught her sister up in a dance. "We've passed the treaty, Beatrice! That means Dudley and Jed will be home soon!" She stopped to look at Markus and Jack. "They will, won't they?"

"The paper says the signed treaty is already on its way back to England. Once it arrives, the prisoners should be set free."

"Five or six weeks to England if the weather is foul, and no more than five back," Hannah calculated. "Jed could be home by the middle of May!"

"Dudley is coming home!" Beatrice ran her hands over her shivering arms. "I need to get home in plenty of time to make things perfect for his homecoming."

"And Myrna?"

Beatrice chuckled. "I think she's ready to return to her own home as well."

"There's more news," Markus said. "Prices are already dropping on British goods, and our banks are paying out record dividends because we can freely trade again. And what's more, the British tried to take the Mississippi around New Year's by attacking New Orleans, just like Jenny said. I should never have doubted her."

Hannah laughed playfully. "You're making up for it now."

The comment brought a blush to Markus's cheeks. "I'm not good at courtin'. I'll have ta write and tell her the news. Maybe some information she gave helped our side down there. We sure gave them worse than they gave us at Bladensburg. They outmanned us and outgunned us, but General Jackson and our troops sent them runnin' back to their ships. Casualties were high on the British side. Sadly enough, it seems the battle was fought after the peace treaty was signed, but neither side knew it."

"What a waste," Hannah said. "All those lives lost, and for nothing."

"Not nothing, Hannah. If the British would have won that battle, they'd refuse ta ratify the treaty, and with them controllin' the Mississippi, this war would have escalated enormously."

"I just want Jed and Dudley home."

"And Frannie and Jenny," Markus added.

Hannah's smile faded. "I wonder if Frannie will come home."

"Or Jenny," Markus mumbled. "She's probably bein' courted by some Brit."

446

Jack produced a sizeable stack of mail from under his coat. "The neighbor picked these up in Calverton. Maybe there's word in there about when they're coming home."

Everyone clutched his or her treasured letters and stole off to read. Hannah headed into Jed's office, the last quiet spot in the crowded house. One of the letters was from an attorney, and she opened it first. The heading alone told the story: "To the heirs of the estate of the deceased, Major Andrew Robertson."

Tears sprang to Hannah's eyes as she read the details of how her former beau had died a hero at the Battle of New Orleans, hurtling himself over two young Kentuckians to protect them from an incoming rocket that claimed his life instead. It was so like Andrew, the consummate soldier, who once exhibited the same tenacity when pursuing her. Blinded by love for her, even after her marriage to Jed, he had been a passive accomplice in the plot that caused Jed to be hurt in the bridge explosion. But when he was taken captive by the British, it was Andrew who sought redemption by offering to receive Jed's fifty lashes in his stead.

The final paragraph proved how tenderly those events marked his life.

> *To Mrs. Jonathan Edward Pearson goes one half of my estate, to be placed in a trust fund for the education of her children, that my life may leave a continued good mark on this world. And the other half I bequeath to West Point Military Academy in honor of Jonathan Edward Pearson III, to keep America strong so we all have a land to which to come home.*

CHAPTER 45

Monday, March 3, 1815
London, England

The news distressed Jed. It was assumed the American congress was as anxious as Britain to be done with the war, and that the treaty bearing the president's signature was likely already on its way back to Great Britain, but events were constantly changing the political landscape, and nothing was certain.

Most distressing was the news of Napoleon's escape from Elba. The war to capture and detain him the first time had already broken the British treasury, costing the nation eight hundred million pounds, and now they were chasing him again. Jed feared the same financial need that caused them to covet America's vast resources would make them slow to surrender her now. The timing was doubly worrisome since the report of the catastrophic British loss at New Orleans, where the losses in men, armament, and ships had wrought a devastating toll. By all estimates, the treaty should arrive by April 1st. Until then, Jed would continue to worry.

It was time to go home. The weather had slowed the arrival of Hannah's letters, and without the comfort and closeness they provided, Jed relied more and more on his dreams of Hannah to get him through each day.

Jenny was languishing as well, so Arthur arranged for her to sing at a local pub in the evenings. She became a popular attraction—so popular, in fact, that Jed wondered if she would return to America with him. He knew that if she did not, she would break the heart of his Irish brother.

Frannie was an altogether different matter. Some days he felt certain she would return home with him. On others it seemed a wedding might be forthcoming. As it was so often with Frannie, her life and choices wearied him, and since Jed had no voice in her decisions, he turned his attention elsewhere.

He and Arthur visited British farms to provide some space between Arthur and Frannie when tensions rose between the pair. Jed kept copious notes about crops and livestock and equipment he might want to incorporate back at the Willows. Other days when Arthur was free, the pair would visit William Wilberforce so Jed could pose more questions about his experience in ending the British slave trade. Also satisfying was the news that a portion of the Treaty of Ghent included the desire of both countries to work together to abolish the practice of slavery worldwide. Jed felt the time was near. It simply had to be.

He had made a few decisions. He would set up the old hunting cabin as a refuge for runaway slaves, stocking it with clothing and supplies and details on similar places of safety. Hannah never went there, and Frannie wouldn't go alone. Markus, Jack, and Abel would have to be told about the plan, but other than that, it would need to remain a secret.

The biggest decision Jed had made would shock Hannah far more than the news about him hosting a freedom station. He had decided to pursue Timothy's and Dr. Foster's suggestion that he run for political office. If his goal was the abolishment of slavery, he knew he must place himself in the best position to effect change. Jed wasn't sure how Hannah would receive the news, but he felt certain she would accept it when she understood his reasoning.

He spent the next four long weeks reading books and legal precedents recommended to him by William, until he felt he had a solid grasp on the economic and social arguments he would need to confront. Arthur came along on his trips to the libraries and courthouses where the documents were kept, and their time together afforded the men time to speak candidly and alone.

A crisp breeze clipped along the banks of the Thames as they walked to the courthouse on the last Friday in March. They drew their scarves and coats more tightly around themselves, enjoying what could be some of their last hours alone.

"It seems your path is set now," Arthur said. "Is it comforting to have a sure vision of your future?"

Jed considered the point and smiled. "No matter what, farming will always be my first love, but God gave me a gift through my imprisonment, correcting my perspective. You see, I once believed I could be a good man if I treated my slaves fairly and housed them and fed them well. Hannah knew how ludicrous my thinking was when she was but a young girl. It took me longer to recognize my folly, and until now to become intolerant of it. I've discovered that captivity, even in a home as lovely as yours, is still captivity. And the torment I experienced on the ship taught me how far man's humanity can fall. It all must change, Arthur, and I believe America's hour is at hand.

"And what of your future, Arthur? Will you return to the ministry or will you manage your father's shipping business?"

Arthur kicked at a pile of snow. "I've tried not to allow my circumstances to diminish my faith in God, but I confess I bear a measure of sorrow and—let's call it what it is—self-pity unbecoming to a man of the cloth. I can serve God without taking ministerial vows that bind me to one faith and one dogma. America's religious freedom has opened my mind on the topic of God. I want to explore it. And I need to keep an eye on the McGowans to be sure Jervis isn't lurking about, seeking a way to use them to hurt me. So I plan to run the shipping company."

Jed raised his eyebrows. "A farmer becomes a politician, and a vicar becomes a merchant."

"Our vocations could serve mutual goods. My ships can move your tobacco, and my captains will be in every port. I'll know who is smuggling slaves and who is not."

"An excellent set of propositions." Jed smiled, binding the unspoken deal by shaking Arthur's hand. "If all goes as planned, the treaty should arrive any day, and I will soon be leaving. But I must ask you, Arthur, will Frannie be sailing with me, or should I plan to give her away to you?"

Arthur moved to a bench and brushed the snow away so the pair could sit. "Did you know she cries sometimes late at night? I stand outside her door, not knowing whether to rush in and take her into my arms, or to pack her bags and send her away. Instead of doing either, I stand outside her door and cry as well."

Jed saw the tears welling in Arthur's eyes over the confession. "There are other ways to show love, Arthur, and children who need homes and parents. Life could still be full and rich."

Arthur hung his head and nodded. "I've said the same to myself. I just . . ." His voice broke and his shoulders began to shake. " I just love her so much, Jed. It pains me to think of all we'll never know." His sorrow came in wrenching sobs that caused his entire body to tremble. Jed placed his arm around Arthur's shoulders to steady him, unable to offer any adequate words of consolation.

Later that evening, when they arrived back at Arthur's home, they found Captain Smith waiting for them. The women had kept him well entertained around the piano, but as soon as the men entered the parlor the mood instantly sobered.

"Captain Smith," Arthur greeted, though his eyes were riveted on Frannie. "What brings you here?"

"I've wonderful news! I wanted to deliver it personally before the papers print it. The signed treaty arrived from Washington today. The prisoner exchange agents are readying ships to carry the prisoners home as we speak. Mr. Corvas volunteered his ship to sail you home. The accommodations there will be more favorable for the women. I assumed you'd want to leave as soon as possible, so he's scheduled to leave in two days. It will be all three of you, correct?"

The anticipated thrill of the moment reverberated in Jed's heart, but he denied his inclination to openly express it, knowing the agonizing decisions the news now precipitated.

Arthur's eyes never left Frannie's face. "Captain, may they answer you in the morning?"

Captain Smith evidently noticed the painful exchange as his own demeanor grew sullen. "Of course. I'll ask the captain to hold the berths until noon. Send your reply by then."

Jenny and Jed escorted the captain out and headed upstairs, leaving Frannie and Arthur alone to sort out the hand they had been dealt.

Arthur stretched his hand out to Frannie. "Come here to me. I need one answer before we decide what to tell the captain."

"Ask me. Ask me anything. I'll tell you the truth. You know that."

He heard the tremor in her voice as she fought her tears. "I know, but this answer can't be had by asking. Come to me." He leaned against the piano, gazing at her, recalling the way she looked that day at the Willows cabin two years ago, poised against the trees with the sun in her hair, smelling of the same perfume she now wore. She was now more woman than she had been then—stronger, more vulnerable, more loving—but she was also less in ways that pained him—less vibrant, less hopeful, less happy. Arthur needed to know what a shared life could offer if he set his own fears aside to focus solely on diminishing Frannie's.

He reached for her hand, and the feel of her skin on his made him shiver, but he did not retreat. Instead, he drew her to him, allowing her nervous arms the freedom to slide around him until no sliver of light separated them. He closed his eyes and drank her in—her scent, her feel, the rhythm of her heart thrashing against his chest. His head leaned back as the enormity of his want nearly crushed him, but still he did not retreat.

Looking down, he met her confused eyes and knew she was struggling to be and do whatever would correctly answer his unspoken question. His hands crept into her hair, disappearing into the auburn tangle. Leaning closer, she met him halfway, no longer seeming tentative or fearful that he would withdraw his lips and deny her this one remaining passion. And as they touched, he heard her softly moan, and he answered her in kind.

Their gentle kiss sparked greater need, and the kiss hardened as her fingers tightened into his back. When he pulled away and looked into her love-filled eyes, he had his answer. Stepping away abruptly, he wiped his hand across his hungry lips and gasped. "I'm not enough."

She shuddered and caught her breath. "Don't say that. You are everything to me."

"And still not as much as you want or deserve." He cradled her against him and whispered softly, "Loving one another is not the issue. The concern is whether that love makes us happier than being apart. Some love harrows our soul, Frannie. I would bear it if it were only my soul that was being torn. But it wounds yours as well, and I could never abide that."

Frannie clung to him more closely. "What does that leave us?"

He kissed her head and laid his own atop it. "Every possibility, just not together."

She jerked away and tearfully challenged him. "Can you dismiss us so easily, Arthur?"

He drew her close, pressing his lips to her hair. "Can you feel me trembling? I assure you, Frannie, there is nothing easy about this, but it is right, and it is best—for both of us."

"You're wrong, Arthur. You're consigning us each to live wasted, lonely lives."

The resignation in her voice caused Arthur to reconsider the plan. "Then let's consider our separation a postponement—a ten-year engagement without obligations, during which you must seek out your options and allow men to court you and give yourself the opportunity to marry and have a family. And if at the end of that time you have not given your heart to someone else—if you still choose me and what I can offer you—then I will gratefully make you mine."

Frannie stepped away from him again, offering no argument. "Will you write?"

"Every day, but I'll only post one letter to you a year."

A single sob broke free from her lips. "Can I visit you?"

Arthur drew her to him once more. "Not until the tenth year. You must set me aside and use this time to open your heart to other possibilities. If I'm to offer you this limited life, I need to know you have chosen me after fully examining what other options love can offer you."

"Are you sending me away now?"

"Yes, Frannie. In two days you must sail home."

CHAPTER 46

Monday, May 15, 1815
Liverpool, England

Emotion ran heavy on the journey to the Liverpool docks. Though the sky was gray, the day was warm, yet Arthur shook as if he were freezing. Frannie's concern for him seemed only to add to his emotional distress, so she didn't argue her case again. She stood stoically by as the luggage was loaded, watching as Arthur completed the arrangements with Juan Corvas. When Arthur returned to her his mouth was twisted with emotion. She fell against him and felt his arms tighten around her. She thought he might actually ask her to stay after all, but those words didn't come. Instead, he struggled to say, "Be happy, my love," which melted her withering resolve.

Across the dock stood Richard "Jervis" Porter, who gloated over the scene. "So, you love Miss Pearson, do you, Mr. Ramsey? Well, now, don't that just change everything?"

Wednesday, June 7, 1815
The Atlantic

Frannie's broken heart had seemed to seek the grave. Disinterested in food of any kind, she had withered for the first shipboard week

455

until Jenny began to fear for her. By week two, determined to win Arthur back, Frannie had resigned to endure her ten-year test. She spent time with Juan Corvas learning about the renewed vitality of the free-trade markets, and she planned ways to capitalize on the ensuing ten years. By the time they reached Baltimore, she had set her sights on becoming a woman of commerce to prove to Arthur that she had not simply pined away for him.

The travelers stood at the ship's bow when the first glimpse of the American shoreline appeared. "Finally, home," Frannie uttered as she pointed to Fort McHenry's striped banner.

"And hope," Jenny said.

Everything, thought Jed.

The group bid farewell to Juan Corvas, who had proven to be a most honorable man. "I will come to this port from time to time," he said. "I hope our paths will cross again."

Jed embraced the man who had saved his life. "You're welcome at my home anytime, Juan. I hope you'll come often and meet my family."

Corvas set them off in a dinghy. An hour passed as they sat at the harbor awaiting the skiff that would carry them up the Patuxent.

At one point, Frannie waved her arm across the panorama. "I'm going to buy as much of this city as I can, Jed. The dawn is rising on a new day for America, and I'm going to be a part of it."

"Can I tell you a secret? I'm planning to run for the Maryland State Senate."

Frannie nudged him playfully. "I bet those old gentry biddies' ears are burning now."

"I suppose they are," Jed teased back. "And what of your career? Is Francesca retiring?"

"I think it will be awhile before I can sing a love song without crying."

Jed understood. Perhaps that was why the ride up the Patuxent was spent in silence, allowing each of them—Jenny included—to set the past behind while preparing to embrace a new day.

The skiff docked in Calverton, where Jed received a hearty welcome. Frannie and Jenny did their best to remain obscure, avoiding the complications that would arise if Jenny were recognized. They heard the owner of the mercantile call out to his customers, asking if anyone headed north could carry the hero Jed Pearson and his group to the Willows. A burly farmer from Nottingham offered, and soon they were on the last leg of Jed's homecoming.

As the wagon rounded the first Willows bend, Jed found himself rubbing goose bumps from his arms and staring at every budding leaf with wide-eyed wonder. Nine months had passed since he had been home, and while some of the damage Dupree had inflicted was still visible, all Jed felt was joy.

He peered in every direction, anxious for the first glimpse of Hannah, but it was the children who saw him first. He leapt to the ground and ran up the lane ahead of the wagon, greeting each clamoring child. Sookie and Royal rushed in on him next, then the two men knowingly steered the children away as they pointed toward the house where Hannah was.

Jack and Markus were in the barn attending to the tobacco seedlings when they heard the children's squeals. Jack barreled across the front lawn to meet Jed in a tearful embrace, while Markus arrived in measured strides with his arms spread wide. The two fell into one another's arms, but Jed quickly broke free, wanting to get to Hannah and Johnny.

Bitty was on the front porch peeling potatoes. She set her knife down and rose when she saw him, her face breaking into a tearful smile. Jed rushed up and kissed her across the railing.

"She's in the back yard, tending her garden," Bitty said through moist eyes.

Jed slowed down to take in every glimpse and sound of the moment. Pushing back the rope-like strands of the willow trees, he saw a blue quilt spread out beside a plot of freshly turned earth, dotted with plants. Lying on it was a wriggling, six-month-old bundle of busy arms and legs. Hannah lay beside him on her side, tickling his face with a strand of her long, dark hair. Still barely able to accept that he was actually home, Jed scarcely breathed for fear he would burst the moment and shatter the dream. He was awed by Hannah's appearance. Everything about her spoke of womanhood and love—her sing-song voice as she played with their son, the earthy roundness of her nursing body, the wind-tossed strands of her loose hair, but most of all, the peace that radiated from her face.

Jed stepped out from the tree and called to her. "Hello, sweetness."

Hannah bolted upright and scanned the perimeter to find him. She froze as their eyes met, and then she raised her arms, beckoning to him. He ran to her and pulled her up and against him, ringing her wet face with kisses as her arms reached around his neck, holding fast to him as she uttered his name a thousand times.

His kisses slowed and she pressed her head into the crook of his neck, nuzzling close as she felt his body relax. Looking up, she saw the reason for the change. His eyes were fixed on his son, who was investigating his toes.

Hannah pulled back and beamed. "I think Bitty's right. He looks just like his father."

The notion inspired a broad smile that returned to a look of wonder.

"Would you like to hold him?" Hannah asked.

Jed scooped her against him and pressed his hungry lips over hers, pulling them down to their knees on the blanket. Then Hannah slid her hands under the busy little body and held him up to make the first introduction. "Johnny, this is your father, the finest man I've ever known."

Without hesitation, Jed took his son in his arms and cradled him near. "He's wondrous," he said as he traced the baby's face with his finger. He looked back at Hannah, studying her face more closely now. "How are you, really?" One hand drew her head near as he pressed his brow to hers. "When I got the letter about

Johnny's birth . . ." His voice became husky. "Oh, Hannah! What if I had lost you?"

"I had the same worries every day you were away from me."

Jed pressed her hand to his mouth and kissed her palm. "I can't imagine what I've put you through. I'm so sorry. I love you, Hannah. You are my world. I'm going to spend the rest of my life making you feel safe and loved."

As if in defiance, the echo of a gunshot split the air near the front of the house. Jed bolted to his feet and handed Johnny back to his mother as he placed himself between his family and the sound. "Wait here," he said, then moved along to the front of the house, where he saw the cause of the commotion. A man was aiming a rifle at Markus, whose arm was wrapped protectively around Jenny. Jed felt sure he recognized the gunman from the mercantile, and he assumed the man had followed them home when the owner called out for drivers to take Jed and the women to the Willows.

"The next shot won't go in the air, Jenny. Come here to me now or I'll kill your dandy."

"No, Jeremiah!" she screamed. "Please!"

"Maybe I'll just kill this Irishman for touching my wife."

"I'm not your wife. How did you find me?"

"This address was all over those divorce papers your lawyer sent. I figured you must be doing real good for yourself if you had money enough to pay for a fancy attorney. Now get in the wagon. I'm taking you home."

Jed watched the events from thirty yards away. His mind kicked into battle readiness as he searched the area for some tactical effort he could employ. He felt Hannah press herself along his back, her arms wrapping around him to hold him in place.

"No," she cried. "You just returned to me."

Jed twisted to face her. "All I wanted was to be free and to come home to you."

Moments passed as the two young lovers mourned their brief peace. "It's just not ever going to be as easy as that, is it?"

He kissed her brow and touched her lips with his finger. "I'll be all right. I can't believe God brought me home to let me die today. Stay here."

Bitty's knife still lay on the railing. Jed slipped it in his belt before moving into the tree line that ran to the right of the altercation. He saw Sookie and Royal in the fields further to the right, with the frightened children gathered around them. Then he saw Jack near the barn to Jeremiah's left. Jack stooped to pick up a rock, but as soon as his fingers closed around it, Jeremiah swung his rifle around and leveled a shot near Jack's feet. As Jeremiah reached to reload the rifle, Markus sprang at him. The man pulled a pistol from under his buckskin jacket, stopping Markus cold.

Jed moved stealthily until he was hidden in the trees twenty feet behind the man. He gripped the knife over and over until it felt balanced in his hand. Then he watched and waited.

"She's not goin' with you," Markus said. "She's not your property and you're never goin' ta hurt her again."

"Think you know her better than I do?" Jeremiah glared at Jenny, who cowered behind Markus. "If you don't get in that wagon I'll just kill him and take you anyway."

Jenny's fingers slowly began releasing from Markus's hands. He tightened his grip on her but she hunched her shoulders and pulled away. "Don't do this, Jenny."

"You're the only man that ever loved me the right way. I can't let him kill you."

Jeremiah grabbed her arm and yanked her to him, snapping her head back and violently thrusting his mouth against hers. After shoving her away, he shot a wad of tobacco spittle to the ground and back-handed her, drawing blood. Markus jerked forward with his hands clenched, and again the gun was raised to his chest. Jed crept from his cover and crouched behind the wagon. Markus saw him but his eyes didn't disclose Jed's new position.

"Run and get your money," Jeremiah ordered Jenny, "or I'll shoot your beau."

460

Jenny raced to the house and returned just as quickly, shoving the bills at Jeremiah. He counted the money and stuffed it into his shirt. "Get in the wagon."

"You've got what you wanted. Leave her and go!" Markus ordered.

"This?" he scoffed. "She's worth far more to me than that." He pulled out a deed. "There's her half of the trading post and all the money she fetches me working the camps. Or did you not know she has other talents than just singing?"

Jenny looked at Markus and shriveled before crawling into the wagon and crouching in the corner.

Jeremiah pointed the gun at Markus's thigh. "If I maim you right you won't be as likely to follow—"

Jed sprang from his hiding place and grabbed Jeremiah from behind, holding the knife to his throat.

"I believe I can take it from here," Markus said as he wrenched the gun from Jeremiah's hand and threw the weapon to the ground. When Jed released Jeremiah, Markus landed three solid punches to Jeremiah's head in quick succession. Jed hauled the dazed man to his feet and threw him against the wagon bed, where Markus stood nose to nose with him. "Leave here and never come back."

Jeremiah cackled. "There are warrants out for her. I'll let the law fight my battles."

"Warrants you swore out against her!" Markus extended his hand to Jenny, coaxing her from the wagon. "Will ya marry me, Jenny? All I have in this world is here on this farm, but if you're willin' to surrender everything else, I'll do my best ta make ya happy."

She threw her arms around his neck and held fast to him. "What more is there than that?"

Markus tore the deed from Jeremiah's hand. "I'm givin' ya two choices, and both of them involve the sheriff. Jenny will sign over her share of the trading post in return for you droppin' the charges against her. Or we can go down and I'll file a charge of attempted murder against ya. I'd advise ya to choose option number one."

CHAPTER 47

Tuesday, July 4, 1815
Baltimore, Maryland

"Congratulations on your purchase, Frannie. Now what will you do with this forty-acre field you've bought in the middle of nowhere?"

Frannie gave Jed a playful shove. "Don't mock a visionary, Brother. This was the closest acreage to the monument site that was for sale. Mark my words, someday Baltimore will sprawl this far north to the monument and beyond, and my land will be worth many times what it is now." She turned to face south, growing pensive as she did so. "Perhaps I'll build a home of my own on this rise, so I can see the flag at Fort McHenry every morning. And I may open a shop featuring European fashions like those I saw in Belgium and London. My life is filled with those options Arthur asked me to explore. But today I just want to sing once more."

Hannah looked at the clock tower. "You'd best hurry, Frannie. It's nearly noon."

"I need to rehearse with Ferdinand and Charles. Then I'll meet you at Howard's Woods."

"We'll be there." Jed flung the tails of his jacket aside and tugged on his new trousers, then stooped to comfort Johnny, who fussed in his carriage.

"She's still aching. I wonder what will become of her and Arthur in ten years—or any of us for that matter," Hannah mused as she closed her parasol and clutched Jed's hand. "Sometimes when you rise before me and I awake to find your side of the bed empty, I pause for a moment and worry that this is all a dream, that you're still a prisoner and the war is still raging."

Jed stood and tipped her chin, then placed a lingering kiss on her lips. "This is a dream, but a lovely one. It was dreaming of you that kept me alive."

"I followed you the other morning. Frannie stayed with Johnny, and I saddled Figaro and followed you up to the hunting cabin. I saw you unload bundles of clothes and food. I know you're establishing a station to hide runaways. I'm very proud of you, although the risk you take frightens me."

Worry crossed Jed's face. "Please promise me you won't go there again. I want you to remain uninvolved in the event I get caught. Since smuggling Titus's family across the Pennsylvania line, and after being held captive on the *Iphigenia,* I can no longer bear the thought of enslaving any innocent human being. Even Abel, a free man, has limited rights to justice, though he was trying to save all you women and children. We must begin legislating change."

They turned to eye the flag flying proudly over Fort McHenry. "We have a long way to go to fulfill the dream of 'one nation under God,'" Hannah said, "but we are now becoming the *United* States of America. It does frustrate me that some newspapers are calling the war inconsequential because all lands returned to their original boundaries. They aren't accounting for the changes in America's people—changes that can't be measured on a map."

"Hopefully our children will recognize that these were the days that brought that change. We are finally a nation—not just a federation of states, but a republic that recognizes a flag as the symbol of our freedom. So does the world now. And repelling Britain has won us international respect. Some argue that Britain would never have occupied us and changed our government. I only know what we felt during those two years—that our way of life was endangered."

"You may need to add all this to your speech today to woo next fall's voters," Hannah said with a smile.

"It's as if I can see America's purpose, but I've many rivals for that state senate post."

"Oh, they'll elect you. Remember your birthmark? You're charmed. You'll be a Maryland state delegate at twenty-five years of age with a long career ahead."

Jed laughed, tightening his hold around her. "Whatever the future brings, we'll do it all together, all right? You've always seen the future more clearly than I. I need you, Hannah."

She wrapped her arm in his and they strolled to the dedication site of the first monument to George Washington in the nation. Howard's Woods was teeming with nearly thirty thousand guests, and dozens of reporters and artists recorded the events. Large banners hung between the trees, and flags waved from every corner. Jed settled Hannah and the baby in a seat reserved in the front row. Markus joined her, tugging on his shirt collar and straightening his cravat.

Hannah smiled approvingly. "You look very handsome, Markus."

He rolled his eyes and blushed. "What can I say? I'm butter in my bride's hands."

"Aren't we all?" Jed winked at Hannah. "I see the announcer waving me up to the podium. I suppose it's time to take my seat."

Jed was seated beside Robert Mills, the architect from South Carolina who had designed the monument. Mayor Johnson sat a few seats down. Jed still couldn't abide the man personally, but he had to admit that Baltimore's plan had preserved the city while many others had fallen.

The announcer introduced the program. Frannie, Jenny, Ferdinand Durang, and Samuel Renfro moved to center stage, accompanied by Charles Durang on flute, and a drummer. The crowd rose as the harmonies mingled over the stirring words of Key's anthem. Few eyes remained dry. With each strike of the drum Jed considered the rockets that had rained down fire over their homes, and the bombs that had pummeled the region. He thought of those who had died—Jerome and Harvey Baumgardner, and Hannah's parents—and of those who would continue to suffer the war's effects—Light Horse Harry Lee, Frannie and Arthur, and Dudley Snowden. Jed thought of the scarred land, the charred city of Washington, and the cemetery at Bladensburg. But underscoring it all was the knowledge that America and her people had prevailed.

A moment of silence hung in the still air as the anthem's lyrics sank into the hearts of those assembled. Then a mighty cheer went up and the thunderous applause began, continuing for a full minute. After the prayer was given and before the mayor spoke, the announcer introduced Jed.

"We are pleased to have with us today Mr. Jonathan Edward Pearson III. Many of us are contented customers of Pearson's splendid Willows-grown tobacco, but Jed also served us well during the war. As we celebrate the erection of this monument to George Washington and the freedom he framed and preserved, it seems fitting to hear from a man who offered his own life in similar service as a soldier and a prisoner of war. Please welcome Mr. Jed Pearson."

Jed set his eyes on Hannah, who beamed at him from below as Johnny tugged at his booties. Behind them, the applauding crowd spread like a sea, with the flag waving far away in the background. He saw Jack, Bitty, and the children standing beside Abel, who was dressed in his uniform and looking as proud as a man had ever looked, while steps away slaves worked to provide refreshments for their seated owners. The entire moment was so surreal that Jed coughed three times to clear the emotion from his throat. Imperfect as it was, hope was in the air. He wondered if everyone else could feel it as well. Gripping the podium, he began by repeating these words:

> *"Then conquer we must, when our cause it is just,*
> *And this be our motto—'In God is our Trust,'*
> *And the star-spangled banner in triumph doth wave,*
> *O'er the land of the Free, and the Home of the*
> *Brave.*

"My dear, beloved countrymen, we speak in a variety of accents and dialects. We stand in a variety of colors, united by one common dream—to keep America free and strong. Though battered, we are not broken, and though our land and people bear the scars of war, we stand proudly together today, fellow Americans all.

"It is fitting that we are gathered here on the day our independence was declared, to honor the father of this great land—George Washington. As it is today, it was sweltering in Independence Hall that summer of 1776. Today, it is the peak of summer, when new crops dot the lands, when ships' bellies are filled with goods rather than cannons, and when the economy soars. Today is a new day of independence!"

The crowd swelled in euphoric response.

"We celebrate our success, as we have a right to do, but let us also be wise and prudent. We must never become complacent, allowing our privileges to lower our guard. We've been given a glorious new beginning for America. The question is, what will we do with this moment?"

Sources

A complete list of the sources used in the research of *Oh, Say Can You See?* was too extensive for inclusion in this volume, but the comprehensive list of sources and notes is available at www.laurielclewis.com. Major sources include:

Gleig, George Robert. *A Subaltern in America; Comprising His Narrative of the Campaigns of the British Army, at Baltimore, Washington, &c. During the Late War.* Philadelphia and Baltimore: Carey, Hart & Co. 1833.

Pitch, Anthony. *The Burning of Washington.* Annapolis, Maryland: Naval Institute Press, 1998.

Sheads, Scott. *Fort McHenry.* New York: Evelyn Hill, 1998.

Svejda, George J., Ph.D. *The History of the Star Spangled Banner from 1814 to the Present.* Washington, DC: United States Park Service, 1969.

Taylor, Lonn. *The Star-Spangled Banner.* New York: The National Museum of American History, Smithsonian Institution, with Harry N. Abrams, Inc., 2000.

The Fort McHenry National Monument and Historic Shrine site (see http://www.nps.gov/fomc/historyculture/)

Various pages on the American Memory Project site (see http://memory.loc.gov/ammem/index.html)

Laurie (L.C.) Lewis was born and raised in rural Maryland, surrounded by history-rich Philadelphia, Washington, and Baltimore. She and her husband, Tom, reside in Carroll County, Maryland, where they raised their four children.

Oh, Say Can You See? is Laurie's sixth published novel. Her other novels include *Unspoken* (2004), *Awakening Avery* (2010, as Laurie Lewis), and the first three volumes in the *FREE MEN and DREAMERS* series: *Dark Sky at Dawn* (2007), *Twilight's Last Gleaming* (2008), and *Dawn's Early Light* (2009). *Dark Sky at Dawn* and *Twilight's Last Gleaming* were finalists in the 2008 USA Best Books competition. The fifth and final volume of *FREE MEN and DREAMERS* is scheduled for a spring 2011 release.

Laurie is a popular historical speaker and workshop presenter. She is a member of the LDStorymakers authors' group as well as ANWA, a writing group for Latter-day Saint women. Laurie combines all her loves—LDS and American history, travel, family, and interesting locations—to produce family and historical dramas. She loves hearing from her readers and may be contacted through her website, www.laurielclewis.com, or her blog, www.laurielclewis.blogspot.com.